How Negotiations End

Whilst past studies have examined when and how negotiations begin, and how wars end, this is the first full-length work to analyze the closing phase of negotiations. It identifies endgame as a definable phase in negotiation, with specific characteristics, as the parties involved sense that the end is in sight and decide whether or not they want to reach it. The authors further classify different types of negotiator behavior characteristic of this phase, drawing out various components, including mediation, conflict management vs. resolution, turning points, uncertainty, and home relations, amongst others. A number of specific cases are examined to illustrate this analysis, including Colombian negotiations with FARC, Greece and the EU, Iranian nuclear proliferation, French friendship treaties with Germany and Algeria, Chinese business negotiations, and trade negotiations in Asia. This pioneering work will appeal to scholars and advanced students of negotiation in international relations, international organization, and business studies.

I. WILLIAM ZARTMAN is Jacob Blaustein Distinguished Professor Emeritus of International Organizations and Conflict Resolution at Johns Hopkins School of Advanced International Studies. He is the author and editor of such books as *Preventing Deadly Conflict* (2015), *Arab Spring: Negotiating in the Shadow of the Intifadat* (2015), *The Global Power of Talk* (2012), and *Negotiation and Conflict Management; Essays on Theory and Practice* (2010), amongst others.

How Negotiations End

Negotiating Behavior in the Endgame

Edited by

I. William Zartman
The Johns Hopkins University

CAMBRIDGE
UNIVERSITY PRESS

University Printing House, Cambridge CB2 8BS, United Kingdom

One Liberty Plaza, 20th Floor, New York, NY 10006, USA

477 Williamstown Road, Port Melbourne, VIC 3207, Australia

314–321, 3rd Floor, Plot 3, Splendor Forum, Jasola District Centre, New Delhi – 110025, India

79 Anson Road, #06–04/06, Singapore 079906

Cambridge University Press is part of the University of Cambridge.

It furthers the University's mission by disseminating knowledge in the pursuit of education, learning, and research at the highest international levels of excellence.

www.cambridge.org
Information on this title: www.cambridge.org/9781108475839
DOI: 10.1017/9781108567466

© Cambridge University Press 2019

This publication is in copyright. Subject to statutory exception and to the provisions of relevant collective licensing agreements, no reproduction of any part may take place without the written permission of Cambridge University Press.

First published 2019

Printed and bound in Great Britain by Clays Ltd, Elcograf S.p.A.

A catalogue record for this publication is available from the British Library.

Library of Congress Cataloging-in-Publication Data
Names: Zartman, I. William, editor.
Title: How negotiations end : negotiating behavior in the endgame / edited by I. William Zartman.
Description: Cambridge, United Kingdom ; New York, NY, USA : Johns Hopkins University, 2019. | Includes bibliographical references and index.
Identifiers: LCCN 2018045933 | ISBN 9781108475839 (hbk) | ISBN 9781108469098 (pbk)
Subjects: LCSH: Negotiation. | Decision making.
Classification: LCC BF637.N4 H687 2019 | DDC 302.3–dc23
LC record available at https://lccn.loc.gov/2018045933

ISBN 978-1-108-47583-9 Hardback

Cambridge University Press has no responsibility for the persistence or accuracy of URLs for external or third-party internet websites referred to in this publication and does not guarantee that any content on such websites is, or will remain, accurate or appropriate.

Contents

List of Figures	*page* vii
List of Tables	viii
List of Contributors	ix
Acknowledgements	x
About the Processes of International Negotiation (PIN) Network at the German Institute for Global and Area Studies (GIGA)	xi
Introduction I. WILLIAM ZARTMAN	1

Part I Cases   25

1 The Iranian Nuclear Negotiations 27
   ARIANE TABATABAI AND CAMILLE PEASE

2 Greek–EU Debt Dueling in the Endgame 46
   DIANA PANKE

3 Colombia's Farewell to Civil War 62
   CARLO NASI AND ANGELIKA RETTBERG

4 Chinese Business Negotiations: Closing the Deal 83
   GUY OLIVIER FAURE

5 France's Reconciliations with Germany and Algeria 104
   VALERIE ROSOUX

6 Closure in Bilateral Negotiations: APEC-Member Free Trade Agreements 122
   LARRY CRUMP

Part II Causes   147

7. Crises and Turning Points: Reframing the Deal   149
   DANIEL DRUCKMAN

8. Managing or Resolving? Defining the Deal   164
   MICHAEL J. BUTLER

9. Mediating Closure: Driving toward a MEO   185
   SINIŠA VUKOVIĆ

10. Mediating Closure: Timing for a MHS   201
    ISAK SVENSSON

11. Facing Impediments: Information and Communication   208
    ANDREW KYDD

12. Facing Impediments: Prospecting   221
    JANICE GROSS STEIN

13. When is "Enough" Enough? Uncertainty   238
    MIKHAIL TROITSKIY

14. When is "Enough" Enough? Approach–Avoidance   256
    DEAN G. PRUITT

15. When is "Enough" Enough? Settling for Suboptimal Agreement   265
    P. TERRENCE HOPMANN

16. Lessons for Theory   287
    I. WILLIAM ZARTMAN

17. Lessons for Practice   295
    CHESTER A. CROCKER

References   304
Index   341

Figures

I.1	Effects of reframing and of high or low security points.	*page* 10
5.1	The Franco-German and Franco-Algerian contexts compared.	119
6.1	Network image of APEC member FTAs.	127
6.2	Closure in complex bilateral negotiations.	142
8.1	Life-cycle of an intractable conflict.	176
14.1	Approach and avoidance tendencies at different points in a journey.	259
14.2	Approach–avoidance conflict when the approach tendency dominates the avoidance tendency.	261
15.1	Leaving value on the table: suboptimal agreements.	267

Tables

3.1 Timeline of partial agreements in the Colombian peace
    process   *page* 63
6.1 Bilateral FTAs in force between APEC-member
    economies   126
8.1 Types of conflict triggers   177
8.2 Typologies of closing behavior and associated strategies   180

Contributors

MICHAEL BUTLER, Clark University

CHESTER A. CROCKER, Georgetown University

LARRY CRUMP, Griffith University

DANIEL DRUCKMAN, George Mason University

GUY OLIVIER FAURE, Université de la Sorbonne

P. TERRENCE HOPMANN, SAIS-Johns Hopkins University

ANDREW KYDD, University of Wisconsin

CARLO NASI, Universidad de los Andes

DIANA PANKE, Freiburg University

CAMILLE PEASE, Georgetown University

DEAN G. PRUITT, George Mason University

ANGELIKA RETTBERG, Universidad de los Andes

VALERIE ROSOUX, Université Catholique de Louvain

JANICE GROSS STEIN, University of Toronto

ISAK SVENSSON, Uppsala University

ARIANE TABATABAI, Georgetown University

MIKHAIL TROITSKIY, MGIMO University

SINIŠA VUKOVIĆ, SAIS-Johns Hopkins University

I. WILLIAM ZARTMAN, SAIS-Johns Hopkins University

Acknowledgements

I am grateful to my wonderful colleagues in the PIN group for letting me move ahead with the idea of this book, which has been pursuing me for a long time. I am pleased to thank the Diplomatic Academy of the Ministry of Foreign Affairs of Montenegro, and its director Ms. Satka Hajdarpašić, for hosting the initial Workshop on this project in Cetinje in July 2015. It was also good to have the initial research assistance of Constance Wilhelm and the indexing of Rona Vaselaar.

About the Processes of International Negotiation (PIN) Network at the German Institute for Global and Area Studies (GIGA)

The PIN Program, formerly at IIASA in Laxenburg, Austria, and then Clingendael, The Hague, the Netherlands, is located at the German Institute for Global and Area Studies (GIGA) in Hamburg. Since 1988, it has been conducted by an international Steering Committee of scholars and practitioners, meeting three times a year to develop and propagate new knowledge about the processes of negotiation. The Steering Committee conducts one to two workshops of scholars from a wide spectrum of disciplines and nationalities every year devoted to the analysis and improvement of the practice of negotiation. These workshops are part of the process of creating a book each year on aspects of negotiation.

It also offers mini-conferences on international negotiations in order to disseminate and encourage research on the subject. Such "Road Shows" have been held at the Argentine Council for International Relations, Buenos Aires; Beida University, Beijing; the Center for Conflict Resolution, Haifa; the Center for the Study of Contemporary Japanese Culture, Kyoto; the School of International Relations, Tehran; the Swedish Institute of International Affairs, Stockholm; the University of Cairo; University Hassan II, Casablanca; the University of Helsinki; the UN University for Peace, San José, Costa Rica; Toledo Center for Peace; the Paris Biennale at Negocia; the Montenegro Foreign Ministry Summer Program Young Diplomats; Johns Hopkins University School of Advanced International Studies in Bologna; Beçeşehir University in Istanbul; and others.

The PIN Network publishes a semiannual online newsletter, *PINPoints*, and sponsors a network of over 4,000 researchers and practitioners in negotiation. Past Projects and the Program have been supported by the William and Flora Hewlett Foundation, the Smith Richardson Foundation, the US Institute of Peace, UNESCO, the Carnegie Corporation, and the Carnegie Commission for the Prevention of Deadly Conflict.

Members of the PIN Steering Committee

Cecilia Albin, Uppsala University
Mark Anstey, Michigan State University in Dubai, formerly Nelson Mandela University, Port Elizabeth
Moty Cristal, NEST, Israel
Guy Olivier Faure, University of Paris V – Sorbonne
Paul Meerts, The Netherlands Institute of International Relations, Clingendael
Amrita Narlikar, GIGA–Hamburg
Valerie Rosoux, Catholic University of Louvain
Rudolf Schüßler, Bayreuth University
Mikhail Troitskiy, MGIMO University, Moscow
I. William Zartman, The Johns Hopkins University
Markus Kirchschlager, GIGA–Hamburg

Emeritus Members

Rudolf Avenhaus, The German Armed Forces University, Munich
Gunnar Sjöstedt, The Swedish Institute of International Affairs
Franz Cede, University of Budapest
Mordechai Melamud, CTBTO

PIN Publications

Zartman, I. William (ed.). 2019. *How Negotiations End: Negotiating Behavior in the Endgame*. Cambridge University Press.
Rosoux, Valerie & Anstey, Mark (eds.). 2018. *Negotiating Reconciliation in Peacemaking*. Springer.
Troitskiy, Mikhail & Hampson, Fen Osler (eds.). 2017. *Tug of War: Negotiating Security in Eurasia*. Center for International Governance Innovation.
Zartman I. William (ed.). 2015. *Arab Spring: Negotiating in the Shadow of the Intifada*. University of Georgia Press.
Melamud, Mordechai, Meerts, Paul & I. William Zartman (eds.). 2014. *Banning the Bang or the Bomb? Negotiating the Test Ban Treaty*. Cambridge University Press.
Faure, Guy Olivier (ed.). 2012. *Unfinished Business: Why International Negotiations Fail*. University of Georgia Press.
Zartman, I. William, Anstey, M. A. & Meerts, P. (eds.), 2012. *The Slippery Slope to Genocide: Reducing Identity Conflicts and Preventing Mass Murder*. Oxford University Press.
Zartman, I. William & Faure, Guy Olivier (eds.). 2011. *Engaging Extremists*. US Institute of Peace Press.

Faure, Guy Olivier & Zartman, I. William (eds.), 2010. *Negotiating with Terrorists.* Routledge.
Aleksy-Szucsich, A. (ed.). 2009. *The Art of International Negotiations.* Żurawia Papers Volume 14. Institute of International Relations, University of Warsaw.
Avenhaus, R. & Sjöstedt G. (eds.). 2009. *Negotiated Risks: International Talks on Hazardous Issues.* Springer.
Bercovitch, Jacob, Kremenyuk, Victor A. & Zartman, I. William (eds.). 2008. *The SAGE Handbook of Conflict Resolution.* Sage.
Avenhaus, R. & Zartman, I. William (eds.). 2007. *Diplomacy Games. Formal Models and International Negotiations.* Springer.
Zartman, I. William & Faure, Guy Olivier (eds.). 2005. *Escalation and Negotiation in International Conflicts.* Cambridge University Press.
Zartman, I. William & Kremenyuk, Victor A. (eds.). 2005. *Peace versus Justice: Negotiating Forward- and Backward-Looking Outcomes.* Rowman and Littlefield.
Spector, B. I. & Zartman, I. William (eds.). 2005. *Getting It Done: Post-agreement Negotiations and International Regimes.* US Institute of Peace Press.
Meerts, P. & Cede, F. (eds.). 2004. *Negotiating European Union.* Palgrave Macmillan.
Sjöstedt, G. & Lang, W. (eds.) 2003. *Professional Cultures in International Negotiation. Bridge or Rift?* Lexington Books.
Faure, Guy Olivier. 2003. *How People Negotiate: Resolving Disputes in Different Cultures.* Kluwer Academic.
Avenhaus, R., Kremenyuk, Victor A. & Sjöstedt, G. (eds.). 2002. *Containing the Atom: International Negotiations on Nuclear Security and Safety.* Lexington Books.
Kremenyuk, Victor A. (ed.). 2002. *International Negotiation. Analysis, Approaches, Issues* (second edition). Jossey-Bass.
Zartman, I. William (ed.). 2001. *Preventive Negotiation: Avoiding Conflict Escalation.* Rowman & Littlefield.
Sjöstedt, G. & Kremenyuk, V. (eds.). 2000. *International Economic Negotiation: Models versus Reality.* Edward Elgar.
Zartman, I. William & Rubin, Jeffrey Z. (eds.). 2000. *Power and Negotiation.* The University of Michigan Press.
Berton, P., Kimura, Hiroshi & Zartman, I. William (eds.). 1999. *International Negotiation: Actors, Structure/Process, Values.* St. Martin's Press.
Zartman, I. William (ed.). 1994. *International Multilateral Negotiation: Approaches to the Management of Complexity.* Jossey-Bass.
Spector, B. I. (ed.). 1993. *Decision Support systems in Negotiation,* special issue of *Theory and Decision* XXXIV(3).
Spector, B. I., Sjöstedt, G. & Zartman, I. William (eds.). 1994. *Negotiating International Regimes: Lessons Learned from the United Nations Conference on Environment and Development (UNCED).* Graham & Trotman/Martinus Nijhoff.
Faure, Guy Olivier & Rubin, Jeffrey. Z. (eds.). 1993. *Culture and Negotiation. The Resolution of Water Disputes.* Sage.
Sjöstedt, G. (ed.). 1993. *International Environmental Negotiation.* Sage.
Mautner-Markhof, F. (ed.). 1989. *Processes of International Negotiations.* Westview Press.

Introduction

I. William Zartman

"How do negotiations end?" is a subject that has eluded any systemic research attention.[1] Yet it is, after all, the basic question in the study and practice of negotiation. How negotiated outcomes are determined is the underlying concern of negotiation analysis, and the question of negotiators' behavior in obtaining closure focuses on the last lap in the race. Closure is the point where Ikle's (1964) three-fold option – Yes, No, Keep on Talking – is collapsed into the first two; talking will continue until the end but is now focused – like Oscar Wilde's hanging – on the immediacy of yes or no. This study focuses on that final phase of the negotiations or the endgame. It seeks to understand how and why negotiators act when they see themselves in a meet-or-break phase of the negotiations in order to bring about a conclusion (successfully or not).

"Endgame" (like "ripeness") is a frequently used term, the title of some 250 books, half of them on Chess, where the term has a special meaning, another half on Go, and one by Samuel Beckett (1957) that is of little help in understanding closure. Like "love" and "war," everyone knows what it means but can't easily define it. In diplomacy, it is often invoked in a general sense, but with some hints at specialty. In the collective account of the Iran hostage negotiations in 1979–1980, Robert Owen (1985, 311) picks up "Final Negotiations" as "one last crash campaign to resolve the matter within the thirty days remaining," creating a deadline before the passage of presidential powers. "The process during those final two weeks ... was essentially that of amending and supplementing" (314), the endgame that McManus (1981, 205) calls "the final dickering," as the parties drove toward a joint declaration (314). Warren Christopher said of that period, "'I think they finally

---

[1] The best treatment, of use in the present discussion, is, as usual Pillar (1983, 119–143), looking at concession rates. The penultimate chapter in Ikle (1964) concentrates mainly on behavior in the main part of the process. Shell (1999) examines closure tactics. Gulliver (1979, 153–168) also looks at concession behavior. What is remarkable is that none of these approaches has been pursued into a fuller analysis, or followed by any literature in the past thirty years.

developed a willingness' to end the crisis" (McManus 1981, 206). The same mode of activity characterized the twenty days at Dayton in 1995, although Richard Holbrooke's account (Holbrooke, 1998) does not seems to identify any moment when he sensed that an end was ever likely, only (as in Iran) necessary. Chester Crocker (1992, 397–398) in "Reflections on the Endgame, 1988" of the Namibian negotiations recalls that "by July and August, we had established our rhythm, ... engaged in nearly round-the-clock improvisations, bending with the moves and signals." In the Sudanese negotiations, Norwegian Minister Hilde Frafjord Johnson (2011, 139, 141) notes that in April 2004 "the break had been useful ... Both sides felt that they were very close to agreement" and John Garang mixed his images: "We have reached the crest of the last hill in our tortuous ascent to the heights of peace," to which Johnson adds, with a different geography, "the road ahead was flat; the Protocols marked a paradigm shift." All of these elements – anticipation, deadline, turning points, trimming, rhythm, break, reframing, direction – will come up in the following analysis. Although they do not always appear with the punctuality of an alarm clock, the fact that they do sometimes and are generally identifiable indicates the usefulness of the concept of an endgame.

This inquiry is particularly relevant to some exciting instances of major negotiations that have recently taken place. Of major significance in international politics are the negotiations between the P5+1 and Iran over nuclear disarmament that drove to an agreement, the Joint Comprehensive Plan of Action (JCPOA), analyzed here by Ariane Tabatabai and Camille Pease of Georgetown University. Once total and immediate withdrawal of sanctions and total elimination of enrichment capabilities were seen as unlikely to be attained, the endgame hung on how much of each was necessary for an agreement. Of major significance in international economic relations were the negotiations between the EU and Greece, a clear case of dueling over two conflicting economic philosophies before our eyes in the headlines, analyzed by Diana Panke of Freiburg University. On the level of intrastate conflict, equally significant was the peace process between Colombia and the FARC, which was, after many previous tries, brought to fruition during the four years after 2012. It was only in the last year that the endgame appeared, when the parties sensed that each was ready to attack the two remaining issues of accountability and transitional justice that stood as a stone wall before agreement. But then a second endgame was forced by the rejection of the agreement in a national referendum, and the parties then rapidly completed an acceptable outcome, an analysis developed by Angelika Rettberg and Carlo Nasi of Los Andes.

While these are the headline cases that make the inquiry so timely, other instances stand out as well to attract attention. In negotiating friendship treaties with Algeria and with Germany, a recall of the deep scars derailed the process at the end in the first case but not in the second, as analyzed in Chapter 5 by Valerie Rosoux. Closure is a major issue in Chinese–Western business negotiations, where the relation is the key and the agreement itself is incidental and epiphenomenal, and is marked by typical but personal behaviors, as Guy Olivier Faure shows in Chapter 4. Larry Crump shows that endgame in trade bilaterals is sharpened by deadlines and taken over by political decision-makers.

Endgame, or the closure phase of the negotiations, occurs when the parties, after having taken stock of where they are in the process, come to the conclusion that an end – positive or negative – is in sight and they need to address their behavior to making it happen. The upcoming round(s) will move to a conclusion, and holding out thereafter for further major gains would be costly and unproductive (Pillar 1983; Gulliver 1979). This phase is usually introduced by a Turning Point of Closure as the negotiations turn from formula to details; as usual, the point may be sharper in concept than in real time but nonetheless is of relevance. It is sometimes preceded by a break in the negotiations to take stock and produce a reframing of the issues, or by an important concession that breaks the deadlock and opens the way to lesser, reciprocal concessions. At this point negotiators sense an acceptable end toward which they are driving, still trying to inflect it in a jointly or separately preferred direction or otherwise bring the negotiations to an end, although they may also be engaging in a dueling or Indian wrestling game for competing outcomes.[2]

There is no telling when that realization will arrive; it is a sense that the negotiators come to during the process, alluded to using the same term "sense" by Faure in Chapter 4. The conflict/problem and relevant pro posals have been thoroughly aired, the preliminaries are out of the way, diagnosis and pre-negotiations have been handled and the negotiations

---

[2] Pillar's (1983, 119, 128) identification is "The first transition [Turning Point of Seriousness] occurs when the bargainers come to view an agreement as possible; the second [Turning Point of Closure] marks the moment they begin viewing it as probable. At the end of Phase Two, the gap between the two positions has narrowed to where they can now see the conclusion of the negotiation – most likely a successful one but a conclusion in any case. The slack is gone from the negotiations, the remaining differences are as clear as they will ever be, and the parties see their subsequent decisions as resulting possibly in the breaking off of talks but not in their indefinite prolongation. Phase Two usually ends with one side making a major concession that ends the waiting game and makes the overall shape of the agreement clear for the first time ... There will be overall reciprocation which was largely absent in Phase Two."

have been going on for a while, the positions and interests have been made clear, the formula (or competing formulas) have been established, everything is on the table, and the dimensions of a Zone of Possible Agreement (ZOPA) are clear and shared, although these understandings may be revisited during the ensuing process. That sense of closure can come as a prospective view, looking forward from where things stand and the direction in which they lean: "there gradually emerged a sense that a moment of new opportunity might be presenting itself" in the words of Harold Saunders (1985, 289) on "The Beginning of the End" of the Iran hostage negotiations But it can also come retrospectively, counting back from a deadline that would close the process: "A great agreement is within their [Bosnians'] grasp ... We must give everyone a drop-dead time limit. I mean really close Dayton down. This should not be a bluff," said Secretary Warren Christopher, and Richard Holbrooke (1998, 304–305) told them as he left, "We must have your answer within an hour ... Not suspend – close down. In an hour."

If there is an agreement it will be overall less than the parties wanted but enough to justify conclusion, either by signing or by leaving. Closure situations come in two types: negotiations that reach an agreement when Not Enough in comparison with original hopes and demands is still enough to make an agreement (Type I), and those that do not reach agreement because Enough was not enough (Type II). In the successful cases (Type I), the parties agree even though they do not reach their stated goals or bottom lines; a partial agreement was deemed sufficient to provide a positive outcome. In the unsuccessful cases (Type II), the parties settle important issues but even that amount of agreement is not sufficient to warrant a final positive outcome. Under what conditions do parties agree to agree on what (and what not) to agree on and under what conditions is the progress insufficient to constitute the basis for an agreement, and how do they behave in the last round?

Obviously the situations are on a spectrum, with extremes at either end. There may be situations where both parties can get all they came for; it is assumed that such situations are rare and, for present purposes, uninteresting. There may also be situations where what they came for is something else than an agreement, that there is no agreement on anything, the parties are not ready to negotiate, and may be acting for side effects (time, publicity, reputation, etc.) (Ikle 1964). These too are outside this inquiry. But the assumption is that most cases of negotiation are in the big gray area in the middle, where the parties cannot get everything they want or thought they deserved, where red lines have to be breached in spots, and yet they sense that the/an end is near and attainable, where the rising question, as the end approaches, is whether

Introduction 5

there is enough to constitute an agreement and how do they behave to attain it? Why stop here, now? Should one continue to negotiate to try to get more, would pushing further push agreement out of reach, is there just or not quite enough to make for a positive outcome? As indicated, there is no way of knowing that the end is really available or how long it will take to get there, but, as the accounts testify, the sense that it is there is usually palpable. Nor is there any way of telling – not even the seriousness of the remaining issues – how long the endgame will take, although it is generally short compared with the previous phases of the negotiations.

Patterns of Closure

Once the negotiations enter into this final phase, how do they proceed? The initial quotations and others' analyses indicate that specific behaviors appear to be associated with the move toward closure, which are different from behaviors during the previous course of negotiations (Douglas 1962; Gulliver 1979; Zartman & Berman 1982; Pillar 1983; Bartos 1976). Endgame behaviors look ahead toward the conclusion to which they are aiming or heading and act strategically in order to get there, a characteristic shared with endgame strategies both in Chess and in Go (Frey 2016; Shotwell 2005). Such behaviors of course relate to the basic process (as also in Chess and Go), to distributive and integrative bargaining, to conflict management and conflict resolution, to payoff maximizing or satisficing, etc. But whatever the particular outcome pursued, the negotiators select various patterns of behavior to move them to closure. What behaviors are typical and required to get the parties to Yes (to refer to the title of a book that does not focus on this point in the process)? What variables are helpful in analyzing the situation? In a word, how do negotiators behave when they feel that they are close to the end of negotiations, and why? Are there common dynamics and identifiable patterns of behavior in the endgame? These are the questions that this study addresses.

Some such modes stand out; others may appear less prominently, but several predominate. Five different patterns of behavior appear very clearly in model form (and muddily but nonetheless distinguishably in reality): *dueling, driving, dragging, mixed,* and *mismatched.*[3] The first two patterns are reciprocal; the parties react to each other in the same terms and expect that reciprocation: toughness leads to toughness, as in

---

[3] Somewhat similar modes from different angles have been advanced in Pruitt (1981), Shell (1999), and Ury, Brett, & Goldberg (1987).

dueling, and softness leads to softness, as in driving (Pillar 1983, 101; Zartman 2005). The other patterns are not reciprocal or matched: toughness leads to softness and vice versa. The first two are related to Rubin & Brown (1975): High Interpersonal Orientation (competitive) and High Interpersonal Orientation (cooperative), taken as behaviors rather than as personality types, with similar results identified for mismatching (see also Shell 1999, although there is relevance but less of a direct equivalent with his five styles or Thomas–Killmann categories); dragging may be related to Low Interpersonal Orientation behavior if it covers the whole endgame and not just a single issue. The behaviors may appear in parts before the Turning Point of Closure; in the endgame they tend to become focused.

Three of the patterns can be appreciated by their behavioral characteristics, sometimes a bit caricaturally:

Dueling	Driving	Dragging
Confrontation	Cooperation/convergence	Disengagement
Cliff hanging	Regular progress	Don't like where this is heading
Hanging tough	Hanging positive	How can we end this gracefully?
End in doubt	End in sight	Approach–avoidance
Steely nerves	Creative mind	Soft landing
Hold out, face it off	Move ahead, wrap it up	Prepare LCD outcome
Classical chicken	Creative chicken	Chicken stalemate
Uncertain information	Exploring information	Uncertainty
Harden support for position	Prepare support for outcome	Prepare for failure or LCD
Threaten	Warn: If not, I'll have to …	Disengage
Ball is in your court	Ball is in our court jointly	Ball is in the net
Deal is far	Deal is attainable	Deal is avoidable
Bad cop	Good cop	Backing out
Late compromise, if at all	Early compromise	LCD compromises
Demand more	Reciprocate	Second thoughts
Emphasize bad collapse	Emphasize good agreement	Emphasize gentle collapse
Re-examine BATNA/security point	Explore ZOPA	Strengthen BATNAs
Entrapped in commitment	Caught up in dynamics	Slow down dynamics
Deadline	Extend deadline if progress	Time running out
Prepare home for failure	Evaluate success so far, crest	Cut losses, make best of it
Concession	Compensation, construction	Set issues aside

The choice of the pattern is path determined by the previous bargaining behavior of the parties. Thus the patterns capture both the individual parties' behavior and also the behavioral pattern of the encounter if shared. The patterns of behavior are not sealed trains in a tunnel; the parties can shift, probably inducing a shift or at least a strain in the other's behavior, but they cannot shift very often without destroying the engagement of the other. A shift can occur at the very end: dueling in the crunch after almost complete agreement by driving, or driving at the edge of the cliff after the dueling has run its course, but such shifts probably require a shift in negotiating or deciding personnel as well.

One pattern is *dueling* (Kitzantonis & Alderman 2015; de Gaulle 1962), also known as cliff-hanging and brinkmanship, in which the parties face each other down to the wire until one of them blinks. This is a pattern of reciprocal behavior, in which toughness has led to toughness, and a low critical risk on the part of both parties leads the process either to confirmed deadlock or to a prolonged shoot-out before one side gives in (Bishop 1964). In critical risk terms, each side bets on the chances of the other side's capitulation and of the acceptability of a deadlock if it does not capitulate.[4] This is a hardened version of a Chicken Dilemma Game (CDG) (only portrayable in a cardinal, not ordinal, depiction), which incorporates the capitulation calculation but not the relative cost of deadlock. Thus dueling parties attempt to persuade the opponent that they will not move and that a deadlock would be quite acceptable to them, that is, to each the "expected cost [of breakdown] equals [or is less than] the expected benefit [of victory]" and each party is indifferent between the two, and they also try to convince the other that its calculation is wrong and that deadlock is indeed costly to the other (Pillar 1983, 92–93). Expressed as security points, the Best Alternative to a Negotiated Agreement (BATNA) for each is – or at least is portrayed as – equivalent to or higher in value than an agreement, so the parties are equal in power and work to reinforce their indifference rather than seeking an accommodation with the other party's position, thus setting up a situation of deadlock or surrender. As a result, an interesting aspect of the dueling pattern is that it drives the parties to bargain on their security points rather than on the terms of a possible agreement, pointing out quite publicly how acceptable for them deadlock

---

[4] There are a number of calculations for critical risk; the most complete one is the ratio of the difference between victory and losing (the southwest and northeast corners in a Prisoners' Dilemma Game matrix) and the difference between victory and deadlock (the southeast corner) (Zeuthen 1930, 147; Pillar 1983, 93; Snyder & Diesing 1977, 49–52). Critical risk is a useful heuristic but more difficult to calculate than its definition would suggest.

is as an alternative and how unbearable the concessions needed to come to an agreement, especially on the other party's hard-line terms, and how awful deadlock would be for the other, without doing much to improve the terms of an agreement. In other words, both parties proclaim that they really don't need an agreement, at least on the other's terms.

Another characteristic of dueling is that there is no agreement on a Formula going into the endgame. The parties still hold different notions of the nature of the problem, the terms of trade, and the notion of justice underwriting the negotiation and hence the agreement. The parties never got out of the competitive stage into a cooperative frame of mind (Pruitt 1981, 133–134; Zartman 1997a). Hence the duelers have an overcharged agenda with little to have built up in preparation for cooperation. If there is finally an agreement among duelers, it is most likely to favor one of the parties.

Decisions in each pattern will have their characteristics. Decisions in dueling will be strategic, i.e. determined by examining (intrapersonal) or comparing (interpersonal) BATNAs, or personal/political, i.e. determined by the strength of commitment to oneself or to the home audience, portraying the offers, deadlines, and BATNAs as fixed reference points. Strategic decisions depend on uncertain information about what one's and the other's security point really is; political decisions depend on a judgment of what one can get away with without breaking commitments. Dueling may take place over a single issue but is more likely to occur over an entire agenda or general concern or relationship that is not subject to decomposition or fractioning, making compensation more difficult. Even when a single issue is, literally, the stumbling block, it tends to take its importance from its representation of the entire relationship. Parties will run down to the wire (and push the wire if possible) to show their unshakability, strengthening their position by public commitments, throwing away the steering wheel in their chicken course while underscoring the catastrophe in the other party's security point (Schelling 1960; Coddington 1968). Thus, the cost of capitulation increases as the parties move toward a decision.

Dueling is done before a public audience and is used to enforce commitment; negotiators are always looking over their shoulder to create a public opinion that then holds them prisoner. There is no question of handling the major issues or any others early to create a positive bargaining atmosphere; the Big One stands to the end as the symbol of the confrontation. Various devices of presentation and misrepresentation as highlighted by prospect theory will be employed (McDermott 2009; Kydd and Stein in Chapters 11 and 12 of this volume). Parties are unlikely to have similar purposes in the negotiation; concessions are the only alternative to one side's giving in completely, but the posture of the parties makes concessions difficult;

compensation may be worth exploring and construction (reframing) is uninteresting. Furthermore, there is no room for mediators in a dueling encounter. They are not welcome, and if they do perchance appear in the hope of being helpful, they are ignored, or worse, by one or both parties, as the fate of Romeo reminds us.

Not surprisingly, the best examples of dueling come from failed encounters, although the Cuban Missile Crisis negotiations were a concise case with a positive outcome. The 2015 Greek debt negotiations, including some interesting manipulation of the public to back the dueling, are a sharp case of dueling examined by Diana Panke in Chapter 2. Negotiations over Kosovo at Rambouillet in February 1999, over Syria in Geneva I and II in February 2012 and February 2014, and negotiations in Sri Lanka in 2006 through 2008 were all cases of dueling. In the first two cases talks were later revived when the situation on the ground (including the disposition of external players) had changed. For this reason, the choice of the EU–Greece case is particularly instructive; one side finally capitulated. Negotiators can of course stop dueling any time they want, but they have to make sure that the decision to change is reciprocated, i.e. that both sides agree to change, or else one party's move will simply be seized upon as capitulation. So duelers can come to an agreement, since their mode is reciprocation if they snap, after appropriate and delicate soundings, to an outcome that takes the best of both positions into account. This may involve selected concessions or, better yet, compensation through an exchange of items to which they assign different values (Nash 1950; Homans 1961). The breakout of the deadlock in the first (2005) Iranian negotiations was accomplished this way and permitted a pattern of driving in the second (2013–2015) round. Examples are also to be found in Chapter 6 by Crump. An unusual, well-executed reciprocated change from dueling to driving occurred after the opening of the Israeli–Palestinian talks at Oslo in 1993 (Zartman 1997b). Like all the others above and below, illustrations are illustration, not perfect fits.

The second pattern is *driving*, in which the parties push and pull each other gradually toward a convergence point, matching concessions and compensations, as the parties work on each other down toward an agreement. This too is a pattern of reciprocal behavior, in which softness has led to softness and a high critical risk on the part of both parties leads the process toward agreement, although only a comparison of the critical risks can tell how long the concession game will go on or which side the outcome will favor (if at all). In critical risk terms (Zeuthen 1930; Pillar 1983), each side bets on the chances of the other side's concessions and of the acceptability of a deadlock if it does not concede. This is an enlightened version of a Chicken Dilemma Game (CDG) where the parties want to avoid a deadlock and so see the situation as an incitement to create a mutually enticing outcome (MEO) (Goldstein 2010) (again only a cardinal depiction of the CGD can show which side the MEO will favor, if any). Thus driving parties attempt to establish an ethos of requitement, persuading the opponent that they will reciprocate any positive move and expect the other to do the same, and also that a deadlock would be quite unacceptable to them; that is, the expected cost of breakdown is much higher than the expected benefit of agreement (Pillar 1983, 92–93). In terms of security points or alternatives, when the alternative to a negotiated agreement (BATNA, XSlo and YSlo in Figure I.1) is – or at least is portrayed as – lower in value than an agreement and both parties are

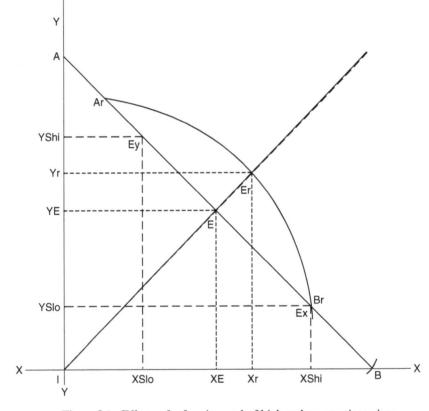

Figure I.1. Effects of reframing and of high or low security points (BATNAs). AEB = zero-sum frontier; ArErBr = reframed positive-sum frontier; YShi or YSlo = Y's high or low security levels/BATNAs; XShi or Xlo = X's high or low security levels/BATNAs.

motivated by this shared difference, they play their bargaining against it to gain concessions and arrive at an agreement (E) better than their unnegotiated alternatives, both sides caught between "it cannot fail" and "we cannot give in." This element of undergirding agreement is possible because in driving the parties have come to an understanding on the Formula for their negotiations (Zartman 1997a). They are now in the stage of details and, although they can backtrack if the Formula is not adequate, they have a basis on which to bargain as they seek to correctly implement the Formula.

However, where the agreement will land depends on the position of one party's security point relative to the others', and on the parties' ability to reframe their issues to produce a more positive sum than before, as often happens within an endgame, as Druckman develops in Chapter 7. If one party can get much the same result without negotiating and so its security point is high (XShi in Figure I.1) and the other's is low (YSlo), a likely agreement (Ex) would be more favorable to the first (X) than to the second (Y). If the reverse obtains (XSlo/YShi), the reverse outcome (Ey) is likely to eventuate. However, if the parties are able to reframe the issues in a way that produces benefits for both of them (the Ar/Br curve instead of A/B), an outcome more attractive to both can be produced, with fewer unaddressed issues left on the table, even if the security points of both parties are high (Er), as discussed further in Chapter 15 by P. Terrence Hopmann. (Figure I.1 also shows that, if both parties' BATNAs are high, as portrayed in the dueling pattern [XShi, YShi], they will need to reframe the issues if they are to reach an agreement [Er] at all).

Decisions in driving will be creative and goal-oriented, looking for possibilities of reframing the issues if necessary, enlarging an outcome and crafting an agreement that maximizes the reach toward the minimum requirements of the parties. They will depend on an evaluation of accumulated benefits, against "must-have red lines" and low BATNAs. Although operating under the shadow of their security points, parties tend to be convinced of the value of the agreement within their ZOPA and decide individual issues on the basis of their requirement and the issues' contributions to maintaining the landing pad in prospect. As agreement is given a value of its own, the cost of failure increases (i.e. BATNA drops) as the parties move toward closure. Negotiators try to maintain confidentiality during the final process to avoid misleading leaks that would help spoilers; nothing is revealed until all is revealed, in principle. The stage is cleared of minor issues at the beginning and even issues of middling importance are handled early, to create momentum and atmosphere. But at the same time, controlled communication is important to keep public confidence but manage expectations, assuring support but controlling information. Parties try to build mutual trust to facilitate the process, although they may turn tactically to dueling as a threat or goad to remind of the push of a painful stalemate – but not too much or too often or they will create a mismatched pattern and destroy trust, as F. W. de Klerk did in South Africa in 1992.

Driving parties may have shared or different purposes, but will look for concessions and compensations to build an agreement; where different purposes make these difficult, parties will seek construction to reframe the issues. In a driving encounter, parties tend to take apart issues and handle them either seriatim or grouped for trade-offs. Focal points such as split-the-difference will be useful where other, substantive criteria fall short of agreement (Schüßler 2018). Working groups on individual issues inhibit compensation among issues but facilitate mosaic agreement. Deadlines can have a catalytic effect in producing agreement but can be postponed to make eventual agreement possible as well, as Angelika Rettberg and Carlo Nasi discuss in Chapter 3, and Larry Crump discusses in Chapter 6. Although these actions appear positive, they require effort and creativity to construct an agreement over stringent "red lines," playing against low security points for both sides, where the deep unattractiveness of no-agreement (southeast corner) in the chicken game creates a strong incentive to fill the northwest box with a mutually enticing opportunity (MEO), as Andrew Kydd discusses in Chapter 11. Deadlock on a stumbling block to the whole package often requires a senior political figure to take over the bargaining and make for closure, as shown a number of times in Chapter 6 by Larry Crump and in the Sudan negotiations (Johnson 2011). The 2015 Iran non-proliferation negotiations for a Joint Comprehensive Plan of Action (JCPOA) are a rich case of driving.

Again not surprisingly, driving is likely to produce a MEO somewhere between the parties' positions going into the endgame, although it must not be thought that the parties will lock arms and dance to an agreement or that the endpoint will be exactly in the middle. The preceding sentence gives the key to the hard bargaining as each side, knowing/believing that the other wants an agreement and therefore is willing to accept less than its maximum, moderate, or even bottom demands, tries to publically wave the danger of collapse at their opponents – again the matter of critical risk. It is at this point that the danger of approach–avoidance analyzed in Chapter 14 by Dean G. Pruitt comes into view, threatening to turn the driving process into a sudden duel. At some point, a "crest" or final turning point may occur, after which the rest of the items are rapidly resolved and the general feeling is one of being in the "home stretch" (Zartman & Berman 1982, 188; Druckman 1986; Johnson

2011, 141). A crest is a point in the negotiations where enough is agreed upon to constitute an acceptable accord, whatever else may be raised (and is therefore a temptation to raise whatever else). A rich illustration is found in the JCPOA negotiations of 2014–2015 with Iran. French negotiations with Algeria versus Germany vividly illustrate how negotiations at the crest can be either upset or untouched by external events, depending on the strength of the commitment built up to that point, as laid out in Chapter 5 by Valerie Rosoux. The 1990–1994 negotiations between the National Party and the African National Congress in South Africa, with all their ups and down, are another example, as were the Northern Ireland negotiations of 1998. The examples amply show that driving often produces an agreement but does not guarantee that outcome, and does not obviate hard bargaining along the way.

For that, it may require third-party attention, so that the mediator becomes the driver, bringing the conflicting parties along in its efforts. Although mediation was seen to be unwelcome in dueling, there is frequently an important place for it in creating a driving pattern, as Chester Crocker emphasizes in Chapter 17. The most important phase of the mediator's work, at the beginning of the mediation and before the endgame, is to ripen the parties' perception that they are in a stalemate and it hurts, and that a way out is available. Only then can the mediator turn to helping fashion a MEO in the endgame. Thus, the mediator needs to awaken the parties' awareness to all the elements – reciprocity, requitement, ZOPA, realistic security points – that they would have developed by themselves in preparation for a directly negotiated endgame but could not, and to keep them on track to the end. In a word, the mediator begins by wanting an agreement more than the parties, contrary to the popular assumption, and then has to transfer that desire and need to the parties – or they would not need a mediator. This was the case in the Namibian Angolan negotiations, beginning in 1980 with the endgame in 1986–1987 (Crocker 1992), in the Sudanese negotiations beginning in May 2002 until the endgame from October 2003 to May 2004 (Johnson 2011), in the Mozambican negotiations beginning in the last version in July 1990 with the endgame between August and October 1992 (Hume 1994), and in the Mindanao negotiations in the latest round in 2010 with the endgame in 2014–2015 (Hopmann & Zartman 2014), among others. In these and other cases, closure was completed through the action of the mediator as the driver.

The same two types, but unilaterally and non-reciprocally mismatched, produce a different pattern when one party behaves as a dueler and the other as a driver. Each party expects the other party to operate on the same model; if this is not the case, the bilateral logic of the behavior is destroyed, or indeed betrayed, and the parties become suspicious and hostile of the other in mismatching. Each expects to find requitement in his own terms, but when it is not forthcoming, the relationship turns very sour. The dueler sees the driver as a softy and a patsy, the driver sees the dueler as an exploiter, and the pattern is upset since it is not clear which pattern is dominant (Rubin & Brown 1975, 158–159.) Gorbachev and Reagan at the end of Reykjavík and Frederik de Klerk and Nelson Mandela at the end of the CODESA phase are telling human examples. These are interpersonal illustrations but, when the two sides meet, each may be bearing a different pattern and expectation. Prime Minister Menachem Begin came to Camp David I as a dueler and President Anwar Sadat as a driver; the mediation of President Carter aside, the meeting would have fallen apart if Begin's staff (as opposed to Prime Minister Begin) had not been bent on driving and despite the fact that Sadat's staff (as opposed to President Sadat) was mainly bent on dueling (Quandt 1995). Many negotiations are mismatched, leading either to collapse or to mutual socialization in one direction or another. The socialization-on-the-job has to be dominated by one side/pattern or the other, lest it merely solidify and intensify the mismatching. Parties and Western mediators have often worked on rebel groups with no sense of negotiation except dueling, to try to inculcate some ideas of driving behavior, as in Darfur, Rwanda, El Salvador, Colombia, Bahrain, Casamance, Sri Lanka, and elsewhere.

The third pattern is dragging, in which the parties alone or severally come to see the outcome toward which they are heading as undesirable and realize that they do not like it. They then work instead to provide a soft landing that ends the negotiations without damage. The realization can come in many terms: that the Formula is not really agreed or adequate, that the details do not lend themselves to an agreement that translates the Formula, that the negotiations are simply not heading toward an enticing outcome, that insistence on a precise solution or an issue would derail the rest of the agreement, and so on. The result can be an effort to call it all off, or simply to push an issue or several aside, putting off for later attention or inattention. Reciprocity, critical risk, and Formulas do not play a systemic role, if they play any role at all. Camp David II was not a case either of dueling or of driving but simply of Arafat's reluctance to negotiate at all, while everyone else was busy coming up with ideas. Reagan dragged on the Strategic Defense Initiative (SDI) at Reykjavík in 1986 and dragged down the entire pending agreement when Gorbachev threw in the issue at the last minute.

Dragging can also be partial and positive, indeed the key to an outcome containing all the other points on which agreement was possible

Introduction 15

but omitting the bone that got stuck in all parties' throats. The question of what issues to include without breaking the back of an agreeable agenda is crucial; it is unlikely that the Jerusalem question could have been included at Oslo or the Kosovo question at Dayton, but the decision to put off a resolution of Brčko at Dayton (1994) and of the Panguna mine at Arawa (2001) were the keys to the last lock on the Bosnian and Bougainville negotiations. Constructive ambiguity on key issues permitted agreements on German unification in 1990, at Oslo in 1993, on the Ukraine in 20013, and even on Iranian weapons denuclearization in 2015, as detailed in Chapter 13 by Mikhail Troitskiy. The same type of calculation can go into agenda setting in preparation for the endgame, leaving out a major issue or aspect of the conflict and then going on to seek closure on the remaining matter. Michael Butler in Chapter 8 divides outcomes into demotion of the means of conflict from violence to politics (Conflict Management [CM]) and settlement of the ends or issues of the conflict (Conflict Resolution [CR]), showing that if, for several reasons, parties decide they cannot take on the latter, they can at least settle for the first.

Decision in dragging – Type II negotiations where not Enough is enough – will depend on calculations of BATNAs and also accumulated and foreseeable benefits. When it appears that a satisfactory agreement in whole or in part is unattainable, parties will attempt to draw down negotiations rather than stalk out with a fuss. The outcome may simply be a petering out of bargaining but is more likely to end in a lowest common denominator (LCD) or ambivalent agreement. Dragging can also apply to only a part of the negotiations, as in a decision to drop certain issues and move on to a less significant outcome on items where agreement can be achieved. The chapters by Dean Pruitt, Mikhail Troitskiy, Michael Butler, and Siniša Vuković explore this effect at various points in relation to the endgame, with examples.

Every dichotomy or other sharp categorization always needs to contain a residual category, in this case, mixed. None of these patterns is pure and consistent; they are general characterizations of behavior in a given instance and are perceptible not only to the analyst but to the parties involved as well. But the parties can switch or slip from time to time, sometimes without destroying the pattern, at other times confusing the train of events and expectations. Duelers may well slip in a driving moment to bring the opponent's guard down or to take advantage of fatigue on the part of the opponent. More frequently, drivers may turn to dueling on a crucial point, at a crucial moment, at a special time in the process. Again, Gorbachev did at Reykjavík, and he failed. Parties cannot switch too often, or they will confuse the other and destroy the process.

16 Introduction

The other patterns are already not sharp enough in the assumptions and characteristics that mixing is less upsetting. The list may not be complete; possibly other patterns (but not too many more, in the name of parsimony) and certainly other traits could be added, but the direction of development is indicated.

Four analytical contexts bring these devices together. One setting is a game of security points (BATNAs, the ingredient of critical risk calculations). Negotiators continually ask themselves (or at least they should), what happens if there is no agreement? This is first an intrapersonal question asked in the large and in the small. The comparison or framing point is one's own level of acceptability, as Janice Gross Stein develops in Chapter 12. In the large, it refers to the whole complex of negotiations; if negotiations break down totally, does the situation go back to war/ conflict, the looming threat (BATNA) as in Colombia 2014–2016, El Salvador in 1992, Namibia in 1988, Cuba in 1962, and Iran in 2016, and how bearable or desirable is this outcome? Does a breakdown of negotiations mean that they are irretrievable, are component elements all lost ("Nothing is agreed until everything is agreed"), or a point where the parties can pick up where they left off? In the small, it does not seem likely that the same question would apply to every issue and negotiating point, concerning whether the particular issue can be decided bi/multilaterally. Thus, the security point question would seem to apply to the sum of the whole impending agreement rather than to its individual parts and would be of little help in the individual decision-shaping process. While one is unlikely to find a favorable BATNA to specific questions, one can ask whether one's side is better off with no agreement, all things considered, and use that as a guideline for specific decisions. However, it should also be an interpersonal question: What is the other party's security point, and how does it compare with mine? What will the other do if there is no agreement, and how does it like that? Critical risk is defined as a comparative calculation. BATNAs are waved about tactically in dueling but are hovering over the proceedings in all the other patterns.

Another contextual setting is a game of chicken, or rather a game of a flock of chickens (Goldstein 2010). This is an interpersonal question, on whether the other side is likely to blink first, first on the specific issue and then on the balance of the whole agreement as it is shaping up (Goldstein 2010). Blinking can be a hard-eyed confrontation, as among duelers such as President Nixon and Chairman Khrushchev at the SALT Talks, or a soft intimation as among drivers such as the JCPOA negotiators in Round 2. The Chicken Dilemma goes back to the previous game: Is breakdown the worst option or only second worst to agreeing (both swerve) or giving in (swerve first)? Chicken can either characterize the classical feud of parties heading to disaster (lower right box of the game-theory matrix) if one or the other does not change course, or as a mutually hurting stalemate it can incite the parties to calculate and communicate to define joint movement to a newly defined agreeable outcome (upper left box) (Zartman 2000, 2006). Again dueling parties play chicken by focusing on the threat of no-agreement, whereas driving parties assume that threat and focus on creating a mutually enticing opportunity in an agreement that will enable them to avoid the threat; dragging parties assume that the cost of no-agreement, their security point, is more bearable than it is in reality. This is a crucial difference in negotiators' frame of mind.

The third setting is a game of echoes, sensing how particular moves and then the whole outcome will ring back home in face of skeptics, opposition, and outright spoilers. More than any other point in the negotiations, endgame is subject to vigorous scrutiny and debate at home. The referent group may be internal to the decision-makers who mandate the negotiators. Or it can be the larger body politic, including the opposition and voting public, as well as others bent on destroying the negotiating party and an agreement, believing the public to be better off without than with any agreement (comparative security points again). The considerations are important in all four signal cases in different forms – the strong conservative nationalist home opposition in Iran and the United States, the personal and political opposition of the Uribistas and also the truce-breakers among both the FARC and the army in Colombia, the domestic audience in Greece and the grumblers over German tactics in some of the other EU members, and the external echoes from observing legislatures in the French–Algerian and French–German negotiations. This aspect of the setting is examined more broadly by P. Terrence Hopmann in Chapter 15.

The fourth is the game of deadlines. Every negotiation, and especially every endgame, has a deadline, formal or informal, vague or precise, felt or explicit, rock-fixed or postponable, externally or internally established. Informal, distant, flexible, internally established end dates have their influence on behavior, as much as do formal, proximate, fixed, externally imposed deadlines. Behaviors are affected by either extreme and in between. It has been found that, in multilateral negotiations, the existence of a deadline was the most important factor in producing agreement (Wagner 2008), but often at the price of achieving no more than the LCD. The impact of deadlines on negotiating behavior in the endgame can be triangulated depending on a number of factors. On one hand is the substantive importance of the issues and the agreement itself; on the other is the agency establishing the deadline, including its flexibility. The interplay of substantive content and procedural restraints is a major determinant of endgame behavior, illustrated by Crump and discussed by Hopmann.

Two sister channels of inquiry might also be examined for inspiration on endgame but they rather highlight differences. One is the growing attention to the When question at the other end of the negotiation process. Ripeness theory, and the associated attention to readiness, addresses the conditions necessary for negotiations to begin (Zartman 2000). Indeed, without belaboring the theory, one can consider the opening of the endgame as a ripe moment, when the parties are in a mutually hurting stalemate (MHS) within the process and see a way out or the possibility of a mutually enticing opportunity (MEO). At this point negotiations are stuck but the possibility of an outcome is up for the seizing. Thus, ripeness for closure is not an externally defined contextual situation, akin to the objective elements of an MHS; it is an internally created stage in the process. Ripeness theory does not, however, look into the appropriate and customary behaviors associated with the situation.

The other related channel of inquiry is the attention devoted to explanation of how wars end (Ikle 1971; Licklider 1993; Fixdal 2012; Kreutz 2010; Rose 2012). The event studied is different enough, however, that the terms of analysis do not seem to offer much insight into the question of how negotiations end. A well-constructed analysis (Faure 2012) of why negotiations fail is closer to the closure problem, both substantively and in its organization. Since failure is overdetermined, Faure (2012) examines a number of cases for specific reasons of failure and then presents a dozen functional or disciplinary answers, each using its own terms of analysis. No common thread is sought, no doubt wisely, but they do add up to some insightful regularities, in the causes presented.

A complicating problem is that while analysts know how far the parties are from a conclusion because it has happened, negotiators do not, because they are only trying to establish that point. Closure behavior concerns how parties act when that point comes into view, however dimly, as they are trying to set and reach it, and the analyst should put himself in the parties' position, as well as the reverse. How do they act in trying to make it so? Just as for the broader question, there are doubtless many answers, depending on the terms of analysis, although the search for a single consolidating answer that is meaningful is tempting. Until one is devised, answers to the question will have to be found in various analytical variables and approaches that impinge on the whole, closing process.

Introduction

Causes of Closure

A search for an understanding of closure behavior can draw on a number of groups of concepts that can throw light on parts of the activity. One group looks at defining components indicating when endgame begins, such as turning points and agenda setting. Another group highlights processual impediments that complicate progress toward completion, such as motivational contradiction, communication ambiguity, information distortion, and critical risk. A final group concerns closing effects that affect the end of the game, such as deadlines, uncertainty, task completion, and principal–agent relations – the game of echoes.

Reframing and Defining the Deal

Turning points are stocktaking moments when negotiators break off talks, consider where they are and what is ahead, and then decide either to return to complete the negotiation or give it up (Druckman 1986). Turning points can occur frequently during negotiations, including within the endgame; however, the endgame itself tends to be introduced by a more significant turning point, the Turning Point of Closure, when the parties individually examine progress and conclude that an agreement may be in sight, for the reaching, as examined in Chapter 7 by Daniel Druckman. It is clear that what is involved is more than a cost/benefit tally sheet but also an estimate of the chances of making progress and the value of the projected endpoint, a salient critical risk calculation. Previous turning points, if any, focused on the prospects of continuing negotiations; the turning point that leads to the endgame posits the prospect of ending them. Druckman introduces an additional element, of reframing, particularly significant in cases of driving, as took place in the Iranian JCPOA negotiations. When the negotiations are stuck on their present course, the cause of the break-off, they may be restored by constructing a new frame for the issue(s) that sets them off on a productive track, avoiding a duel. This is characterized as "the way Navajos decide important questions. When an issue is that sharply divided, it's traditional to say, 'We have to come up with another plan.'" (Hedden 2016).

The perception that the negotiations are entering the final phase also involves defining the type of outcome toward which the parties are heading, whether conflict management (ceasing violence) or conflict resolution (handling issues). Conflict management through ceasefires and truces leaves time under better conditions of suspended violence to work for a solution to the problem, but parties may not want to give up violence as their only money with which to buy concessions until they know what direction efforts at resolution of issues are taking. By engaging with both processual and contextual variables, parties may tend to find management strategies better associated with dragging and dueling. Dueling parties can find preliminary agreement in a ceasefire to attenuate their duel, as was tried in the Syrian sparring in 2014–2016, whereas driving parties may be able to establish conflict resolution, after management early in the endgame, with occasional ruptures, since the shape of the outcome is already in distant view. Michael Butler analyzes this situation in Chapter 8.

Mediating Closure

Even when an endgame strategy is chosen, negotiators may be unable to find a conclusion by themselves. As in any negotiating phase, mediation can be necessary for progress, but, special to endgame, the mediator can invoke deadlines that threaten or promise an end to the process. At the same time they can help identify mutually enticing opportunities (MEOs), a continuation of the reframing undertaken at the initiation of the closure. Other tactics of timing are helpful in the hands of the mediator to move the process along the various modes of endgame negotiation, as examined in Chapter 9 by Siniša Vuković. Progress along the road to the end depends on the costs and benefits to the mediator as well as the parties, as posed by the concept of critical risk related to timing, which is significant in the analysis of Isak Svensson in Chapter 10. The ratio of the difference between victory and losing and the difference between victory and deadlock, even if reduced to an estimation of the relation between losing and deadlock, comes to the fore in the evaluation of mediation in the endgame. Timing informs the decisions, as the balance sheet of closure becomes clearer to the parties as they near the end and are faced with the need to decide whether Not Enough is enough (or Enough is not enough), analyzed by Isak Svensson. Chester Crocker returns to the theme of mediation in Chapter 17 in his conclusion on Lessons for Practice in emphasizing the role of the third party in ripening perceptions of a MHS.

Processing Information

Advancing through the endgame requires processing information, through communication between the parties and evaluation by each of them. Conveyance of information is skewed by its strategic function. Much behavior can be explained by the effects of information availability and its use within the negotiation process, analyzed by Andrew Kydd in Chapter 11. In the case of closure, information of BATNAs and security points, and of the other party's intentions, comes to the fore, as information is manipulated so as to provoke either break-off or completion. Communication of offers and demands has three functions: to indicate a position, to attract the other party, and to signal the degree of flexibility, as a party uses its control over information to draw the other party to a conclusion on its terms. Whereas in the beginning, negotiators withhold information on their offers and demands, at the end they release it to produce closure, at a particular point, or avoid it.

Further information distortion is inherent in the gap between value to the sender and to the receiver, and between differential evaluation of gain vs. loss, the latter carrying overvaluation and risk aversion. Such effects, highlighted by prospect theory as developed in Chapter 12 by Janice Gross Stein, impose a heavy impediment to the final determination of Enough through the process of giving something to get something in negotiation (Stein & Pauly 1993; McDermott 2009). Differential evaluation also makes difficult any estimation, by the party and by the opponent, of either party's security point (BATNA), the most important reference point in the negotiation process and one that tends to move as a prospect comes into view in the endgame. Criticizing the assumption of linear expectations of concession rates and fixed reference points, Coddington (1966, 1968), commenting on Cross (1969), suggests that negotiators behave differently at the end, changing their expectations and notably allowing for brinkmanship, a very non-linear and chicken-like variable.

When is "Enough" Enough?

As the parties near the end of the endgame, the Enough question looms large. Unachieved goals, scuttled bottom lines, and unclaimed gains lay on the table (Thompson 2009). Do parties close – sign or break off – leaving potential gains on the table and why, missing potential gains from the agreement either way, or do they clear the table and under what conditions? Are the decisions made out of ignorance (why?), out of some preconceived blockage against pursuing unclaimed gains (why and within what limits?), or out of a calculation that claiming more benefits might upset the balance of mutual cost/benefit calculations? How do they make the decision between satisficing and optimizing? It may be that the negotiators' calculations change completely in the endgame, as they shift from seeking the best outcome obtainable from the other side to finding an outcome that can be sold back home. Under certain conditions, deadlines are known to facilitate agreement, but they may facilitate a meaningless agreement in dragging behavior. How much can they impose substantive agreement and how much is it a matter of simply procedural agreement to sign anything in order to have signed and to satisfy the source of the deadlines, often dragging to a Lowest Common Denominator (LCD) or framework agreements? The principal–agent setting becomes an additional – and overlapping – element in the final decision. The agent turns attention to the principals, to tell them "Face it, this is the best we can get. Fish or cut bait." But it also asks itself, "Will my boss accept this? How much does he value an agreement? Can he wait and shall I try for something better?" In addition to the usual understanding of deadline as an externally imposed cut-off date, deadline can also be imposed by the evolution of the conflict: It's now or never. These are the closing questions analyzed by P. Terrence Hopmann in Chapter 15.

Or the outcome never can become larger and Enough turns into Not Enough as it comes into clearer view at the end. The motivational ambiguity embodied in the approach–avoidance effect indicates that progress becomes more and more difficult as parties come close to the final issue (substance) or the final agreement (procedure). The goal to which they had been working seems less and less acceptable as it is approached, a behavioral complication investigated by Dean Pruitt in Chapter 14. The effect is most evident in dragging, but it dogs driving as well and reinforces the intrinsic nature of dueling; even the small concessions normally produced toward closure become more difficult and give way to retractions (Jensen 1978, 314). The US started the whole climate change control process with the Framework Convention on Climate Change (FCCC) but had second thoughts on the way to Kyoto and after. Under Norwegian and Centre for Humanitarian Dialog (CHD) mediation, the Acehnese and Indonesians balked at the idea of "special autonomy," but then mediation by Martti Ahtisaari moved them on to accept "self-government"; about the same time, the Tamil Tigers (LTTE) and the Sri Lankan government engaged in negotiations, then pulled back from agreement and fought to the finish (of the LTTE). But before the last hurdle which appears bigger and bigger as one approaches it, negotiators can take stock of where they are and where they want to be, weighing these values against the fearful hurdle, and decide to go for it. (Following the Turning Point of Closure in the 1992 All-White referendum authorizing de Klerk to enter the endgame, he overcame avoidance and moved ahead to the Memo of Understanding and then to the final agreement on South Africa.) What type of behavior is associated with either reaction, and how do negotiations leap the avoidance barrier to move on to agreement?

Finally, a way out of the crunch imposed by the momentum of the negotiations before a deadline, in any of the patterns identified, is to retreat into ambiguity. When the previously discussed matters of prioritizing and agenda-setting issues still leave stumbling blocks in the last moments, constructive fudging can provide a way of kicking the can down the road, as analyzed by Mikhail Troitskiy in Chapter 13. When the end is not the end, negotiations need to leave a way for them to go on, putting a dragging conclusion to an issue in an otherwise driving or dueling pattern. Endgame has its drama, *Capriccio* instead of *Pagliacci* in operatic terms.

So the behavior of negotiators flows after being oriented into the endgame. Rocks and shoals mark the whole course of negotiation up to the final phase, but behavior in the final flow becomes focused, channeled by the sense of entering the endgame and aimed at an end in sight. Strategies are calculated to make closure come alive and to then decide whether it is enough. The following accounts of cases and causes will help flesh out the dynamics of that final phase. It is no surprise that the result does not answer all questions or predict all behaviors and outcomes. But it opens the subject to the first full view and to further productive inquiry.

Part I

Cases

1 The Iranian Nuclear Negotiations

Ariane Tabatabai and Camille Pease

Few arms control and non-proliferation negotiations have made as many headlines as those seeking to curb the Iranian nuclear program. The "Iran talks," as they have come to be known, kept hundreds of officials, experts, and journalists in a dozen countries busy for almost fifteen years. For each of the parties involved, directly or indirectly, the endgame of the negotiations was different. For Iran, the ultimate goal was to maintain key elements in its nuclear program, while normalizing its international status and economy. For the six countries – the five permanent members of the United Nations Security Council (UNSC) and Germany, known as the P5+1 – sitting across the table from Tehran, the goal was to make sure the Islamic Republic would not build a nuclear weapon in violation of its international obligations under the Treaty on the Non-Proliferation of Nuclear Weapons (NPT) and its Comprehensive Safeguards Agreement concluded with the International Atomic Energy Agency (IAEA).

Despite being united in the ultimate endgame of the negotiations, bringing Iran back into compliance, each of these six players also had its own interests to secure. The United States, the leader of the talks on the P5+1 side, was driven by its deep distrust of the Iranian regime dating back to the 1979–1981 hostage crisis, in which members of its diplomatic corps were held by Iranian revolutionaries, and disbelieved its willingness to curb its nuclear program. Under President Barack Obama, the White House was also motivated by political considerations, namely viewing the Iran deal as its potential foreign policy legacy (Phillips 2015). Russia, another key player in the talks, was driven by a number of geopolitical, security, and economic considerations. These included its aligning interests with Tehran in the Middle East and the Caspian region, as well as vis-à-vis Washington. Moscow also had a number of economic and defense interests at stake, including maintaining its semi-monopoly in the Iranian nuclear program, and its stronghold in supplying Tehran with aeronautic and defense technologies (Ryabkov 2015). China was predominantly guided by its economic interests in Iran (Singh 2015). Beijing filled the vacuum created in Iran when the 1979 Islamic

Revolution transformed the country's status from friend to foe in Washington's eyes. Chinese companies secured a large presence on the Iranian market. The remaining members of the P5+1, the three European countries, had common goals but diverging interests. On the one hand, they had a lot to win at a low cost and little to lose. Unlike the United States, Russia, China, and Iran, the European governments did not have to make any major concessions; they were well positioned to strengthen their presence on the promising Iranian market, and did not have the political considerations of Tehran and Washington. Despite being eager to reach a deal, Germany and the United Kingdom took a backseat in many instances throughout the 2013–2015 talks. France, however, was the most hard-line member of the P5+1. Foreign Minister Laurent Fabius deeply distrusted the Islamic Republic, to which he attributed a number of terrorist attacks throughout the 1980s, some during his tenure as prime minister (Irish 2014; Pfeffer 2015). Moreover, Paris had increased its ties with two key stakeholders, which were not part of the negotiations but had considerable influence on the process: Israel and Saudi Arabia.

Neither Israel nor Saudi Arabia was officially part of the process. Yet, these two governments played a key role in shaping the discourse on the nuclear negotiations and resulting deal. They consistently warned against reaching an agreement with Tehran, which they denounced for harboring regional hegemonic ambitions and fanning the flames of destabilizing sectarianism (al-Faisal 2015). A nuclear Iran, Israeli Prime Minister Benjamin Netanyahu (2015) argued, would be a vital threat to the Jewish nation akin to another Holocaust. Riyadh warned that, "whatever the Iranians have, we will have, too" (Sanger 2015b). But for Israel as for the Kingdom, the main problem of the negotiations was the fear of abandonment resulting from a rapprochement between Washington and Tehran and a return to the pre-1979 regional dynamics: a strong Iran backed by the United States, with Iran being reintegrated into the international community.

This chapter explores the endgame of the negotiations over Iran's controversial nuclear program for these actors. It explains that the first round of negotiations (2003–2005) collapsed because of the unrealistic answer given by the EU-3 – the name given to the P5+1 process when the EU states were leading it during that period – to the question "How much is enough?" At the time, Washington fixed the goal of "zero enrichment," thus effectively closing the door to any negotiated solution (Bush 2005; Borhani & Fung 2014). This period was characterized by dragging. This first phase is then compared and contrasted with the 2012–2015 negotiations, where the turning point of closure started when the United States decided to forgo zero enrichment and the moderates came to power in Iran in August 2013.

The Iranian Nuclear Program: A Timeline

The Iranian nuclear program was launched in the 1950s in partnership with the United States as part of President Dwight Eisenhower's Atoms for Peace initiative. Washington supplied Iran with the Tehran Research Reactor (TRR) and highly enriched uranium (HEU) fuel in 1967, after signing an agreement in 1957, while the Germans began construction on the Bushehr Nuclear Power Plant, the first such plant in the Middle East (Iran Watch 2011). Punctuating Iran's international nuclear cooperation was its entrance into Eurodif, a multinational consortium that would enrich uranium in France and sell it to the partners.

By the late 1970s, revolution was brewing in Iran and its leaders saw nuclear energy as a waste of resources for the oil-rich nation. So the country halted the program (Rouhani 2011, 27). But when Saddam Hussein's Iraq attacked Iran with alarming brutality, bombing cities and using chemical weapons against Iranian soldiers, Tehran changed its mind. But suppliers had left and Eurodif did not sell Iran nuclear fuel. The country waited a decade to be reimbursed after taking legal action. The experience made self-reliance a key objective (author interview with Javad Zarif, New York, September 20, 2014). Iran turned to A. Q. Khan, the father of the Pakistani nuclear weapons program and the head of the world's largest illicit nuclear trafficking network, for advice and blueprints (Sanger 2004). By the early 2000s, Iran was building its own centrifuge models, an enrichment facility in Natanz, and a heavy-water reactor in Arak (Nuclear Threat Initiative 2018).

These facilities were revealed by a dissident group in 2002, opening the Iranian nuclear file (Sinha & Campbell Beachy 2015). In 2003, Tehran and the EU3 attempted to reach a negotiated solution (Davenport 2014; Sinha 2005). Hassan Rouhani, who became the country's seventh president in 2013, led the Iranian negotiators, supported by his future foreign minister and chief nuclear negotiator Javad Zarif. The negotiations collapsed in 2005. The conservative Mahmoud Ahmadinejad replaced the reformist President Mohammad Khatami. Unlike his predecessor, Ahmadinejad had little interest in engaging with the West. His rhetoric and policies deeply isolated Iran for eight years.

The next year, the Iranian nuclear file had made it to the Security Council, and the UN began ramping up sanctions against Tehran. After the passage of the final resolution, UNSCR 1929, in June 2010, the list of UN sanctions against Iran included a complete arms embargo, inspections of all vessels suspected of carrying prohibited cargo to Iran, asset freezes on dozens of companies and individuals, individual travel bans, and bans on a number of dual-use items (S/RES/1696 [2006]; S/RES/1737 [2006]; S/RES/1747 [2007]; S/RES/1803 [2008]; S/RES/1835 [2008]; S/RES/1929 [2010]). This was in addition to unilateral US and EU sanctions, which also prohibited trade in Iranian crude oil and natural gas – some of Iran's largest sources of wealth (HR 3107, 104th Congress; HR 61998, 109th Congress).

Yet Iran continued work on the nuclear program and increased its enrichment capability, as its economy was crumbling under the weight of sanctions. By 2013, Tehran was effectively isolated from the international market and financial infrastructure. That year, the presidential candidates' campaigns focused almost exclusively on improving the economy. Rouhani won the election with a mandate to strike a nuclear deal, put the country's economy back on the path to recovery, and normalize its international relations. One hundred days into his presidency, he delivered the Joint Plan of Action (JPOA). In July 2015, the parties signed the Joint Comprehensive Plan of Action (JCPOA).

First Series – Dragging, 2003–2006

When Iran declared Natanz and Arak to the IAEA and opened them up to inspectors in May 2003, the Agency declared that Iran had not technically violated the NPT. The country was following IAEA Safeguards Agreement Code 3.1 and had not yet agreed to follow the modified version of Code 3.1 with the Additional Protocol, which would have required earlier notice. But that summer, IAEA inspectors found traces of HEU at two different sites, after which the IAEA Board of Governors adopted its first resolution on Iran's nuclear program (GOV/2003/69), calling on Iran to adopt and implement the Additional Protocol (IAEA 2003; Kerr 2003).

Following these events, Iran concluded a voluntary agreement ("The Tehran Declaration") with France, Germany, and the United Kingdom to suspend enrichment and sign the Additional Protocol, including voluntary implementation of the modified Code 3.1. In November, the IAEA announced that it had not found evidence for the existence of a clandestine nuclear weapons program in Iran. The following month, Tehran signed the Additional Protocol without ratifying it. As the EU-3 and Iran were negotiating, a devastating earthquake occurred in the city of Bam. The United States offered humanitarian assistance as an overture of goodwill, prompting Mohammad Reza Khatami, then deputy speaker of the Majles and brother of President Mohammad Khatami, to suggest that "goodwill will be answered with goodwill" (Astill & Younge 2004). Both parties seemed to be signaling their willingness to engage in reciprocity with the other, where softness led to softness. President Khatami asserted Iran's inherent right to enrichment, while signaling a willingness to cooperate with the IAEA. But, by June 2004, the IAEA had issued a resolution criticizing Iran's lack of "full, timely, and proactive" cooperation with the Agency (IAEA 2004).

Nevertheless, by the winter, Iran and the EU-3 had signed the Paris Accord, in which Tehran restated its commitment to nuclear non-proliferation and announced it would voluntarily suspend uranium-enrichment activities and allow further IAEA inspections (Sinha & Campbell Beachy 2015). One week later, IAEA inspectors confirmed that the suspension was in place and that it had not found any evidence of an Iranian nuclear weapons program, but that undeclared facilities could still exist. Iran also allowed partial IAEA access to the Parchin military complex, which it had previously rejected on the grounds that as a military base Parchin was not covered by IAEA safeguards. It also made a proposal to the EU-3 Political and Security Working Group, which included a commitment not to pursue WMD and to cooperate on counterterrorism and regional security. In return, Iran asked the EU-3 to remove restrictions on the transfer of conventional arms and dual-use goods, as well as a commitment not to attack, threaten to attack, or sabotage Iran's nuclear facilities (Davenport 2014). These efforts were oriented toward facilitating reciprocity: Iran would take certain steps, some – like allowing access to Parchin – out of goodwill in the expectation that the EU-3 would in turn take steps benefiting Iran.

Iran made another proposal to the EU-3 in March, which included more concrete steps, including Iran's adoption of the Additional Protocol, a limit on enrichment, and an offer to immediately convert all enriched uranium to fuel rods. It reiterated many of the March proposal's points in a third proposal in April (Davenport 2014). None of the three was accepted by the EU-3, which effectively killed hope for reciprocal negotiating and began a spiral of dragging. Indeed, the Iranian proposals were more focused on short-term measures, rather than long-term ones that would address the issue more substantially.

The Iranian Parliament adopted a non-binding resolution favoring the resumption of uranium enrichment for peaceful purposes in May. Two months later, President George W. Bush signed Executive Order 13382, "Blocking Property of Weapons of Mass Destruction Proliferators and Their Supporters," which was later used to impose economic sanctions on Iran. In August, Ahmadinejad assumed the office of President.

Just before he was sworn in, the EU-3 proposed to Iran the "Framework for a Long-Term Agreement," a detailed offer to support Iran's development of peaceful nuclear energy technology as well as trade, political, and security benefits, if Tehran would agree to end uranium enrichment. Iran rejected the proposal days later, as it did not recognize the right to enrichment as interpreted by Iran under Article IV of the NPT. It proceeded with enrichment, breaking the suspension agreement with the EU-3 and ending negotiations. The following month, the IAEA adopted a resolution, "Implementation of the NPT Safeguards Agreement in the Islamic Republic of Iran," characterizing Iran's history of concealment and reporting failures as constituting "noncompliance," and urging it to declare its facilities and activities (IAEA 2005).

In October 2005, Russia proposed a joint enrichment venture under which Iran could enrich uranium in a facility located in Russia, but without access to enrichment technology and without any indigenous enrichment capability. The proposal was supported by the Bush administration, but rejected by Tehran (Parker 2012). The Iranian Parliament then required the government to stop voluntary implementation of the Additional Protocol. A new EU-3 proposal allowed Iran to convert uranium at Isfahan and ship the resulting UF_6 to Russia for enrichment for Iran's reactor fuel. Tehran rejected the proposal after resuming nuclear fuel research at Natanz under IAEA monitoring. The IAEA then reported Iran to the Security Council for non-compliance due to its failure to fully declare its nuclear activities.

The United States, China, and Russia joined the EU-3 in June to create the P5+1, and proposed in Vienna a plan for comprehensive talks with Iran. Preconditions included Iran's suspension of enrichment and re-implementation of the Additional Protocol. The next month, the Security Council adopted the first of seven Resolutions, UNSC Resolution 1696 (UNSC 2006a), requiring Iran to suspend all enrichment activities within one month. Iran rejected the terms of the proposal because of its prerequisites, but noted that it contained useful foundations for cooperation.

In October 2006 President Bush signed the Iran Freedom Support Act (HR 6179), which codified sanctions against Iran and amended the Iran and Libya Sanctions Act of 1996. The act further contributed to Tehran's distrust of US intentions, underlining the idea that Washington's ultimate goal lay in toppling the Islamic Republic. The Iran Act also further reinforced the idea in Tehran that the nuclear crisis was only a cover for regime change. The Security Council's second resolution on Iran's nuclear program in December, S/RES/1737 (UNSC 2006b), imposed the first UN sanctions on Iran and called for immediate suspension of all uranium-enrichment, heavy-water-reactor, and plutonium-reprocessing activities.

The first round of talks did not lead to a negotiated solution or even significant progress or momentum, although both sides made overtures of goodwill. However, a pattern of mismatching dominated the process. The two parties alternatively drove or stalled negotiations, communication remained poor, there was insufficient willingness to compromise, mistrust remained the leitmotif of the process, and, in the end, each attempt at negotiation turned sour. Eventually, with Ahmadinejad's election, the parties turned to dragging. It would take another seven years and new leaders in both Tehran and Washington to set a different pattern.

Second Series – Driving, 2012–2015

Iran and the P5+1 met on and off since the failure of the first series of negotiations, but talks were infrequent and did not produce any substantial progress. Following an October 2011 IAEA report that raised further concerns over the nature of the nuclear program, the EU in January 2012 broadened its restrictive sanctions against Iran by banning the import, purchase, and transport of Iranian crude oil and petroleum products (EU 2012). The EU had previously accounted for 20% of Iran's oil exports. Just three weeks later, chief nuclear negotiator Saeed Jalili sent the P5+1 a letter stating Iran's readiness to resume contacts (Labott 2012; Crail 2012). But, in February, the IAEA released a report outlining serious concerns over Iran's stepped-up enrichment program at the Fordow Fuel Enrichment Plant. Iran originally designated Fordow to the IAEA as a facility for enriching UF_6 to 5%, later revising the designation three times before finally indicating that the plant would enrich UF_6 both to 5% and to 20%. The IAEA report cast a pall of doubt over the tentative plans between the P5+1 and Iran to hold a new round of talks, but the talks eventually did begin, in Istanbul.

This time, the P5+1 pushed for Iran to cease 20% enrichment, but did not necessarily require the complete termination of all enrichment, a condition that had caused the collapse of previous diplomatic efforts. The removal of the demand was for Iran a prerequisite to proceed, as it viewed the dismantlement of its enrichment program as a red line (author interview with Iranian officials, Vienna, May 14, 2014). Instead, Tehran was ready to accept limitations on the program, including the suspension of activity for more advanced centrifuges and a cap on the number of centrifuges it could operate (Davenport 2014). The parties agreed to meet again in Baghdad, where Iran continued to push for concrete steps for quick lifting of sanctions, but the United States and the EU refused to lift sanctions without certain steps from Iran to ensure suspension of 20% enrichment first (Richter 2012; Borger 2012). Meanwhile, the IAEA released in late May a report that discussed the results of a February 2012 environmental sample analysis at Fordow, which showed the presence of particles with enrichment levels of up to 27% U-235, higher than the levels declared in Iran's Design Information Questionnaire (IAEA 2012a). In response, Iran stated that such high levels of enrichment may happen for technical reasons beyond the operator's control.

Despite the report, the P5+1 and Iran resumed talks in Moscow, where Iran signaled that it might be willing to halt 20% enrichment in exchange for recognition of its "inherent right" to enrich uranium and for concrete steps to ease sanctions. The P5+1 showed a willingness to consider the expanded terms of trade and ease some sanctions in exchange for Iran's suspension of 20% enrichment and export of existing stockpiles of 20%-enriched uranium (Davenport 2015). Although the positions of the parties had softened, the talks produced no major breakthroughs and were described as "inconclusive."

The United States announced additional unilateral sanctions against Iran's nuclear and missile programs in July, specifically targeting a group of alleged front companies and banks (US Treasury Department 2012). The following month, an IAEA report (IAEA 2012b) addressed the detection of 27%-enriched particles in environmental samples previously reported in May, stating that "Iran's explanation [a result of 'technical reasons beyond the operator's control'] is not inconsistent with the further assessment made by the Agency since the previous report." However, the report did raise concerns about the sanitization of suspected sites at the Parchin military complex, which would degrade the IAEA's ability to investigate the complex. In a November statement to the United Nations General Assembly, IAEA Director General Yukiya Amano (2012) declared that while the IAEA continued to verify that Iran's declared nuclear material was not being diverted from peaceful purposes, Iran was not providing the necessary cooperation to establish credible assurance about the absence of undeclared nuclear material and activities. The next month, the US Treasury Department imposed additional sanctions.

The IAEA finally concluded its talks with Iran in January 2013 without agreement to clarify possible testing of nuclear trigger mechanisms at Parchin. Iran continued to assert that it was not obligated to open the Complex to inspectors (Kelley 2013). The US Treasury Department (2013) then announced new sanctions against the Central Bank of Iran, even as the P5+1 and Iran met at Almaty. In this round of talks, the P5+1 appeared to have dropped the demand for Iran to transfer its entire stockpile of 20%-enriched uranium out of the country, stating that Iran could be allowed to keep enough for a medical-isotopes research reactor. Further enrichment to 20% would still have to be suspended. The parties agreed to meet again for further talks in the spring, but the meetings in Almaty ended without any substantial progress, or even a next meeting date. In April, Iran began uranium mining at the Saghand Mine and yellowcake production at the Ardakan Plant, progressing further toward a complete indigenous fuel cycle. The United States imposed sanctions on the Iranian rial under Executive Order 13645 in June 2013, just twelve days before Rouhani's election. In the few weeks between the election and his inauguration, Washington further expanded sanctions against Iran to include trade in gold, to prevent Iran from continuing to exploit a loophole in the oil and gas embargo by exchanging oil and gas for gold.

Upon his election, Rouhani gave the nuclear file to the Foreign Ministry, tasking the US-educated and apt diplomat Zarif with concluding a nuclear deal and closing the nuclear file. Zarif had a different approach to negotiations: He did not believe in a zero-sum solution and instead frequently highlighted the importance of reciprocity and mutual understanding (author interviews with Iranian officials, Lausanne, March 18, 2015; Vienna, June 29, 2015). The difference between the Jalili and Zarif teams' approaches did not go unnoticed by the P5+1 negotiators, who saw a window of opportunity to finally find a ZOPA. P5+1 negotiators described Jalili as "kicking the can down the street" and "wasting time" rather than looking for a ZOPA. For Jalili, the negotiations were about the P5+1 alone making compromises (author interviews with EU and US officials, Vienna, Paris, and London, June and July 2015). He was not ready to negotiate, did not see the failure to reach a deal as a problem, and was acting for side effects (showing that Iran was negotiating while stalling the process).

In contrast, Zarif's team recognized that it could not get everything it wanted or thought Iran deserved and that redlines could not be set in stone; they would be breached in spots. He also believed that the BATNA was the continuation of the deterioration of the Iranian economy, while the worst case scenario was an all-out war with the United States. And this view was shared by the P5+1. The Obama administration had inherited two devastating wars in Afghanistan and Iraq, and, with the Syrian conflict brewing, Obama was reluctant to commit more blood and treasure to a further conflict that would only create more instability in the Middle East. Moreover, the status quo was not sustainable, as it meant a possible tenth nuclear-armed state, located in a volatile region. The administration also approached the talks by evaluating and presenting accumulated benefits, against "must-have red lines" and low BATNAs. It pushed for an agreement within its ZOPA.

In September, following meetings on the sidelines between the P5+1 and Iran at the UN General Assembly, President Obama called President Rouhani to discuss negotiations on Iran's nuclear program. This call marked the first time a US president had spoken directly to an Iranian president since the 1979 Revolution. This was a turning point in the long-standing negotiating deadlock, as it signaled the importance of the negotiations as well as mutual desire to reach a ZOPA and opened the endgame in the negotiations. It indicated the importance of reaching a deal to the two capitals, as both Rouhani and Obama saw the deal as their chief foreign policy legacy (author interviews with Iranian officials, Lausanne, March 18, 2015; Vienna, June 29, 2015; Maddux 2014). The talks entered their driving phase, characterized by cooperation, regular progress, outcome support preparation, reciprocation, extended deadlines, and the view that a deal was attainable.

The phone call propelled the talks to the headlines of major newspapers, and various P5+1 partners became involved in each other's domestic politics, and induced leaders of countries outside the talks also to seek to influence the process. Each individual, party, interest group, and nation brought its own endgame to the table, making finding a ZOPA more difficult. But the phone call enabled official diplomatic channels to be created between Washington and Tehran. Soon, US Secretary of State John Kerry and Zarif were meeting regularly in Vienna, Lausanne, and Geneva. Their strolls in Geneva made headlines, angering hard-liners (RFE 2015). But the creation of this channel was key to the successful conclusion of the deal. It allowed the two parties to directly discuss their respective domestic challenges and to seek solutions that would enable them both to sell the talks and emerging deal to their capitals. In other words, the two sides began preparing to support the outcome of the talks from early on. The language of the final deal reflects this fact. The channel was also instrumental in avoiding escalation during and after the talks over related issues. This was a defining element of the talks, as it allowed the settling of disputes before they derailed the process. It also facilitated and signaled the importance of conflict resolution, cooperation, and convergence.

Part of reaching a ZOPA was finding an acceptable compromise between the original positions of the two sides. The United States under President Bush originally demanded zero enrichment, while the Iranians were committed to their "right" to enrich. One negotiator noted that the

Iranians particularly wanted to keep buildings and tangible equipment – the visible, tangible signs of a nuclear program – but were more willing to give up fuel or other low-visibility elements of their program (Sanger & Gordon 2015). In practice, Iran was even willing to give up some elements of its program that were key to its capabilities in return for the preservation of its more politicized, less defining components. Albeit never advertised and acknowledged by Tehran, this was no secret to the P5+1 (author interview with US officials, Washington, DC, March 2015), and was key in providing the two sides with a ZOPA. The US Department of Energy was crucial in finding creative ways to reframe the issues and establish a ZOPA, working within nuclear physics to change the focus from the number and type of centrifuges Iran would be allowed to operate to the length of Iran's "breakout" time – the time it would take Iran to produce a single weapon's worth of fissile material (Sanger & Gordon 2015). A deal could therefore keep more centrifuges than the United States originally preferred in place if Iran agreed to ship out a larger quantity of its enriched-uranium stockpile. This allowed Iran to maintain a certain number of centrifuges, which served as a symbol of the program, while also lengthening the breakout time. The Iranians could say the program was preserved, while the Americans could claim that Iran's weapons capability was delayed significantly.

The P5+1 and Iran next met in Geneva in November, and almost finalized an agreement. France refused to sign the agreement, stating that the proposals were not tough enough on Iran. Specifically, Paris objected to what it viewed as its partners' concessions on Arak (Crumley 2013). In the meantime, Iran and the IAEA completed their set of negotiations by signing the Joint Statement on a Framework for Cooperation Agreement on 11 November, which aimed to increase transparency with respect to several aspects of Iran's nuclear program (IAEA 2013). This may have given the P5+1 talks a boost as well, as the parties agreed to a six-month-long Interim Agreement/Joint Plan of Action (JPOA) upon the resumption of talks two weeks later.

The JPOA was significant in several respects. It represented a major achievement of early compromise in the process of the second round of negotiations and established preliminary parameters of a ZOPA. It helped convince the parties of the value of an agreement, and provided an agreed-upon basis from which further negotiations could take place. Finally, the JPOA increased the cost of failure. The existence of an agreement, despite its temporary nature, raised the stakes and gave each of the negotiating parties something more to lose. As part of the JPOA, Iran agreed to freeze its enrichment program, downblend its 20% stockpile into 5% or turn it into uranium compounds unsuitable for further enrichment, halt construction on the IR-40, freeze installation of centrifuges at enrichment facilities, and provide the IAEA with information and access to sites it had not had access to under Iran's Safeguards Agreement. In exchange, Iran was allowed to repatriate $4.2 billion in oil-sales proceeds from foreign accounts, and the P5+1 agree to temporarily suspend sanctions against sales of petrochemicals, gold, and other precious metals, and against Iran's auto sector (US State Department 2014a). This reciprocity is a hallmark of the driving pattern of negotiations, in which each side makes exchanges in order to build confidence and set a precedent of mutual benefits.

Following the JPOA's implementation, the IAEA released a report verifying Iran's compliance with the interim agreement (IAEA 2014c). Progress continued in February as the P5+1 and Iran met in Geneva and agreed on a framework to guide the talks in the coming months. The IAEA released a report indicating Iran's compliance with the six initial practical measures that were part of the IAEA's Framework for Cooperation with Iran. In a sign of progress, the United States provided compensation to Iran by releasing $450 million of frozen Iranian funds following IAEA reports that Iran was in compliance with its JPOA commitments (Harf 2014; Dunham 2014). In May, Iran and the IAEA (2014b) agreed on five additional practical measures as a part of their Framework for Cooperation, to be implemented by August 25. Some of these measures addressed potential military dimensions of Iran's program, which had also come up as a negotiating point in Iran's talks with the P5+1. Washington and Tehran held talks in Geneva in June, in the lead-up to the next round of talks between the P5+1 and Iran (BBC 2014). In this round, the negotiators agreed to intensify the frequency of talks in July, and set July 20 as the deadline for reaching a final agreement. It appeared the end was in sight. There was a strong effort to maintain confidentiality of the talks to ensure that negotiators did not suffer from vocal domestic constituencies' raising protests before they had the opportunity to come to a full and complete agreement – nothing is revealed until all is revealed.

As the July 20 deadline neared, the parties agreed that there was enough progress to justify a four-month extension to the talks, with a self-imposed deadline of November 24. This was the first such extension. A key feature of these extensions was the two sides' emphasis that the aim was not to simply attain an agreement, but to attain a good one. Under the terms of the extension, Iran would convert all of its 20%-enriched LEU stockpiles into fuel plates for the Tehran Research Reactor. In exchange, the P5+1 would repatriate $2.8 billion (US State Department 2014b). Some important details were left unresolved: the extent of

Iran's enrichment capacity, the timeframe of a deal, and the schedule for sanctions relief.

The IAEA released a report in September indicating that Iran was continuing to comply with JPOA measures. However, only one of the five practical measures Iran was required to take through the Cooperative Framework had actually been implemented by the deadline of August 25. Two additional measures were implemented after the deadline, and discussions for implementation of the two additional measures were ongoing (IAEA 2014d). The P5+1 and Iran resumed talks on the sidelines of the UN General Assembly meeting, including one-on-one talks between Kerry and Zarif, but no further progress was made. A number of stumbling blocks continued to stymie subsequent talks in Vienna in October, stemming from disagreements over the limits of Iran's enrichment capabilities, the timeframe of a potential deal, and the sequencing of sanctions relief. The negotiating parties took time to regroup and come back with fresh ideas on how to move forward.

The IAEA's last report (IAEA 2014c) on Iran prior to the extended deadline for the P5+1 talks, on November 7, verified Iran's continued compliance with the extended JPOA, although it stated that two of the five practical measures had not yet been implemented. When the November deadline came, after additional meetings in Vienna, Iran and the P5+1 announced that negotiations would again be extended. They expressed the view that progress had been made and both sides saw a way forward. Neither side blamed the other for missing the deadline, signaling a political will to continue the process in good faith. The new goal was to reach a political (framework) agreement by March 2015, and complete the technical details by June 30. Both sides agreed to continue implementing the JPOA as well as to implement five new practical measures in the next step (EU 2014; IAEA 2014b).

Talks restarted in Geneva in December and continued through February 2015 in both Geneva and Vienna. A late-February IAEA report (IAEA 2014c) confirmed that Iran was abiding by the terms of the interim deal, including the additional provisions agreed to in November 2014 (IAEA 2014e). In the weeks leading up to the second deadline, there was a spoiler scare when Senator Tom Cotton (2015) and forty-six other senators signed an open letter to Iran, warning that "the next president could revoke such an executive agreement with the stroke of a pen and future Congresses could modify the terms of the agreement." Despite the unrest in Congress, talks between the P5+1 and Iran continued in Lausanne, and the monitoring regime, the timeframe of the agreement, and the number of centrifuges Iran would be able to keep were settled. Sanctions relief remained a sticking point, while research and development remained another when the talks resumed in November 2014. Iranian negotiators could sense the pressure felt by their American counterparts, as their constituency pushed back against the process (author interviews with Iranian officials, Vienna, June 29, 2015). The Iranians' perceived toughness and new demands from the Americans led them to in turn adopt a tougher stance. This tactical dueling was triggered by the United States' pushing back on research and development, after reports indicated a possible breach of the JPOA by Iran (Albright & Stricker 2014; Lewis 2014; Psaki 2014). Ultimately, Washington stated that Tehran had not violated the terms of the JPOA but asked Tehran to refrain from those activities. Iran accepted (Psaki 2014).

The negotiations changed course in February, when Iran announced that it would send Ali Akbar Salehi, chairman of the Atomic Energy Organization of Iran, to join the negotiation team (Balali 2015). Salehi possesses both detailed technical knowledge regarding Iran's nuclear program and a close relationship with Ayatollah Khamenei, which gave him significant authority in the proceedings (Sanger 2015a). In response, the United States sent Ernest Moniz, the US Secretary of Energy and a nuclear physicist, to engage in negotiations on the technical dimensions of the agreement. US officials, first taken aback by the Iranian decision to include Salehi, then welcomed the opportunity to have a technical channel between Salehi and Moniz, in addition to the existing diplomatic channel between Zarif and Kerry.

The inclusion of Salehi and Moniz was crucial for closure for a few reasons. First, the engagement of technical experts suggested that the negotiating partners had settled the major points of an agreement and reached some of the hardest and most detailed issues left to be decided (Sanger 2015a). Their firm grasp of the science behind strategic political considerations generated more options. According to Salehi, if he and Moniz had not been willing to spend long periods of time negotiating on the technical issues and been empowered to sign off on their agreements, the talks would not have reached a conclusion (Karami 2015). Second, Salehi and Moniz reportedly worked well together, with Moniz stating that they have a "good rapport" (Sanger 2015a). The two men shared an experience at the Massachusetts Institute of Technology (MIT), where Salehi had studied and Moniz had taught. Salehi's short absence in June further proved his importance, as talks were "getting nowhere" until Zarif made a quick trip to Tehran and returned with Salehi (Sanger & Gordon 2015).

After eight days of marathon talks in Lausanne, on April 2, the P5+1 and Iran announced a framework deal. During that week, negotiators on both sides understood they had arrived at a meet-or-break moment:

Domestic pressure on both sides was increasing, as the US Congress received Netanyahu, who denounced the emerging deal, while hardliners in the Iranian parliament mirrored Congress's tough talk. But both sides also saw the stakes as too high and the endgame as too close not to push through. The framework was contingent on reaching a final agreement by June 30, and all sanctions would remain in place until the implementation of such an agreement. Under the outline deal, to last ten years, Iran would reduce its enrichment capacity by two-thirds, modify the Arak reactor and export the spent fuel, reduce its stockpile of LEU by 98%, and accept intrusive monitoring mechanisms. Iran was allowed to keep Fordow open as a research and nuclear physics lab. Iran also agreed to allow inspectors into Parchin (Arms Control Association 2015). The agreement was endorsed by a UN Security Council (UNSC) resolution superseding all previous UNSC measures on the Iranian nuclear program.

Moniz continued to be important domestically in the administration's efforts to secure support within the United States, as he was well respected in Washington and adept at dealing with Congress (Mufson 2015). His credibility as an experienced nuclear physicist was invaluable in supporting assertions that the deal will indeed block Iran's pathways to a nuclear bomb, adding scientific rigor to the political arguments in favor of the deal. He is also lauded for his ability to explain complicated scientific issues to non-experts, another asset for the administration's efforts to lay out the deal to both Congress and the public (Dixon & Everett 2015).

However, opposing public statements by officials in the United States and Iran suggest that not all is settled. Foreign Minister Zarif (2015) tweeted and made statements to the press after the deal was announced that the West would immediately lift all sanctions on Iran's banking and oil sectors once Iran's compliance had been verified, a position echoed in an Iranian "fact sheet" published in Farsi and released to Iranian media,[1] while Secretary Kerry said it would occur in phases (Erdbrink & Sanger 2015). Ayatollah Khamenei later made his own statement on sanctions, declaring that they would be lifted as soon as Iran began to implement the deal. Khamenei also stated that Iran would not allow inspections of military facilities, including Parchin, contradicting what Iranian negotiators had supposedly agreed to (Fitch, Solomon & Lee 2015; Mostaghim &

---

[1] According to Iranian Foreign Ministry officials, the "fact sheet" produced by some Iranian media outlets was leaked and not officially endorsed by the negotiating team (author email interview with Iranian official, July 2015). For a discussion of the differences between the US and Iranian statements, see Gordon (2015).

Richter 2015). And behind closed doors, it seemed like the two sides had entered another tactical dueling phase. At that stage, the Iranians were particularly frustrated by the lack of clarity on the sanctions provisions. Later, Iranian officials recognized that had they involved economists on their end throughout the process, as they had on the technical front, that stage of the talks would have gone more smoothly (author telephone interview with Iranian official 2016).

The End of the Game: The Comprehensive Deal

The P5+1 and Iran finally reached a comprehensive deal (Joint Comprehensive Plan of Action – JCPOA) in July 2015 (US State Department 2015). The JCPOA went beyond the framework agreement of March 2015 in many ways. Its language was meticulously worked to allow both sides to sell the deal at home. In the United States, this was more difficult given some lawmakers' insistence that anything short of zero enrichment would constitute a "bad deal"(Corker 2015; Herszenhorn 2015). In Iran, this was made easier by the vague and semi-flexible red lines fixed by the Supreme Leader. Among these, the Iranian negotiating team could highlight certain key achievements, including Iran's ability to keep all the facilities, preserve the enrichment program, and continue research and development.

Under the JCPOA, Tehran could operate 5,060 IR-1 centrifuges at Natanz to enrich uranium, while 1,040 IR-1 centrifuges in Fordow would operate without enriching uranium. Of these 1,040 centrifuges, 348 would spin, but would enrich materials other than uranium for production of medical isotopes (JCPOA §6). This limitation would last ten years. These numbers were higher than those expected by some members of Congress, but were substantially below the starting point of 19,500 centrifuges installed at Natanz and Fordow at the time of the interim deal. Of these, about half were spinning and enriching uranium. For Iran, the number was below what it had hoped to receive at first. However, Tehran was willing to compromise the quantity and quality of its enrichment program in order to preserve all its facilities and keep Fordow open. For the US government, the ideal plan was to have Iran limit its enrichment levels to less than 5% and its stockpile below 300 kg of 3.5%-enriched uranium, with no stockpile of 20%-enriched uranium. Iran's starting position was that it had the right to enrich at any level, but it would agree to cap its level to 5% for the interim deal. Under the framework agreement, Iran had accepted not to enrich over 3.5% and to limit its stockpile to 300 kg for fifteen years. Under the comprehensive deal, it conceded not to enrich over 3.67% for fifteen years and to limit its stockpile of nuclear material to 300 kg of UF_6 enriched up to 3.67%. It also undertook to sell the excess UF_6 in return for natural or diluted uranium. The fuel rods for the country's reactors would not be counted in these figures (JCPOA §7).

Iran entered the negotiations unwilling to compromise on the essence of research and development. It was, however, willing to scale it back. In the 2003–2005 talks, Tehran proposed maintaining 500 centrifuges for research and development, with the option to increase to 3,000 centrifuges over time. The United States' preferred outcome would have been for Iran to suspend its activities temporarily. The issue of research and development became especially problematic during the weeks leading to the framework agreement being reached. Ultimately, it was agreed in the JCPOA that Iran would limit its research and development with advanced centrifuges for ten years. Iran would be able to continue working on its IR-2m, IR-4, IR-5, IR-6, IR-7, and IR-8 centrifuges, all of which will be hosted in Natanz, and conduct computer modeling and simulations of new centrifuge models beyond those specified. After 8.5 years, Iran could increase the number of IR-6 and IR-8 centrifuges to thirty of each type, but would not be able to stockpile the enriched uranium produced by these centrifuges (JCPOA §3 and Annex 1).

A key area of controversy in the lead-up to and during the talks was the Arak Heavy Water Reactor (Dahl 2013). For the US Congress (but also France and Israel), Arak was a facility that needed to be shut down. Indeed, although it is a more vulnerable target than the enrichment sites, Arak would generate substantial amounts of radioactive fallout if hit once it became operational. As former Israeli military intelligence chief Amos Yadlin said, "Whoever considers attacking an active reactor is willing to invite another Chernobyl," referencing the disastrous 1986 reactor accident in Ukraine that spread radioactive particles over much of the western USSR and eastern Europe (Dahl & Williams 2013). The US government position was different: Requiring Iran to close the reactor would drive it away from the negotiating table. The administration position was that Arak could operate but would not be able to produce plutonium; Iran's starting position was that the reactor would be completed and would operate. A possibility put forward by some experts was to convert the heavy-water reactor into a light-water reactor. Iran rejected this premise, noting that it would need to rely on the outside world to operate a light-water reactor, as it did not have that know-how domestically (author interview with Javad Zarif, Vienna, June 2015). The two sides settled on Arak's being redesigned and modified so as not to produce weapons-grade plutonium, with the spent fuel rods being shipped out of the country for the lifetime of the reactor. Iran formalized its commitment not to reprocess spent fuel and to refrain from building additional heavy-water reactors for fifteen years (JCPOA §8).

The JCPOA included a robust inspection and monitoring regime. Iran accepted to voluntarily implement the Additional Protocol, as it had briefly in the past, while committing to take steps to ratify the document through its legislative branch. Tehran also agreed to abide by the modified Code 3.1 of the Safeguards Agreement, which requires countries to submit design information for new nuclear facilities to the IAEA as soon as the decision is made to construct or authorize construction of the facility (IAEA 2011). Previously, Iran had been following the original 1976 Code 3.1, which requires a declaration of the existence of a nuclear facility "not later than 180 days" before introducing any nuclear materials (Ford 2012). Routine measures include daily IAEA access to declared facilities, ranging from uranium mines and mills and centrifuge assembly workshops (an unprecedented measure) to enrichment facilities. It was agreed that 150 IAEA inspectors will be present in Iran long-term in order to carry out these inspections. Iran also agreed to surveillance of centrifuge construction for twenty years and a mechanism to ensure speedy resolution of IAEA access concerns for fifteen years (JCPOA §15).

The IAEA verified on January 16, 2016 that Iran had shipped over 8.5 tons of enriched uranium to Russia, disabled more than 12,000 centrifuges, and poured concrete into the core of Arak, leading President Obama to declare "every single path Iran could have used to build a bomb" had been cut off (*New York Times* Editorial Board 2016).

Conclusion

It took two rounds of negotiations over the course of more than a decade to reach a comprehensive solution over Iran's nuclear program. Different moving parts had to come together for this, including domestic politics, political will and capital on both sides, the cooperation of key countries and the broader international community, economic incentives, and the involvement of the right individuals. These different pieces did not fall into place until August 2013, when Rouhani came to power, putting an end to a decade of mismatch between the parties. When Khatami was willing to engage, the United States of President George W. Bush saw Iran as part of an Axis of Evil that needed to be isolated. Later, President Obama's outreach to Ahmadinejad fell flat and the Iranians started dragging. Finally, the Rouhani–Obama overlap and the creation of two individual yet interconnected channels, one technical between Salehi and Moniz, and one diplomatic between Zarif and Kerry, helped create the right political environment for the deal. These two channels stemmed from and contributed to the willingness and ability of two parties to find a ZOPA and begin an endgame.

The turning point in closure was summer 2013, when the driving phase started. During that period, both parties had a clear understanding of the other's redlines, reciprocated goodwill with goodwill, were willing to compromise, and saw the costs of deadlock or a failure of negotiations as being unacceptably high. They further maintained confidentiality to avoid misleading leaks that would help spoilers. They often extended deadlines as both parties saw the end in sight and believed they were making progress. The low-hanging fruit was tackled and settled early on to create momentum. Moreover, the controlled communication by the two sides helped manage expectation and built support for the process. Both parties emphasized the importance of striking a good deal, not just any deal.

The resulting deal is a complex document with over 150 pages. It is a flawed document. But it was precisely the acceptance of a possibly flawed deal over a perfect one that allowed the two sides to get to closure.

2 Greek–EU Debt Dueling in the Endgame

Diana Panke

This chapter sheds light on the endgame in the negotiations between Greece and the EU over the conditions for financial bailout in 2015.[1] In a first section, it summarizes how the economic and financial crisis evolved and why Greece has been hit hard. On this basis, it studies the negotiations between Greece and the EU. First, it provides an overview of the first and second bailouts and introduces the major actors and institutional arenas for the 2015 bailout negotiations. It then examines the negotiation dynamics. From the beginning in 2015, the Greek–EU negotiations were regarded as an endgame, since the second bailout package had been proven to be insufficient and the solvency of Greece had an expiration date coinciding with the end of the second bailout program. In this context, the negotiations turned into dueling. Both sides exchanged demands and proposals on a regular basis and usually under the eye of the public. The negotiations were very confrontational, but both sides were entrapped in commitments to hold off the Greek crisis and prevent negative economic and financial consequences for the EU at large (for a theoretical discussion on entrapments, see Panke 2015).

Nevertheless, because of the public attention and the high stakes, no side wanted to make major concessions deviating from the ordo-liberal approach (the Eurogroup) or deviating from the Keynesian approach (Greece). The negotiators were throwing balls into each other's field, not only exchanging threats and limited compromises, but also externalizing responsibility. Blame shifting did not solve the problem, and the default of Greece was looming. Greece could not leverage up vis-à-vis the EU side in a two-level-game fashion despite having held a referendum on the bailout conditions in which the Greek citizens rejected them. After the failure of this last escalating negotiation move, the Greek side had to make concessions. They lost the negotiation endgame. In August 2015, the Greek government ended up agreeing on conditions for a third

---

[1] For proofreading and research support, I would like to thank Matthias Büttner and Elliott Bourgeault.

bailout that were more demanding than a compromise proposal put forward by the EU at the end of June.

How the Crisis Evolved

The Greek crisis, leading to the negotiations between the EU and Greece over financial bailout conditions concluded in August 2015, had a long history. In 2007, the US housing-market bubble burst as the underlying financing structure ceased to be viable. Whilst initially being a "local" problem, the impact was soon to be felt across the Atlantic as well. Greece was one of the countries severely affected by the US crisis, along with Ireland, Portugal, and Spain. Public and private endeavors were not backed up by adequate securities, and investors doubted that the structure of home financing, building, and other economic sectors, as well as banking, was viable. Greece came under severe pressure, as it already faced severe structural and economic problems prior to the international economic and financial crisis of 2007/8. Most notably, the state's spending had been high while income through the domestic economy and taxation was limited. For example, the Greek gross public debt changed from 111.37% of gross domestic product (GDP) in 2005 to over 115.80% in 2006, 113.08% in 2007, and 117.38% in 2008 (OECD 2015). Thus, not only were credits for private and public enterprises insufficiently backed up by guarantees, but once the creditors stopped prolonging credits, the debtors were unable to pay off their debts.

Owing to the weak state of the Greek economy, the limited budget, and the governmental debts, the Greek government could not step in and fill gaps in the credit chain (Christodoulakis 2015). As a consequence, unemployment rates went up (from 8.4% in 2007 to 9.6% in 2009 and 24.5% in 2012), tax revenues stagnated, and the Greek economy almost came to a halt (Eurostat 2015a).[2] The situation was severe, and the system came close to collapse. In response to risks of sovereign default, credit rating agencies downgraded the government debt of Greece, reaching high-yield bond status in 2010. Thus, by mid 2010 Greece had *de facto* no access to the private capital lending market anymore. Since not all EU members were affected as strongly by the financial and economic crisis, there was no concerted EU response to tackle the crisis and stabilize the countries in the EU's periphery that suffered from severe turbulence. Instead, in 2007/8 and 2009, the response to financial

---

[2] The Greek GDP (in millions of euro) declined as follows: 2007: 232,831.1; 2008: 242,096.1; 2009: 237,431.0; 2010: 226,209.6; 2011: 207,751.9; 2012: 194,203.7; 2013: 182,438.3; 2014: 179,080.6 (Eurostat 2015b).

and economic difficulties was national rather than European in character and turned out to be inadequate.

The euro prevented the struggling Eurozone countries from downgrading their currency as a means to ease pressure. At the same time, severe financial turmoil in Eurozone countries put the strength and reliability of the Euro at risk. Consequently, initially domestic crises in the EU periphery turned into a European crisis and triggered a European response. Yet no system had been established to deal with economic and financial crisis of the magnitude Greece and others experienced from 2007/8 onwards.[3] The Economic and Monetary Union (EMU) lacked a crisis-management system under which Eurozone members under pressure could obtain substantial funds and credits to stabilize their respective economies. Thus, in December 2010, the Heads of States and Government in the European Council agreed on establishing a European Stability Mechanism (ESM) and also established the European Financial Stability Facility (EFSF) as a temporary instrument to cope with debt restructuring and financial support of Eurozone members in crisis. The EFSF was quickly operational and supported Greece, Ireland, and Portugal by issuing bonds on capital markets and thereby providing liquidity (EFSF 2013; BBC News 2012; European Commission 2015a).

From October 2012 onwards, the ESM, which was equipped with €80 billion, was operational (ESM 2015a). It took over the principal tasks of the EFSF in issuing debt instruments and mobilizing funds for Eurozone countries to overcome sovereign debt crises. Thus, through the ESM the Eurozone members could finance loans and organize financial assistance to struggling member states, which were expected to also apply for similar support from the International Monetary Fund (IMF) at the same time. The ESM financially supported Cyprus (€8.968 billion) (ESM 2015b) and Spain (€41.3 billion) (ESM 2015c), and provides guarantees (that can total around €500 billion) that enable Eurozone countries in crisis to obtain credits on the world's financial markets. Yet, in accordance with Article 136 of the Treaty of the Functioning of the European Union, ESM financial assistance is conditional upon domestic economic reforms overseen by the Troika of the European Commission, the European Central Bank, and the IMF (ESM 2012, 2013, 2014).

---

[3] The Treaty of Amsterdam 1997 put forward the Stability and Growth Pact (SGP) to further specify the convergence criteria of Maastricht and ensure budgetary discipline among the future members of the Eurozone. In 1998 the European Central Bank (ECB) was created to organize the introduction of the euro in 1999–2001 and take over responsibility for the single monetary policy.

Despite obtaining assistance (mode details are given in the section below), the Greek economy had not reached the necessary productive level,[4] the unemployment rate remained very high (2014: 26.5%) (Eurostat 2015a), and tax evasion was still a problem in late 2014 (*The Economist* 2012, 2014). As a consequence, the public revenue was too limited to pay back loans and to avoid a gap in the budget sheet of the Greek state. Knowing this, Greece was in dire need of financial support through the ESM. The negotiations between the EU on the one hand and the Greek government on the other for an additional bailout started in 2014 and continued in 2015. In line with the focus of this volume, a special focus is placed on the endgame of the EU–Greek negotiations which took place in 2015. Did the negotiations resemble dueling, driving, or dragging? Which dynamics took place, and how can they be accounted for?

The Negotiations between Greece and the EU

The Context: Previous Bailouts

Since 2010, two bailouts had taken place. Greece received a *first bailout* loan of €110 billion in May 2010, to which the Troika attached austerity measures including structural reforms and privatization of government assets (European Commission 2015a; Wearden 2010; Bharati *et al.* 2010). In 2011, it became apparent that the first bailout was not sufficient. To help Greece overcome the recession, a *second bailout* loan of €130 billion was agreed upon between the Troika and Greece in February 2012 (which was once more conditional upon structural reforms and austerity measures by the Greek government).[5] In total €240 billion was meant to be transferred to Greece at regular intervals by December 2014. This plan did not work out. Not only did Greece fall behind with implementing austerity and reform measures, its economic condition worsened as well. Thus, in December 2012, Greece received an *additional loan* from the IMF (€8.2 billion to be provided between January 2015 and March 2016), while the EU reduced Greek debt (53.5%/€105 billion) (Bundesministerium der Finanzen 2014;

---

[4] The development of the Greek real GDP growth rate was as follows: 2008: −0.4%; 2009: −4.4%; 2010: −5.4%; 2011: −8.9%; 2012: −6.6%; 2013: −3.9%; 2014: 0.8% (Eurostat 2015d).

[5] The second bailout included a bank recapitalization package totaling €48 billion and all private creditors with Greek government bonds took a haircut by which the deadlines for the payback of lowered interest rates were extended, leading to a face-value loss of about 50% (Castle 2012; Guo and Zhang 2012; *Financial Times* 2012).

Plickert 2015). In early 2014, the Greek economy improved (by 0.9% economic growth in the first quarter) and the unemployment rate declined (decreased in the second quarter 2014 by 4.6% compared with the first quarter and by 3.6% compared with the previous year to 26.6%), only to be back in recession in the fall and winter of the same year (unemployment increased by 1.6% compared with the previous quarter to 26.1%, and the GDP decreased (seasonally adjusted) by 0.4% compared with the previous quarter) (Eurostat 2015c; Hellenic Statistical Authority 2014a, 2014b). Hence, in the second half of 2014, negotiations between Greece and the Troika took place in order to fill the calculated gap in the financial balance sheet of Greece in the years to come. The negotiations covered the state of implementation of the conditions in relation to structural reforms and austerity measures attached to the previous bailout programs, the activation of the last bailout tranche in December 2014, and a *third bailout*. This cumulated in a domestic political crisis leading to new elections.

While SYRIZA (Coalition of the Radical Left/Synaspismós Rizospastikís Aristerás) opposed existing and potentially new bailout conditions (austerity measures, structural reforms), other political parties were in favor of continuing the path of the former Samaras government (New Democracy/Nea Dimokratia; Panhellenic Socialist Movement/Panellinio Sosialistiko; The River/To Potami). On January 25, 2015, the left-populist party SYRIZA together with the junior coalition party ANEL (Independent Greeks/Anexartiti Ellines) formed the government under Alexis Tsipras as the new prime minister. In line with their electoral manifesto, the new coalition did not accept the terms of the previously negotiated bailout agreements and wanted to renegotiate the terms of the bailout (Horvat 2014). In response, the Troika temporarily suspended scheduled loan payments either until the Tsipras government accepted the conditions attached to the bailout programs or until a new deal had been negotiated and agreed upon by the EU and Greece. In the meantime, the Greek economy suffered and government bonds were further downgraded so that – similarly to what had occurred in 2010 – the Greek government could not become re-liquidized through the private capital market. Thus, *de facto*, the only viable way to receive loans and avoid sovereign default for Greece was to regain access to the EU's bailout fund.

The Actors

The main actors in the endgame negotiations of 2015 on the third bailout of Greece were the following.

On the one side are the Troika consisting of the European Commission, the European Central Bank (ECB), and the International Monetary Fund (IMF). From 2015 onwards, the term "troika" was not used anymore, having been replaced by the term "institutions." The Troika members have different functions, since the bailout treaties or loans are formally signed by the European Commission, the IMF, and Greece, but not the ECB, with the latter having only a consultative function in the Troika. The Troika actors were Jean-Claude Juncker as President of the European Commission, Olli Rehn as Vice President of the European Commission, Matthias Mors as Commission negotiation leader, Mario Draghi as President of the ECB, and Klaus Masuch as negotiation leader for the ECB, as well as Christine Lagarde as IMF President and Poul Mathias Thomsen as IMF negotiation leader.

While the Troika, or more specifically the European Commission and the IMF, had to formally sign agreements with Greece, the bulk of negotiations were taking place in the Eurogroup. Thus, for the EU, the most important negotiating actors included the Eurogroup president (and Dutch finance minister) Jeroen Dijsselbloem and Wolfgang Schäuble (German finance minister) for the Eurogroup, Donald Tusk (President of the European Council since December 1, 2014, successor of Herman Van Rompuy) for the European Council, and Jean-Claude Juncker (European Commission President) for the European Commission. In addition, Dijsselbloem was acting on behalf of the ESM's Board of Governors and Board of Directors (which he chairs as the President of the Eurogroup) in the endgame negotiations.

On the Greek side, the major actors were Alexis Tsipras, the prime minister, from the SYRIZA party as well as his finance minister, Yanis Varoufakis, also from SYRIZA. Varoufakis was in office until July 6, 2015, when Tsipras accepted his resignation and replaced him with Euklides Tsakalotos. The prime minister himself was in office until August 27, having resigned on August 20 after losing support from MPs of his own party.

The Institutional Negotiation Arenas

The 2015 negotiations between Greece and the EU on the conditions for a third bailout took place in various arenas. These included the Eurogroup, an informal setting in which the nineteen finance ministers of the countries with the common European currency meet to discuss issues related to the common currency and economic growth (Generalsekretariat des Rates 2015). The Eurogroup generally convenes in Brussels on a monthly basis, usually the night before the Council for Economy and

Finance meets. During the crisis, and especially during the 2015-endgame stage, the Eurogroup got together more frequently in order to negotiate with Greece. While the IMF is not a member of the Eurogroup, Christine Lagarde as the IMF president was sometimes present at meetings. Apart from the Eurogroup meetings in Brussels, the negotiations between the EU and Greece also took place at flexible venues, including bilateral or multilateral diplomatic meetings in various capitals, as well as meetings during the G7 in June at Schloss Elmau in Germany.

Negotiation Dynamics

Initially the last tranche of the EFSF funding was due to expire in January 2015, but the dire economic and financial situation in Greece called for additional loans in order to avoid insolvency in the medium term (European Commission 2015a). Since the newly elected government under Prime Minister Tsipras objected to the bailout conditions from the 2014 negotiations, an agreement on a third bailout was not in easy reach in January 2015. In this situation, the Eurogroup decided to extend the second bailout program by four months, in order to buy time to renegotiate bailout terms and bring about a third rescue package.[6] These renegotiations were planned to be finalized by the end of April. Thus, the EU–Greece negotiations of 2015 had been framed as an "endgame" from early on. The actors on all sides knew that the negotiations could not continue endlessly, not even into late 2015 or 2016, as a failure of swift agreement would have made the object of negotiations and therefore further negotiations along the same lines obsolete: Without further bailout funds, the Greek state would have been bankrupt, and sovereign default on a major scale could not be remedied with a third bailout package.

However, despite widespread perceptions of the EU–Greek negotiations as an endgame and despite the initial optimism that the negotiations could be concluded quickly and with a compromise satisfying both sides,[7] the negotiations proved to be difficult from the start. The Greek

---

[6] See Lynch (2015) and *The Economist* (2015a).
[7] For example, a newspaper reported "Jeroen Dijsselbloem said he's 'very confident' the government in Athens will demonstrate commitment to reforming the country's finances. Under a draft agreement on Feb. 20, it had until midnight Greek time to complete a list of policies in return for continued funding. A Greek government official said it will be sent to the finance ministers on Tuesday. 'The Greek government has been very serious, working very hard the last couple of days,' Dijsselbloem, who is also Dutch finance minister, said in an interview at an event in Tilburg, the Netherlands, on Monday. 'We need it to be strong enough to work on the next couple of months. I am always optimistic.'" Cited in Chrysoloras & Pals (2015).

government, especially finance minister Varoufakis and Prime Minister Tsipras, made the point that they were elected with the popular mandate to significantly ease austerity measures and refused to agree to strict bailout conditions.[8] On the other hand, the head of the Eurogroup Dijsselbloem, and German Finance Minister Schäuble, backed by many of the Baltic states of the Eurogroup, maintained their austerity policy and continued to insist on ordo-liberal structural reforms in Greece as bailout conditions (Agence France-Presse 2015; *Financial Times* 2015; Kollewe & Wearden 2015).

Thus, in the first quarter of 2015, Tsipras and Varoufakis played a two-level game. Characteristic for such a negotiation approach is that each of the negotiators has access to two levels at the same time, namely the respective domestic arena and the international arena, so that each actor can use her information advantage and justify demands in the international arena through references to domestic-arena constraints or vice versa (Schelling 1980; Putnam 1988). Accordingly, the Greek government insisted that it had the backing of its electorate or even more strongly the mandate to avoid "damaging austerity measures" and demanded that the EU must respect the democratic decisions of an EU member state (Traynor 2015; Hewitt 2015; Chibber 2015). However, the tied-hands strategy failed and did not sufficiently strengthen the Greek bargaining position at the negotiation table in Brussels (Traynor 2015; Hewitt 2015; Chibber 2015).

The ordo-liberal majority of the Eurogroup, under the informal lead of the German Finance Minister Schäuble, did not accept the political framing that EU demands would undermine democracy in Greece. Instead, they emphasized that European solidarity has been and still is strong, and that the EU wants to help the Greek people, but that they themselves have an obligation to the EU citizens (*The Economist* 2015c). Thus, the Eurogroup insisted that they needed to ensure that taxpayers' money is not wasted but used to invest in a better Greek future, which can only be reached through the combination of suggested structural reforms (liberalization, competition, privatization, prevention of tax evasion) and austerity measures (cutting government spending in regard to public welfare, military expenses, etc.). Dueling took place as the two economic policy approaches held by the two sides were incompatible and irreconcilable, irrespective of how many proposals and counterproposals

---

[8] For example, Tsipras is quoted as having stated that "he is committed to honoring the Greek people's mandate, which he received in January's general elections. On this basis, the Greek PM reportedly said that he will continue to seek an agreement with European partners." Cited in Protothema (2015).

both sides made, pitting the Eurogroup's ordo-liberalism and the Greeks' Keynesian approach of achieving economic growth through deficit spending against each other (Gourevitch 1989, Hall 1989, Siems and Schnyder 2014). In February, the Eurogroup extended the terms of the second bailout by one month, now reaching to June 30. Not only did the Greek tied-hands strategy fail in using the Greek domestic public opinion in order to gain leverage vis-à-vis the Troika, their attempt to put pressure on the EU to make concessions to Greece in order to avoid collaboration between Greece and Russia failed as well; to this end, Tsipras visited Putin in Moscow in April 2015 (Alderman & Herszenhorn 2015).[9] The move was very confrontational in character. Thus, it was possible that this move was never intended to further the negotiations with the European partners in a constructive manner, but rather was meant as a show of strength for the benefit of the Greek domestic audience, signaling that Greece had possible alternatives to the unpopular negotiations in Brussels.

Since the renegotiations between the EU and Greece were not concluded by the end of April, it became unlikely that the last financial tranche of the second bailout package was going to be paid out by the end of June as initially planned. This phase of the dueling dynamics was characterized by cliff-hanging as the uncertainty of the stakes was rising for both sides. By May 2015, Greece was heading for a sovereign default as its international credit ratings were on the lowest possible level, rendering access to the private capital market close to impossible, whilst public loans were not provided by the EU (or the IMF either). Talks about a possible "Grexit" were widespread in media outlets across Europe and beyond, according to which Greece would leave the Euro and re-establish its own currency (e.g. Ewing 2015; *The Guardian* 2015). Confrontation was also part of the dueling nature of the EU–Greek negotiation endgame, and Greece resorted to this strategy once more. Thus, Tsipras did not seek reconciliation with the negotiation partners from the EU in May 2015,[10] but instead openly criticized the EU,

---

[9] For example, the Greek finance minister stated in an interview "We negotiated with the troika, the representative of the IMF, the ECB and the EU Commission. It is not true that they made concessions and we made concessions and that there is a deadlock. They made no concessions. When we met the first time in February they came up with pretty much what they have now offered. Then we had months of negotiations in the so-called Brussels group. And there was a lot more convergence there." (Simantke & Schumann 2015).

[10] For example, *The Guardian* wrote about Tsipras "It hasn't helped that his government's negotiating tactics have become overwhelmingly perceived as having more to do with posturing and lecturing than with readiness to find a compromise"(*The Guardian* 2015).

especially the Eurogroup and the European Commission, for having been overly technocratic (Tsipras 2015).

Cliff-hanging is a dangerous sport, albeit an integral feature of dueling negotiation dynamics. Thus, to avoid a financial and economic disaster, Tsipras and Varoufakis revitalized the staggering negotiations with the Troika around mid June 2015 (Simantke & Schumann 2015; Smith 2015). This time, the bargaining position of Greece was even worse than in the period between January and April 2015. Also characteristic of dueling negotiations is that more or less the same arguments were exchanged by both sides, despite the chances of persuading the opponent of the appropriateness and value of one's proposal being close to non-existent (*Spiegel Online* 2015; Stewart 2015a). Yet the Greek need for additional loans was considerably more urgent in early June 2015. Sovereign default was looming (Lienau 2015; Clements 2015). The Greek government risked running out of liquidity, which would have brought their banking sector and the economy to the brink of collapse. Since such events would also have negative consequences for the common currency and the Eurozone economy, the negotiation situation showed features of a "chicken game."[11]

In June, Greece was initially willing to negotiate until a compromise could be reached, on the basis of which the Eurogroup could decide on the authorization of a third bailout fund. Thus, the Troika (the European Commission, the ECB, and the IMF) as well as the Greek government exchanged compromise proposals, again resembling dueling features of negotiation dynamics. On June 22, Tsipras proposed to reform the VAT system (unify the rates to 23% [which would be an increase, especially for restaurants] and eliminate discounts, especially for the islands) and to change the retirement system by stopping early retirement and increasing the regular retirement age step by step to sixty-seven (European Commission 2015b). Yet, the European Commission, the ECB, and the IMF did not regard these proposals as being sufficient to raise enough revenue for the Greek state and to close the Greek budget deficit in the short, medium, or long term. Nevertheless, negotiations continued and Tusk (General Secretariat of the Council 2015a) remained cautiously optimistic: "For now, I can only say, that work is under way and for sure it will need still many hours. The last hours have been critical but I have a good

---

[11] A newspaper article even explicitly portrayed the negotiation as a game of chicken as "With just seven weeks remaining before Greece's current rescue runs out, it is unclear who might blink first. Will Athens bow to pressure and accept tough new economic reforms to release the remaining €7.2bn in the programme and refill its dwindling coffers? Or will Greece's increasingly divided creditors succumb to fears over 'Grexit' and give Athens a pass?" (*Spiegel Online* 2015).

hunch that unlike in Sophocles' tragedies this Greek story will have a happy end." Similarly, Tsipras spread optimism: "I think that European history is full of disagreements, negotiations and at the end, compromises," said Tsipras. "So, after the comprehensive Greek proposals, I am confident that we will reach a compromise that will help the Eurozone and Greece to overcome the crisis" (cited in Steinhauser & Dendrinou 2015a).

Yet, the situation was about to change and "hopes of a breakthrough were fading even before the ministers sat round the table. Arriving at the meeting, Germany's Finance Minister Schäuble said Greece had moved backwards, a message that was echoed by the German chancellor Angela Merkel" (Rankin & Traynor 2015). The positions prepared on June 24 did not allow much room for compromise. Finally, in the evening on June 25, the EU made a compromise offer. The creditors proposed to release €15.5bn of bailout funds, €1.8bn of which would have been made available immediately to avoid the sovereign default of Greece. This "extraordinarily generous" offer (Angela Merkel, German chancellor, quoted in BBC News 2015a) was conditional upon Greece being willing to accept the unaltered reform demands of the Troika, including the highly contested pension reform and increasing VAT. While this could have been a late compromise, ending the nerve-racking dueling negotiation endgame, it was not accepted as such by the Greek government, which held an emergency meeting on the night of June 25 in Athens to discuss the bailout proposal.[12]

Instead of accepting the Eurogroup's latest compromise as a BATNA on June 26, the Greek delegation haltered the internal negotiations and communicated to the Eurogroup that they would terminate the discussions with the EU. Conditions on a third bailout were still not agreed upon. On the same day, Tsipras announced a referendum (which was approved by the Greek parliament on June 28), in which the Greek citizens should decide whether or not to accept the Troika offer from June 25 as a preliminary negotiation outcome (Hellenic Republic Prime Minister 2015; Kitsantonis & Yardley 2015). Again, following the logic of a two-level-game tied-hands strategy, the Greek government recommended a no vote ("οχι") on the conditions on the basis of which they could negotiate a new, better deal with the EU. Such a new, better deal should not only be less conditional with respect to reform and austerity

---

[12] Most likely Tsipras did not make strong arguments in his government to accept the proposal as he is quoted of having "accused the lenders of blackmail, saying: 'Europe's principles are not based on blackmail and ultimatums,' he said. 'In these crucial hours, nobody has the right to put these principles at risk'" (cited in BBC News 2015a).

measures required in exchange for loans, but should also include substantive debt-relief measures for Greece (new "haircuts"). Yet, the Eurogroup leader openly rejected the possibility of further compromises in order to secure a yes vote in the Greek referendum, and the position of the Eurogroup hardened.[13] Moreover, the EU also rejected the Greek request to further extend the current bailout by five months in order to allow more time for renegotiations. Thus, the endgame nature of the EU–Greece negotiations had not been changed.

The Greek referendum was scheduled for July 5, while the second bailout was due to expire on June 30. Thus, members of the Eurogroup, most prominently Wolfgang Schäuble, reacted to the announced referendum by highlighting that if both sides, the EU and Greece, failed to agree on new terms, the object of the Greek referendum was void, as it would no longer be a viable option for the EU side (Hooper 2015). Schäuble and the Eurogroup put pressure on the SYRIZA government, pointing out not only that it was unprecedented that a party break off negotiations unilaterally, but also that it was politically risky to do so, as the Eurogroup were no longer bound by the old terms (their compromise proposal from June 25) after June 30.

On June 27 the Eurogroup adopted an official position, which, however, entailed a built-in compromise (General Secretariat of the Council 2015b, 2015c; Jacobsen 2015). They insisted that they were willing to further extend the second bailout, paving the way for a third bailout if the referendum in Greece supported the conditions, but only if the EU and Greece reached a compromise on the conditions for a third bailout program before June 30. This move is also consistent with the dueling nature of the EU–Greek negotiations at large, since it reflects the entrapped commitment of European political leaders, most notably German Chancellor Merkel, to keep Greece in the Eurozone if at all possible.

Although the negotiations between the institutions and Greece did not continue at that point, the ECB announced that Emergency Liquidity Assistance would be available to Greek banks as long as the June 30 deadline for agreement on a third bailout had not passed, but also that emergency funding would not be increased (Blackstone 2015;

---

[13] "'Europe can still ask Greek people to vote 'yes' to an improved proposal' for financial aid, said Mr. Varoufakis, who left the meeting after a first round of talks Saturday afternoon. Mr. Dijsselbloem, however, ruled out the possibility of a new proposal with easier terms. Even if the Greek people voted 'yes' in the referendum, he said, there would be 'grave problems of credibility' over the government's willingness and ability to implement the measures demanded by the creditors." (Steinhauser & Dendrinou 2015b).

The Economist 2015b). At the same time, the Eurogroup publicly announced that they would not extend the bailout program beyond June 30. Since Greek loans worth €1.6 billon from the IMF were due to be paid back on the same day, sovereign default was looming more than ever. Greece was about to run out of liquidity, risking financial and economic breakdown. Accordingly, Greek citizens were lining up to withdraw cash from their bank accounts, further accelerating the risk of illiquidity of the Greek state. On June 28, the Greek government reacted. They announced that banks were closed from June 29 until July 6, and they installed capital controls, prohibiting most foreign transactions and limiting the amount of euros that could be withdrawn from bank accounts through ATMs (€60 per day per person). These measures affected the payment of salaries and of pensions, and led to public protests in Athens and elsewhere in the country.

The referendum took place on July 5 and had a turnout of 62.5%. A majority (61%) of the Greek electorate rejected the provisional bailout terms (as offered by the Troika on June 25). For most Eurogroup members, this result came as a surprise, and they had no immediate response. The international financial and capital markets, however, responded immediately, leaving Greece worse off. A Grexit was now a real political possibility, no longer pushed only by individual finance ministers, but widely debated (Ghosal & Thomas 2015; BBC News 2015b; Sinn 2015; Kirby 2015). Yet, Tsipras did not favor a Grexit and therefore restarted the negotiations with the EU, albeit with a different lead negotiator as Euclid Tsakalotos replaced Varoufakis.

From July 7 onward, both sides were back at the negotiation table. Although the EMU did not foresee any procedures for how a country could leave the common currency, it was now openly discussed whether Greece would be better off outside the Eurozone (Eddy 2015). Yet, a Grexit was something the Greek government and especially its Prime Minister Tsipras were eager to avoid, since Greek public opinion seemed to be in favor of remaining in the Eurozone.[14] Thus, Tsipras was entrapped in commitment as well: abandoning the common currency and leaving the Eurozone was no viable alternative. This opened the door for a late compromise and a negotiation marathon lasting until July 13 took place. On this day, an agreement on the conditions for a third bailout through the ESM was reached. The third bailout agreement would have a volume of about €82 billion (and could be increased to a

---

[14] Not least since by now concrete plans of how to manage a possible Grexit existed (for the controversy around Schäuble's proposal of a temporary Grexit, see Maas 2015; Becker & Weiland 2015; BBC News 2015b).

total of €86 billion) and would be paid in phased tranches between 2015 and June 2018 (Guarascio & Maltezou 2015; Wearden 2015; Thompson 2015). The payment of tranches was conditional upon a strict set of structural reforms (e.g. of the justice sector, of the pension system, privatization of state assets estimated to be worth €50 billon, liberalization) and austerity measures (e.g. introduction of massive cuts in public spending).[15] In addition, laws put in place by the SYRIZA government

---

[15] The conditionality was to be updated on a quarterly basis, taking into account the progress in reforms achieved over the previous quarter (European Commission 2015c). The European Commission stated the bailout conditions in a press statement which had been coordinated with the IMF and the ESM (*European Commission* 2015c): "*Restoring fiscal sustainability*: Greece will target a medium-term primary surplus of 3.5% of GDP to be achieved through a combination of upfront parametric fiscal reforms supported by an ambitious programme to strengthen tax compliance and public financial management, and fight tax evasion, while ensuring adequate protection of vulnerable groups. A major reform of the pension system will eliminate disincentives to work, and address sizeable imbalances which threaten fiscal sustainability. In pursuit of this medium-term goal and taking into account the deterioration in the economic situation, the authorities will accordingly pursue a new fiscal path premised on a primary surplus balance targets of −¼, 0.5, 1¾, and 3.5 percent of GDP in 2015, 2016, 2017 and 2018 and beyond, respectively. The trajectory of the fiscal targets is consistent with expected growth rates of the Greek economy as it recovers from its deepest recorded recession. *Safeguarding financial stability*: Greece will immediately take urgently needed steps to tackle the non-performing loan (NPL) problem in the banking sector. The extraordinarily high level of NPLs and the related over-indebtedness of the private sector divert significant resources from more productive uses and prevent the banking sector from providing the necessary credit in support of a recovery of growth. In addition, a recapitalisation process of banks, to be completed before the end of 2015, will contribute to a stabilisation of the situation in the banking sector. This will be accompanied by concomitant measures to strengthen the governance of the Hellenic Financial Stability Fund (HFSF) and of banks. Together with other programme policies this is expected to foster a normalisation of the liquidity situation in the banking sector, allowing a concomitant gradual easing of capital controls. *Growth, competitiveness and investment*: Greece will design and implement a wide range of reforms in labour markets and product markets (including energy) that not only ensure full compliance with EU requirements, but which also aim at achieving European best practices. There will be an ambitious privatization program, and policies that support investment. The structural reform package to be enacted is significant, particularly in the area of business environment and competition policies, which are key for unlocking the growth potential of the economy. *A modern State and public administration* shall be a key priority of the program. Particular attention will be paid to increasing the efficiency of the public sector in the delivery of essential public goods and services. Measures will be taken to enhance the efficiency of the judicial system, including by implementing the recently adopted new Code of Civil Procedure, and to upgrade the fight against corruption. Reforms will strengthen the institutional and operational independence of key institutions such as revenue administration and the statistics institute (ELSTAT). The agreed strategy takes into account the need for social justice and fairness, both across and within generations. Fiscal constraints have imposed hard choices, and it is therefore important that the burden of adjustment is borne by all parts of society and takes into account the ability to pay. Priority has been placed on actions to tackle tax evasion, fraud and strategic defaulters, as these impose a burden on the honest citizens

which are incompatible with the bailout conditions had to be revoked, leading commenters to state that the Greeks needed to "grant veto powers over much legislation to international inspectors." (Stamouli & Bouras 2015).

Without viable political alternatives on the table, Greece had to re-examine the BATNA. Entrapped in the commitment to avoid bankruptcy and sovereign default on the one hand, and stay in the Eurozone on the other, Tsipras finally accepted the conditions for the third bailout, although they were stricter than the compromise proposal by the Troika from June 25. Having lost the negotiation endgame and having to accept major concessions, Tsipras prepared home for failure and rallied for support of the bailout agreement. The Greek parliament agreed to the bailout conditions on August 14, but to pass the agreement, Tsipras had to rely on the support of oppositional MPs, given that thirty-two SYRIZA MPs voted against it and eleven abstained (Hjelmgaard 2015; *Kathimerini in English* 2015; *Spiegel Online* 2015). Tsipras stated that "The country had no choice. This was not a triumph, he said, but nor was Greece in mourning" (cited in BBC News 2015c). On August 20, 2015, Alexis Tsipras resigned.

Conclusions

From the beginning in 2015, the major actors were aware of the endgame character of the Greece–EU third rescue package negotiations. From early on, dueling dynamics evolved in which proposals and counter-proposals were exchanged on a frequent basis, but more often than not without creating room for compromise and concessions. The negotiations took place in front of a public audience: the Greek people and the citizens of the other EU member states. Both sides, the EU and Greece, had negotiation constraints as they were both entrapped in

and companies who pay their taxes and loans on time. Product market reforms seek to eliminate the rents accruing to vested interest groups: through higher prices, these undermine the disposable income of consumers and harm competitiveness. Pension reforms have focused on measures to remove exemptions and provide incentives for continued labor market participation [and to] end early retirement. To get people back to work and prevent the entrenching of long-term unemployment, the authorities, working closely with European partners, will initiate measures to boost employment by 50,000 people targeting the long-term unemployed. A fairer society will require that Greece improves the design of its welfare system, so that there is a genuine social safety net which targets scarce resources at those who need it most. The authorities plan to benefit from available technical assistance from international organizations on measures to provide access to health care for all (including the uninsured) and to roll out a basic social safety net in the form of a Guaranteed Minimum Income (GMI)."

commitment: Greece was committed to staying in the Eurozone and avoiding sovereign default, while the EU side was committed to avoiding negative financial and economic consequences for the Eurozone countries and the EU at large. Moreover, both sides emphasized that the collapse of negotiations and the financial and economic breakdown of Greece would be bad for everyone involved.

Although deadlines for the end of the second bailout were looming from the start of the negotiations in early 2015, the negotiation style was in large part confrontational, with both parties throwing the ball into the other's field whenever possible. No side was prepared to make (major) concessions, and the interaction soon resembled a game of chicken, in which whoever moves first loses. Blame shifting for the lack of success of negotiations became an integral part as well. The negotiation dynamics went into an escalating spiral after the Greek government tried to leverage up in a two-level-game fashion. They held a referendum on June 30 in which the citizens rejected the proposal of the Eurogroup from June 25 that was designed to avoid the sovereign default of Greece, hoping to use this as a means to leverage up on the negotiation table in Brussels. This strategy did not work. The ECB provided limited emergency funds, but the economic and financial downward spiral became severe for Greece nevertheless. In this context, a Grexit was increasingly becoming a potential solution to the failure of the third bailout negotiations. Yet, this was not a price the Greek government was willing to pay. They were strongly committed to staying in the Eurozone and in this sense entrapped. Without any alternatives left, they returned to the negotiation table. Without much bargaining power left, the Greek government took up the proposal of the Eurogroup to negotiate a new deal. They lost the endgame negotiations. Thus, the third bailout package that has been agreed upon in August 2015 bears the hallmarks of ordo-liberalism and its conditions are more stringent than the June 25 compromise proposal that prompted the Greek government to call for a referendum.

3 Colombia's Farewell to Civil War

Carlo Nasi and Angelika Rettberg

The government of Juan Manuel Santos and the Fuerzas Armadas Revolucionarias de Colombia Ejército del Pueblo (FARC-EP) – the largest and most important insurgent force that Colombia has ever had – engaged in prolonged and complex peace negotiations that ended with the signing of a definitive peace accord in Bogotá, on November 24, 2016. Since then, the rebel group has engaged in the process of demobilizing and disarming and is firmly *en route* to becoming a new political party, while the Colombian government is working on the implementation of the agreement.

It was not easy to reach this point. In October 2016, the first agreement that had been signed was rejected in a popular referendum, which handed the "no" side a razor-thin majority. The political turmoil surrounding the referendum and the following months have made visible the many ways in which Colombian society is divided over issues ranging from the course of the economy and corruption to the separation between Church and state, the rights of sexual minorities, and the role of gender in determining family values. Most of these issues are unrelated to the aspirations and contents of the peace agreement, but were brought to the front of the public debate during the negotiations, profoundly shaping the final phase of the talks and the ongoing implementation process.

In this chapter, we describe the endgame of the negotiation process between FARC and the Colombian government. We argue that the endgame began in September 2015 with the signing of the partial accord on victims and transitional justice (Mesa de Conversaciones 2015). We suggest that this accord was the final and most important turning point of the peace process, providing a solution to the dilemma between the search for peace and the need to serve justice. Although the parties had reached agreement on various topics of the agenda in previous years, disagreements on how to approach transitional justice had made the process stall. Thus, reaching an agreement on victims and transitional justice was a major achievement that ushered in the endgame of the negotiations.

Table 3.1 *A timeline of partial agreements in the Colombian peace process (2012–2016), according to whether parties were dueling or driving*

Dueling and Driving	October 18, 2012	Beginnning of formal peace talks
	May 26, 2013	**First partial agreement: Integrated rural reform**
	November 4, 2013	**Second partial agreement: Political participation**
	May 16, 2014	**Third partial agreement: Illicit drugs**
Dueling	March 7, 2015	Agreement on demining
	September 23, 2015	**Fourth partial agreement: Victims – Transitional Justice**
Dueling and Driving (endgame)	May 12, 2016	Agreement to provide security and legal stability to the Final Agreement
	May 15, 2016	*Agreement on the Separation and Reintegration of Children from the FARC*
	June 10, 2016	*Agreement to launch a joint effort of voluntary crop substitution in Briceño (Antioquia)*
	June 23, 2016	**Fifth partial agreement: End of conflict and demobilization**
	September 26, 2016	Signature of Final Agreement in Cartagena
	October 2, 2016	Victory of "No" in national referendum
	November 24, 2016	Signature of adjusted agreement in Bogotá
	December 8, 2016	President Santos awarded the Peace Nobel Prize

We argue that different types of interactions between the government and FARC characterized the various stages of the peace process (see Table 3.1). Interplay between a dueling and a driving mode prevailed during the first two years of the negotiations, when the parties were able to solve problems and show results despite holding contradictory view points on various topics. Between May 2014 and September 2015 the negotiation lost traction and became deadlocked. While neither party seemed to consider a return to full war as a viable option, stumbling blocks related to transitional justice provided the background for prolonged dueling. Solving the transitional justice issue introduced the final phase of the negotiation – endgame.

Despite the parties' belief in the imminence of closure – or precisely because of it – this phase was anything but smooth: dueling resumed, causing repeated crises. Unlike the first stage of the negotiations, in which the parties tended to tone down their disagreements and swiftly reach compromise solutions on various items of the agenda, there were many stand-offs during the endgame. The parties were more vocal and often issued public statements on their disagreements, fostering public debates on pending (and sensitive) issues related to disarmament, demobilization, and reintegration (DDR), the terms of political participation by the FARC-EP, and implementation of the peace accords.

Table 3.1 describes the timing and main contents of the partial agreements reached prior to the signing of the peace accords.[1]

In the following pages we examine the Colombian peace process and its endgame. In the first section, we provide background information on previous Colombian peace processes. In the second section we analyze the factors leading president Santos to negotiate, as well as the pre-negotiation and first stage of the peace process, in which the parties signed three partial agreements. In the third section we focus on the period of deadlock and intense dueling, explaining why the parties found it difficult to reach an agreement on a formula of transitional justice. A fourth section focuses on the final stage of the negotiations, illustrating the particular dynamic of the endgame of the negotiations. In the conclusions we summarize our findings and identify directions for future research.

No Newcomer to Peace Talks: Three Decades of Negotiations in Colombia

Colombia has provided a fertile ground for insurgency. From the late 1940s to the early 1960s a conflict between Colombia's former main political parties, the Liberal and the Conservative, underwent severe escalation and led to the formation of Liberal guerrillas, leaving over 200,000 people killed (Wilde 1978; Sánchez & Meertens 1983; Pizarro Leongómez 1990). This cycle of violence ended in 1958, when Liberal and Conservative politicians devised a power-sharing agreement known as the Frente Nacional (National Front, NF) that provided stability to Colombia for a few years (Hartlyn 2008; Wilde 1982).

However, in the mid 1960s Colombia entered a second cycle of violence (Chernick 1999; Vargas 2000; Pizarro Leongómez 1990). To begin with, the spread of Communism in Latin America and the Cuban revolution helped to radicalize university students, peasants and members of labor unions, who became eager to join revolutionary organizations. High levels of poverty and inequality further fueled radicalism,

---

[1] All partial agreements and other documents are available at www.altocomisionadoparalapaz .gov.co/Prensa/Paginas/2018/Biblioteca-del-Proceso-de-Paz-con-las-Farc-EP.aspx.

as did the discrediting of the NF (due to its exclusion of third parties from government, corruption, and the inefficient delivery of public goods). The spread of insurgency was also facilitated by Colombia's vast territory, which includes inaccessible mountains and jungles marked by weak state presence.

Thus, in the 1960s several (for the most part Communist) rebel groups were formed: in 1962 the Revolutionary Armed Forces of Colombia (FARC-EP); in 1964 the Popular Liberation Army (EPL) – inspired by Maoism – and also the National Liberation Army (Ejército de Liberación Nacional, ELN) – inspired by the Cuban revolution; and in 1974 the Movimiento 19 de Abril (Movement April 19, or M-19, an urban guerrilla organization), after Conservative candidate Misael Pastrana had allegedly resorted to fraud in order to win the presidential election of 1970 (Comisión de Superación de la Violencia 1992; Chernick 1999).

The proliferation of rebel groups was met with repression by different governments, but this did not suffice to militarily defeat the various insurgencies (Bejarano 1995). In fact, since the mid 1980s and partly due to their active participation in the drug trade and in various resource-related war economies, various guerrilla organizations underwent a significant expansion (Pecaut 1997; Nieto 2001; Chernick 1999).

In the context of rising insurgency, various governments attempted to find a negotiated solution to Colombia's armed conflict. The government of President Belisario Betancur (1982–1986) was the first to sign a short-lived truce with the rebel groups M-19, EPL, and FARC, but the peace talks ended in failure (Bejarano 1995; Pizarro Leongómez 1990; Chernick 1999).

In 1988, the government of Virgilio Barco started a new peace process that produced the demobilization of the M-19 in 1990. Other revolutionary organizations followed suit, as was the case for the EPL, PRT (Partido Revolucionario de los Trabajadores), MAQL (Movimiento Armado Quintin Lame), and later the CRS (Corriente de Renovación Socialista), which disarmed in the early 1990s (Leal 1993). The end of the Cold War (which helped to question the viability of socialist models promoted by the insurgent groups), Barco's well-crafted negotiating strategy, and also the involvement of the military in the negotiations as a measure to prevent and counteract spoiling help to explain why this peace process concluded successfully (Pardo 2004; García 1992; Presidencia de la República de Colombia 1988). In addition, a popularly elected National Constituent Assembly paved the way for peace: various rebel groups were offered the opportunity to participate in the assembly and take part in the crafting of institutional reforms if they gave up the armed struggle (Villamizar 1997).

However, the war against the FARC-EP and ELN continued. Between 1991 and 1992, President César Gaviria again attempted to reach a negotiated settlement with the FARC-EP and ELN, but his endeavor failed (Kline 2007). The war greatly intensified between 1994 and 1998, during the government of president Ernesto Samper, in which both the rebel groups and right-wing paramilitary groups (sponsored by drug traffickers, large land owners, and some members of the Armed Forces) grew in numbers and underwent territorial expansion.

Faced with conflict escalation and an unprecedented humanitarian crisis, in 1998 the government of Andrés Pastrana attempted to find a bargained solution to Colombia's armed conflict, starting a peace process with FARC (and later with the weaker ELN) (Valencia 2002; Kline 2007). However, Pastrana's endeavors ended in yet another failure: while FARC were at their strongest militarily and negotiated only tactically (that is, as part of a war strategy), Pastrana committed many mistakes in design and strategy (Nasi 2009). After three years of escalating violence and blatant lack of progress, talks were called off in 2002.

The ensuing conflict dynamic was qualitatively different from any previous period. The US-funded Plan Colombia, an aid package aimed initially at curbing the drug trade in Colombia (Rosen 2014; Tickner 2003), substantially improved the offensive capacity of the Colombian military forces (Isaacson 2010), helping the government to deliver unprecedented offensives against the FARC-EP.

Pastrana's successor, president Álvaro Uribe, considered no option other than militarily defeating FARC and the ELN. Uribe, a charismatic, right-wing politician, used inflammatory rhetoric to blame guerrillas for all the country's problems. Uribe's success in improving security and economic indicators helped his re-election in 2006. Under his continued leadership, the Colombian military were able to undermine FARC's military capacity and kill some of the rebels' leaders.

However, Uribe never attained total victory against the rebel forces. FARC was weakened, but not defeated. Between 2003 and 2006 Uribe carried out negotiations aimed at disarming Colombia's right-wing paramilitary groups, which were partially successful (Bagley and Restrepo 2011; Nussio 2012), although some former fighters later rearmed to profit from illegal economies.

During the end of Uribe's second term, his government attempted to launch talks with FARC, aided by Cuba. Initial contacts were made, however unsuccessful. In the end, Uribe left office with some of the highest public approval ratings historically speaking, but also left behind a deeply polarized country.

The Peace Process of Juan Manuel Santos, 2012–2016

It was left to Juan Manuel Santos (who had been Uribe's Minister of Defense) to re-approach FARC for fresh peace talks. Santos was a member of Uribe's political party, and had been hand-picked by Uribe as his political heir. He was expected to continue with a hard-line approach toward FARC, as many believed either that it was impossible to reach a peaceful settlement with FARC, or that defeating the rebels was only a matter of time.

Santos maintained a militaristic approach to conflict during the first part of his government. But the president, a political liberal, was also a pragmatic politician, aware that the road to victory remained treacherous and uncertain. The Colombian Armed Forces had taken down several first- and second-tier guerrilla commanders, thereby contesting the myth that the rebel group was untouchable.[2] But FARC had shown a great deal of resilience. In addition, the military strategy against the Colombian guerrillas had been yielding diminishing returns since 2008 (Granada, Restrepo & Vargas, 2009). Finally, the attacks and mass kidnappings of the 1990s had shown FARC's inhumane treatment of dozens of captive soldiers and policemen, fueling domestic and international anger and reducing the group's political legitimacy (Haspeslagh 2016). In this context, senior (and ageing) FARC leaders searched for a dignified way out of protracted war.

In addition, the electoral successes of several Leftist parties across Latin America – in Venezuela, Ecuador, Bolivia, Brazil, and Argentina – instilled hope in FARC leaders that they too could be elected in a democratic scenario. But in order to participate in democratic politics, FARC had to give up insurgency.

For its part, the Colombian government realized that negotiating peace was a rational course of action. But Santos had to be very cautious. As FARC had repeatedly cheated in the past, and all previous negotiations had ended in failure, to sit down for talks was tantamount to assuming a sizable political risk. Santos was aware that he might provoke the wrath of former president Uribe and alienate his own constituency.

The killing of Alfonso Cano, FARC's top leader, created a window of opportunity and a strong position for Santos to secretly propose

---

[2] The downturn of FARC had begun in 2008, when the founder and top leader, "Manuel Marulanda Vélez" (a.k.a. "Tirofijo") died of natural causes. A few months later the Colombian military killed FARC's second in command, Raúl Reyes, who was hiding in Ecuador. Then, in 2010, the military killed Reyes' replacement, "Mono Jojoy." And in November 2011, government troops located and killed FARC's top leader, "Alfonso Cano."

peace talks to Cano's replacement, Timoléon Jiménez ("Timochenko"). Timochenko agreed.

The Pre-negotiation and the Setting of the Agenda

A period of secret pre-negotiations in Venezuela and Cuba began, during which international actors as well as Colombian facilitators helped bring the two sides together. The government's team sought reassurance that FARC had renounced its strategy of negotiating merely tactically and that the rebels had understood that the bargaining table was no longer the place to pursue a revolutionary agenda.

After six months of pre-negotiations, the Colombian government and FARC crafted a framework agreement that included the following key principles: (1) "nothing is agreed until everything is agreed" (a disincentive for reaching only partial accords, instead of striving for a comprehensive settlement); (2) "this will be a negotiation by Colombians and for Colombians" (a statement of local ownership of the peace process, despite the decision to negotiate in Cuba under the observation of Cuba, Chile, Norway, and Venezuela); and (3) "negotiations will take place amidst conflict" (no ceasefire was agreed prior to the launching of talks).

In addition, the parties agreed to negotiate confidentially (with the guidance of international observers), to issue joint and mutually agreed statements, to periodically invite experts and stakeholders, and to convene parallel thematic commissions to discuss issues such as demining, the substitution of illicit crops, and efforts to locate disappeared persons. All these rules were aimed at facilitating progress and controlling information emerging from the bargaining table.

As soon as Santos disclosed to the public that he was negotiating with FARC, Uribe and his aides formed a break-away political party, the Centro Democrático (CD), in order to protect Uribe's legacy and political capital. Any concessions to FARC were deemed unacceptable. The support of Venezuela – a socialist-run neighbor country – fed fears that Colombia would follow suit.

But Santos had carefully planned the negotiation strategy. For instance, the framework agreement specified a limited number of topics to be included in the bargaining agenda. The idea was not to repeat the mistakes made during Pastrana's peace process, when not only had FARC hoped to achieve at the bargaining table a "negotiated" revolution, but also the government conveyed the idea that the agenda was open (Nasi 2009).

Yet Santos could not frame the peace negotiations in minimalist terms (which is contrary to what former president Uribe had aspired to do).

FARC was not a defeated rebel group and would have rejected negotiating a peace accord aimed solely at handing in weapons in exchange for a reduction of prison sentences. Eventually, the government and FARC agreed on a more limited agenda, covering six issues.

The first one concerned rural reform. Colombia has had a history of failed agrarian reforms, and FARC has mostly been a peasant guerrilla movement (even though FARC cannot credibly claim to represent the Colombian peasantry, but only a very specific fraction of peasants). Given that in Colombia agrarian policies systematically failed to address deep-rooted rural problems – which partially explains the resilience of FARC – the topic was put at the top of the bargaining agenda (Machado 2009).

A second topic referred to guarantees of political participation. This was a topic of deep concern for FARC. In fact, during the first attempt at negotiating peace during the government of President Betancur, FARC had created a legal political party, the Patriotic Union (Unión Patriótica, UP). But FARC formed the UP without disarming, that is, as part of a strategy to take power by both legal and illegal means. Right-wing paramilitary groups and extremist factions of the Colombian armed forces killed about 3,500 leaders and followers of UP because of their proximity to FARC – and also because it was far easier to attack unarmed supporters of the rebel group than the actual guerrillas in the jungle (Dudley 2008). This explains why FARC has been so apprehensive with regard to political participation and democracy. The guerrillas fear that their members will be killed if they disarm and form a political party (Gómez-Suárez 2007; Gómez-Suárez and Newman, 2013).

Both items – rural reform and political participation – have not been exclusive concerns of FARC. Even the World Bank and the International Monetary Fund converge around the fact that land is unequally distributed in Colombia, that the agrarian infrastructure is insufficient to provide a living income for rural populations or to boost the country's international competitiveness, and that most large areas of land are unproductive and inefficient (World Bank nd). The political system also faces criticisms. Although Colombia has maintained a democratic regime for many years, the barriers encountered by new parties willing to compete in elections, along with low levels of turnover in political leadership and rampant corruption, have caused profound concerns about the quality of the polity (Nasi 2007; Botero 2010).

The third topic was illicit drugs, which relates to FARC's involvement in and profiting from drug trafficking. This has been one of the main concerns of the US government, and a few FARC commanders have been extradited to the United States for judicial prosecution on drug-related charges. The future of FARC's relation with the drug trade was thus at the heart of its willingness to give up territorial control and hand in their weapons.

Fourth was the issue of victims and transitional justice. Whereas victims were largely "invisible" in most previous peace negotiations, an international normative consensus has emerged which underscores the importance of hearing the voice and addressing the needs of those who have suffered the brunt of conflict (Rettberg 2015). While this was easy to agree on, the point of victims was coupled to a debate on transitional justice, which stands at the core of the dilemma of how to induce a rebel group to give up their armed struggle *and* hold perpetrators accountable.

Guerrillas, paramilitary groups, and members of the Colombian Armed Forces have committed human rights violations throughout the conflict. Parties had to craft a formula of transitional justice that reconciled the seemingly contradictory goals of effective demobilization of FARC fighters (which required alternative forms of justice and some impunity), a social preference for punitive justice, and an international context marked by international normative principles seeking the punishment of all perpetrators.

Finally, the agenda included a section on effective conflict termination, referring to DDR, and the ratification and implementation of the peace accords by Colombian citizens. These were procedural issues that established the conditions under which FARC would cease military operations and hand in their weapons.

The First Stage: Between Dueling and Driving

The bargaining table was installed in Havana in October 2012 and made steady progress until May 2014. In the beginning it was difficult to start actual negotiations due to FARC statements that were both rhetorical and quarrelsome. However, a spirit of collaboration and increasing trust among members of the negotiating teams gradually emerged, while progress was made on issues such as demining (which begun in the municipality of Orejón with the collaboration of FARC guerrillas) and efforts to locate forcibly disappeared persons. An interplay between driving and dueling prevailed in this period. At times, FARC assumed a defiant attitude, as when the negotiators of the rebel group interpreted in a very loose sense some parts of the preamble of the bargaining agenda, hoping to negotiate more topics than the ones originally agreed upon with the government (Gómez 2012).

The government rejected such moves by repeatedly telling FARC that the peace talks were facing time constraints: If the bargaining table failed to make tangible progress, Santos was willing to abort the process. And only by showing results could Santos dispute Uribe's claim that negotiating with FARC was pointless.

In this period the parties reached partial agreements on three topics of the agenda, concerning rural reform, political rights, and drug trafficking.

Agreement on Agrarian Reform: This accord facilitates access to land and credit for landless or land-poor peasants, helps formalize land titles, creates special tribunals to resolve ownership conflicts, creates peasant land reserves, and includes social development plans with massive investments in rural regions affected most by armed conflict, as well as economic incentives for rural development and food security. In short, this is an important rural reform to spur development, although it is not a radical agrarian reform, because it does not entail expropriations of landowners or the abolition of private property.

Agreement on Political Participation: This accord improves rights and guarantees for opposition political parties and social movements, creating temporary special electoral districts to promote minority representation, electoral reform, and equitable access to mass media, as well as mechanisms to improve electoral transparency and political accountability, and a Statute of the Opposition specifying the rights of opposition parties. FARC leaders will have special measures of protection in the transition from guerrilla organization to political party, and the rebel group will be granted for two consecutive terms ten seats in Congress (without participating in elections) as a reward for laying down weapons. In short, this agreement aims at deepening democracy and improving both transparency and accountability, while giving FARC temporary privileges in the electoral contest.

Agreement on Illicit Crops: This accord purportedly aims at finding a "permanent solution to the problem of illicit drugs in Colombia." However, it would be naive to believe that a peace agreement with FARC will suffice to bring an end to the drug trade in the country, as many criminal groups are engaged in this lucrative business. None of the proposed policies is fundamentally different from what has historically been attempted. The accord commits the parties to ongoing interdiction efforts and punitive measures against drug traffickers, while peasants and drug addicts shall be handled in a non-punitive manner, with efforts to substitute alternative – legal – crops for coca.

More than the specific content of the agreement, this item is important because it will help clarify the role of FARC in the drug-trafficking chain. Guerrillas are expected to sever all their ties to drug trafficking, help the government locate illegal fields and laboratories for processing coca in the jungles, and also contribute to identifying distribution routes. And if FARC changes from being an illegal organization involved in drug trafficking to being a legal group collaborating with the Colombian government against drug trafficking, this might be a way to cater to US political interests and to prevent the future extradition of guerrilla leaders.

Reaching these partial agreements helped to curb skepticism vis-à-vis the peace process in its early stage. In fact, in mid 2014 Santos' first term was ending, and Colombia was heading for presidential elections. Uribe's party backed Óscar Iván Zuluaga as presidential candidate, hoping to defeat Santos in the electoral contest for re-election and overhaul the entire peace negotiation. In the end Santos, was re-elected in the second round by a small margin, which ensured the continuation of the peace process.

The very fact that the elections of 2014 imperiled the peace process might have worked as a stimulus for the parties to "show results," and so it did. But, after this promising start, the bargaining dynamic changed. In fact, not only did Santos' re-election ease the pressure on the bargaining table, but also the parties were approaching sensitive issues (concerning transitional justice, DDR, and guarantees of compliance with the peace accords), which resulted in prolonged deadlock.

Approaching the Endgame: From Prolonged Deadlock to Breakthrough

In mid 2014 it seemed that the negotiations could maintain a fast pace. Redressing victims' rights did not seem difficult: In principle, the government and FARC could craft an agreement to improve policies that had been adopted in the past. Since 2005 (in the context of the demobilization of paramilitary groups), the government had jump-started an ambitious reparations program to address the needs of almost eight million Colombians registered in the state's registry of victims. Then, in 2011, President Santos promoted a Law for Victims and Land Restitution, which elevated the administrative status and capabilities of the office in charge of victims. Victims acquired greater visibility and started to receive more benefits from the government. It was also Santos' initiative to include the issue of victims in the bargaining agenda with FARC.

Of course, the issue entailed complexity: Finding a way to protect the victim's rights while maintaining the fiscal viability of the state was a significant challenge. However, if the problem was circumscribed to the allocation of limited resources for the benefit of victims, the parties would have worked out a solution.

But the issue of victims was linked to the judicial fate of perpetrators, which led to prolonged deadlock.[3] Colombia had ratified the Rome Protocol, which impaired granting blanket amnesties to perpetrators of gross human rights violations. It seemed that international norms had deprived the Colombian government of the required flexibility to end the armed confrontation.

Sending the guerrillas to jail at the end of the peace process, however, was not an option. FARC leaders had made the point that they would not be the first (and only) non-defeated rebel group to end up in prison after a successful peace negotiation. To complicate matters, at the outset of the talks FARC had stated they were to be considered the prime victims of state violence and oppression by the Colombian oligarchy, and that they were not willing to spend "even one day in prison."

Only little by little did FARC acknowledge some responsibility in the atrocities that they had committed, a concession that can be partially credited to pressure from victims' organizations, international actors, and the national government (Europapress 2014).[4] FARC's acceptance of their responsibility for the violence may also reflect their understanding that, should they be held judicially accountable at a later date, having recognized their victims at an early point may earn them a more lenient sentence.[5]

In any event, FARC negotiators underscored that they were not the lone culprits of human rights abuses. They wanted to shed light on the state's responsibility in Colombia's humanitarian disaster (both by action and by omission), and also on the blame of multiple and diverse actors, including the military forces and sectors of civil society and the private sector which had supported and funded paramilitary groups (Rettberg 2016).

---

[3] The international Human Right NGO Human Rights Watch, for example, made it a point to underscore Colombia's obligations to international law, www.hrw.org/es/americas/colombia.

[4] The exact wording was "reconocemos explícitamente que nuestro accionar ha afectado a civiles en diferentes momentos y circunstancias a lo largo de la contienda, que al prolongarse ha generado mayores y múltiples impactos" (Europapress 2014).

[5] Illustrative of this change is a closed event that was held in Bojayá in December 2015. There, FARC had carried out one of the worst attacks against civilians in 2002, killing seventy-nine people, forty-eight of whom were children. During the event, FARC faced the local community and asked for their forgiveness (Molano 2015).

The bargaining table promoted a national debate on the question of who was responsible for Colombia's decades of violence.[6] This helped to emphasize that many groups shared this responsibility, and that the negotiations were not only about seeking retribution against FARC. Yet these initiatives did not suffice to answer the question of how to apply justice to FARC guerrillas once they had demobilized. A commission made up by experts who had not previously been engaged in the negotiations was crucial in finding a novel solution to the dilemma of peace vs. justice (El Tiempo 2015).

Agreement on Victims and Transitional Justice: The agreement on victims and transitional justice was a key turning point that propelled the peace process into the endgame phase. In the agreement, the parties committed themselves to amending the harm caused to victims of the armed conflict.[7] FARC agreed to contribute their illicit properties – money and land – to victims in restitution. In addition, the parties decided to create a Truth Commission[8] and a Special Peace Jurisdiction (including a Special Tribunal) in order to deal with past human rights abuses.

No blanket amnesty was handed out, as crimes against humanity, war crimes, genocide, and crimes against International Humanitarian Law need to be adjudicated by the courts. However, perpetrators of such crimes – including members of the guerrillas, the state, and civil society – who confess all their wrongdoings will not necessarily face time in jail, but instead be subjected to an "effective restriction of freedom" lasting from five to eight years in restricted areas. Perpetrators who confess to all the crimes committed, but not in a timely manner, will have to spend from five to eight years in jail. And all those who do not confess their crimes and afterwards are found guilty by the courts will have to spend up to twenty years in jail.

This formula has been very controversial, as many people (Colombians of all walks of life and also NGOs such as Human Rights Watch,

---

[6] For instance, the United Nations and the National University of Colombia hosted four meetings to discuss the issue of victims (more than 3,000 participants attended such meetings), and later sixty individuals who had been victimized by different perpetrators traveled to Havana to have their plight made known.
[7] Comunicado Conjunto #64. La Habana, December 15, 2015 (www.altocomisionadoparalapaz.gov.co/mesadeconversaciones/PDF/comunicado-conjunto-64-15-de-diciembre-de-2015-1450190009.pdf).
[8] In addition to the Comisión Histórica del Conflicto y sus Víctimas (Historical Commission on Conflict and Its Victims), which had produced a report in February of 2015 on all possible causes of the armed conflict. See http://pazfarc-ep.org/pdf/Version%20final%20informes%20CHCV.pdf.

not only Uribe's followers) denounced the concession of a great deal of impunity, a critique that is universally levied against transitional justice arrangements. Anyway, the agreement will have to prove its efficiency in allocating responsibilities as well as its effectiveness in bringing closure to Colombia's conflict – instead of perpetuating social divides.

With the signing of this accord in September 2015, it seemed that the main obstacle to the negotiations had been overcome, and that bargaining on the remaining – for the most part procedural – issues would proceed rather quickly. A sense of optimism, irreversibility, and impending closure of the peace process materialized. Shortly after reaching this agreement, Santos and Timochenko publicly announced that they had agreed on a date for signing the final comprehensive peace agreement: March 23, 2016 (CNN 2015).[9]

The Endgame: Security Dilemmas and Dueling Redux

Security dilemmas often arise in the final stage of negotiated settlements to civil wars (Licklider and Bloom 2013; Walter 1999). In fact, as only the rebel groups are expected to hand in all their weapons and afterwards have to coexist in the same territory with former enemies, their sense of vulnerability increases. Once they have disarmed, they might be annihilated by vengeful military and paramilitary forces; alternatively, by handing in their weapons, they lose their sole means to make the government comply with the peace accords. If the government cheats, there is nothing that a disarmed guerrilla can do to exert pressure for the implementation of the peace accords (other than threatening a return to war, which is extremely costly once a DDR process is under way).[10]

But if a rebel group drags its feet during the DDR process due to such security concerns, other security dilemmas arise. Time and again different rebel groups have negotiated only tactically, that is, in order to regroup and better position themselves to keep on fighting (Regehr 2015). If a guerrilla organization shows reluctance to hand in its weapons in the final stage of a peace process, a government has plenty of reasons to fear that the negotiations merely provided an opportunity for prolonging the war.

---

[9] The exact words were "estaremos dando el adiós definitivo a la guerra más larga de Colombia y del mundo" (CNN 2015).

[10] The literature on conflict resolution has suggested different mechanisms to cope with such security dilemmas, which often involve a role for external guarantors, but this does not always suffice to ensure the survival of disarmed guerrillas and/or compliance with the peace accords (Licklider and Bloom 2013; Wallensteen 2011).

The endgame in the Colombian peace process was rife with dueling in such security dilemmas. There were repeated stand-offs between the government and FARC. At some points it seemed that, after having reached agreement on most of the issues of the agenda, a definitive peace accord still remained out of reach.

A first crisis erupted in February 2016, when FARC leaders were expected to meet with various guerrilla units in order to instruct the rank-and-file on the content and implications of the peace accords. One such meeting, held in the town of *El Conejo* (Guajira), turned out to be a political rally, in which armed FARC leaders addressed local dwellers.[11] Way before disarming, FARC was already acting as if they were a political party, prompting fears in the government that the rebel group was resorting once again to the "combination of all forms of struggle" (Cosoy 2016). This was deemed unacceptable by the government and fueled fears among the opposition. The impasse was solved in March, with the crafting of a protocol that specified that any meetings of FARC leaders with the rank-and-file would not involve people other than guerrillas, nor take place in populated areas, and would include the accompaniment of international guarantors, such as the International Committee of the Red Cross (ICRC).[12]

While the parties were able to overcome this stand-off, the self-imposed deadline for signing the final accord was fast approaching, and the bargaining table was not making progress on the remaining topics of the agenda. Government and FARC delegates grew increasingly frustrated and impatient and started issuing statements to the media. When Timochenko announced that due to continuing gridlock on topics related to the DDR process, FARC and the government would not comply with the deadline of March 23 for signing a definitive peace agreement,[13] a sense of pessimism set in. It turned out that the parties were dueling on various remaining topics, namely the following issues.

- **Disarmament**: While FARC accepted (for the first time ever) that signing definitive peace accords entailed turning in all their weapons, they were reluctant to set specific dates for doing so.[14] While rebel leaders cited security concerns (pointing to the Unión Patriótica

---

[11] See "Gobierno levantaría suspensión a las FARC una vez se ajusten los protocolos," in Semana.com, February 24, 2016.
[12] See "Segunda oportunidad a las FARC y sus visitas pedagógicas," in Semana.com, March 3, 2016
[13] See "Timochenko descarta que se pueda firmar algún acuerdo el 23 de marzo," in Semana.com, March 12, 2016.
[14] See "¿Qué tiene embolatada la firma del acuerdo?," in Semana.com, March 23, 2016, and also the interview of FARC leader Carlos Antonio Lozada, "Vamos a dejar hasta el último fusil," in Semana.com, March 27, 2016.

experience), the government argued that leaving an open-ended deadline for the disarmament of the guerrillas was unacceptable. There was also serious disagreement on the timing of the suspension of arrest warrants and judicial pardons for guerrillas responsible for crimes (other than crimes against humanity). While the rebel group expected the government to take such measures right after the signing of a definitive peace accord, the government considered that any judicial benefits to FARC would have to wait until the rebel force's complete disarmament.

- **Concentration of rebel forces**: In the course of DDR, FARC rebels were expected to concentrate in some well-defined areas in order to make the transition to civilian life. However, there was serious disagreement on both the number and the location of those areas, and on the activities permitted to FARC guerrillas in those places. FARC delegates argued that, since they were going to form a political party, they should be allowed to interact with the population of nearby towns in order to disseminate their political project. The government, in turn, argued that disarmament should be a requirement for political rallies to be held.
- **Implementation of the peace accords**: While the government had long argued that, once a definitive peace agreement was signed, it would have to be ratified by citizens through a plebiscite (which would be the condition for legislation by Congress), FARC had always rejected such a proposal.[15] In fact, even if most of the Colombian citizens had approved the agreement, this would have only a symbolic value and did not entail any compulsory judicial consequences. And even if Congress were able to approve laws for the implementation of the peace accords, they could be changed (or overturned) at a later date (Rettberg & Quiroga 2017). In consequence, FARC's proposal was to hold a National Constituent Assembly. This would be the path to include in the Constitution and safeguard the various norms derived from the peace accords. However, there was also the risk that this might allow major changes in the accord.

Disagreements on these issues were solved in different ways. Concerning *disarmament*, for some time a joint technical sub-commission of active members of the Colombian Armed Forces and high-ranking FARC leaders had been discussing DDR. This sub-commission had been advised by the Swedish Agency for Peace, Security and Development (Folke Bernadotte Academy), and came up with a roadmap for

---

[15] Ibid.

completing the DDR process (Folke Bernadotte Academy 2016). In January 2016 the parties announced that the UN, in alliance with the Comunidad de Estados Latinoamericanos y Caribeños (CELAC),[16] would oversee and verify the disarmament process (United Nations 2016).

But this did not suffice to address the security concerns of FARC, and the fear that many guerrillas could be killed in the aftermath of a DDR process. Furthermore, FARC resented the government's denial of the existence of paramilitary groups that posed a threat to disarmed guerrillas.[17] Even if the paramilitary groups were less threatening than they had been in the past, it remained a fact that many human rights defenders, leaders of social movements, and peasants seeking the restitution of their lands were still being killed by criminal groups (Human Rights Watch 2013; OAS 2016). From the standpoint of FARC, if the government not only denied the existence of paramilitary groups, but had also been unable to protect human rights defenders and leaders of social movements, how would it protect demobilized FARC guerrillas? There was prolonged deadlock on this issue: FARC refused to set specific dates for its disarmament, citing security concerns,[18] while the government considered that the rebel group was making up excuses to postpone the end of the war.[19]

This hurdle was overcome through reciprocal concessions. The government stated that it did not control and therefore could not dismantle at will the criminal (or paramilitary) bands (also known as "BACRIMS") that were still operating in some regions. But Santos pledged to undertake strong-hand policies aimed at fighting these groups (Semana 2016). A meeting of FARC leaders with the US Secretary of State, John Kerry, during US president Barak Obama's visit to Cuba in March 2016 further reassured the guerrillas that the US government was supporting the peace process and would contribute to the personal security of demobilized guerrillas (El País 2016). FARC then agreed to hand in weapons gradually to the UN, over a period of six months after signing the final accord.[20]

---

[16] A regional organization composed of all American states except the United States and Canada.
[17] See "FARC piden acción contra paramilitares para destrabar la paz," in Semana.com, April 6, 2016.
[18] See "'Timochenko' rechaza fijar fecha para desarme," in Semana.com. April 8, 2016.
[19] See "Gobierno exige fecha 'fija, precisa y clara' para que las FARC se desarmen," in Semana.com, April 8, 2016.
[20] See "Histórico: Santos y 'Timochenko' sellan el fin del conflicto," in Semana.com, June 23, 2016.

As regards the *implementation of the peace accords*, FARC was concerned about the stability of any agreements reached. The rebel group understood correctly that what had been agreed with the government at the bargaining table might later be rejected by Congress, or by a new President, or even by the courts.

This impasse was resolved through a complicated legal formula proposed by FARC that stirred a great deal of debate in Colombia. In short, the specific provisions of the peace accords would be transformed into laws by Congress, but congressmen would not be allowed to introduce any amendments to the propositions. Afterwards, constitutional review would define whether the new laws were in accordance with the Constitution. Finally, the peace accords would acquire the status of international accords and would be incorporated as part of the Geneva Conventions. The final accord would be part of the National Constitution with the status of an international treaty, thereby making change extremely difficult and less vulnerable to the vagaries of the Colombian domestic context.[21]

However, this solution for a specific problem at the negotiating table was hugely unpopular with the opposition, which accused Santos of violating the Constitution, ruining democracy, and betraying his political mentor (Uribe).[22] At the same time, though, it led FARC to abandon its demand for a Constituent Assembly, and to accept the government's proposal of calling for a plebiscite to ratify (or reject) the peace agreements, with the understanding that the legal status of the accords did not depend on the result of the plebiscite, but on the agreed-upon legal formula.

Finally, the debate with regard to the areas where FARC fighters would concentrate in the demobilization process, the activities that they would be allowed to carry out, and who would be in charge of FARC's physical security was resolved with the help of international actors. Up until the very end FARC demanded a number of locations four times higher than the one offered by the government. Ultimately, a cost argument made by the UN – which would actually pay for staff and installations – settled the matter, and an agreement was reached to have FARC fighters gather at twenty-three sites in various municipalities.[23] Critical in

---

[21] For the specifics of this agreement see Rodrigo Pardo, "Ahora sí se desbloqueó el proceso," in Semana.com, May 12, 2016; and "Acuerdo Especial: 'No fue un acto de locura ni de improvisación,'" in Semana.com, May 17, 2016.

[22] See "'Es un golpe de Estado a la democracia': uribismo," in Semana.com, April 12, 2016.

[23] www.elespectador.com/noticias/infografia/asi-estaran-distribuidas-zonas-donde-se-concentraran-fa-articulo-639694.

the decision about these zones were criteria such as their distance from international borders (to avoid spill-over into neighboring countries as well as the possibility to access illicit transnational economic activities), and absence of illegal mining or illicit crops, which was very imperfectly achieved.

In short, the breakthrough accord on victims and transitional justice was followed by repeated crises, illustrating both FARC's fear of closure and of facing the consequences of DDR and the government's need to protect international commitments and address domestic criticisms. Dueling was the prevailing mode, and in the view of many analysts the peace process was clearly running out of steam. However, the parties managed to resolve these crises, resuming a driving mode of negotiation.

On June 23, the parties reached an agreement on a bilateral ceasefire, and on September 26, 2016 they signed what they expected to be a definitive peace accord in Cartagena (Colombia), under the hopeful eyes of the international community and of numerous political and social leaders.

The End of the End

However, enthusiasm was short-lived. In a referendum carried out on October 2, 2016, a majority of voters rejected the peace accords. Indeed, after an effective campaign spreading fear and misinformation,[24] matched by government incompetency to provide appropriate peace pedagogy and a tropical storm that flooded many Caribbean towns and kept voters from accessing the ballot boxes, Uribe's followers and several Pentecostal churches were able to pull out a razor-thin majority: 50.21% of voters rejected the accords, while 49.78% approved (turnout was less than 38%, indicating that most Colombians either did not care about making peace with FARC, or did not understand correctly what was at stake).[25] Adding to the political rollercoaster, just five days after the accord had been rejected in the polls, the Nobel Peace Prize was awarded to President Santos.

---

[24] This was even confirmed by the Colombian high courts. Those who campaigned against the peace accords spread lies such as that the peace accords would cut down subsidies to peasants and tax pensions to Colombians in order to benefit FARC; some Catholic groups even said that a satanic rite was conducted to "seal" the peace accords. See "Las mentiras de la campaña del No según el Consejo de Estado," in Semana.com, December 19, 2016.

[25] "Las razones por las que el No se impuso en el plebiscito," BBC Mundo, October 3, 2016.

Given the results of the referendum, the Santos government was forced to change course. Meetings were held with members of the "No" camp, in order to acknowledge their complaints and adjust the text of the peace accord. Notably, after all the bickering during the endgame, the victory of the "No" camp confronted the two sides at the negotiation table with the harsh reality that everything could be lost if concessions and adjustment were not made to accommodate the arguments of the opposition. Thus, in a short lapse of time, the government renegotiated with FARC various items of the accords, backed by massive social mobilizations demanding the prompt resolution of the crisis. The renegotiation involved efforts to clarify aspects of the peace accords, as well as significant amendments: The peace accords would not become part of the Constitution, nor be considered as international agreements; and the government would pass laws through Congress following a fast-track procedure.

On November 24, 2016, in a much more discrete and toned-down ceremony, the government and FARC signed a "new" peace agreement in Bogotá, which was later approved by the Colombian Congress, thus avoiding a new plebiscite. Since then, the accords have entered the implementation stage. However, the "No" camp continues to feel that the will of the majority was ignored. Despite having been able to make unprecedented progress in bringing the armed conflict to a close, Colombia thus approached the presidential elections in 2018 as a profoundly divided society.

Conclusion and Remaining Challenges

This chapter has described the endgame of the negotiations between the Colombian government and FARC. Almost five years of negotiations paid off both in terms of building sufficient trust among the parties and in establishing mechanisms and procedures to address substantial concerns and overcome bottlenecks.

To successfully reach closure required increased creativity on both sides, and was marked by intense bickering and stand-offs. However, once the partial accord on transitional justice had been signed, negotiations entered a point of no return. Surprisingly, the greatest challenge in this phase came from outside the negotiation table, with the blow provided by the referendum results.

Huge challenges remain for peace in Colombia, stemming from domestic politics (the role of the opposition and of sub-national authorities, and the difficulties FARC will face in transforming into a political organization), as well as from the technical, financial, and legal difficulties associated with implementation. It is thus likely that, while the negotiation was able to enter a driving mode in the final phase, especially after the failed referendum, dueling will resume in the implementation phase, as new veto actors – including Congress, the opposition, public opinion, and sub-national authorities – have emerged. This adds to other remaining challenges, such as the fate of remaining rebel and criminal groups, which may attempt to fill the power void left after FARC's demobilization in key strategic regions (such is the case of the ELN, the last remaining guerrilla group). Sustainable peace in Colombia will require that all these challenges be dealt with in a timely manner.

4 Chinese Business Negotiations: Closing the Deal

Guy Olivier Faure

Negotiating in China offers a huge variety of situations and opportunities for closing a deal. In China, everything is negotiable and everything has to be negotiated. It is not a possibility linked to specific circumstances but a way of life (Fang 1999). The law imposes itself to a very relative extent in economic transactions, and its fuzziness in interpretation may be another reason for negotiating. Friendship and the quality of the personal relation are often put forward, but sometimes may serve to extract more concessions to the foreign party, especially in the ultimate phase of the negotiation. The process develops on all possible registers, strategic, structural, cultural, and psychological. It leads to outcomes that are not necessary win–win, and one needs to overcome obstacles such as deadlocks, power games, identity issues, and misunderstandings (Lavin 1994; Blackman 1997; Chung 2011). Furthermore, the process may be punctuated by dirty tricks, and may also be subject to time pressure and to external influences, which greatly complicate situations that were already not simple from the start (Mann 1989; Shapiro *et al.* 1991; Leung and Yeung 1995; Blackman 2000; Clissold 2010).

Several negotiation cases will be presented first, illustrating the major types of business that can be carried out in China: a technology transfer, a joint-venture set-up, and a typical purchase. The focus will be on the final part of the process, the endgame. These cases will be studied with the help of analytical categories pertaining to negotiation theory. Then, broader conclusions will be drawn to contribute to a better understanding of the operating rationales in this ultimate phase of the negotiation process that is the closure.

Although all negotiations follow the same basic rationale, business negotiations have some specifics compared, for example, with diplomatic negotiations. It is easier to reach an agreement because most of the time each side can benefit from a rather high BATNA. It is relatively easy to find a substitute as a supplier, as a joint venture partner, etc. This is, of course, not the case between two states, where the decision-making process is usually longer. Companies have often a much stronger sense of urgency, as time and investment really are money. The weight of the past and of history is usually not so important unless governments come to interfere. There are no issues of sovereignty to take care of, and the financial dimension is often essential and provides a clear focus.

Considering the various stages a negotiation has to go through (pre-negotiation, formula, details, implementation), China as a high-context culture (Hall 1976) offers some particulars. The pre-negotiation leading to the negotiation table raises a cross-cultural issue since the main point is to develop a common understanding of the project. Hidden agendas may further complicate the task (Chung 2011; Fernandez and Underwood 2012). Establishing a formula for the agreement is a fuzzy and ever-changing stage as goals may be very different between parties and untold. The formula may long look elusive, unstable, and somewhat opaque. The stage dealing with details, which means fine tuning on each of the issues selected, usually happens to be highly competitive, very much played win–lose in the Chinese way and mitigated only by the quality of the relationship. What will happen during the implementation stage is very much linked to how much trust and how much control each side has regarding the other and the ensuing possibility of retaliation if the counterpart does not execute the agreement as expected.

Negotiators through their experience acquire a sense for when it is time for closing the deal (Chen & Faure 1995). Before, opportunities for gains may be wasted. Later, too many harsh tactics may have been used and hope for reaching an agreement may have been reduced almost to nothing. Thus, the negotiation process would be at best dragging until no one sees any reason to carry on with further discussions.

First Case: "Buying Rabbit Furs"

A French company wanted to buy furs in China because of the highly competitive prices offered by Chinese companies. Negotiations were necessary to deal with the type of pelt, quality, quantity, and terms of delivery. The Chinese company showed samples of all sorts of furs and discussed the qualities of the rabbit furs at length, offering to sell a huge amount much beyond the needs of the buyer. This tactic was probably meant to put the French company in a weaker position by showing that the discount related to big quantities could not be applied. Then, the Chinese gave a price that the French perceived as very high and quite outside the expected ZOPA. This was a very tough opening position, leaving room for a considerable amount of haggling. Knowing that the price is an obsessional focus in China, this was not a surprise for the French company. Further on, delivery time became a base of contention:

The French company buyer was in a hurry and wanted to get the whole amount free on board (FOB) within three weeks. On the other hand, the Chinese supplier kept stating that normal practice required a delivery time of four months.

The first real deadlock arose about quality, which is often a problem in China and for which the traditional affected modesty is not the order of the day. It was solved by resorting to an external expert of foreign origin, a Russian. On the other issues, the Chinese company did not openly contradict the potential buyer but did not make any move, after they had filled up the days with a lot of irrelevant discussion. After some time, the French became convinced that the Chinese were trying to exploit foreign impatience by resorting to stonewalling, another well-known tactic. The French set a deadline for closing the negotiation.

The Chinese side tried to show that they were not playing "black heart and thick skin," by inviting the French for a banquet followed by a karaoke session. Another time, they all went for a foot massage in order to recover the fluidity of everyone's qi (the vital energy that animates the body according to Chinese medicine) and the fluidity of the negotiation.

The delivery time remained a difficult issue throughout the discussions and finally led to another deadlock. The Chinese party explained that the time they needed was linked to the necessary formal approvals from the many bureaus involved, and that it was the way exportation is carried out in China. Furthermore, the French delegation realized that the Chinese counterpart was not the real decision-maker, that he wanted to take no risks, and that one of his goals was to show the big boss how good he was at resisting western greed. It turned out to be a face issue, and the French knew they would have to make some concessions to maintain the reputation of the negotiator within his company.

Slowly, a sort of package was designed in an informal way. The French company still hesitated to sign the agreement and looked for some external advice. In the meantime, probably thinking that they might lose the business, the negotiators of the Chinese fur company offered a huge cut in prices, as a "take it or leave it" deal. The French gave an oral agreement. Then, the Chinese company started reconsidering every issue that had informally been agreed, as if everything had just been tentative and conditional. For the French negotiators, it had taken several weeks of rows, shouting, and door slamming to find themselves nowhere. They got furious and simply threatened to abandon the business.

This time, the Chinese counterpart took the threat seriously and sent a new negotiator, an experienced lady, to handle the situation. She looked extremely different from the farmers who had been involved at the start of the negotiation. She dressed in a very modern fashion, put on a lot of makeup, used a lot of kind words, and generously distributed smiles of all calibers. She invited the buyers to a banquet that she called "a feast for the eyes and the palate," during which a "little dragon," in reality a snake, was among the main delicacies. The animal was first skinned alive in front of the guests. The blood and the bile of the snake were mixed with some strong liquor and drunk accompanied by a special toast mentioning that these were the best drinks for the health of people and, of course, for the common project as well.

During the whole banquet she tirelessly held more "ganbei" (bottom-up toasts) to the health of everyone and to the success of the deal. Not to be outdone, the French guests focused the conversation on the only two subjects that inflame any decent Shanghainese lady: speculation at the stock exchange and real-estate investments. At the end of the feast, she handed over to the leader of the French delegation a written paper saying, "Please do not waste any time before conveying to your great leader my deepest appreciation for the cardinal virtues that you display for our mutual benefit." In the evening, she took the French delegation to a Beijing Opera show.

The next day she kept on applying the basic principles of the Chinese way of negotiating, which consist for instance of "not trying to save candle wax and run the risk of bumping into something in the dark" or "to catch a cub one has to go into the tiger's den." She brought to the discussions the most fanciful data with the greatest self-confidence and, considering that she had done a smart, shrewd, and effective job, she left the stage.

Assuming that the relationship had been properly restored, the Chinese supplier adopted a more realistic attitude because he well knew that "one should not take the fog on top of Tai Mountain for the entrance of the celestial paradise." Thus, he invited everyone to get back to the negotiation table and gave in to most of the French demands. The French team then wondered whether they were going to experience a winner's curse. Later on, the Chinese side came up with a written version of the contract in which some terms had been changed and a couple of additions made, leading to another round of negotiation.

As a result of time pressure and of getting tired of the endless haggling, the deal was finally signed. However, it was not the end of the negotiation because, after no more than a couple of days, the Chinese side indicated that circumstances were changing, due to an extra military order for rabbit shapkas and a sudden pandemic affecting the livestock of rabbits. To compensate for the further delay, they promised better business conditions for the next deal. The French side did not accept the argument and traded off the new delay against another cut in the price.

This negotiation was carried out very much according to a zero-sum game rationale with a lot of haggling, tricks, lies, cheating, playing the clock, threats, and restoration tactics to avoid the final collapse of the deal. The Chinese side borrowed considerably from the register of classical stratagems that have successfully stood the test of time (Pye 1982; von Senger 1991; March & Wu 2007) and also from lessons from famous Chinese strategists such as Sun Tzu (McNeilly 1996).

At some stage the parties had to leave the technical ground. Obviously, the supplier did not believe that it was more than a one-shot deal, and tried to extract as much benefit as possible from the foreign buyer. However, this had to be done within certain limits, because at any time the French side could call it all off, even if it would not have been easy to find another reliable supplier. As the saying goes, "a man without a smile should never open a shop"; the Chinese company did not want either to have the foreign company complaining to their ministry in charge of exports. They knew that the foreigners would not get anything from such a procedure but the local company might ultimately face considerable troubles with the ministry for not taking enough care of the reputation of China.

Ultimately a measure of last resort, the classical Chinese stratagem of the "beauty trap," in this case sending an attractive woman, was used to lower the level of vigilance of the foreigners and to take their mind away from the current annoying issues (von Senger 1991).

The overall negotiation pattern was definitely "dueling," with a certain amount of posturing, affected indifference, and tough tactics. The driving force leading to a closing came from the exhaustion of means to influence the other side, weariness, reduction of expectations, and being convinced that the other side had reached its bottom line. In Chinese terms, it was simply illustrating the formula "enough is enough, and fair enough for both parties." The implementation phase was again a mere reflection of the negotiation process itself.

Second Negotiation Case: A Technology Transfer

Electron is a French company dealing with high technology and one of the two world leaders in this very specific market. The Chinese knew about the quality of the equipment manufactured by this company because they had already bought some in a more or less legal way. The point for them was to produce this equipment on an industrial scale and, in order to do this, they needed to buy the license. They had accumulated a large technology lag from a technical point of view, and they badly needed to jump to a superior new technical level. This could be achieved only with the help of Electron. On its side, Electron had already saturated its market in the West and had now met some financial difficulties. Its shareholders were thinking about selling the company before it was bound to file for bankruptcy. Trading its technology had become a most urgent matter, knowing that the gains will be net profits as the intellectual investments had already been amortized.

After some preliminary contacts and the required banquets accompanied by flowery speeches, the French side went to the plant where the equipment was supposed to be manufactured. The journey took a two-hour flight, then a night by train, followed by a final four-hour drive to reach a place in the countryside, where part of the Chinese industry had previously been moved in case of a Soviet invasion. The first negotiation that took place was to persuade the Chinese side not to stick any longer to the strategy of the "third front" (the most remote and less vulnerable part of China for an invader) but to move the site of production from this ill-located place. An agreement was reached to have the equipment made in Nanjing, the former capital of China, a much easier place to reach by international flights. Then the Chinese party sent a team to the Electron plant near Paris to learn how to use the equipment. Afterwards, a draft contract with technical annexes was sent to the Chinese side. Then, the two parties decided to negotiate, and a team of four people from Electron was sent to Beijing.

The licensing procedure included the following issues: manufacturing rights, plans, methods, technical assistance, transfer of know-how, and rights of use. After a few discussions followed by banquets, kind words, and great libations, the Chinese side called the whole offer into question and sent the negotiation process back to square one.

The French side suggested organizing sub-groups working in parallel on each of the main issues. The Chinese side objected to the method and required a sequential approach, dealing with one issue then another. They wanted to work from a cost-price base to which a negotiated profit would be added. The French wanted to include a profit in each of the issues to be negotiated. The four members of the Electron Company were facing a group of seventeen Chinese people in a special room of a big hotel. Communication was carried out through interpreters. The Chinese side kept asking question after question, splitting hairs and reconsidering what had already been agreed. Obviously, the Chinese had not been convinced that the French had made all the possible concessions. The negotiation continued with a persistent impression of distrust, and only the engineers seemed motivated to reach an agreement.

The French side played the good cop/bad cop tactic to try to overcome the deadlock, while the Chinese side waited out the clock. The Chinese also considered that only concrete things such as materials and equipment should be bought. The license itself should not be sold. The Chinese side did not understand that on top of the cost of French engineers come social security and expatriation costs, and they wanted to take the salary of Chinese engineers as the reference for the coming discussion. The guarantee of means was for them not sufficient, and they called for a guarantee of results, which was impossible to accept when one does not have control of the production itself since Chinese workers will make the product in China.

Weeks passed, and the visas of the French negotiators had to be extended for four more weeks. At the expiry date, the French decided to go, leaving the Chinese party stunned and helpless. When the negotiators had gone back to France, the head of the Electron delegation received a message from the Chinese side stating that the negotiation was very near to having come to a close, and that they were invited to come back as soon as possible. The French returned after three weeks for a second negotiation phase, which resulted in a series of sessions of price crushing engaged in by the Chinese with the utmost energy. The Chinese also resorted to the tactic of blowing hot and cold. They took a very tough stance in the morning, and in the afternoon celebrated the encounter with kind words such as the "historical relations between our two countries," "the traditional friendship between our peoples," and "the deep respect that each company has for the other."

Discussions were still carried out when strolling on the Great Wall. When a price had been agreed upon, the Chinese negotiators tried to redefine the provision of services to which it was related. Then, on each issue one had to restart from scratch.

One evening, the Chinese delegation did not stop the negotiation at 6 p.m. as usual. Their head negotiator kept sweating heavily, smoking frantically, and made a series of substantial concessions. At 8 p.m., agreement on the first negotiation subject, the know-how, was reached. The two other subjects, spare parts and machine tools, were much easier to deal with, as the French party knew the purchasing price and was able to establish a ceiling price under which it would not be interesting to strike any deal. There commenced a negotiation dance, which quickly turned again into a tough confrontation. In very low spirits, the French broke out, spent the weekend shopping, and got ready to leave the next day. A few hours before their departure time, the Chinese relaunched the bargaining process with a new session, but still based on stonewalling tactics and ending up with no result, until suddenly there appeared a prospect for an agreement, but no contract was signed. Ultimately, the French team left for the airport, but at the very moment of passing the police controls, the head of the Chinese delegation agreed to sign the protocol of agreement.

Such a negotiation was characterized by a number of protracted deadlocks. Several tactics were used to overcome them and did not produce the expected result: the good cop/bad cop routine, the social-relational dimension, blowing hot and cold, threatening, bluffing, stonewalling, resorting to a deadlock, waiting out the clock, speaking on behalf of a country. Tactics of exhaustion, of harassment, and playing on the transaction costs did not help either.

The overall pattern was "driving," with both parties working at reaching a convergence point through developing a ZOPA and combining it with a process of exploration and information exchange. However, it included a number of periods of "dueling" with cliff-hanging games, brinkmanship, and simulated chicken games. Even at the last moment in the closing process the "dueling" pattern remained apparently dominant through deadlocks. A game of deadlines real or invented, credible or unbelievable, was also used with some effectiveness to put pressure on the counterpart.

The major obstacle was of a cognitive nature and no solution could be found at the tactical level. A learning process that took months had to be carried out, in order to make progress by getting rid of the distrust concerning the other. The Chinese saw the French as prowlers coming to enrich themselves at the expense of China, as had previously been done in the nineteenth century by the foreign powers tearing apart their country. The French tended to perceive the Chinese as a team of tricky people, cunning, shrewd, slick, and shameless when it came to seeking advantages, and, furthermore, not very familiar with the rules of international business.

Third Case: A Joint-Venture Set-up

A European multinational company started setting up a series of joint ventures in China to take a strategic position in this new market. Its competitive advantage lay in its advanced technology and its international experience. On its side, the Chinese counterpart was a privately owned company from Jiangsu province that realized that it could not ensure its future development without access to a higher level of technology and was not able to achieve this by its own means. The owner had tried every way to improve the performance of the company, which still, in the eyes of the Westerners, looked poorly organized, with no clear-cut job designations and a rather weak coordination.

People worked six days a week, sometimes seven, but most often twelve hours a day. If workers got sick or pregnant they might be fired. If someone had an accident, he would be lucky if he only lost his bonus. The slogan stating that "if employees do not work hard now, later they will be looking hard for another job" had become a kind of mantra. As most of the workers were migrants coming from the countryside who were not supposed to take jobs outside their village, they remained submissive. People tended to believe in line with the newly promoted values that to die poor is a sin and that one had to spare no effort to make money. Some of the employees, too young to be accepted for work in the factory, had managed to get a job by borrowing the ID card of an older relative.

A joint venture seemed to be an excellent formula for meeting the needs of both parties as, until now, this Chinese company had been quite successful in its market. However, negotiating to set up the joint venture was a long and complex operation because there were no fewer than 150 main issues to be negotiated, addressing, for instance, domains such as the equity split, the representation on the board, the operational control of the joint venture, the technology transfer, training and technical assistance, equipment, etc.

The owner of the Chinese company was at the negotiation table. This was a great advantage, because thus the foreign party was directly in contact with the decision-maker, enabling both parties to save time and develop good communication. However, this owner, who was a former farmer in his fifties with a handsome gaunt face, shaggy eyebrows, and tired eyes, was most active, entrepreneurial, creative, and extremely smart but not at all familiar with the practices of Western companies. He had difficulties to understand and to accept a western system of management. For instance, as he was heavily resorting to kickbacks and "red envelopes," his accounting was far from being transparent, and he was not keen to disclose the real figures. He had to be persuaded that it was not a matter of personal distrust, that everyone believed what he said but that, in international business, there were formal procedures one had to abide by. He ended up accepting the need to disclose the real accounting after a much protracted deadlock lasting several months.

Drinking plays an important role when doing business in China. Negotiators must learn to absorb devastating liquors and practice "ganbei" (bottom-up toasts) between the negotiation sessions. The members of the foreign side were not prepared to have their livers destroyed to serve the interests of their company, and relations remained formal and distant for quite a while. As Chinese people have the reputation of being extremely patriotic, to please their counterparts the foreign side stated that all Chinese people were good people. The Chinese owner reacted by objecting, and added that seventy percent of Chinese people were bad, leaving the foreigners rather puzzled and embarrassed.

It was through development and strengthening of personal relations that the negotiation could finally restart. One October morning, the Chinese owner came to see his foreign counterparts with a big basket of hairy crabs, the delicacy of the season. It was a strong signal that something had changed, and the Europeans, on their side, reciprocated by organizing a banquet during which people spent hours shelling crustaceans, while chatting on every unimportant subject they could think of.

In a "marriage in heaven," which is what a joint venture normally should be, there are many potential misunderstandings well expressed through traditional sayings such as "same bed but different dreams." It was not easy for the Chinese company to pay for the technology transfer, as it was often running short of cash. One asset the Chinese brought to the common venture was the right of land use. In this case, the plot was not large enough for expanding the future plant. Thus, a plot had to be acquired next. For the time being, it was being used, probably illegally, by farmers who immediately asked for half a million US dollars of compensation! The matter was finally solved at the level of the municipality, which, expecting taxes, jobs, and a positive image, did not want the foreigners to leave and invest elsewhere. Finally, the farmers were firmly invited to drop their demand and did so.

Another issue was about what to do with the future profits of the joint venture, namely cash them in or reinvest. Cashing them in was too small a benefit for a multinational company and not worth the trouble of having come to China, but, for a Chinese entrepreneur, it was important to end up with cash either for marrying off his son or for starting another company. Finally, the decision was left to the future, because above all it would depend upon the amount of profit generated.

In the meantime, an unexpected detail again froze the negotiation process. The foreign side, realizing that it was the rainy season and intending to make a friendly gesture, offered to the Chinese party umbrellas (made in China) with their western company logo on them. In the local culture an umbrella (in Mandarin "yu san") is an object that should never be offered because the pronunciation of "san" is similar to that of the verb "separate." The foreign side came to know about this only later with the help of a consultant. Then, they could repair their mistake by first telling their hosts about their ignorance and sincere goodwill, and then organizing another banquet with expensive drinks such as Moutai and French cognac, all meant to "open the souls."

Technology and power issues remained stumbling blocks again for several months. The discussions went on in a circle with each party endlessly repeating the same arguments. One day, the one in charge of the negotiation on the foreign side, infuriated by what he perceived as obvious bad-faith behavior, lost his temper. He started shouting how tired he was of hearing something one day and just the opposite the next day. On the other side of the table, there was a young lady, assisting the main negotiator, who, when she heard the fit of anger, all of a sudden burst into tears. Everyone became silent and a sense of uneasiness invaded the whole room. Each side had the feeling that things had gone too far. The Westerners could not imagine that, behind an apparently impassive public appearance, Chinese people could be so emotional. The negotiation was interrupted for the day. At the next meeting the discussions restarted on a more positive tone.

A divergence arose on the production costs of the future joint venture. The foreign side considered that night work and Sunday work had to be paid at a significantly higher rate than work during normal hours. The Chinese side took this view as a joke and categorically refused to integrate it into any further financial forecast. Tired of being so poorly understood, the foreign side ended up dropping this issue when confronted with the persistent laughter of their counterparts.

The Chinese owner had only one company, so the risk of technology leakage was small, as there was no ghost company which could illegally benefit from it. The power split related to a different kind of problem. The Chinese company was a family enterprise and its owner wanted to stipulate that the day he was no longer in charge, the responsibility for the management would be transferred to his elder son. The European company did not want to abide by a principle of dynastic inheritance for the future joint venture. The deadlock seemed impossible to overcome, because what was at stake was a millenary Confucian tradition. Ultimately, it was another belief pertaining to the Chinese culture that helped to disentangle the situation. During the discussions, it was indicated to the Chinese owner that this joint venture would be the sixty-eighth signed by the foreign company. As the number six refers to harmony and the number eight indicates prosperity, the Chinese counterpart unexpectedly stated that he could not pass up so propitious and unique an opportunity. The final agreement was signed with no further discussion. Later on, he disclosed that he had visited a fortune teller who was positive on the overall project, erasing his last concerns about the future of the venture.

The solutions to the various deadlocks are linked to the very nature of the problems met. Most of the deadlocks encountered in this negotiation were of a cultural nature. A foreign party had to somehow adjust to the Chinese traditions and beliefs when operating in China and, when appropriate, make effective use of them. This reality led the multinational company to take some distance from the usual economic rationality on which an enterprise normally bases its approach with regard to a market (Kirkbride, Tang & Westwood 1991; Baker 1993; Lee, Yang & Graham 2006; Chung 2011). A major deadlock occurred because the foreign party was not careful enough to hide its distrust when the Chinese owner stated that the real benefit was substantially higher than the official figure showed. "Each person has a face like a tree has a bark" according to the proverb (Earley 1997). Then, once the issue had been cleared up, the challenge became to restore the face of the owner, a crucial issue in Chinese culture (Brunner and Wang 1988). If a Chinese person loses face, it is not just an individual matter but the damage is to the whole family, the company, or even the country (Ho 1976; Lu 1980; Hwang 1987; Lip 1995; Chung 2008). In this case, a way to handle the problem was to publicly recognize the merits of the owner, praise his achievements, and strongly underline his personal qualities.

By resorting to the authority of the Party at the municipality level, both sides found a solution to the obstacle posed by the farmers, operating thus at the strategic level with the introduction of a third party, the municipality. This municipality, which had its own vested interests, entered the process as a biased mediator (Faure 2011). Finally, the relational aspect played its part too, by replicating at the joint-venture level the metaphor of a couple starting a family on the basis of selective affinities and shared emotions.

At the closing stage, the dominant pattern was "driving," with a sort of soft confrontation in which tough tactics were not applied but replaced by a "dragging" stance that would normally lead to a silent disengagement. Several times, the foreign party perceived the deadlock occurring as a soft way to break off and had almost lost any hope of reaching an agreement. The effectiveness of the symbolic argument invoked at the very end came as a surprise, illustrating the widespread belief that in China anything can happen at any time, even a good agreement. A powerful symbol in Chinese culture overshadowed all the remaining obstacles, putting enough weight in the balance that the Chinese side decided to sign up. What happened was nothing less than a process of unlocking a situation by resorting to symbols.

Business Negotiations Closure in China: An Analytical View

Seldom do negotiations in China go smoothly with no deadlock at some stage of the process. Divergences of interests, cultural differences, and structural constraints make it inevitable that these negotiations will not flow smoothly, and a number of hazards may arise (Chu 1991; Gao 1991; Lip 1991; DeBruijn and Jia 1993). The closing phase is, thus, a complex phase and certainly not a one-time event. Several aspects of it can be distinguished. First of all, just as animals can smell fear in humans, a seasoned negotiator has a sense of when a situation has matured enough to offer a final deal. Before, it would be too early and the counterpart would still have further expectations or was not really convinced that the negotiator had reached his bottom line. No mathematician can predict much about it. Only sensitivity and empathy can somehow help. This sense is inextricably linked to the ability of a negotiator to hear what has not been said. The existence of a hidden agenda (Chung 2011; Fernandez & Underwood 2012) makes it far more difficult to know whether the process has really reached its closing stage.

On the basis of one's experience, one may consider that the time has come to offer a final package deal when goals are met. One can try to get a little more but there is no point in continuing to haggle *ad nauseam* if the negotiators get what they wanted. Also, a turning point is reached when someone has made all the concessions that could possibly be granted. Then, it is time to offer to close the deal or walk away. When one gets deeply convinced that the other side is running out of steam, and has absolutely nothing more to give, it is time to close. Still, the final offer has to be presented as a strong emotional moment, as the form might greatly help to enhance the substance.

If the final offer appears as win–win, leaving no loser at the negotiation table, if a sense of fairness has been developed through, for instance, shared efforts to reach a potential agreement, if the dominant feeling is positive, not prone at a later stage to resentment, there will be a high probability that it will be accepted by the other side. There are a number of signals that may reveal that the counterpart is willing to close the deal. Attitudes revealing stress, nervousness, anxiety, feverish agitation, sweating, and smoking compulsively show that the counterpart is expecting something important. A new conciliatory tone, an emphasis on common interests or on shared efforts, and unexpectedly offered gifts may also indicate that the process is getting into its final stage.

As long as uncertainty is not sufficiently reduced, the negotiation process will go on as an exploratory process suitable for data collection. When the Chinese party has gained enough certainty about the object of the negotiation, the value of the concessions made, and the limits reached, he will consider closing the deal. Thus, reducing uncertainty limits risks and facilitates the deal.

Strategic Obstacles to Closing a Negotiation

One of the most common causes of deadlocks in the case of a joint venture is a conflicting vision of the project (Eiteman 1990; Purves 1991; Shapiro *et al.* 1991; Lewis 1995; Faure, 2000a, 2000b, 2009). For instance, should it be, first of all, a way to make profit and cash it in, or should it be a way to slowly grab a larger market share? In the first option, it is a short-term view; in the second option, the point becomes to increase investments and play the longer term. Usually the foreign party comes to China with long-term views and tends to invest as much as possible. The Chinese party may be more interested in obtaining quick cash and might start by itself another company, sometimes a direct competitor to the joint venture. Such conflicting goals are not prominent at the beginning of the negotiation process, but become more visible at a later stage and lead to heated discussions, even to deadlocks. The road to closing the deal with an agreement is taken again when both parties realize that what is at stake, if the negotiation leads nowhere, is simply the existence of the project.

Negotiating in order to set up a joint venture often carries with it hidden intentions. The basic principle is to join forces and attack the market together. Sometimes, the Chinese side tends to think that it is going to be easier first to get advantages from the partner before tackling a competitive market by, for instance, using the foreign technology for its own benefit (Shapiro *et al.* 1991; Faure 2009; Clissold 2010). The story of the hen and the pig that want to start a joint venture tells us something about what could happen. To the banker, who has been asked for a loan to start the business, the hen indicates that the plan is to sell bacon and eggs. When asked to be more precise, the hen adds that it will provide the eggs, while the pig will provide the bacon. Investment and consequences are obviously not of the same nature.

Among the many tricks used to extract money from the partner, the Chinese side may pretend that it has to hand over a substantial amount of money to the "fat rats" (officials) in order to secure some authorization or accelerate some procedure. No one really knows into whose pockets the "red envelopes" go.

In any type of negotiation in China, unless the parties have a special link or know each other very well, the process starts with many polite smiles, but under a high level of mistrust (Fang 1999; Chung 2008). A learning process has to be built up in order to substantially move on toward a positive end. The foreign party will take a considerable amount of legal precautions, as if the counterpart were a criminal. The Chinese side that is anxious not to cooperate with a predator coming to China just to make money at the expense of its country (as was the case in the nineteenth century with the foreign concessions and the "unequal treaties") will only come out of a stage of hesitations and deadlocks through the development of a true personal relation. Dinners, banquets, tourist visits, and evenings spent in karaoke will be most helpful (Seligman 1990; Hsieh and Liu 1992; Yang 1994). The foreigner might join in for a foot-massage session during which for an hour both people will be stretched out next to each other, giving them an opportunity to carry on with more informal and friendly exchanges, while expert hands will take care of their feet.

Reaching a satisfying level of trust may definitely help in switching the process to its final stage. In China cognitive trust is a basic condition to be fulfilled to reach that stage. Limiting risks enables both parties to consider signing a deal. However, affective trust can work as a most effective trigger to conclude, a driving force to push the negotiation until its closure.

If trust has not been built, one should prepare for the worst even if it is never certain that it will happen. Trust has to be built from scratch as the legal system is quite insufficient to do the job or is not properly applied to protect companies from wrongdoings. Such trust does not take place between companies but between people. The process leads one to "open one's soul," for instance by way of libations or shared leisure activities.

Building up a strong power relation may facilitate the closing of a negotiation even if it is perceived by the other as very much a constraint or as an unfair situation. For instance, if the foreign side has a technology that the Chinese company absolutely needs, this creates a dependence that helps to get out of the deadlock. On the other side, if the Chinese company is the only one that can control the distribution channels of the products manufactured by the joint venture, it could much more easily impose the terms of the agreement. Thus, a power relation based on the control of necessary resources will facilitate the closing of a negotiation (Faure & Chen 1999; Zartman and Rubin 2000; Faure and Ding 2003).

If the matter is simple business, such as purchasing and selling, resorting to basic negotiation tactics usually enables one to get out of a deadlock and move on to a closure. For instance, the bad cop/good cop routine could pay off through lowering the level of expectation of the other side. In the Beijing Opera, these are classical figures called red and white faces. The "red face" negotiates in a very tough way, using highly distributive tactics, pushing to demands to the extreme limit and then, at the very moment that it appears that the whole negotiation will collapse, leaves the stage. Then, comes the softliner, the "white face," who smartly capitalizes on the psychological situation built up by the "red face" by getting a few more concessions at the closing stage.

Another technique that can help the reaching of an agreement consists of stepping back from action, using the "helicopter effect." The point is to take some distance from the issue that is the bone of contention and help the counterpart to do likewise. Grasping again the overall picture may help one to realize that spending so much energy to fight on a small issue may not be worth the trouble. Bringing the dispute back to its real importance may greatly help both sides to close the deal.

Another option to help to get out of a protracted deadlock and move on to closure consists of changing the negotiators. Negotiating is a human relationship, and sometimes difficulties occur because of poor chemistry. Changing the people at the negotiation table may help to change something in the personal relations and facilitate the agreement. However, it may increase the transaction costs because the new negotiators have to be briefed, and the process must somehow be restarted from scratch.

Invoking a real or fictitious competitor to the supplier counterpart may also be sometimes quite effective, because the discussion gets out of the technical domain and the buyer may thus improve its bargaining position.

Resorting to values may also occasionally help to overcome some deadlocks. In business, interests are taken care of according to economic rationality. Values operate at a different level, that of the heart, of the emotions. Thus, one may call on friendship, the necessity of cooperation, long-term interest, mutual respect, and fairness (Zartman and Faure 2005). Changing the state of mind of the parties involved in the negotiation may help to restart the process and close the deal without having to make extra concessions.

There are also techniques to facilitate closure, such as bringing one's own superior to the negotiation table, as also seen in the following accounts by Larry Crump and Siniša Vuković, in Chapters 6 and 9, respectively. Such a move confers a higher status on the negotiation and encourages people to go beyond the usual bargaining tactics and tricks. If the counterpart also brings in his manager, this is also a way to disentangle deadlocks as bosses are not bound by petty commitments made by their subordinates. Furthermore, getting the negotiation process out of the rut, out of its stalemate, is for them a way to show how effective they are.

When the deadlock is especially painful for both parties and the necessity of reaching an agreement is urgent and crucial, they may call upon a third party acting as a mediator, in order to facilitate the restarting of the discussions, and incidentally suggest solutions, as discussed in the following chapters by Vuković and Janice Gross Stein (Chapter 12). In China, one may thus call upon a common acquaintance, someone who belongs to one's own network ("Guanxi") and that of the other party (Solomon 1987; Hsieh and Liu 1992; Graham and Lam 2003). It has to be someone who has sufficient competence and credibility to take on the task. Of course, at some point, in one way or another, the mediator will have to be compensated.

To overcome deadlocks and reach closure, the social–emotional treatment may be quite effective. Banquets with very particular dishes of a high symbolic value, special toasts, foot massage, karaoke, and personal gifts are tools likely to relaunch the negotiations on the road to agreement (Faure 2008). Even if the conflict is not personal but interest-based, in China it easily contaminates the relational sphere. As a consequence, the exit from the crisis, the restarting of the negotiation, has to be carried out simultaneously at two levels: relational and substantial. To the extra status, respect, and face brought to the other must be added a new package for agreement, based either on concessions or on a new formula addressing the problem at stake. It is the reconstructed relation that will make the new offer audible and possibly acceptable.

Whether made up by the negotiators or imposed by external conditions, deadlines may greatly help at least to create a momentum for closing the deal. When they are credible, they add pressure on the negotiators, pushing them to make more efforts toward reaching agreement, by changing their attitude and possibly their strategy. Thus, deadlines operate in a similar way to threats and warnings.

Cultural Obstacles

Negotiating in China for a foreigner is not, contrary to what some people have written, tantamount to walking a tightrope in a maze with blindfolded eyes, but it is still a very particular challenge. Several levels of difficulty have to be distinguished. The first level is all that concerns behaviors and their interpretation; the second level relates to beliefs and values shared or not shared by the parties, as well as the symbols that could be manipulated consciously or unconsciously during the exchanges; and the third level encompasses identity, pride, the sense of belonging to a group, a social entity, a civilization (Faure and Rubin 1993; Baker 1993).

Chinese society is highly ritualistic and behaviors, whether in doing business or in a private relationship, are strongly codified (De Mente 1989; Yang 1994; Chung 2011). The challenge for foreign counterparts is to know these codes and to conform at least to some of them. The closing of a negotiation is part of a culturally marked out itinerary in which one has to signal to one's counterpart by various means such as facial expressions, gestures, and dramatic statements that one has reached one's bottom line and that it would really be a waste of time and energy to expect any more concessions. Then, the point becomes to send to the other signs of statutory recognition, respect, and consideration. It addresses the personal dimension of the negotiation, the purpose being to give enough face to the other to enable him or her to turn the result of the negotiation into a positive reference in his or her professional résumé.

One has to reach a stage where "yes, but" no longer means "no, for the time being," but really does mean "yes, but," with emphasis on the "yes." When the smile is no longer a smile of polite derision or defense but a positive signal, then the closure of the deal is not far off. When the relations become less formal, more personalized, when the "souls" have been revealed through more open exchanges, the ways to the agreement start opening. Going to the "Great Wall" and contemplating together the vastness that separated the Middle Kingdom from the territory of the Mongols, or enjoying together a foot massage, adds a soft and smooth note to the cold accounting of business.

Chinese and Westerners share a number of values but diverge on others especially in their understanding of what business is, what a company is, and what constitutes a fair deal (Buchan 1998; Faure 2000a; Clissold, 2010; Cremer and Faure 2017). Either the negotiation process has enabled both sides to come closer at the level of values, or both parties have reasonably set them aside and, in spite of the absence of such potential glue, the community of interests has been sufficient to lead to the agreement. If, for instance, the Chinese counterpart attaches a real importance to a practical philosophy such as "Feng shui" (geomancy), the foreign side will have to conform to its requirements and avoid considering objective and rational criteria as the basis for decision-making when the point of choosing a date for the signing ceremony, for the grand opening of the plant, or for revealing the layout of the buildings is reached.

About religious beliefs, in his *Analects* Confucius (1996) reminded everyone to "respect gods but to have as little to do with them as possible." Nowadays, this advice applies again as no one really knows how much traditional beliefs are still active in the minds of business people at the negotiation table.

Finally, China is a western name invented to describe a country that only calls itself the "Middle Kingdom" or the "Center of the World."

Now this country and its people are returning to the historical position they occupied in past millennia. Then, the point, especially in the last stage of the negotiation, is to give to China what it estimates the World owes it, at least in terms of national pride. For instance, the practical translation of this requirement would be to sign an important agreement only on Chinese soil, and according to Chinese rituals with ceremonies, speeches, and banquets. The Chinese identity is what has survived all the hazards of history and all the calamities the country has had to bear. The point is to acknowledge its reality and importance until the very end of the process leading to the agreement.

Finally, signing a contract does not put an end to the negotiation, for it is not unusual in Chinese culture to renegotiate an agreement, knowing that the contract is only the mark of an equilibrium point accepted at a given time within a relationship that is meant to last far beyond (Faure & Chen 1999).

Conclusion

In the closing phase, the dominant pattern varies according to the type of negotiation. For a business such as buying/selling it is more "dueling" with the use of tough tactics that can belong to the register of the chicken game and can be completed by the constant threat of breaking off. When the point is to set up a joint venture, the dominant pattern is rather "driving" because the point is to seek convergences between parties who will afterwards work together to confront the market. The technology-transfer case presents a mix of these two patterns, and the range of tactics used is the widest as long as confrontation prevails on the idea of the negotiation as a joint project.

Several characteristics play an important role at the closing stage of the negotiation process. Negotiating in China is as much a relational game as a strategic game. When the parties get near agreement, this relational aspect becomes even more influential. One has to set up a feedback system enabling one to know something about the views of the other party on oneself and on the negotiation progress by, for instance, resorting to a third party.

Time in China, as in the West, is now becoming money, and may be used strategically to put pressure on the other side (Faure 2008). As Chinese negotiators have a special talent in exercising patience and resistance, sometimes the negotiation is played like the quarter of an hour of Nogi, the famous Japanese general who won the Port Arthur battle against the Russians (1894). He explained that he was victorious simply because he was able to stand suffering for a quarter of an hour longer than his opponent. Resistance and patience are basic requirements with Chinese counterparts. Before getting to the agreement, they absolutely need to make sure they have tested all the limits, have tried every tactic they can think of, have been convinced about the sincerity of the foreigners, and have fully explored all the dimensions of the deal.

The negotiation closing is very much linked to the possible variations of the level of expectations. Foreigners still tend to see China as a new Eldorado and come with high expectations. Part of the process on the Chinese side is to lower the magnitude of the goals the foreigners want to achieve. If done properly, at some point the foreigners will realize that one cannot "negotiate one's skin with a tiger" ("yu hou mou pi"), and then they will revise their level of expectation in a more realistic way and eventually come up with an agreement.

The security point is a major concept in closure theory because of the role it plays. One cannot expect concluding negotiations before everyone is deeply convinced that he or she has reached the security point of the other. Thus, the challenge is to be able to identify signs indicating this subjective reality: protracted deadlock, breakaway, warning, threat, and resorting to a third party/mediator. The point is for the other to send signals as if they were revealing a reality that one would not wish to display.

To build up a joint project, both sides have to develop a forward-looking approach. However, the Chinese side will always keep on considering the past to evaluate the quality of the coming agreement. The contract does not create the relationship but is the consequence of it. Thus, Chinese negotiators operate according to Western inverted negotiation logics (Faure and Fang 2008).

The feeling of having invested so much in the negotiation process in terms of time, money, and energy, and the desire not to have done it for no result, may be a powerful driving force to reach an agreement and to accept the necessary sacrifices. This attitude relates to a situation of psychological entrapment (Zartman and Faure 2005).

It is indispensable that the Chinese counterpart become convinced that the foreigner has given away all the concessions he could to accept getting into the closing phase. If ever he discovers, after the signature of the contract, that there is still a possibility of obtaining some additional advantage, he will not hesitate to call into question the current agreement (Faure 1998, 2006). This is why in China "yes" must not be taken as an answer. Finally, if the foreign side takes advantage of a position of weakness of the Chinese party to get particularly advantageous concessions, he runs the risk of having to pay a high price for it later on. If the balance of power reverses, there are consequences because in the Chinese memory nothing is ever forgotten.

Beyond objective factors including goals met or the value of the potential agreement's superiority to the absence of agreement, there is what can be called the psychological moment, which is a combination of subjective factors. For instance, the feeling of having tried all possible options and having carried them out to their limits; that the other will not make any more concessions; that all possible agreement formulas have been explored; a sense of the necessity to get out of the process; a sense of urgency to finish; the impression that the other is (and may only temporarily be) in a positive state of mind; that the agreement may signal a stage in the career of the negotiator; that the agreement is quite defensible with his superior; that finally both sides could meet each other again by chance and not feel embarrassed.

There is always some ritualistic dimension in any negotiation, and in China this is more so than anywhere in the West. The closure stage can be somehow understood as the scenario of the end. The script has been written in the mind of everyone and the sequence of the final moves is quite standardized. One must play it properly and have the feeling that the other is behaving accordingly. The joint show must not elicit any regret. It refers to an esthetical evaluation of the mutual performance.

Negotiating the closing stage of an agreement in China may go much beyond ordinary rationality as understood in the western way (Faure & Fang 2011). Traditional wisdom, cultural beliefs, and symbols may play an important part in the final decision-making. Clearly negotiation involves people, with their culture and psychology, resorting to strategies and tactics. Some of these strategies and tactics are rather universal and some are genuinely Chinese, making negotiating in China a very unique experience.

Finally, a sense of a possible closing opportunity comes with the impression of having reached not an optimum but rather an equilibrium that makes agreeing acceptable. An equilibrium includes gains but also efforts produced that cannot be simply measured by concessions made or received but comprise intangibles such as acceptance of the other, mutual respect, compatible representations of the situation, and, last but not least even in China, shared emotions.

5 France's Reconciliations with Germany and Algeria

Valerie Rosoux

> *War es gestern unsere Pflicht Feinde zu sein,*
> *ist es heute unser Recht Brüder zu werden*   Charles de Gaulle[1]

The purpose of this chapter is to compare the failed Treaty of Friendship between France and Algeria with the successful Élysée Treaty between France and Germany. Why was closure impossible in one case and not in the other? To answer this question, the chapter focuses on the endgame behavior in the two negotiations. It seeks to explain how the parties behaved in the run-up to engagement or disengagement in the final stages, showing how the final-round negotiations were different from the earlier stages.

Both case studies clearly illustrate the scope and the limitations of conflict-transformation processes. Among all the historical cases of reconciliation, Franco-German reconciliation is often considered to be *the* success story. On the international stage, the rapprochement between these European "hereditary enemies" is frequently presented as a textbook case to be studied and replicated. Whether in Tokyo, Karachi, Islamabad, or Warsaw, the Franco-German case is depicted as an inspiring model and even sometimes as "the biggest product of reconciliation in history" (Kurbjuweit 2010). However, can this historical reconciliation be replicated in any circumstances?

Since the end of the Algerian war in 1962, French and Algerian authorities have frequently referred to Franco-German relations as a model for moving forward. In November 1983, Chadli Bendjedid undertook the first ever State visit by an Algerian President to France, and directly described Franco-German relations as a model of how to deal with a tragic past: "Why couldn't there be identical relations between France and Algeria?" (*Le Monde*, November 6–7, 1983). However, twenty years later, the failure of the negotiations leading to a Friendship

---

[1] "If yesterday it was our duty to be enemies, today it is our right to become brothers" (Hamburg, September 7, 1962).

Treaty shows that the Franco-German model did not turn out to be an effective model. For what reasons? An analysis of the endgame of the negotiations initiated by French President Jacques Chirac and Algerian President Abdelaziz Bouteflika reveals a number of variables that explain why Franco-Algerian relationships can apparently not be "normalized."

This analysis is divided into three parts. The first examines the Franco-German process which started in 1958 and ended in January 1963 with the signature of the Élysée Treaty. It illustrates the first closure situation described in the Introduction of this book: French and German negotiators reached an agreement that was obviously "not enough" in comparison with original hopes and demands, but "still enough" for them to make an agreement. The second part focuses on the Franco-Algerian process that started in 2003 and was abandoned in 2007. It exemplifies the second closure situation where "enough is not enough," since French and Algerian negotiators abandoned their project despite having achieved agreement on major issues. The third part stresses four critical factors that explain why closure was possible in one case and not in the other: leadership, context, domestic resistance, and the nature of the past violence. This last variable goes far beyond the framework of the negotiation endgames. However, the assumption underlying the whole chapter is that closure cannot be completely understood without taking into consideration the long-term relationship between the parties. Such a widening of the analysis seems useful to explain the intensity of the resistance faced by the negotiators at the very end of the game.

The Franco-German Case: The Fear of a New Common Enemy

In a devastated Europe, the decision to favor a rapprochement was not a matter of altruism but, rather, was seen as being in both French and German national interests. France and Germany needed each other, as Konrad Adenauer and Charles de Gaulle readily recognized. In September 1962, Chancellor Adenauer described national interest as the "key factor" that drives any foreign policy and, he continued, "thank God, the interest of France coincides with the interest of Germany." President de Gaulle explained later that "it is clear that our interests meet and will meet more and more. Germany needs us as much as we need it" (Peyrefitte 1994, 154).

The complete and radical nature of Germany's defeat explains its crucial need for political rehabilitation and return of sovereignty. Moreover, to German leaders, the economic future of their country was an additional reason to favor the normalization of relationships with their neighbors as quickly as possible. In this particular context, a rapprochement with France was perceived as indispensable. For France, also, it was a question of necessity. Since the end of the war, French grandeur was being called into question. France's economy had been reduced to half its previous size, its infrastructure was devastated, its demography had been undermined by the human cost of the conflict, and its colonies were close to being lost. The two countries needed one another.

In addition to these domestic issues, the configuration of the broader international system was also propitious to a rapprochement between former enemies. Among the political, economic, and security considerations that encouraged this process, one was particularly significant: the existence of a common enemy – the USSR – and therefore external, mostly American, support for rapprochement. Protection from a third-party threat is a crucial incentive for cooperation. Just as France and Great Britain cooperated at the beginning of the twentieth century to counter the emerging power of Germany, it was time for France and Germany to work together.

The Franco-German rapprochement proceeded in three "waves" (Grosser 1967, 6). The first was that of a small minority of pioneers. The second consisted of the "Europeanists." The third occurred under Charles de Gaulle and Konrad Adenauer.

Process

The resolute actions of both leaders indicated that the reconciliation did not come only from multilateral institutions or specific private circles but was also the outcome of direct bilateral initiatives. From that perspective, the signature of the Friendship Treaty was a turning point (Druckman 2001). Rather than being *the* founding moment of the Franco-German reconciliation, it crystallized the rapprochement and still determines the ongoing negotiation process between Paris and Berlin.

Preliminary contacts between 1958 and 1962 by de Gaulle and Adenauer involved considerable efforts to persuade the public of the necessity for a Franco-German rapprochement. They carried out frequent trips on both sides of the Rhine to help their populations overcome preconceived ideas and fears rooted in past events. Charles de Gaulle's State visit on September 4–9, 1962 was an unprecedented success. Whether in Duisburg, Hamburg, or Munich, Charles de Gaulle did not hesitate to speak German to his audiences. He finished all his speeches by throwing his arms up in the air and shouting out in German "Es lebe Deutschland! Es lebe die deutsch-französische Freundschaft" ("Long live Germany! Long live Franco-German friendship!").

Each time, this vibrant exaltation of Franco-German friendship brought cheers from the crowd.

One of the most important speeches of the trip was delivered at a youth meeting in Ludwigsburg. The General stoked the enthusiasm of his audience by denouncing any form of collective condemnation and denying Manichean and simplistic readings of the past. In his view, the great mistakes of the past could not erase the fact that Germany had "spread around the world fruitful waves of thought, science, art, and philosophy; enriched the universe with countless inventions, techniques and much work; and had displayed in peacetime actions and during the hardships of war the treasures of courage, discipline, and organization" (September 9, 1962). Since the war, no other foreign statesman had rehabilitated the German nation in such an outspoken way.

This attitude of openness on the part of the officer who, in 1940, had embodied resistance against the occupier aroused a great deal of emotion in Germany. The reactions of German officials confirmed the emotion expressed by the population. In hailing General de Gaulle, the Minister-President of Baden-Württemberg, Dr. Kiesinger, asserted "You have won the hearts of German children with one touch of your hand, which erases all the past" (*La Croix*, September 11, 1962). The president of the German parliament, Eugen Gerstenmaier, echoed this feeling: "It was the gesture the German people had expected the least, and his generosity touched deep layers of our history and our emotions that no other person had reached before. It not only put an end to the chapter from 1940 to 1945. More than that, a debt two centuries old was erased" (Gerstenmaier 1964, 2).

This trip can be considered as a precipitating factor leading to the Élysée Treaty. In a joint communiqué on September 7, 1962, Charles de Gaulle and Konrad Adenauer announced that they wanted to take "practical measures" to strengthen the ties that already existed between the two countries. On September 19, 1962, the French President sent the German Chancellor a draft version of a protocol calling for closer cooperation between the two countries in two specific areas: foreign and defense policy on the one hand, and youth and cultural issues on the other. Four months later, this initiative resulted in the Friendship Treaty, which was signed on January 22, 1963.

Argumentation between September 1962 and January 1963 focused the main discussion between French and German experts on the modalities of a new audacious linkage: the requirements for regular official consultation and the promotion of interaction on a "people-to-people" level. (1) The institutional mechanisms provided for by the Élysée Treaty created a structure of constant dialogue through biannual meetings of

Heads of State, with consultations between foreign and technical ministers as well as joint councils in all fields. The intention of the two Heads of State was to create a habit of talking together regularly in order to get used to searching for common ground. The purpose of these meetings was to favor mutual understanding among official representatives but also to impact generations of French and German civil servants. (2) The negotiations also led to the creation of the Franco-German Youth Office, which was set up to vitalize youth exchanges, conferences, and reciprocal language teaching.

Beside these consultative mechanisms, most discussions concerned two specific subjects, namely European affairs and NATO. Knowing that Charles de Gaulle was eager to provide France, and Europe, with an independent foreign and defense policy, "anti-Gaullist" Germans were unwilling to frighten off their European and Atlantic partners. Two years before, de Gaulle had proposed the Fouchet Plan, an intergovernmental arrangement for European foreign and economic policy coordination. This project was perceived as a way to create a European counterweight to American "domination," and was therefore rejected by his European partners. He then considered that the Franco-German couple would be the core of such an independent foreign policy. From this perspective, de Gaulle's plan was perceived as a way to ensure French leadership in Europe. Furthermore, de Gaulle consistently opposed closer relations with Britain. This fundamental tension toward London and Washington explains why the German negotiators, and in particular the Federal Foreign Minister, Gerhard Schröder of the Christian Democratic Union (CDU), proposed that the final agreement between Paris and Bonn could take the form of a Treaty. To them, this was a way to make sure that the agreement would ultimately be backed by ratification in the Bundestag.[2]

The endgame came as a provocative crisis before the deadline. At a famous press conference on January 14, 1963, Charles de Gaulle's veto of British entry into the Common Market provoked a crisis in Franco-German circles. However, Konrad Adenauer's determination was not shaken. His objective was to sign the Treaty before the end of his mandate. The symbolic deadline that both Charles de Gaulle and Konrad Adenauer

---

[2] In France, the choice to negotiate a treaty rather than a standard agreement did not only make a difference in terms of the degree of official importance. It also affected the negotiation process, since the French Constitution (*titre VI*) distinguishes between treaties, which are negotiated and ratified by the French President, and agreements, which are not directly negotiated by the president and are approved by the Government (art. 52). Thus, this procedural distinction reinforced the crucial importance of leadership (*vide infra*).

had in mind was the changeover in Bonn. This eagerness to reach an agreement was not affected by the increasing opposition of the German people, who wanted to clearly set the Treaty within the general Atlantic framework. The Élysée Treaty was signed on January 22 as planned. The Bundestag ratified the Treaty on June 15, adding a Preamble that stipulated "the maintenance and consolidation of understanding between free peoples, with particular close collaboration between Europe and the USA," "joint defence within the framework of the North Atlantic Treaty Alliance," and "the unification of Europe following the path traced by the creation of the European Community and including Great Britain and the other nations willing to accede" (quoted by Fackler 1965, 30), suddenly extending an endgame to the negotiations that had been considered ended.

Consequences

This addition of the Preamble was severely criticized by Charles de Gaulle. However, it did not prevent the Treaty acting as an impressive force to generate a "shared sense of purpose" and develop "habits on both governments to keep the relationship productive" (Wallace 1986, 137). From 1963, the numerous political crises that had affected Franco-German relations were a thing of the past. In the field of youth and culture, the outcomes of the Treaty were impressive. In 1964 alone, the Franco-German Youth Office contributed to meetings of 180,000 youths from both countries at 6,500 gatherings, seminars, and study trips – a process that gradually affected all levels of society. In just a couple of decades, the Franco-German relationship had reached an unmatched level of intensity. Each country is now the other's most important trade partner. More than 2,500 towns are involved in twinning programs and partnerships. Almost seventy-five percent of the French and German populations live in twinned cities or towns, while more than seven million young people have been involved in student exchange programmes.

The Franco-Algerian Case: The Need for an Intimate Enemy

The Franco-German case is often referred to when discussing Franco-Algerian relations. In 2001, the former French President wondered how to emulate Franco-German relations, to turn the page on a difficult past: "The weight of the past finally fades with time. The weight of the past was much more difficult to erase between Germany and France [...].

The dispute was age-old, considerable and added up to millions and millions of dead, during successive wars. Thus I am deeply convinced that the relation between France and Algeria is in the nature of things [...] and that it can develop" (Algiers, December 1, 2001). Two years later, Jacques Chirac again underlined the same belief: "What I wish is that we emphasize the elements that unify us, without forgetting those which could divide us naturally, but these belong to history – as we could do with Germany" (Paris, March 1, 2003). From that perspective, it was not surprising that Jacques Chirac explicitly called for an "Élysée Treaty in the Franco-Algerian style" (*Le Point*, August 19, 2004).

Process

Preliminary contacts. As in the Franco-German case, the first major steps were taken by the French and Algerian Presidents. They undertook trips on each side of the Mediterranean. Abdelaziz Bouteflika was welcomed in Paris in 2000. Without trying to downplay the "wounds of history," Jacques Chirac referred to the common heritage of the two nations and recalled a legacy "that history has done and cannot undo" (June 14, 2000). In 2003, Jacques Chirac paid a state visit to Algeria, the first by a French president since Algerian independence. Throughout his stay, the president spoke warmly of the "key moment in history" in which two nations "who loved each other and were torn apart, find themselves" at last. He called on the two countries to confront the "complex, yet painful past" from the conquest of 1830 to the years of a "murderous, sometimes unforgivable war," to move on toward the future and organize a "community of destiny" (March 4, 2003). In a joint declaration, the two leaders undertook to draw up and finalize a Treaty reflecting their willingness to establish an "exceptional partnership" (*partenariat d'exception*), respecting their history and their identity (March 2, 2003). This Algiers declaration can be seen as a precipitating factor, leading to the negotiations of the Friendship Treaty, which began a couple of months later.

In argumentation, neither party was acting for side effects such as reputation, publicity, or time. From April 2004 onwards, experts from both sides met regularly in order to prepare the document. Five main issues were to be discussed. The first concerned regional cooperation between the two sides of the Mediterranean in the framework of the Barcelona Process. The second related to an economic and financial partnership. The third referred to cultural and scientific cooperation between the two countries, especially the establishment of the "Franco-Algerian High Council for university and research cooperation."

The fourth concerned the movement of people between France and Algeria. This issue was particularly sensitive in the eyes of all Algerians living in France, and above all those waiting for visas to become residents in France. The fifth and final issue was the nature of the "memory work" – or rather the work on *memories* in the plural – to be carried out by France and Algeria.

The endgame came as a fatal crisis before the deadline. Neither Bouteflika nor Chirac mentioned an explicit date for signature of the future Treaty. However, all observers expected an official closure – in all senses of the term (technically and symbolically) – before the end of the French president's mandate in 2007. At the end of December 2004, most technical aspects of the projects were already settled. Several observers foresaw the signature of the Treaty in 2005. However, on February 23, 2005, French MPs passed a law that highlighted certain "positive effects of colonization" (Art. 4, para. 2). This unanticipated event, which was the result of an initiative by a group of French settlers who had been repatriated after Algerian independence, was immediately perceived as a scandal in Algeria. The gulf between what Algerians considered to be an unacceptable law and the "memory work" that they expected quickly jeopardized negotiation of the Friendship Treaty. The endgame had begun.

Two days after the voting through of this controversial law, the French Ambassador in Algiers gave a historic speech in Sétif, an average-sized town in the Eastern part of Algeria, where the French had committed a massacre on May 8, 1945.[3] His words were unprecedented in the French official narrative: "I have to bring to mind a tragedy that plunged your region into mourning. I mean the massacres of May 8, 1945, almost sixty years ago: an unforgivable tragedy" (Sétif, February 27, 2005). In Algeria, this official acknowledgement was hailed as a historic event. However, it did not calm Algerian claims. The powerful victims' association, the "8 May 1945 Foundation," for instance, considered that it was not enough and insisted that France should not only acknowledge the inhuman acts committed from 1830 to 1962 (i.e. the colonial period) but

---

[3] In Algeria on May 8, 1945, just as people were celebrating the allied victory over Germany (in which Algerian native troops had participated), banned demonstrations of Algerian nationalists took place in several towns. In Sétif, the demonstration turned into a riot after the police forces intervened. Ninety French settlers were killed. The severe repression organized by the army left many thousands dead – between 10,000 and 45,000 victims, according to different sources. In the view of Algerian writer Kateb Yacine, who witnessed "this horrible slaughter" (*Le Monde*, March 9, 2005), the Sétif massacre was the founding moment of Algerian nationalism. Some historians even consider that the Algerian war of independence did not start on November 1, 1954, but on May 8, 1945.

should also ask for forgiveness, along the lines of the official acknowledgement made by Jacques Chirac in 1995 regarding French responsibility in the deportation of Jews during WWII.

In July 2005, the two chambers of the Algerian Parliament condemned the French law. The French Minister of Foreign Affairs, Philippe Douste-Blazy, attempted to break the deadlock in the negotiations by demanding the establishment of a commission of historians. As shown by this development, the dynamic was then reduced to a strictly backward-looking negotiation process (Zartman 2005). In September, Bouteflika himself considered French repentance to be a condition for signing the Friendship Treaty (Batna, September 20, 2005). Under pressure from victims' associations and military circles, the Algerian President officially required the full acknowledgement by French representatives of the sufferings inflicted on the Algerian people during 132 years of occupation.

The French President attempted to change things by disavowing the law of February 23, 2005. To him, the accentuation of the positive aspect of the colonial legacy was "unjustified," if not "indecent" (Chirac 2011, 435). In January 2006, he decided to abrogate the disputed article in the law. Nonetheless, he did not accept the principle of a Treaty Preamble based on formal repentance by France, as was required by Bouteflika. Chirac could not accept an "official recognition of guilt" in the Treaty (quoted by Pervillé 2014, 89). The concession that he was ready to make was a distinct declaration (separate from the Treaty) to highlight the "hardships and the torments that history had imposed on both countries" (quoted by Pervillé 2014, 89). They had reached a total impasse. There was clearly no zone of potential agreement (ZOPA) between the parties. Heavily constrained by the wishes of their populations, both presidents were stuck in their respective positions somewhere between the requirement for full repentance, on the one hand, and the recognition of the hardships imposed by history, on the other.

Consequences

From then on, the entire pattern of behavior shifted: from *driving* to *dragging*, *mismatching*, and then *dueling*. Having initially been involved in a process of convergence, both parties considered that the expected cost breakdown was much higher than the expected benefit of a Friendship Treaty. In terms of security points or alternatives, neither party estimated that the negotiation process could fail. The voting through of the law in February 2005 interrupted this driving phase. Pushed by various pressure groups, the Algerian President dragged on to such an extent that negotiation rapidly mismatched. Jacques Chirac remained a *driver*, while Bouteflika progressively adopted the role of a *dueler*.

The French president tried several times to relaunch the project. For two years, French representatives went to Algeria in order to find an acceptable compromise. In January 2007, Jean-Louis Debré, who was then the President of the National Assembly, called upon French and Algerian citizens to undertake "essential memory work": "Any great country has to deal with its history," "with its glorious pages" and "with its dark times." "France, like many other nations, will not fail to do so" (*Le Monde*, January 20, 2007). These initiatives could not prevent an escalation of the tensions between the two sides of the Mediterranean. Obviously disappointed, Abdelaziz Bouteflika gradually adopted a more aggressive attitude toward the former colonial power that had committed "a genocide against the innocent Algerian people." On several occasions, he made it clear that in such conditions Algeria was better off with no treaty.

This posture was followed by a drastic step backward when Nicolas Sarkozy was elected. Refusing categorically to express guilt, he did not agree to consider memory issues as conditions for negotiating further agreements. In a press conference with Bouteflika, he claimed that young generations on both sides are "forward looking and not backward looking," and symbolically stopped the whole process of negotiating a Treaty: "I never thought that the Friendship Treaty was a solution." "When we have friends, we don't need to write it down, we need to live it. [...] So let us not divide the future by resurrecting the past" (July 10, 2007). *Dueling* – which had characterized the Franco-Algerian relationship for decades – was back. Neither party could be creative enough to develop a ZOPA or reframe the issues. It was not even possible to find a lowest common denominator (LCD). Outright spoilers from both sides had the last word.

Four Main Variables

This analysis of the case studies indicates the significance of four critical factors: leadership, timing, domestic resistance (discussed further, in Chapter 15, by P. Terrence Hopmann), and the nature of past violence.

Leadership

In the Franco-German case, both Charles de Gaulle and Konrad Adenauer understood that it was in their national interests to favor a rapprochement with the "hereditary enemy." Both individuals had sufficient historic legitimacy to entitle them to condemn Nazism. They became deeply involved in a personal friendship that would demonstrate the possibility of a dramatic change in attitude toward the other and established a ZOPA.

In the Franco-Algerian case, both Chirac and Bouteflika considered the Friendship Treaty as a historic opportunity to turn the page on the colonial past. Both had fought during the Algerian War. Chirac was twenty-four years old when he was sent to Algeria: "From this experience," he explained, "no one came back really unscathed" (Paris, November 11, 1996). For him, the effect of time was decisive: "Thirty years, forty years," "it is a time when, for those who have known the stupor of hardship, efforts to survive and attempts to forget, comes the hour of serenity and appeasement" (Paris, November 11, 1996).

On the other side, Bouteflika was one of the closest collaborators of Houari Boumedienne. As a former *moudjahid*, he largely based his legitimacy on his fight against the former colonial power. After the vote passing the French Law of 2005, his eagerness to become the equivalent of "Charles de Gaulle" in Algeria gave way to a much more traditional anti-colonial posture. This evolution during the final stages of the process demonstrates that the initial determination of both leaders could not overcome the resentment that remains a major feature of the relationship between the two countries. Whatever shadow of a ZOPA had been taking shape in the beginning was torn apart.

Context

In the Franco-German case, most protagonists agreed on the "absurdity of dueling" (Binoche 1990, 143). The communist threat encouraged a more concessionary approach, which remained constant, even during the final stages of negotiations. This ability to move toward each other's position was scarcely to be seen in the last stages of the Franco-Algerian process. Even though the standard arguments of realpolitik (whether in the field of economics, geopolitics, or strategy) pressed Paris to work for reconciliation with Algiers, and vice versa, neither party could escape the sparring and the subsequent impasse.

One major distinction between these cases is the political instability that characterized Algeria during the bloody civil war which devastated the country during the 1990s. In September 2005, Bouteflika launched a referendum on the "Charter for Peace and National Reconciliation" in order to bring closure to the civil war, by offering an amnesty for most of the violence committed during the black decade. The Charter was implemented as law in February 2006. In these circumstances, as numerous specialists observed, the constant condemnation of the French "neo-colonial attitude" became a way to calm down internal crises. In other words, Bouteflika could have been using the anti-colonial – and therefore anti-French – feeling in order to increase his legitimacy among the population.

In this regard, these two parties were not at all equal in terms of BATNA. Chirac expected to achieve a turning point in the relationship between the two countries. Giving up the Treaty was a personal failure for him, whereas it provided a heroic fighting posture for Bouteflika, which is apparently appreciated by most Algerians. This complete shift in attitude during the final stages of the process largely explains his systematic focus on the unfairness of the past.

Domestic Resistance

The two case studies vary greatly in terms of their popular basis. Both in Germany and in France, the Treaty of Friendship was supported by a vast majority of the population. The concerns expressed by the "anti-Gaullist" Germans did not prevent the signature of the Treaty. A creative solution was found thanks to the addition of the Preamble. The strength of this popular support was initially greatly influenced by pioneers who fought on both sides in favor of the rapprochement. Thus, numerous members of the French Resistance stressed the critical need to respect German prisoners after the war. Often they had just returned from German prisons and concentration camps. They did not believe in collective guilt, and immediately denounced any attempt to take revenge. From the same perspective, some French and German historians quickly gathered in order to favor a rapprochement. Inspired by an international institution for the revision of textbooks created in 1926 in Amsterdam, historians from both countries met for the first time in 1950 and engaged in the arduous task of revising national representations of the past. In a series of conferences over the years, these joint historical commissions attempted to critically scrutinize the myth of a "hereditary enmity" between France and Germany. Non-governmental organizations in both countries also provided avenues by which victims and victimizers could address their collective grief. Such initiatives, for the most part sponsored by religious associations (both Catholic and Protestant), focused on collective mourning (Ackermann 1994).

The organizers of these Franco-German meetings encouraged links between people working in embassies, in ministries, on the staffs of newspapers, and in the leadership of the unions, political parties, and professional organizations of both countries. In doing so, they revealed themselves to be real mediators between the two civil societies and constituted the "human infrastructure" of the rapprochement (Grosser 1967, 35). Thanks to their actions, attitudes evolved surprisingly quickly. In 1961, to give only one example, 76% of the Germans questioned in a poll considered that they could trust France in case of war, while 57% of the French expressed their confidence in the Germans. In 1955, these confidence figures were only 37% and 38%, respectively (Puchala 1970). Since then, all surveys have confirmed the high degree of mutual confidence across age groups (Ku 2008).

The Franco-Algerian context is radically different. At first glance, relations between the countries have pretty much been normalized. France is Algeria's largest trading partner. Hundreds of thousands of Algerians live in France. Both Presidents were originally convinced that a Friendship Treaty was critical. Experts from both sides of the Mediterranean rapidly drew up the document to be signed. However, domestic spoilers constantly interfered. The adoption of the controversial law by French MPs following the initiative of a group of *pieds-noirs*, and the subsequent indignation expressed by the Algerian population, illustrate the intensity of the resistance to any form of rapprochement/closure. Many testimonies remind us that the wounds described by various groups (*pieds-noirs*, former moudjahids, *harkis*, former French combatants) remain open. The Algerian Minister of Foreign Affairs, Mohammed Bedjaoui, emphasized this point in April 2006: "The objective and subjective conditions that are necessary to the signature of a Treaty are not sufficiently favourable today." In his view, "this Treaty is not a treaty between two presidents but between two peoples. We have to prepare public opinion to arouse the adherence of all the actors of our societies" (April 11, 2004).

This absence of ripeness (Zartman 2000) is tragically illustrated by the incompatible perceptions of the *harkis* (Muslims who fought alongside the French against their fellow Algerians). Following the French withdrawal, up to 150,000 *harkis* were slaughtered in Algeria.[4] More than 40,000 *harkis* were able to escape to France after the war, but they were badly treated once they had arrived. Most of them described a double betrayal (not only by Algeria but also by France), and considered themselves as second-class French citizens. The descendants of the *harkis* nowadays insist on the long-term impact of this double rejection: financial distress, a high unemployment rate, and a high frequency of suicide in their families. To them, this issue is far from being closed. During the

---

[4] The figures still vary according to the source.

negotiation process, Jacques Chirac suggested that the *harkis* be mentioned at the moment of the signature of the Treaty, while Algiers did not want to hear anything about these traitors.

The *harkis* are not the only group that expresses frustrations and resentment regarding their status. The *pieds-noirs* also depict themselves as "historical victims of social exclusion." Testimonies are abundant in this regard: "We are actually the losers, we have been manhandled, misled, humiliated, tortured, imprisoned, broken, rejected, caricaturized"; "We are a dead people. Without geography, there is nothing left" (Baussant 2002, 424, 433). The feeling is the same in the mind of former French combatants who do not feel like former combatants of WWII because people are not interested in them. A lot of them lament that their fight did not make any sense, 25% of them considering that their stay in Algeria was actually useless (Jauffret 2000, 329). As all these reactions show, one of the features of the Franco-Algerian case is the lack of psychological closure.

Past Violence

The initial assumption behind this chapter is that the intensity of domestic resistance toward a rapprochement with the former enemy directly depends on the nature of the past violence. In the framework of the Franco-German wars, the other was the *enemy* to fight. In the colonial context, the other – as depicted by the colonial authorities – was a backward *child* to be educated and/or a *barbarian* to be exploited. These representations are not incompatible. However, they do not have the same long-term effects on the affected population. Many observers use the same label of "reconciliation" both in the Franco-German case and in the Franco-Algerian case. They explain that both contexts involved massive human rights abuses (be it during WWI, WWII, or the Algerian war) and thus that there was a common need for a Friendship Treaty. However, these contexts differ fundamentally as regards the figure of the *other*.

For centuries, the German enemy was a basic component of French national identity and vice versa. The *other* was the negative reflection of qualities that each nation attributed to itself. Three cruel wars, without counting those of the Napoleonic era, made the antagonism seemingly irremediable. It was with that historic relationship in mind that Charles de Gaulle considered the nations to be naturally conflicting. According to him, their opposing temperaments and behaviors inevitably implied a "visceral mistrust" and an "ontological incompatibility" (de Gaulle 1944, 22–23). General de Gaulle drew portrait after portrait of Germany and pulled no punches: "We knew that the German is German. We did not doubt his hatred, nor his ferocity. We were certain that these unbalanced people could not restrain their nature for long, and that they would go right to crime at the first crisis of fear or anger" (October 23, 1941). Germany was depicted in his speeches as "a brutal neighbour, cunning and jealous," "intoxicated with pride and wickedness" (January 24, 1941). "By nature, it continues to exude Bismarck and Wilhelm II or Hitler" (November 11, 1942). Besides these descriptions, traditional songs on both sides of the Rhine revealed not only a constant competition between national powers, but also a genuine hatred between the nations. This hostility was particularly palpable after the end of the WWI. Stereotypes abounded and echoed the fears, frustrations, and resentments of the French and Germans with regard to one another.

However, this hatred is not sufficient to depict the true depth of Franco-German relationships. One of the key facets of this case lies, indeed, in the ambiguous fascination that captivated both peoples. Interestingly enough, this fascination was not incompatible with the detestation of the enemy. A paradoxical mixture of hatred and esteem was especially obvious among officers from both sides. To Charles de Gaulle again, fierce hostility did not prevent "a particular attraction" between the people of Germany and France; "Perhaps that is due to our origins or due to our vicinity." It also resulted, he explained, "from the genuine esteem that we had for one another, despite all our struggles" (July 12, 1967). This dissimilarity results from a cultural admiration that is apparent not only among German officers. In fact, respect for French culture was commonplace among the German elite. Likewise, a long tradition of French intellectuals and artists expressed their admiration for German writers and composers. This reciprocal admiration, ambivalent as it was, guaranteed a form of symmetry between the enemies despite the battlefields and even the defeats. It indeed allowed the development of a kind of empathy felt for the vanquished by a minority of intellectuals within the conqueror's camp. In France, Germaine de Staël offered an idealized image of Germany as a land of poets and thinkers. This uneasy symmetry, made up of a mixture of hatred and respect, would be decisive in creating the favorable conditions for a post-war rapprochement.

Once again, the Franco-Algerian context is totally different (see Figure 5.1). First, colonization can hardly be characterized as a period of reciprocal admiration. Scorn and humiliation were felt on a day-to-day basis. Secondly, the nature of the war was very different. Far from being a war between similar combatants on both sides (as in the case of Verdun during WWI, for instance), the fighting between the French army and the *fellagha* cannot be qualified as symmetrical. Thirdly, the war ended in

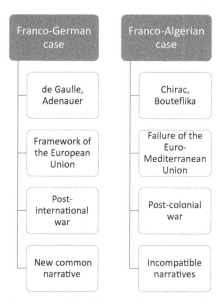

Figure 5.1. The Franco-German and Franco-Algerian contexts compared.

a particular way. In Algeria, the hostilities ceased after a negotiated agreement (the Évian Accords in 1962), and not after a crushing defeat by one of the parties. From that perspective, the notion of winners/losers is obviously less relevant than in other circumstances. Therefore it seems appropriate to question the notion of friendship. Does friendship imply an ability to move forward together and/or an ability to acknowledge the inflicted sufferings to "purge" the past? Besides, is friendship possible – and even necessary – in all circumstances?

Conclusion

The contrast between the endgame behavior in the Franco-German negotiations and that in the Franco-Algerian negotiations is telling. In the first case, the driving continued to the end despite the opposition and criticisms expressed until the very last day of the process. In the second case, the parties did not resist an escalation of symbolic violence and thus shifted to dueling. This divergence cannot be fully understood by considering exclusively the long-standing difference between the cases. In this regard, numerous specialists insist on the importance of common projects between former enemies. The European Union was created, while the Union for the Mediterranean failed. However, this element cannot explain the ultimate trajectory of the negotiations. If we try to generalize this framework, it is striking that Germany and Israel managed to normalize relationship reasonably quickly after the war (Reparation Agreement in 1952, diplomatic relations in 1965) despite the lack of common political or economic projects and the magnitude of past violence. The comparative analysis shows that, beyond these elements, it is the endgame dynamics that actually determined the distinctive outcomes in the two case studies. In adding a Preamble *after* the signature of the Franco-German Treaty, the German authorities did not completely jeopardize the rapprochement with France. In requiring a Preamble as a condition *before* the signature of a Treaty, the Algerian government endangered the whole process of negotiation. In refusing the principle of formal repentance, the French authorities definitely condemned it. In both cases, the question of an additional clause coming at the very end of rather successful discussions became crucial to confirm or derail the rapprochement.

One of the main points made in this chapter is that the broadening of the analysis does not only concern the future. It also depends on the representation given of the past. In the Franco-Algerian case, the explicit objective of closure precipitated the failure. As the Algerian Minister of Foreign Affairs, Mohammed Bedjaoui, explained, the purpose was ambitious: "We must purge the past of negative reminiscences," since "it is not a banal treaty that we want, it is a treaty to re-found the relationships between our two countries and our two peoples, which will *definitively* allow us to turn the page" (RFI, April 11, 2006). Is this objective too ambitious? How can people definitively close a tragedy where both sides still feel victimized?

Stressing the nature of past violence does not suggest that the outcome of the negotiation process is contextually ordained. As has been underlined, other variables (leadership, timing, and domestic resistance) are critical. But the two case studies show that among all the factors impacting the endgames, memory issues should be taken seriously into account. The question is then: How do we know whether it is useful to launch a negotiation process despite the weight of the past? How do we know whether the memory issues are explosive? One dimension to consider, among others, is the existence – or not – of a consensual narrative of the past. Between France and Germany, the narrative was clearly based on (a) the distinction between Germans and Nazis, and (b) the notion of European reconciliation (Rosoux 2014). In the Franco-Algerian case, there is absolutely no consensus on the meaning of the Algerian war. The gap is not only between the French and Algerian sides.

It exists also – and above all – between various groups in France ("pro-Algérie française" – and some of their descendants – who did not take part in a mourning process, *harkis* who cannot see the war as a war of liberation, members of the military who felt betrayed by the French politicians who negotiated the Évian Accords, etc.). All these groups are still struggling with the meaning of the past. In such circumstances, a modest and pragmatic attitude can probably be more efficient than a maximalist one. It is only if all the groups affected by the past violence *gradually* negotiate a common narrative that they will finally see an end, and a beginning.

6 Closure in Bilateral Negotiations: APEC-Member Free Trade Agreements

Larry Crump

This chapter begins by reviewing the multilateral literature on closure, as it provides a context for case data containing five bilateral free trade agreement (FTA) negotiations. The multilateral literature on closure or the endgame considers coalition behavior, negotiation complexity, decision-making, leadership, and negotiation deadlines.

Endgame activity is identified within coalition behavior, which is concerned with strategizing and transactions, balancing power, and the use of resources and roles, including leadership (Dupont 1996). Coalitions often serve to reduce complexity, while complexity is often identified as a challenge to be managed within multilateral negotiations (Zartman 1994; Crump and Zartman 2003). Within the endgame, however, complexity is not only identified as a challenge; it is also considered to be an opportunity. Complexity can help break through the last outstanding issues once a long negotiation moves toward a conclusion, as a complicated and vague situation provides negotiators with flexibility regarding the way the outcome is portrayed to constituents (Winham 1987).

Decision-making at the endgame is more a matter of educated political guesswork than a precise calculation of advantage, as the following chapters by Andrew Kydd, Janice Gross Stein, and Mikhail Troitskiy develop. Negotiation delegations experience a transition during the endgame as senior leaders take over, while lower-level technical delegation members – who put much of the deal together – recede to an advisory role. From several dimensions, leadership emerges as a critical issue during the endgame. Delegation leadership requires that a negotiation team be organized in a decentralized manner to effectively study technical issues, and in a centralized and hierarchical manner to take difficult political decisions. This bi-structural requirement presents organizational challenges for party leadership (Winham 1987).

The endgame within the General Agreement on Tariffs and Trade (GATT) Uruguay Round (1986–1994), is perhaps the most intensively studied multilateral trade negotiation (Stewart 1999). Publication of the "Draft Final Act Embodying the Results of the Uruguay Round of

Multilateral Trade Negotiations" – named the Dunkel Draft after its author, GATT Director-General Arthur Dunkel – established the foundation for closure in December 1991, but the actual endgame began only in July 1993 with the appointment of Peter Sutherland as GATT Director-General. He arrived with a singular and repeated message that the last opportunity to conclude the GATT Uruguay Round would end on December 15, 1993 – when US Fast-Track Authority essentially expired (McDonough 1999).[1] This deadline plus the outline of a realistic agreement through the Dunkel Draft drove GATT parties toward a mid-December 1993 agreement, although not all economic sectors achieved closure by the deadline.

The politically sensitive areas contained in the General Agreement for Trade in Services (GATS), including financial services, telecommunications, maritime services, audio-visual services, and movement of natural persons, dragged on in negotiation after the deadline, although Sutherland had firmly established the finality of the December 15 deadline. Yet the GATS closure continued to be elusive. Services negotiations continued beyond the initial deadline, with closure finally achieved just before the GATT Marrakesh Agreement was signed on April 15, 1994 (Reyna 1999).

If a deadline is to be effective it must be perceived as creditable, as discussed in Chapter 15 by P. Terrence Hopmann. Sutherland achieved such creditability by establishing a final date when opportunity would be lost if agreement were not reached. The many GATT negotiators that made up the GATT Uruguay Round responded to this creditable deadline by achieving closure, without which negotiations could have continued to drag – with no agreement in sight. However, once this outcome had been achieved, Sutherland was not so dogmatic as to refuse GATS gains that were achieved through a second GATT Uruguay deadline, which gained creditability through the finality associated with the signing of the 1994 Marrakesh Agreement.

The present study will utilize the multilateral understanding gained through this literature review to examine data from a bilateral environment. We will pay special attention to coalitions, leadership, deadlines, and shifts that might occur from the technical to the political at the endgame. Specifically, this chapter will focus on those negotiations that

---

[1] The US Congress renewed fast-track authority (an up-or-down vote on a trade treaty in the US Congress with no amendments) but only for trade agreements entered into prior to April 16, 1994, which effectively required the US President to notify Congress by December 15, 1993 of an intention to enter into a trade agreement (McDonough 1999). This December 1993 expiration date became the GATT Uruguay deadline that Peter Sutherland effectively promoted.

reach an agreement (when not enough is still enough). The focus of attention is on a domain that has received little scholarly attention within the negotiation literature: regional economic associations (Crump 2013). Bilateral trade negotiations conducted by members of the Asia–Pacific Economic Cooperation (APEC) association provide data for this investigation. The focus of the case presentation is to establish the dynamics that lead to negotiation closure. We examine the unique features of each case to gain further understanding about the specific dynamics that lead to closure. The chapter concludes by describing a process model for closure in complex bilateral negotiations, and offers direction for future research toward understanding the forces that contribute to gaining or losing opportunity in the concluding stage of a negotiation.

Research Setting

This study draws on data from bilateral negotiations conducted between members of APEC. Former Australian Prime Minister Bob Hawke first proposed the idea of APEC during a speech in January 1989. Ten months later, twelve Asia–Pacific countries met in Canberra to establish APEC – a non-treaty organization. Nine additional nations acceded to APEC between 1991 and 1998 to establish a twenty-one-member economic association focused on security, stability, and prosperity through free and open trade and investment (APEC 2015). This association has achieved success and maturity over the twenty-five-plus years during which it has engaged its members.

Distinct from this regional association are bilateral relationships between APEC members, relationships that are sustained in part through association membership. The chapter seeks to understand closure in these bilateral trade negotiations between APEC members, as one way to monitor APEC economic integration and the dynamic interaction within a regional economic association. The present study uses a bilateral and a bilateral–multiparty lens to understand multilateral or regional dynamics (Crump 2006, 2015). Under what conditions do negotiators follow one type of behavior over another?

Each of these twenty-one APEC members has established multiple and diverse bilateral relationships, although the present study is concerned only with negotiations that produced FTAs in force between APEC members.[2] APEC reports, for example, that its twenty-one members have 144 enforced FTAs – but that includes all bilateral and

---

[2] Free trade agreement (FTA) is the most common term to describe these negotiations, but other terms include closer economic relations, economic partnership agreement,

regional agreements that have at least one APEC member as a partner, while non-APEC economies are also included in these 144 FTAs (APEC Policy Support Unit 2015). The present study is concerned with trade treaties that include APEC economies only (with no non-members present). Data gathered from twenty-one APEC-member websites (e.g. Ministry or Department of Foreign Affairs and Trade) identified forty-eight bilateral FTAs currently in force between APEC members as of May 2015,[3] as listed in Table 6.1. In three cases, trilateral relationships are included: economic relations between Canada, Mexico, and the United States (via NAFTA); economic relations between Hong Kong, China, and Chile; and economic relations between China, Hong Kong China, and New Zealand. Trilateral relationships are included in our data set when they only include APEC members.

A network image of this data is presented as Figure 6.1. Papua New Guinea and Russia report that they do not have formal bilateral economic relationships with any APEC member, while the complicated political circumstances of Chinese Taipei preclude formal bilateral economic relations with other APEC member economies.[4] Three other APEC members – Brunei, Indonesia, and the Philippines – each have a formal bilateral relationship with only one other APEC member, namely Japan, while Vietnam has separate FTA relations with Japan and Chile. However, these Southeast Asian countries have multiple economic relationships through membership in ASEAN.

The fourteen remaining APEC members are actively engaged in establishing FTAs with other APEC-member economies, including Australia with eight FTAs, Canada with five FTAs, Chile with eleven FTAs, China with five FTAs, Hong Kong (China) with three FTAs, Japan with eleven FTAs, (South) Korea with six FTAs, Malaysia with four FTAs, Mexico with five FTAs, New Zealand with six FTAs, Peru with nine FTAs, Singapore with seven FTAs, Thailand with four FTAs, and the United States with seven FTAs (see Figure 6.1).

---

economic cooperation partnership agreements, closer economic and partnership arrangement, and related terms.

[3] The APEC website identifies FTAs and regional trade agreements of APEC members at www.apec.org/Groups/Other-Groups/FTA_RTA. This site lists the website links for all APEC members' free trade agreements. Generally, these website links are directed toward the member government's ministry or department of foreign affairs and trade. APEC members make a distinction between their bilateral and regional trade agreements (e.g. ASEAN), although the APEC Policy Support Unit (2015) does not make this distinction.

[4] Note that APEC members are never referred to as nations or countries but as member economies, as one way to include both China and Chinese Taipei (commonly known as Taiwan) in the same international table.

Table 6.1 *Bilateral FTAs in force between APEC-member economies*

	Australia	Brunei	Canada	Chile	China	Hong Kong China	Indonesia	Japan	South Korea	Malaysia	Mexico	New Zealand	Papua New Guinea	Peru	Philippines	Russia	Singapore	Chinese Taipei	Thailand	United States	Vietnam
Australia																					
Brunei																					
Canada																					
Chile	×		×																		
China				×																	
Hong Kong China				×	×																
Indonesia																					
Japan	×	×		×			×														
South Korea	×		×	×																	
Malaysia	×			×				×													
Mexico				×	×			×													
New Zealand	×				×	×				×											
Papua New Guinea																					
Peru			×	×	×			×	×		×										
Philippines								×													
Russia																					
Singapore	×				×			×	×			×		×							
Chinese Taipei																					
Thailand	×							×				×		×							
United States	×		×	×					×		×			×			×				
Vietnam				×				×													

This study investigates five of these forty-eight bilateral FTA negotiations, or around 10%, identified by *dashed lines* in Figure 6.1. These five negotiations were selected as a convenient sample to examine negotiation processes and outcomes between APEC-member economies with a focus on understanding how closure is achieved in FTA negotiations.

The following five bilateral FTA negotiations were investigated in this study to identify similarities and differences to support the development of a framework to understand how closure is achieved in bilateral free trade agreement negotiations:

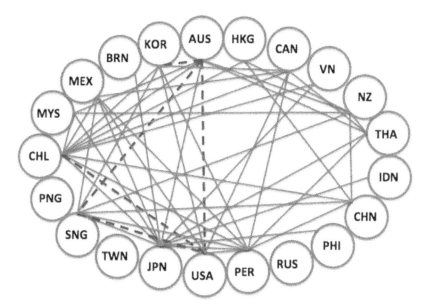

Figure 6.1. Network image of APEC member FTAs.
Note: Forty-eight bilateral relationships (FTAs) are identified (as of May 2015) via connecting lines for all twenty-one APEC member economies. The dashed connecting lines identify the five cases under investigation. ISO 3166-1 Alpha-2 or Alpha-3 country codes are adopted: Australia (AUS); Brunei (BRN); Canada (CAN); Chile (CHL); China (CHN); Hong Kong (China) (HKG); Indonesia (IDN); Japan (JPN); (South) Korea (KOR); Malaysia (MYS); Mexico (MEX); New Zealand (NZ); Papua New Guinea (PNG); Peru (PER); the Philippines (PHI); Russia (RUS); Singapore (SGP); Chinese Taipei (TWN); Thailand (THA); United States (USA); and Vietnam (VN).

- Singapore Australia Free Trade Agreement of 2003 (SAFTA)
- United States–Singapore Free Trade Agreement of 2003 (USSFTA)
- Australia–United States Free Trade Agreement of 2004 (AUSFTA)
- Chile–United States Free Trade Agreement of 2003 (CUSFTA)
- Korea–Australia Free Trade Agreement of 2014 (KAFTA)

All five cases are of Type 1: Agreement was reached, as not enough was still enough. At the concluding stage, three of the cases demonstrate a pattern of behavior that is purely driving (SAFTA, USSFTA, and AUSFTA), a fourth case demonstrates a pattern of behavior that is both driving and dueling (CUSFTA), and a fifth case is mixed, with primarily dueling up to the concluding stage before reverting to a driving pattern of behavior (KAFTA).

This study employed qualitative research methodology in investigating these five FTA cases by conducting field interviews complemented by the collection of documents to construct case studies (Odell 2001; Yin 1989) including a focused comparison approach to data analysis (Druckman 2002; Zartman 2005).

Three periods of field interviews with trade negotiators, trade policy specialists, diplomats, and ambassadors were conducted to construct these five cases. SAFTA, USSFTA, and AUSFTA included eighty-six interviews in Canberra, Geneva, Singapore, and Washington, DC in 2004. CUSFTA included twenty-eight interviews in Santiago and Washington, DC in 2006. KAFTA included twenty-eight interviews in Canberra, Seoul, and Sejong City in 2014–2015. Confidentiality was assured all 142 respondents interviewed to secure data for these five cases.

National governments usually field a negotiation team that includes between twenty-five and ninety members in bilateral trade negotiations. Teams are normally organized into groups of ten to twenty (normally one group per treaty chapter). Interviews with the team leader or chief negotiator, group leaders, and any other officials who sat at the negotiation table were sought. The focus of this field research was on negotiations to draft and sign a trade treaty between two nations. Treaty approval through parliamentary or congressional process is a separate negotiation beyond the scope of this study.

Case Material

The following is a synopsis of five negotiations that achieved FTAs, with special attention paid to endgame. We begin by providing some background on each case before focusing on negotiation closure.

Singapore–Australia Negotiation (SAFTA)

Singapore and Australia announced their decision to commence negotiating a trade agreement on November 15, 2000 on the "sidelines" of the APEC Leaders' Summit in Brunei. Singapore's negotiation delegation was led initially by Vanu Gopala Menon of the Ministry of Foreign Affairs (MFA), and many staff assigned to the Singaporean SAFTA team came from Directorate B, the Trade Division of the Ministry of Trade and Industry (MTI). The Australian delegation was led initially by Donald Kenyon of the Department of Foreign Affairs and Trade (DFAT), and many staff assigned to the Australian SAFTA team came from the DFAT Office of Trade Negotiations (OTN).

The two sides held ten negotiation rounds between February 2001 and October 2002 (normally a round will last for one week, with meeting sites alternating between Singapore and Australia). Halfway through the process (August 2001 to February 2002) the two sides called a hiatus, as the shift from a multilateral to a bilateral trade policy was controversial for many trade officials. On resuming negotiations, Stephen Deady of OTN led the Australian team and Goh Aik Guan of the Deputy Prime Minister's office led the Singaporean team.

Many trade issues were challenging for the seventeen SAFTA working groups. Often we find two or three accepted formulas or templates for a specific trade policy issue. Agreement on the type of template to apply to a given issue minimizes such challenges. For example, in negotiations over goods and rules of origin (ROO), Singapore sought to persuade Australia to adopt a "change in tariff classification system," but Australia refused and so SAFTA (Chapter 3) uses a "value-added system" based on the net cost of a product.[5] Within trade in services, the two most common templates are a "positive list for trade in services" and a "negative list for trade in services."[6] Australia insisted that the treaty adopt a negative list, whereas Singapore argued for a positive list, but eventually relinquished, so SAFTA uses a negative list for managing trade in services (Chapter 7). Investment, financial services, and telecommunications are treated separately within SAFTA (Chapters 8–10), but trade policy in the services chapter establishes a foundation for these other chapters. Reports indicate that negotiations in these chapters were more positional than integrative, as each side sought to protect its own interests. When working groups or their co-leaders could not resolve significant issues, the two Chief Negotiators eventually negotiated these issues. Many issues could be resolved, but some had qualities that required political deliberations.

Closure On the edge of an APEC Ministerial Meeting in Los Cabos, Mexico in October 2002, Australian Trade Minister Mark Vaile and Singaporean Trade Minister George Yeo discussed and resolved the remaining issues, including financial services, legal services, investment, and rules of origin. The 117-page SAFTA treaty (not including annexes

---

[5] Rules of origin (ROO) determine whether a good qualifies for preferential treatment (e.g. a reduced tariff), by establishing a method for defining where a good was actually made. There are several ROO methods, but the most common are the value-added or local-content system, and the change-in-tariff classification or transformation system.

[6] A negative list for trade in services allows for trade in any service unless it is specifically *excluded* in the trade treaty. A positive list for trade in services allows for trade only if a service is specifically *included* in the trade treaty. A negative list is considered to be more liberal in encouraging international trade than a positive list.

and side letters) was signed by these Trade Ministers on February 17, 2003. The process leading up to closure suggests a driving behavior pattern, since each side clearly pushed to achieve a conclusion, as demonstrated by the continual resolution of issues. Negotiations shifted from the technical to the political level at the endgame, as the two Trade Ministers closed the deal on the sideline of an APEC Ministerial meeting.

United States–Singapore Negotiation (USSFTA)

On November 16, 2000 on the sidelines of the APEC Leaders' Summit in Brunei, Singapore and the United States announced that their nations would negotiate a trade agreement. Professor Tommy Koh led Singapore's delegation, and many Singaporean negotiators were drawn from Directorate B, the Trade Division of the Ministry of Trade and Industry (MTI). Ralph Ives led the US delegation, and many US negotiators came from the Office of the United States Trade Representative (USTR). There were forty to fifty negotiators on each side during the negotiation. Each team organized its negotiators into twenty-one working groups, or one per treaty chapter. Eleven rounds were held, mostly in London, with the first round held in December 2000 and the final round held in November 2002. The last substantive issue was resolved in January 2003.

Among the many issues discussed and agreed, a number offered real challenges. From the beginning, the United States insisted that goods be divided into non-textile and textile products. In goods, Singapore sought to eliminate tariffs early and the United States sought to delay tariff elimination. In textiles, the United States forced Singapore to adopt the US Yarn Forward Rule (USSFTA Chapter 5).[7] The United States arrived in Singapore with a twenty-one-page initial position on intellectual property rights (IPR). Singaporean negotiators thought that the US position was very much focused on IPR enforcement where little capacity for enforcement exists, an

---

[7] The US Yarn Forwarding Rule allows a treaty partner to secure raw materials from anywhere in the world, but the yarn produced from this raw material must come from either treaty partner to gain US tariff benefits. Singapore argued that it was highly inefficient to transport yarn from the United States (Singapore does not have a yarn industry) just so Singaporean textile manufacturers can gain tariff benefits when exporting finished products to the United States. The two Chief Negotiators resolved this issue on the final day of the final round, with Singapore's arguments unsuccessful in persuading the United States.

[8] One high-level Singaporean official explained the US position on intellectual property rights (IPR) by stating that Singapore is small and can be bullied by a county like the United States. At the same time, the United States could back up all of its requests with specific examples. Nevertheless, Singaporeans directly involved in IPR negotiations questioned the relevance of the USSFTA IPR chapter to Singaporean conditions.

approach that was not seen to be relevant to Singapore. Nevertheless, much of what the United States sought is found in USSFTA (Chapter 16).[8] In financial services, Singaporean liberalization was a top US priority (USSFTA Chapter 10). For example, the United States successfully persuaded Singapore to liberalize its retail-banking sector and to phase out its wholesale bank license quota system for US banks. However, Singapore refused to allow US banks to acquire local Singaporean banks. In telecommunications (USSFTA Chapter 9), interviews indicate that Singapore and the United States created a state-of-the-art agreement between two open-market economies. In electronic commerce (USSFTA Chapter 14), both sides sought to explore every opportunity to liberalize trade and succeeded in establishing the first trade treaty ever concluded with electronic commerce provisions.

Closure USSFTA negotiations moved toward a conclusion when US Trade Representative Robert Zoellick and Singaporean Trade Minister George Yeo met at an APEC Ministerial Meeting in Los Cabos, Mexico in October 2002, followed by meetings between the US and Singaporean Chief Negotiators. These meetings narrowed the list of outstanding issues from thirty to five issues – competition policy, financial services, investment, intellectual property, and textiles. At the final round, in mid November 2002, Yeo, Zoellick and ten negotiators from each side resolved all but one issue – investment and technology transfer (USSFTA Chapter 15) – which was resolved in mid January 2003. Singaporean officials reported that Zoellick used anger and threats in concluding negotiations with Singapore.

US President Bush notified the US Congress of his intention to sign the USSFTA on January 30, and he and Singaporean Prime Minister Goh signed the 240-page treaty (800 pages when all annexes are included) on May 6, 2003 at the White House. The process leading up to closure suggests a driving behavior pattern, as we find a sustained attempt to resolve and reduce the number of outstanding issues by each side. Negotiations shifted from the technical to the political level at the endgame which began at the 2002 APEC Ministerial Meeting in Mexico, with Ministerial involvement continuing into the following month, although it is important to note that one final issue (investment and technology transfer) was resolved at the technical level two months later.

Australia–United States Negotiation (AUSFTA)

The United States and Australia announced that they would commence negotiating a trade agreement on November 14, 2002. Ralph Ives led the

US delegation and Stephen Deady led the Australian delegation. Many of the sixty to seventy staff assigned to the US team came from the Office of the United States Trade Representative (USTR) and many of the sixty to seventy staff assigned to the Australian team came from the Office of Trade Negotiation (OTN) within the Department of Foreign Affairs and Trade (DFAT). Each team organized its negotiators into twenty-three working groups, or one per treaty chapter. The two sides held six rounds between March 2003 and February 2004 – two in Canberra and two in Honolulu, with the final two in Washington, DC. Each round lasted one week, except the last round, which lasted three weeks.

The two sides confronted a very brief time period for concluding negotiations. The fact that these negotiations could commence and finish in only eleven months can only be explained by the desire of each side to reach agreement and secure US Congressional treaty approval before the November 2004 US presidential election.

Negotiations over goods did not present substantial challenges (AUSFTA Chapter 2) – the focus was on tariff reduction – but some of the most contentious issues involved specific goods such as agriculture, textiles, and pharmaceuticals. Agriculture was the major AUSFTA issue for Australia. The United States claimed that the Australian Import Risk Assessment system served as a non-tariff barrier to trade, while the two sides eventually agreed on an enhanced science-based risk-assessment system (AUSFTA Chapter 7). In specific agricultural sectors Australia achieved no additional sugar exports to the United States and its export quota for beef was increased by 70,000 tons. Australia secured small increases across many dairy product categories, resulting in some gains over a long phase-in period.

Australian negotiators did not think that a national health program such as the Australian pharmaceutical benefits scheme (PBS) should be included in a trade agreement, but the United States insisted, and so it was (as an annex to AUSFTA Chapter 2). The United States was unsuccessful in seeking changes that would increase PBS medication prices, although Australia agreed to enhance PBS processes by involving transparency. The United States was very unsatisfied with this outcome.

The most contentious services issue involved Australia's right to ensure that local cultural content would be presented on Australia media; however, both parties were generally pleased with the outcome they achieved (AUSFTA Chapter 10 including annexes). Within telecommunications (AUSFTA Chapter 12), financial services (AUSFTA Chapter 13), and electronic commerce (AUSFTA Chapter 16), the two sides adopted a cooperative framework that further integrates the two economies.

Investment presented two challenges, as the United States sought to dismantle the Australian Foreign Investment Review Board (FIRB) – an agency that reviews all foreign investments in Australia over $50 million. Australia would not relinquish the FIRB, but it did increase the threshold to $800 million for US companies (AUSFTA Chapter 11). The United States was also unsuccessful in providing investors with the right to seek international arbitration in disputes with governments (Investor–State Dispute Settlement, or ISDS) (AUSFTA Chapter 11). In intellectual property (AUSFTA Chapter 17), Australia basically agreed to the same deal that the United States gave Singapore.

Closure AUSFTA negotiations moved toward a conclusion after missing the initial December 2003 deadline. Negotiations were planned for two weeks but went into three in January and February 2004 in Washington, DC. In the first week, each side sought to narrow the areas of disagreement with their full team. In the second and third weeks, these negotiations were passed up to political leaders on each side, including ministers, secretaries, and ambassadors. AUSFTA team leaders also played an active role in this process, and working-group leaders were brought in when technical expertise was required, although the focus of talks shifted to a search for political solutions. During the final two weeks, US and Australian political leaders found solutions for agriculture, cultural content in the media, the FIRB, investor–state relations, intellectual property, and the PBS. The Australian Prime Minister was regularly briefed and made compromise decisions on several issues. The US President was less involved in the process, as the US side was more focused on delivering a treaty that could gain US Congressional approval. Agreement was reached and negotiations concluded on February 8, 2004.

US President Bush notified the US Congress of his intention to sign the AUSFTA on February 13, and USTR Zoellick and Australian Trade Minister Mark Vaile signed the 264-page treaty (over 1,000 pages when annexes and side letters are included) on May 18, 2004 at the White House.

The process leading up to a conclusion again suggests a driving behavior pattern, as each side was actively involved in reducing the number of outstanding issues. However, unlike the prior two cases, in AUSFTA deadlines played a role in closure, as each side reduced issues by securing compromises from the other side and by reducing demands (letting issues go) in order to meet a self-imposed deadline. A deadline forces each party to examine what they really want and then decide which issue to push and which to let go. Again, negotiations shifted from the technical to the political level at the endgame.

Chile–United States Negotiation (CUSFTA)

Chile and the United States began trade negotiations in 1994 (as part of the Four-Amigo Talks), as Chilean leaders linked their trade aspirations to the recently concluded North American Free Trade Agreement (NAFTA). Complications between US President Clinton and the US Congress did not allow negotiations to proceed, but talks had begun. When the United States and Singapore announced their intention to negotiate an FTA, Chilean leaders immediately reminded the United States that they had been waiting for five years. Shortly thereafter, the United States was concurrently negotiating two separate bilateral FTAs with Chile and Singapore, beginning in November 2000.

Ambassador Osvaldo Rosales led Chile's delegation with ninety to 100 staff assigned to the Chile CUSFTA team that were drawn from the General Directorate for International Economic Relations within the Ministerio de Relaciones Exteriores. Regina Vargo led the US delegation with forty to fifty staff assigned to the US CUSFTA team that came from the Office of the USTR. Each team organized its negotiators into twenty-four working groups, or one per treaty chapter.

There was a rush to accomplish an outcome prior to US President Clinton's January 2001 departure from office, followed by an extended pause as the US Executive Office underwent a change in administration with CUSFTA negotiations recommencing in mid 2001. Talks continued, and ten rounds were conducted in Washington, DC and Santiago, Chile before negotiations were suspended in March 2002 because the USTR lacked sufficient guidance from the US Congress. The US Trade Promotion Authority Act (Public Law 107-210, also known as the fast-track authority) was passed by Congress and enacted into law on August 6, 2002. This provided the guidance the USTR required. CUSFTA talks resumed in September 2002.

Closure Agreement was reached at the fourteenth round, with some of the most difficult issues concerning US financial objectives. For example, the United States was concerned about movement of capital – especially the movement of capital out of Chile. The United States also sought to establish a policy that would allow foreign banks to set up in Chile without committing capital – a proposal Chile successfully rejected (see CUSFTA Chapter 12).

Other issues that were finalized in the last round included the phase-out of the 85% Chilean tax on the custom value of cars above the threshold of US$15,740 and the elimination on the US side of tariffs on copper – Chile's largest export product (see CUSFTA Chapter 3). These final issues were not traded straight across; rather, they were part of a larger bundle or package of issues that also included advantages for Chilean small and medium-sized companies in the US market, among other issues.

Given the financial nature of these final unresolved issues, negotiations were concluded by the Chilean Minister of Finance and the Chilean Chief Negotiator on one side and the USTR leadership and the US Chief Negotiator on the other side. Agreement was reached in principle in December 2002.

However, the bilateral process became complicated the following month, shortly after Chile became a non-permanent member of the UN Security Council. Negotiations were practically concluded, and now each side deployed a team of lawyers to engage in "legal-scrubbing" to convert the agreement into a treaty. Concurrently, the United States began to delay this process to pressure Chile to vote in the UN Security Council in support of a US proposal to initiate war against Iraq. Chile did not cooperate on this US initiative, but still had to manage US attempts to link international trade and international security.

Conclusion of the treaty was delayed, but USTR Zoellick and Chilean Minister of Foreign Affairs Maria Soledad Alvear Valenzuela finally signed it on the sidelines of a Free Trade Area of the Americas Ministerial Meeting in June 2003. The process leading up to closure demonstrates a mixed pattern of behavior that is both driving and dueling, in which each side pushed to reduce issues but, once this had been achieved, the more powerful side unsuccessfully attempted to hold the treaty hostage to secure cooperation in an unrelated venue (the UN Security Council). This tactic shifted a driving pattern of behavior into dueling during the endgame. Just prior to the introduction of this tactic, we find Chilean Ministers and the USTR leadership concluding the trade negotiation, but once these delay tactics had become more apparent (reports indicate), the Chilean President made some of the critical decisions that brought about a conclusion.

Korea–Australia Negotiation (KAFTA)

Korean President Lee Myung-bak and Prime Minister Kevin Rudd announced that FTA negotiations between Korea and Australia would begin in March 2009. Korean Minister for Trade Kim Jeong-hoon met with Australian Minister for Trade Simon Crean in Canberra to officially launch the first round of the Korea–Australia Free Trade Agreement (KAFTA) negotiations in May 2009. Four rounds followed, in Seoul and Canberra, led by Australian Jan Adams, of the Department of Foreign Affairs and Trade (DFAT), and Korean Lee Tae-ho, of the Ministry of Foreign Affairs and Trade (MOFAT). Generally, there were between fifty and ninety trade negotiators on each side during the five KAFTA rounds that occurred between May 2009 and May 2010.

Much was accomplished in 2009–2010, but negotiations stalled and then deadlocked for over three years starting in 2010; several factors explain the delay, but it was a single substantive issue that halted negotiations: Korea could not accept an FTA that did *not* include Investor-State Dispute Settlement (ISDS), while the Australian Labor Party – which then controlled the Australian government – could not accept an FTA that included ISDS.[9]

ISDS was the "Big Issue" in this negotiation, although controversial in Australia and Korea alike; Korea's insistence on including ISDS in KAFTA was based on the US requirement that ISDS be included in the Korea–US trade treaty. Upon accepting this US demand, the Korean government explained to the public that ISDS was a new standard that was widely accepted internationally. Not to pursue ISDS in every future Korean treaty would cause complications between the Korean government and their opposition parties, which could have impacted negatively on Korea–US relations. Korea refused to back down in KAFTA because of these domestic complications.

Closure The September 2013 change of government in Australia broke this deadlock, as the new government wanted to demonstrate to Australia, Asia, and the world that it was *ready to do business*: ISDS was given away by Australia in exchange for a number of Australian offensive interests, including 40% Korean beef tariffs that will reduce to zero over fifteen years, and reductions in dairy, grain, sugar, and wine tariffs. Upon full implementation, 99.8% of Australian products will enter Korea duty-free. Australia also gained access to the Korean services market on terms that are equal to those Korea gave the United States and the EU in Korea's prior FTAs. Korea also achieved gains that included duty-free imports of almost all products into Australia within five years, including the immediate elimination of tariffs on Korean

---

[9] ISDS is a set of policies that assure a corporation's right to take a national government to third-party arbitration if that government engages in behavior (passes a law, changes enforcement of a regulation, etc.) that results in apparent corporate financial loss.

automobiles, televisions, and refrigerators. Further, Korea achieved some protective measures for its agricultural sector within KAFTA, and Korean investors receive the same treatment as is granted to US investors in the Australian market.

A team of high-level negotiators led by the Australian and Korean Trade Ministers put this final package together in November and December 2013. The new Australian Trade Minister Andrew Robb visited Korea and met with Deputy Prime Minister Hyun Oh-seok and Minister for Trade, Industry and Energy Yoon Sang-jick in November 2013; at this meeting, progress was made on several politically sensitive issues. Minister Robb and Minister Yoon concluded negotiations on the sidelines of a WTO Ministerial Meeting in Bali, Indonesia in December 2013. Australian Trade Minister Robb and Korean Trade Minister Yoon signed the KAFTA in Seoul in April 2014.

KAFTA primarily demonstrated a dueling behavioral pattern up to the concluding stage and then it reverted to a driving behavioral pattern. Each side stood its ground for over three years, resulting in a deadlock which was broken only when the political party that controlled the Australian government was replaced. Again we find that negotiations shifted from the technical to the political level at the endgame, as Trade Ministers on each side put the final deal together on the sidelines of the 2013 WTO Ministerial Meeting.

Case Analysis: Closure in Complex Bilateral Negotiations

These five cases provide a rich database by which to investigate the forces and processes that contribute to closure in complex bilateral trade negotiations. We will consider negotiation closure in the context of negotiation party stability and instability, creditable deadlines and linkage dynamics, asymmetrical power relations, exchange of politically sensitive issues, and negotiating bilateral agreements on the sidelines of a multilateral forum. This analysis will provide the foundation for the development of a process model that supports understanding of closure in complex bilateral negotiations.

Party Stability–Instability

The stability or instability of a group or political party that controls a negotiating party such as a national government has a dramatic impact on negotiation-closure dynamics. KAFTA and AUSFTA each illustrate this observation. For example, most of KAFTA was negotiated within the first year, during 2009–2010, and then a stalemate turned into a three-year deadlock primarily over the "Big Issue" – ISDS. It seemed that there was no room to compromise on this issue, as Korea wanted ISDS included and Australia did not. After Korea had elected a new president (although the Korean Saenuri Party remained in control of the Executive Branch) in February 2013, the Australian Trade Minister visited Korea to see whether Korea's ISDS position had changed, and learned to his dismay that the Korean position was still firmly in place.

KAFTA closure became possible only after the Australian Liberal/National Coalition Party had replaced the Australian Labor Party in government in a national election in September 2013. A new Australian Trade Minister visited Korea shortly thereafter, and explained that in the future ISDS would be considered on a case-by-case basis. Essentially the political group that controlled Australia was replaced, which brought about flexibility on a single issue that had deadlocked negotiations. KAFTA was concluded three months later. Australian party instability created the conditions that supported closure (see Crump & Moon, 2017).

ISDS was that stumbling block that created a deadlock. The Introduction in this volume notes that when a single issue creates dueling behavior that issue will tend to take its importance from its representation of the entire relationship. This certainly seems likely, but in this case we find that it was more complicated. The Korean government would have had to manage domestic conflict because after they had included ISDS in their trade treaty with the United States they had explained to the public that ISDS was the new global standard. To then omit ISDS from KAFTA would have raised questions about the government's honesty with the Korean public. The Korean government seemed prepared to "wait-out" Australia forever.

A second example also demonstrates the dramatic impact that party stability or instability can have on negotiation closure dynamics. At the start of AUSFTA negotiations, US President George W. Bush was concerned that AUSFTA treaty ratification through the US Congress would negatively impact upon Republican Party control of the US government, as US presidential elections were scheduled for November 2004. The US agricultural lobby was especially concerned about commencing AUSFTA negotiations. To counter this possibility, the two sides established December 2003 as the AUSFTA deadline – essentially compressing a two- to three-year negotiation into less than a year – this case was absolutely driven by a game of deadlines. Although the initial deadline was not met, negotiations continued non-stop for two weeks in

January 2004, with agreement achieved in early February, thus concluding AUSFTA in eleven months of negotiations. Concern that AUSFTA could jeopardize Republican Party control over the Executive Branch drove the negotiation process through the endgame (see Crump 2007).

Party stability and/or the perception or potential for instability appears to influence negotiation closure dynamics by rapidly driving the process toward closure (AUSFTA), by delaying a process that might lead to closure (KAFTA), and by breaking a deadlock (KAFTA) that contributes to conditions that result in negotiation closure.

Linkage Dynamics: Creditable Deadlines

AUSFTA is the only case of the five that established a creditable deadline, although a deadline was essential in creating closure in the GATT Uruguay round through linkage to expiration of US Fast Track (see footnote 1 above). Seeking to avoid AUSFTA Congressional approval during a US presidential re-election period resulted in a complex negotiation being compressed into eleven months, and created a deadline that forced parties to give up specific offensive interests. The United States wanted, but did not secure, an ISDS clause; nor was it successful in dismantling the Australian FIRB or in dismantling the Australian PBS. The Australians, on the other hand, had hoped to achieve greater market access for their agricultural goods in the US market. A driving pattern of behavior came to an abrupt end, although each side wanted much more, because the risk of delaying closure was perceived to be too great. A delay was unacceptable to the US Executive and the Republican Party, as they each feared that AUSFTA could become too costly an issue in the upcoming Presidential election. Here we observe how a creditable deadline was created through consecutive-future linkage dynamics (Crump 2007).

Deadlines are often created through linkage dynamics, but linkages serve as the foundation for many strategic acts. For example, the United States linked CUSFTA closure to decisions occurring within the UN Security Council. In this case, the United States indicated that it was prepared to delay and perhaps even postpone FTA closure if Chile were unwilling to support the US military agenda within the UN Security Council. This strategy represents a form of brinkmanship in which each side had to carefully calculate its own and the other side's real interests and constraints. This last-minute development added another dimension and substantial complexity to a negotiation that was already rather complex. In the end, the US government realized that it required a stable partner in Latin America more than it needed to punish a "recalcitrant" partner. Traditional issue linkage, as defined within the field of international relations, briefly delayed and almost derailed the CUSFTA closure.

Symmetrical and Asymmetrical Power Relations

Imagine for a moment that Korea refused to cooperate with the United States for over three years. Or that Australia refused to cooperate with the United States for over three years. This counter-intuitive observation seems unlikely because asymmetrical power relations dictate compromise by the less powerful party. On the other hand, Korea and Australia engaged in an extended three-year deadlock. Many factors contributed to the continuation of such a negotiation process, but the current observation suggests that symmetrical power relations played an important role in maintaining this deadlock. Neither side felt compelled to compromise until Australia experienced a change in government (party instability). Such dynamics were not present in Singapore–Australia negotiations, in US–Singapore negotiations, in Australia–US negotiations, and in Chile–US negotiations. It could be said that each of these four negotiations contained asymmetrical power relations, while our only case with symmetrical power relations provides a deadlock as a fundamental element of its process. It is an interesting observation that has implications for our understanding of negotiation closure.

Shift from Technical to Political Negotiations

SAFTA and USSFTA were concluded through an exchange of politically sensitive issues at the ministerial level, indicating that trade diplomats negotiate trade issues and political leaders negotiate politically sensitive issues. Essentially, there were two negotiating teams operating at two hierarchical levels that were engaged in concurrently linked negotiations (Crump 2010). Negotiations are begun at senior levels and then passed down to diplomats to work out the technical details before being taken back over by senior officials who bring an FTA negotiation to a conclusion. This two-level hierarchical dynamic occurred in all five cases, and this same dynamic appeared in the review of the multilateral negotiation literature. It may be that this technical-to-political dynamic serves as a "rule of thumb" within diplomatic negotiations.

We observe this two-level structure on the senior political level at the initiation and conclusion stage, with trade diplomats engaged in between. Political decisions are made with a focus on each side's achieving a "defensible settlement" – a game of echoes. Fundamental is the construction and communication of settlement packages, which may include trades on individual issues or trades involving packages of issues. This system of making trades through a process of give-and-take is fundamental to negotiation and well understood within the literature.

Another way of thinking about the emergence of a defensible settlement package or game of echoes is to understand that senior political leaders are looking for a "landing pad" that is large enough for a politically safe landing. Where a negotiation actually settles on the landing pad is unclear initially, but it is clear that the pad is sufficiently large to hold all the critical elements required for a political settlement and closure. At the endgame this dynamic can be seen to be a game of echoes, but it also demonstrates a desire to manage principal–agent relations so that the principal has greater control over the event being managed by a senior agent.

Venue: Negotiating on the Sidelines

It is interesting to note the role of APEC in providing a venue for bilateral negotiations, while recognizing that many bilateral negotiations are initiated and concluded at senior levels (presidential, ministerial, etc.) in multilateral meetings. Investigating the fundamental nature of these "sideline" negotiations may offer some understanding of how negotiation closure is achieved.

In our study, several bilateral negotiations occurred on the sidelines of regular APEC meetings. For example, the APEC Leaders' Summit in Brunei in 2000 allowed for informal bilateral meetings, which resulted in separate announcements about the commencement of both SAFTA and USSFTA. In the latter case, the USSFTA announcement caused Chile to remind the United States that Chile had been seeking an FTA with the United States since the conclusion of NAFTA (through the Four-Amigo Talks). Negotiations to advance FTAs also occur on the sidelines of Ministerial APEC meetings. The US and Singaporean Trade Ministers were able to narrow the range of outstanding issues at a ministerial meeting held in Mexico in 2002. This achievement shifted USSFTA negotiations into the concluding stage, while SAFTA negotiations between Australia and Singapore actually concluded at this same Ministerial Meeting.

APEC is not the only "sideline venue" where high-level bilateral negotiations occur. CUSFTA was signed on the sidelines of a Free Trade Area of the Americas meeting in Miami in 2003, and KAFTA negotiations were concluded on the sidelines of a WTO Ministerial Meeting in Bali in 2013.

Closure Variables

Figure 6.2. Closure in complex bilateral negotiations.

Bilateral negotiation initiation and closure seem to regularly occur on the sidelines of multilateral and regional gatherings, as this is when and where ministers and secretaries seem to meet. These sideline meetings change the negotiation process by including senior leaders. Ministers see each other regularly at so many meetings (e.g. the Australian and Korean Trade Ministers saw each other regularly for over three years at WTO, APEC, and related meetings, but engaged with each other only at the KAFTA endgame) and then engage with each other when their technical advisors (actually these are the Negotiation Team Leaders) report that a "landing pad" is beginning to appear. At that point a Minister is briefed on the final issues to be resolved and then each Minister engages the other to bring about negotiation closure.

Figure 6.2 presents a model that summarizes what has been learned through the present investigation. Closure variables are identified to the left in this process model. Any one of these variables can bring about closure, although it is also possible that the presence of each closure variable may not be sufficiently potent to bring about closure independently, as closure in a complex negotiation is complicated. On the other hand, each variable may contribute to the establishment of a negotiation landing pad – a defensible settlement or game of echoes at a political level. A meeting of an international or regional organization, such as an APEC Ministerial Meeting, may serve as the final venue for bringing together key leaders on each side to achieve closure.

Case analysis examined the closure venue for complex bilateral negotiations, and the normal give-and-take that brings about closure within a two-part (technical and political) hierarchical system. We have also considered symmetrical and asymmetrical power relations, deadlines and linkage dynamics, and party stability and instability as variables that support negotiation closure.

Conclusion

In this study, we examined closure in five bilateral free trade negotiations that included only APEC members as negotiating parties: Australia, Chile, Korea, Singapore, and the United States. Where, when, and how does negotiation closure occur? As a regional association, APEC regularly serves as a venue and meeting place for presidents, ministers, and secretaries. Often, negotiations are initiated and concluded when senior leaders meet. Specifically, closure is possible when two or more parties negotiate to a point where a defensible settlement or game of echoes for all parties is evident. This potential defensible outcome establishes a negotiation "landing pad" – a landing pad that simply requires a venue for closure. Regional and international summits and ministerial meetings often serve as a venue for bilateral negotiations that occur on the "sidelines."

SAFTA negotiators, for example, built a landing pad prior to the Los Cabos Mexico APEC Ministerial Meeting in October 2002, so Australian and Singaporean Trade Ministers were able to bring closure to SAFTA on the sidelines of that APEC Ministerial Meeting. The US and Singaporean Trade Ministers met at that same venue and were able to reduce the number of outstanding issues from thirty to five issues. Perhaps a USSFTA landing pad was built at the Los Cabos APEC Ministerial Meeting, as USSFTA negotiations concluded two months later in Singapore.

After a very complicated endgame, the United States and Chile concluded CUSFTA negotiations on the sidelines of the Free Trade Area of the Americas Ministerial Meeting in Miami in June 2003. Australia and Korea concluded KAFTA negotiations on the sidelines of the WTO Ministerial Meeting in Bali in December 2013. In each case, sub-process negotiations had progressed to the point where a landing pad had been established and then the final piece of the puzzle was a venue that brought relevant senior political leaders (i.e. Trade Ministers) together to finalize the deal. This shift from technical agents to political agents provides greater control to the principal in concluding negotiations.

It might be useful to study the planning that occurs to create these "sideline" bilateral negotiations. Advisers to ministers, secretaries, presidents, and prime ministers must have protocol or some guiding principles for establishing sideline meetings. Who approaches whom first, how is the agenda established, who is included and excluded, who is available (in person or via video conference), what is the role of Chief

Negotiators, and what is the role of Committee Chairs (for issues in dispute) in sideline meetings? Pulling away from a multilateral gathering to conduct a bilateral negotiation may be more than a scheduling exercise. Do strategic opportunities or constraints exist within side meetings that are held at a multilateral or regional venue, compared with holding a bilateral meeting independently of a regional or international setting? Do strategic opportunities exist that might provide one side or the other with an advantage? We do not know, and such questions may well be worthy of study.

Negotiation linkages are especially effective in creating closure in negotiations, as such dynamics can establish creditable deadlines, although linkages have also been found to delay negotiation closure. A creditable deadline may be the most efficient means for bringing about closure in a complex setting, but what constitutes a creditable deadline? There exists some kind of inherent logic that seems to link the negotiation to some external event or process. When a creditable deadline can be established – usually through some external event or process – it can create a game of deadlines.

Linkages can also delay closure, as was observed in the CAFTA case. In this example, the goals of the more powerful party expanded beyond the agreed-upon trade agenda to include questions of international security within the UN Security Council via issue linkage. Significant research has been conducted on issue linkage, although much of this work is grounded in an international relations tradition. There could be utility in studying issue linkage as a tactic within an international negotiation tradition (Crump 2007, 2013). Issue linkages and deadline linkages were each observed in the present study, while it is possible that other linkage forms could contribute to negotiation closure.

Deadline linkages are also associated with party stability. Party stability means that those groups that control a negotiating party are able to maintain control over that party. For example, in AUSFTA we find an entity (the US Republican Party) that was so concerned with losing control of the US Executive Branch (the branch that controls trade negotiations) that it compressed an FTA negotiation that typically takes two to three years into just eleven months. In this case, the Republican Party feared that its agreement with Australia would damage its re-election goals, so it sought to distance these negotiations from the election by concluding the negotiations well before the traditional US election campaign period. This external event created a game of deadlines.

Party instability means that those groups that control a negotiation party lose control over that party. Party instability can be observed in KAFTA negotiations, where a negotiation deadlock was finally resolved because the Australian Labor Party was removed from office, thus allowing the Liberal/National Coalition Party to take control of the Australian government (the negotiating party) and implement more flexible objectives. Again, party stability–instability served as a factor in creating closure. Gaining further understanding about the relationship between control or loss of control over a negotiating party would enhance our knowledge of closure dynamics.

Many research opportunities exist that can help us to understand how complex negotiations achieve closure. Initially, it is useful to recognize that negotiation closure exists as a sub-process within our understanding of a negotiation process. The present study has offered a preliminary model that is based on too few cases that may be unique to a particular context. Developing a valid context-free process model of closure in complex negotiation will require a larger and more diverse data set.

Part II

Causes

7 Crises and Turning Points: Reframing the Deal

Daniel Druckman

Eleven months of negotiation between Spain and the United States about base rights had transpired when a breakdown occurred in October 1975. The Spanish delegation could not resolve a problem of coordinating with their foreign ministry. The talks were suspended indefinitely. Then, suddenly, their leader, Francisco Franco, died and the West reacted with a sense of urgency to the executions of political prisoners in Spain. These events precipitated a return to the table in December. Bargaining ensued and the US positions prevailed in the face of Spanish desperation (see Druckman 1986).

This case illustrates the power of a crisis to change the course of negotiation. Franco's death led to reconsiderations of strategy and preference changes for the Spanish delegation. Changes in strategy or preferences may be construed as turning points that move the talks toward agreement or dissolution. Although turning points occur throughout the negotiation process (Druckman 2001), they are particularly salient during the later stage of the talks. It is at those junctures that negotiators are confronted with the choice of agreeing, withdrawing, or suspending the talks in hope of reconvening at a later time. Regarded by Iklé (1964) as a three-fold choice, this decision is particularly compelling as a deadline approaches. The time pressure that is exerted by a deadline forces negotiators to decide in the face of uncertainty. It also defines an endgame where the object is to bring closure to the negotiation process.

This chapter focuses attention on attempts made to close a deal.[1] What factors in the negotiating situation influence the choices made to conclude the process: How do negotiators find a way out of a stalemate? Of paramount importance is the forcing pressure of a deadline: It directs attention to the need to choose among the three-fold alternatives. It does not, however, provide insight into the choice that is made. These

---

[1] The experiments reported in this chapter were conducted with Mara Olekalns. Thanks go to Mara for her useful suggestions on this chapter. Thanks also to Bill Zartman and the anonymous reviewers for their helpful suggestions.

insights are suggested by findings about the impacts of alternatives to negotiated agreements (BATNAs), salient solutions or focal points, and visibility: Unattractive BATNAs and salient solutions increase the chances for agreement; visibility hardens negotiators' stances, leading often to deadlock (see Druckman 1993 for a review of these findings.) But, it is also the case that these factors can lead to suboptimal agreements as when unattractive alternatives lead to capitulation or when salient solutions produce compromises. Thus it is interesting to ask when negotiators take initiatives to move the talks in a different direction, toward better agreements. This question is a basis for our current research focus on reframing. Before turning to that research, it is useful to look at the endgame in the contexts of crises and turning points.

Crises and the Endgame

The endgame is often conceived as the culmination of an orderly process that proceeds through stages. This conception assumes that negotiators know when they have reached a point at which an agreement is in sight and begin to hammer it out. Although some negotiation processes take this form – particularly when part of long-standing regional or international institutions – many do not. There is an element of unpredictability caused by sudden ruptures not foreseen in advance. The ruptures may be crises that threaten the sustenance of the talks. Indeed, this was the typical pattern for many of the thirty-four cases analyzed in Druckman's (2001) comparative analysis of turning points. These cases evinced several crises occurring at different points in the process. Each crisis was a moment of decision about the future course of the talks: to abort, agree, or continue. For some cases, the negotiation ended. For others, the negotiation found new life following the crises. Each ushered in a *potential endgame*. In this chapter, the endgame is considered in the context of responses to negotiating crises. It is understood in terms of the ebb and flow of events rather than as the culmination of a staged process.

This dynamic conception of endgames is similar to Iklé's (1964) idea of a continuing three-fold choice. It also resembles Coddington's (1968) cyclical process of expectation–evaluation–adjustment (see Druckman 1977). For both of these theorists, the endgame is a choice that emerges from continuous evaluations of progress. When the choice is either to take the terms on the table or to walk away, the end has occurred. When the choice is an adjustment to disappointed expectations, the negotiation is in jeopardy, as demonstrated by Druckman and Harris (1990). Negotiating crises are forcing events that can lead to an end of the process or provide new life. The end occurs when negotiators agree that it is too

Crises and Turning Points: Reframing the Deal 151

risky to continue. The new life occurs when they agree that a reframing provides hope for an agreement. These alternative choices are the focus of the experiments reported in this chapter.

The choice made following the crisis has implications for an endgame process. A negotiating crisis, like crises experienced in other endeavors, creates a sense of desperation that shortens the timeframe for decision-making and sharpens the available choices. For negotiators, choosing between the alternatives of exiting or continuing the process is a particularly salient first-order decision. Choosing to exit provides a way out that defines an endgame stage. It raises the second-order decision of whether to drag the process to an end by reaching agreement or abort the process without an agreement. Choosing to continue postpones the endgame reframing stage in favor of dueling on toward an eventual agreement. A second-order decision consists of whether to continue the talks along the same path or to depart from that path with new ideas. The choice to depart from the past, referred to as reframing, is considered as a turning point that drives the process toward agreement.

Reframing is regarded as an opportunity to change the direction of the negotiation or to view the issues in new ways. It is intended to drive the negotiations toward agreement. An example comes again from the Spain–US base-rights negotiation, where the delegations resolved a sticking point by combining the different objectives of the parties: The United States accepted Spain's desire to redefine its role in the Western community of nations, in return for Spain's willingness to create a format that would facilitate bargaining. This breakthrough got the talks back on track toward agreement. Another example comes from the Intermediate-Range Nuclear Forces (INF) negotiations between the Soviet Union and the United States. New ideas proposed by Gorbachev propelled the talks to agreement: delinking strategic weapon systems from intermediate-range systems and the "double-zero" option in which all relevant weapons systems deployed in Europe and Asia would be eliminated. Other examples include introducing broad themes that unite the parties, using the window created by a crisis to move quickly to agreement, reversing course from a focus on the past to developing a vision of the future, probing more deeply into each party's intentions, and searching for an integrative agreement, often with the help of a mediator.

Some conditions that motivate the choice made in response to a crisis are elucidated by the experimental research. The decision in the face of a crisis to end the talks at an impasse or with an agreement may be construed as being a desperate choice. Negotiators may weigh the risks of continuing as being higher than the risks of either agreeing or ending without an agreement. The Spanish delegation in the base-rights talks described above took the agreement proposed by the United States in desperation. Those talks needed a major crisis in order for them to conclude with an agreement after an extended impasse. The alternative decision to continue may be regarded as an opportunistic choice. Negotiators weigh the risks of keeping the process in train as being higher than the risks of breaking off the discussions. But it may also be the case that both desperation and opportunity motivate a decision to continue. For desperate negotiators, it may be worth taking a chance on giving the talks another try. This may actually be viewed by them as the less risky choice. For opportunistic negotiators, it is worth taking the chance of breathing new life into the talks. For them, the choice to reframe would seem to provide an opportunity. Reframing is the turning point that has often been found to follow crises (Druckman 2001). It is discussed in concert with a review of the turning-points literature in the next section.

Turning Points in Negotiation

The idea of turning points (TPs) has captured the imagination of scholars in a variety of fields. These analysts agree on a broad conceptual definition of TPs, which may be stated as follows: a clear and self-evident change from earlier patterns in the form of an impactful event or decision taken by one or more parties. This definition, which applies as well to negotiation, suggests a causal sequence from precipitating factors to departures to consequences. The sequence can be traced at several junctures where departures occur during a negotiation process (Druckman 2001). Here, the interest is in the sequences that occur during the later phase of a negotiation process. These sequences are instrumental in reaching agreement or closing the deal.

The case and laboratory research on TPs has been organized in terms of four themes: stage transitions, interruptions, framing, and context (Druckman & Olekalns 2013b). For some negotiation researchers, an agreement is more likely to emerge when negotiators have passed through a defined stage sequence, although they differ with regard to the number and naming of these stages (e.g. Donohue & Roberto 1996; Gulliver 1979; Holmes 1992; Zartman 1978; Zartman & Berman 1982). For other researchers, the momentum needed for agreement is provided by interruptions – breaks or time outs, mediator interventions, or crises emerging from the inside or outside the talks – that disrupt the course of the talks in order to shift from impasse to progress (e.g. McGinn, Lingo & Ciano 2004; Olekalns, Brett & Weingart 2003). The shift may be regarded as a TP.

A third theme focuses on the interpretive frames that are applied to events such as crises. The impact of an interruption on negotiation has been shown to be influenced by the way it is interpreted by the negotiators. Three interpretive frames in particular that alter the process are power, shared identity, and transaction costs (Druckman & Olekalns 2013). Negotiating TPs have also been shown to be influenced by media frames (Putnam & Shoemaker 2007), strategic reframing (Putnam & Fuller 2010), and dialogic processes (Leary 2004).

A fourth theme is context. One feature of the context that has been shown to influence the TP sequence is the source of conflict: Types of precipitants (external or substantive), departures (abrupt, non-abrupt), and consequences (de-escalatory, escalatory) were shown to be influenced by whether the source of conflict was interests, understanding, or values (Druckman 2005). Other contextual features are the distinction between domestic and international settings and the way TPs occur in multilateral negotiations (Chasek 1997; Hall 2014) and escalatory and de-escalatory consequences of departures (Druckman 2001). With regard to the latter, the activity of reframing was shown to be instrumental in setting into motion a multilateral process toward agreement (Crump & Druckman 2012).

The current research considers a further possibility, the interpersonal context. How does the perceived trustworthiness of an opponent influence the choices made by negotiators and what role does cognitive and affective trust play in negotiators' responses to a crisis? Cognitive trust is grounded in an assessment of others' competences, their behavioral patterns, and the likelihood that they will honor promises and commitments. Affective trust is grounded in the perceived values and intentions of an opposing negotiator. Individuals assess affective trust by gauging the extent to which others share their values and are working toward mutual benefit, their benevolence, and their integrity. Past research has shown that, in more routine negotiations such as employment contract negotiations, cognitive and affective trust affect the identification and interpretation of turning points (Olekalns & Smith 2005; Druckman, Olekalns & Smith 2009).

Stages, Interruptions, and Reframing

The current research builds on the themes that have guided the earlier studies on TPs, exploring the nexus between interruptions and decisions to reframe the issues in negotiation. The decision confronts negotiations in the context of a crisis that arises suddenly in the form of a stop-action event and must be dealt with during a break in the talks. A three-fold choice plus one is put before two delegations in a simulated negotiation resembling a situation where Iraq and the United States are trying to prevent a war between them. The alternative choices consist of reaching agreement now, withdrawing from the talks, continuing the talks at a later time to be decided, or reframing the issues for further discussion. When negotiators disengage from the talks they drag each other toward closure. When they opt to continue talking, the dueling goes on until a way out is found.

The earlier TP research encouraged adding a reframing choice to the alternatives proposed by Ikle (1964). That choice provides a way around having to confront the three-fold dilemma, particularly the choice between agreeing or withdrawing from the talks. It is often a creative attempt to move the talks forward and to avoid having to make an endgame choice from among reaching agreement now, withdrawing from the talks, or suspending them to another time and, perhaps, location. They also have in common a key feature of turning points, which is a clear and self-evident change from earlier events in the form of an impactful decision taken by one or all parties (Druckman and Olekalns 2011). What conditions encourage or discourage the reframing choice? The scenario is described before the conditions are discussed.

Experimental Scenario

A scenario based roughly on the negotiation that did not occur between Iraq and the United States was devised to include a crisis in the form of a stop-action event. Negotiators are taken by surprise and must decide how to react to the sudden event. They are confronted with four choices: to agree to the terms on the table, to withdraw from the talks, to suspend the talks, or to reframe the issues.

In the experiments, participants were assigned randomly to the roles of chief negotiators appointed by their foreign ministries to represent their countries, Anice or Izeria, in a bilateral negotiation concerning a number of security issues. Participants received background information about the context for their negotiation. This consisted of a chronology of the key events that occurred from December 2007 to March 2010, a sense of urgency conveyed by their presidents and the UN Secretary-General to reach agreements on the issues, and confidential information about the issues, including their nation's positions and rationale.

Negotiators needed to reach agreement on six issues (five distributive and one integrative). Two of the distributive issues concerned Anice's desire to inspect Izeria's presidential palace; at issue were the number of weapons inspectors and the period of inspection. The other three distributive issues concerned the deployment of an Anicean-led international military force in a border area that lies between Izeria and its neighbor, Kerejistan; the specific questions were the number of troops, the period of deployment, and the amount of budget allocation. The one integrative issue concerned ways to combat terrorism in the region. Both parties were encouraged to consider ways of developing a plan that would be in their joint interest.

The negotiation was divided into two fifteen-minute periods. Negotiators were free to decide on the order for discussion of the issues as well as whether they would be addressed sequentially or in combination. Various positions on the distributive issues were arranged on scales to facilitate the discussion. During the between-round break, each dyad received a "Foreign Ministry Update," which informed them of late breaking news as follows:

The Associated Press reports that the president of Izeria, Sadam Ismaeli, succumbed unexpectedly to a fatal heart attack. This event has thrown the government into chaos as they hurriedly prepare for a succession. The vice president will serve as president until elections can be held. Negotiations with Anice will continue until arrangements have been made for a public funeral.

This message is in keeping with the definition of a crisis as an unexpected event that triggers a possible breakdown in the talks. Without the Izerian president's support the negotiation was in jeopardy. The negotiators were asked to consider the implications of this event for the talks. After negotiators had received the memo from their Foreign Ministry, they were asked to provide advice to their Prime Minister about what to do next, from among four choices (withdraw, agree, continue, or reframe), and to write a short explanation for their recommendation. These decisions and explanations served as the dependent variables in the experiments to be described next.

Motivational Primes

A recent experiment on motivational primes asked about the conditions that would encourage or discourage a choice to reframe in the context of a crisis (Druckman and Olekalns 2013a). Three conditions were compared and embedded in the Anice–Izeria simulation described above. A transaction-costs prime consisted of calling attention to the increasing costs that correspond to the time spent negotiating. A shared-identity prime called attention to shared diplomatic experiences and a good working relationship. An alternatives prime emphasized the unattractive alternatives for each party to getting an agreement in these talks; this prime had the effect of increasing negotiators' mutual dependence. These primes were presented as part of the background information and repeated in the between-round memos that were delivered at the time of the crisis. Impacts were assessed on the four choices and on various perceptions, including affective and cognitive trust.

Strong priming-condition effects occurred on choices following the crisis. First, the way the negotiation was framed affected negotiators' choices, sending them in different directions. Reframing was the preferred choice for negotiators in the alternatives (high mutual dependence) condition, whereas continuing the talks without changing directions was the preferred choice for transaction-cost bargainers. Both frames impose costs on negotiators: in the case of mutual dependence the cost is a relational one, whereas in the case of transaction costs it is an economic one. In both cases, negotiators may be "too much invested to quit" (Teger 1980). The costs may motivate both mutual-dependence and transaction-cost negotiators to strive for a better agreement, but shape how they pursue that agreement. In contrast to these two frames, a shared-identity frame did not elicit a dominant course of action following the crisis. One interpretation of this pattern is that a shared identity gives negotiators greater confidence that, because of their shared values, they will be able to weather the crisis.

An important qualification to these findings is added when we consider the role of trust, which influenced the decisions of mutual-dependence-framed and shared-identity-framed negotiators. Negotiators who were mutually dependent were most likely to opt for reframing when they reported low affective trust in the opposing negotiator. This finding provides additional insight into the relationship, obtained in earlier studies, between crises and turning points. A turning point, in the form of a decision to reframe, may be more likely to follow a crisis when mutual trust is low and mutual dependence is high. Reframing may be seen as a way to repair low-trust relationships when the parties cannot go elsewhere, as in such intractable conflicts as that between the Israelis and Palestinians. In contrast, negotiators with a shared-identity frame opted to continue talks when they reported high affective trust in their opponents. This finding hints at the possibility that high cognitive trust complements the perception that negotiators have shared values by signaling that opponents also have the skills and motivation to navigate negotiations to a successful conclusion.

Tracing the path from the prime to the decision to reframe suggests the following sequence: high mutual dependence → (shared mental model) → crisis event → primed dependence → (emotional reaction) → low affective trust → decision to reframe.

The mutual dependence is created early, as part of the negotiating context. It results in a shared mental model that serves as a lens for interpreting the crisis and an emotional reaction that may trigger perceptions of trust, leading to the decision to reframe. Regarded as speculative, these intervening factors provide further understanding of the crisis–turning-point relationship.

Regulatory Focus

Another direction for insight into the crisis–turning-point relationship comes from the research on regulatory focus. The idea of regulatory focus introduced by Higgins (1987) distinguishes between two motivational orientations, prevention and promotion. A prevention focus is primarily reactive. It seeks to minimize losses by adopting a vigilant, risk-averse course of action. For negotiators confronted with a crisis, this orientation would encourage exiting the talks with or without an agreement. It may also lead them to continue talking along the same lines as before. A promotion focus is more proactive. It attempts to maximize opportunities for gain by adopting a risk-seeking and generally optimistic course of action. When facing a crisis, promotion-oriented negotiators may be eager to try new courses by reframing the issues. For them, reframing is an alternative to the dilemma presented by the choices of agreeing, withdrawing, or continuing. We investigated these orientations in an experiment embedded in the Anice–Izeria scenario.

Partly on the basis of the results obtained from the motivational primes experiment, discussed above, the impact of trust was also investigated. For negotiators facing a crisis, cautiousness is more likely when the parties are oriented toward cognitive trust. Cautiousness is reflected in the choices of agreeing, withdrawing, or continuing. It may also correlate with a prevention focus. Risk-taking stemming from eagerness is more likely when negotiators are oriented toward affective trust. Taking chances is reflected in the reframing choice. That choice is preferred as well when negotiators take a promotion focus. Thus, trust is related to regulatory focus.

An alignment of trust (cognitive or affective) and regulatory focus (prevention and promotion) suggests compound effects on choice: There is a stronger likelihood of making the preferred choice when trust and regulatory focus act in combination. This is the idea of regulatory fit (Appelt et al. 2009). Less risky choices follow from the combination of prevention and cognitive trust. Reframing is more likely to occur when a promotion orientation combines with affective trust. This kind of fit, between the type of trust and regulatory focus, amplifies the dominant choice (agree, withdraw, continue, or reframe). That choice is further reinforced by the crisis event as suggested by research on the relationship between crises and behavioral flexibility (Milburn 1972).

Reframing was evident in a number of historical negotiations, including the 2000 talks to resolve a civil war in Burundi, the 1987 negotiations between the Soviet Union and the United States over intermediate-range nuclear weapons (INF), and the 2013 period in the Iran talks, spelled out in Chapter 1 by Ariane Tabatabai and Camille Pease. In the Burundi case, Nelson Mandela was recruited as mediator when his predecessor, the president of Tanzania, succumbed to a heart attack. Responding to this crisis, he invigorated the talks by conveying optimism (promotion orientation) and by developing the trust needed to move the warring parties on a path toward agreement (affective trust). This combination of orientation and trust (regulatory fit) seemed to be the prescription for the agreement that stopped the fighting, at least in the short term. In the INF case, Reagan developed a proposal, referred to as "double zero," that unfroze the stalemated negotiations. This proposal encouraged the parties to re-conceptualize the issues (reframing). Similarly to Mandela's initiatives in Burundi, Gorbachev increased the parties' optimism that an agreement could be reached (promotion orientation) in an atmosphere of increasing trust between the presidents (affective trust). Similarly, the election of Iranian President Rouhani and the telephone call of American President Obama evidence trust and optimism that opened the Iranian endgame, as Chapter 1 shows. These cases illustrate a relationship between regulatory fit and reframing. They do not, however, demonstrate a causal relationship: The variables are intertwined during the negotiation process, making time lags unclear.

This issue is addressed in two experiments where fit (or misfit) is created prior to the choice made in response in the crisis caused by the death of the Izerian president (see Caspi, Olekalns & Druckman 2017 for details). A first experiment compared the trust and regulatory-focus variables in a two-variable design. Both variables were primed by instructions presented as part of the background material during the pre-negotiation phase of the simulation and again just after the crisis event had occurred. Cognitive trust was created by telling the negotiators that their counterpart is well qualified to lead his/her delegation and has shown professionalism and dedication in earlier talks. The affective-trust instructions emphasized liking for and shared values with their counterpart as well as an expectation of a constructive working relationship. A promotion focus was induced by telling the negotiators that their objective is to protect their country's security by maximizing their opportunities, benefits, and gains. Negotiators with a prevention focus were told to protect their country from risks, threats, or losses in the interest of national security. Negotiators of both types were then asked to write down two ways in which they would meet these obligations.

A second experiment, conducted as an MTurk survey, added a third variable, which consisted of making a distinction between a high and a low level of cognitive or affective trust. The key dependent variable for both experiments was choice following the experience of a crisis. Interesting results were obtained from these experiments. Contrary to the dominant-response hypothesis, regulatory fit in both experiments led to a preference for reframing both for the promotion–affective-trust combination and for the prevention–cognitive-trust combination. Fit *per se* rather than type of fit amplified the riskier and perhaps more optimistic choice following a crisis event. It encouraged the negotiators to take a chance on moving the talks in a different direction in order to secure a better settlement.

The MTurk survey was used to explore several additional variables, foremost among them the level of trust (relatively high or low) that negotiators had in their opponents. The role played by negotiators' cognitions was also explored: how close they believed they were to agreement, as well as their willingness either to take a risk or to compromise in order to reach agreement. Adding these variables yielded two interesting findings in relation to level of trust. First, high trust emboldened negotiators to make riskier choices the further they were from an agreement. Trusting negotiators, as opposed to non-trusting negotiators, were more willing to try something different when agreement was elusive or when they were not making progress toward getting an agreement. Secondly, the level of trust affected the importance of compromising for promotion-focused (but not prevention-focused) negotiators. Promotion-focused negotiators who were far from an agreement favored compromise when trust was high but not when trust was low. These findings suggest that high trust offsets the potential risk of continuing a negotiation that is far from an agreement: Negotiators are more willing to take risks by searching for agreements and compromises when they trust the other party. The finding that this effect is more pronounced when negotiators have a promotion focus highlights the greater willingness to pursue opportunities associated with a promotion focus when the conditions are "right."

Closing the Deal: Implications from the Research

Taken together, findings from the motivational primes and regulatory-focus studies suggest opposite motives for making the reframing choice in response to a crisis. The combination of mutual dependence and low trust suggest a state of desperation following the crisis. A similar state of desperation may be evoked when negotiators are oriented toward a prevention–cognitive-trust focus that highlights avoiding losses. In contrast, the combination of a promotion focus and affective trust may encourage negotiators to seek opportunities in the context of a crisis. Thus, desperation and opportunities are alternative motives for choosing to reframe. Both can lead to a desire for change from the lack of progress toward an agreement. The research has identified some conditions that lead to one or the other perception. It has not explored the way reframing is implemented; nor has it examined the consequences of reframing. The alternative motives, desperation and opportunities, might indeed have implications for the activity of reframing and for its result. This is discussed in the next section.

More broadly, the findings point to the role of fit as an important factor in encouraging individuals to reframe negotiations after a crisis, and suggest that it is immaterial whether this fit might be considered malign or benign. Thus, in the first experiment, poor conditions – no exit options and the absence of shared values – nonetheless encouraged negotiators to reframe the negotiation. In the second experiment, fit between regulatory focus and type of trust similarly encouraged reframing. These findings suggest that interpersonal and contextual factors have an amplifying effect, such that their alignment encourages greater risk-taking in negotiations. Conversely, the results suggest that more conservative actions might follow from an offset effect: When the negotiating context (shared identity frame) and trust (high cognitive trust) offset rather than amplify each other, they encourage negotiators to continue along their previous path.

Choices and the Endgame

The decision to abandon the negotiation, with or without an agreement, precludes an endgame. The negotiators drag their way into disengagement; the negotiation collapses, coming to an end abruptly. The decision to reframe or continue following the crisis provides an opportunity to transition to an endgame that sets the stage for agreement. Whether or not an agreement results from further negotiating is likely to depend on the emergence of another turning point. However, each of these decisions – to reframe or continue – may set in motion different precipitating events.

The decision to reframe can be motivated either by desperation or by opportunity. For desperate negotiators, a variety of levers are at their disposal, including attempts to alter the visibility of the process and to manufacture deadlines. A less visible, more private process – such as a Walk in the Woods or a Walk on the Wharf – has been shown to increase the chances for agreement during the endgame stages of simulated negotiations (Druckman 1993; Goodby 2012). Likewise, creating or enforcing deadlines strengthens the shared perception that there is an end in sight, as discussed by Isak Svensson and P. Terrence Hopmann in Chapters 10 and 15, respectively. Regarded as procedural precipitants, each of these levers can be put into motion with the help of a mediator.

For opportunistic negotiators, agreements are more likely to emerge from a positive view of the future, including the prospects for long-term relationships. This attitude is encouraged by the progress made in reframing the issues and sustained by mediators who engage the negotiators in problem solving (Conlon, Carnevale & Ross 1994; Pruitt 2015). Regarded as substantive precipitants, these activities and interventions drive the process toward agreement. The drive toward agreement is strengthened further when negotiators are encouraged to affirm each other's ideas and visions (Harinck & Druckman 2017).

The decision to continue dueling can also propel the negotiation process toward agreement. The continue decision is more likely to invoke strategic thinking, as negotiators regard the impasse as a stumbling block to be overcome through competitive bargaining. High on the list of strategic considerations is the issue of transaction costs: Time spent negotiating incurs increasing costs through delay in making a decision and further deterioration in relationships. Agreements stop the accumulation of the costly interactions. As with reframing decisions, transitioning to an endgame is helped by installing deadlines as well as insulating the process from public attention. Unlike reframing, the challenge is to overcome pessimistic appraisals of the future. One approach, usually taken by a mediator, is to pause the process. During the pause, negotiators are encouraged to reconsider the reframing option. Such reconsideration may alter their approach, switching from competitive dueling to cooperative driving. Another approach is to change the focus from an emphasis on costs to a consideration of benefits. Examples include the value of realizing joint economic gains, improving the political relationship, and moving on to other issues that also demand attention. These considerations came into play during the Iran nuclear P5+1 negotiations, helping the negotiators to close the deal. They are matters ripe for further research on turning points.

The research has implications for a dynamic conception of negotiation. This conception emphasizes change in the way that negotiators evaluate the prospects for agreement. The evaluations reflect an ebb and flow that is often interrupted by crises. By their reactions to crises, negotiators influence the course by either precluding an endgame process (agree or abort) or encouraging a progression toward an endgame (continue or reframe). Whether motivated by desperation or opportunity, the choice to reframe drives the process forward and continues the dueling or orients the process toward cooperation. A key contribution made by this chapter is to encourage analysts to view negotiators as agents of change rather than as subjects of conditions over which they have limited control. The chapter also suggests some limitations of viewing negotiation as a stage-like progression culminating in an endgame. Potential endgames emerge from a continuing process of evaluation occasionally interrupted by crises.

New Directions

The difference between responding to crises with a sense of desperation or viewing the crisis as an opportunity to restart the stalemated negotiation is intriguing. We discovered some conditions that influence those reactions. More broadly, we can extend the investigation to a variety of other factors in the negotiation situation, the cultures of the parties, the negotiators' past experiences, and the structures within which the negotiations take place. Regarding situations, the role played by risk assessments would seem promising. The assessment can lead either to aversion (withdrawal) or pro-action (reframing). Similarly, the traditions established by socialized or professional cultures may influence the way negotiators respond to crises, notably the distinction between bureaucratized and entrepreneurial cultures. Memories of past experiences may also come into play, particularly with regard to reward histories for responding in passive or active ways. And, incentives may also be influenced by the institutional contexts that define reward structures.

Our research has also uncovered the possibility that interpersonal factors such as trustworthiness affect what negotiators do in the wake of a crisis. We found that when trustworthiness was intuitive, formed on first impressions, both the type and the level of trust affected their choices. However, when trustworthiness was evidence-based (written information) the type and level of trust had independent influences on negotiators' choices. This pattern suggests that how negotiators form impressions of an opponent's trustworthiness (e.g. via spontaneous impressions or preceding reputation) impacts the specific influences that trust exerts on negotiators' willingness to reframe or continue negotiations. Our findings, which hint at this possibility, also identify a fertile avenue for future research.

The second experiment that we described also suggests a role for intrapersonal factors in shaping negotiators' responses to a crisis. We demonstrated that the assessment of distance from agreement influenced willingness to take risks and to compromise. Dyadic negotiation researchers have long focused on the role of expectations in shaping negotiators' actions and outcomes, and our research suggests that drawing on this body of research may give new insights into how negotiators respond to turning points. At the same time, it is possible to go further and consider other intrapersonal variables. We have elsewhere (Druckman & Olekalns 2013b) speculated that resilience, flexibility, and adaptability in the face of adverse events may also play a role in how negotiators interpret and respond to crises. Focusing attention on these behaviors in the next iteration of this research is likely to provide further insight into the conditions under which negotiators continue or withdraw from negotiations following a crisis.

A growing body of research shows that the emotional tone of negotiations plays a key role in how they develop (Olekalns & Druckman 2014). It is possible that some of the effects we reported are linked to negotiators' optimism about the likelihood that their opponents will negotiate in good faith, or that an agreement is possible. An untapped avenue for research is to consider how negotiators' emotions, both before and after a crisis, might influence their willingness to reframe negotiations.

Finally, we focused on one very specific crisis, the death of a key figure known to support the negotiations (the President). This is a discrete temporal event, leaving virtually no uncertainty that "things will change." Crises are not always this blatant, and our understanding of negotiators' reactions to crises may be further enhanced if we expand the kinds of crises that are analyzed.

8 Managing or Resolving? Defining the Deal

Michael J. Butler

The influence of temporal factors on negotiation strategy and behavior is well chronicled (Regan and Stam 2000). Elapsed time is thought to lead to lessened demands and more frequent concessions, particularly when a sense of urgency is introduced through agreeable and feasible deadlines (Colosi 1986). This may translate into a greater possibility for striking an agreement (Kelley, Beckman & Fischer 1967; Pruitt & Drews 1969) through acceleration of the process in a phenomenon known as yielding (Smith, Pruitt & Carnevale 1982). At the same time, the yielding effect is less likely to manifest itself in situations where one or more parties are close to their Best Alternative to Negotiated Agreement (BATNA) (Pruitt 1981), when the issue at hand is basic and fundamental (Burton & Sandole 1986) or intangible (Rubin & Brown 1975), or when ideology or hostility toward the other party (or parties) shapes a negotiator's position (Zubek *et al.* 1989). Apart from their (variable) accelerating effects, time factors are also correlated with turning points or breakthroughs in protracted and seemingly intractable negotiations. Such critical moments or junctures have been associated both with environmental precipitants and with agents themselves (Putnam 2004; Druckman 2004; Watkins and Rosegrant 2001).

Starting from these insights regarding negotiation strategies and behavior, this chapter examines calculations in which leading negotiators engaged in the closing stages of a negotiation in choosing a strategy oriented around containing violence (conflict management) or one aimed at settling the disputes underlying that violence (conflict resolution). On reaching a point at which the end of the negotiations is nigh, what factors impact the decision-making calculus of the negotiation parties such that they perceive one or the other strategy as more (or less) desirable? Do the closing behaviors of dueling, driving, dragging, or mismatching correspond to either of these strategies and outcomes?[1]

---

[1] Some important limiting parameters to this inquiry should be acknowledged at the outset. To start, this chapter is primarily focused on *dyadic negotiated interactions between parties*

Competing Logics of Management and Resolution

Conflict management (CM) refers to any *effort by a third party to control or contain the violence associated with an ongoing conflict* (Burton & Dukes 1990; Ramsbothom, Woodhouse & Miall 2005). CM processes are concerned with making an ongoing conflict less damaging to the parties directly engaged in it; such processes may, but need not necessarily, involve a third party (in the role of mediator, arbitrator, adjudicator, or transitional administrator). CM typically originates from a concern with containing the conflict's damaging and destabilizing effects on other parties ("horizontal escalation") as well as containing the conflict's ascent up the ladder of violent behaviors ("vertical escalation"). The goal of conflict management is to deny "victory" to the aggressor(s), or, perhaps more accurately, to deny the utility of aggression (Butler 2009). Conflict management also presumes that conflict can be contained and controlled through efforts to demote the situation from the arena of expressed violence to the arena of non-violent political contestation.

Negotiators who employ the logic of conflict management – i.e. who seek to identify and secure attainable outcomes containing, minimizing, and ultimately terminating violence *extant* within a conflict – accept the prevailing security landscape arrayed around strategic coercion and competing interests. Within the logic of CM, this is a necessary trade-off for those seeking to shave off the rough edges that stem from the intersection of these forces (Vuković 2015a). The focal point of their efforts thereby becomes management of the deleterious effects of a conflict rather than resolution of its underlying causes; purveyors of CM are therefore attuned to the notion that a conflict can be too complex and intractable to be resolved at a particular juncture (Crocker, Hampson & Aall 2007). In a closing situation, negotiators who have elected to pursue a CM strategy are likely to focus their efforts toward identifying and crafting a Zone of Possible Agreement (ZOPA) defined by coordination of the

---

already engaged in conflict. Additionally, the present investigation is primarily concerned with examining the strategy and behavior of negotiators representing states or political communities seeking statehood. Given the persistence of a largely anarchical international environment, states remain central actors in the international negotiation arena, and state sovereignty remains the primary "currency" in international negotiations (Kremenyuk 2002; Berton & Kimura 1999). An additional delimitation is that the negotiation behavior in question pertains to ongoing cases of armed conflict. As such, while any insights which might emerge here concerning the closing behavior of negotiators could plausibly be extended or applied to other scenarios involving mediators or non-state actors, or to negotiations not tied to armed conflicts, these parameters delimit the analytical scope of the chapter.

parties around containing the violent dimensions of the conflict. The ease of reaching such a coordinated position through negotiation and bargaining is contingent on the presence, absence, or relative degree of ripeness evident (itself a variable which may, but need not necessarily, correspond to the closing stages of a negotiation). The desired outcome of negotiators pursuing a CM strategy is narrow in scope and more attainable in the near term.

Conflict resolution (CR) traces its origins to the fields of game theory (Snyder & Diesing 1977; Axelrod 1984), peace science (Galtung 1969), and social-movement theory (Tilly 1985) as well as to practitioners of non-violence (Sharp 1973; Kelman 1992; Keashly & Fisher 1996). The utility of different approaches to CR varies in accordance with types and/or stages of conflict – and, moreover, the effective practice of CR is typically informed by multiple methods (Keashly & Fisher 1996; Kriesberg 2007). This point of emphasis stems from the recognition that social conflicts are multifaceted, involve numerous parties, and ultimately hinge on a multiplicity of issues (Kriesberg 1982).

Crucially, CR is not simply the inverse of CM; rather, it operates by its own distinct logic. At the analytical center of CR lies the difference between "conflicts" and "disputes," a logical distinction informing the dedication of resources and effort to settling, resolving, or transforming them. "Disputes" are defined by contestation over matters that are negotiable and amenable to compromise, whereas "conflicts" stem from sharp discrepancies between parties over issues rooted in basic human needs (Burton 1990). CR is also defined by a fundamental concern with transforming the relationship between conflict parties. CR includes long-term strategies, short-term tactics, and actions employed by adversaries as well as by mediators, all geared toward attainment of this transformation (Burton 1990). As such, CR differs significantly from CM in its revealed emphasis on inter-subjectivity and the effects of inter-subjective understandings on conflict escalation (or de-escalation). CR outcomes necessarily aim for at least a partial alteration if not a fundamental transformation in the relationship between adversaries. This generates a negotiation process in which the characteristics of individual parties and the encroaching effects of societal forces are necessarily de-emphasized (Jervis 1976; Kelley & Michela 1980). Accordingly, CR outcomes are oriented not only toward minimizing violence, but toward overcoming antagonism between adversaries. Identifying mutually/collectively acceptable outcomes for involved parties and crafting enduring settlements rooted in transformation and resolution of underlying grievances are central objectives (Kriesberg 2007).

While CM and CR are distinct on a conceptual plane, they are not irreconcilable. In fact, CM and its attendant emphasis on containing violence may be employed as a means to the end of a CR outcome (and may in some cases be a prerequisite to it), since the perpetuation of violence is an obvious obstacle to resolving underlying disputes and transforming the relationship between the parties. Conversely, CR processes may, and often do, prove critical to the long-term reinforcement and support of a CM outcome, as adversarial relationships that remain unchanged and underlying disputes that are not resolved are clearly catalysts for recidivist violence.

Strategic Determinants for Management and Resolution

The remainder of this chapter seeks to identify those processual and contextual factors which inform the decision of endgame negotiators to pursue violence limitation or to seek conflict resolution, with each of these approaches representing discernable endgame strategies, and not solely outcomes. While the six factors considered below hardly constitute an exhaustive list, each demonstrates influence on the closing strategy and attendant behavior of negotiation principals. These factors are variable, and may generate unpredictable or counter-intuitive outcomes in select cases. Yet, as the discussion below reflects, it is possible to advance a series of plausible hypotheses about the effects of these variables on the closing strategies of negotiators.

Process Variables

Given the reality of negotiators as inter-subjective agents embedded within an iterative and interactive process, process-oriented factors such as the varying styles available to and employed by negotiators, the track record of interactions between and among negotiators over time, and the influence of domestic factors and considerations via the "two-level game" (Putnam 1988) are likely to be impactful.

Negotiation style varies in part as a function of cultural ideas and practices associated with national or ethnic identity (Berton & Kimura 1999; Faure and Rubin 1993; Cohen 1997), gender (Florea *et al.* 2003; Ruane 2006; Boyer *et al.* 2009), or even regime type (Dixon and Senese 2002). Yet beyond the influence of culture, gender, or political systems on negotiation behavior, norms concerning the nature and objective of negotiation itself shape the styles of negotiation employed by delegations and lead negotiators. The primary point of demarcation is best approximated by the competing models of distributive/positional versus integrative/problem-solving bargaining (Moore 2003; Bartos 1995; Kelman 1990). Each of these broad typologies betrays different orientations toward the nature of the conflicts and disputes subject to negotiation and the place of coercion as a backdrop to bargaining processes (Kriesberg 2007, 65).

Positional bargaining conceives of negotiation as a form of competitive interaction motivated by the pursuit of relative gains and reflective of the conflict endemic under international anarchy. Schelling's seminal work *The Strategy of Conflict* (1960) served as a crucial starting point in the conceptualization of negotiation as a distributive process, along with Iklé's (1964)*How Nations Negotiate*. These works ushered in a period of roughly two decades during which positional and adversarial views of negotiation represented the dominant paradigm in the field, and negotiation was viewed primarily as conflict by means short of war (Grieco 1988; Grieco, Powell & Snidal 1993; Werner 1997). Additional and important variations on the interest-based bargaining paradigm exist, such as those grappling with the best account for strategic interaction (expected-utility models versus prospect theory) within a negotiation setting such as that which produced the Good Friday Agreements (Bueno de Mesquita, McDermott & Cope 2001).

Conversely, integrative styles are rooted in a normative orientation which views negotiation as a tool to be applied to tangible problems by parties interested in identifying fair, equitable, and/or just resolutions (Albin 2001; Hopmann 1995). A key catalyst for this alternative to distributive or hard bargaining was the introduction of a temporal dimension to the Prisoner's Dilemma (PD) model and the possibilities for cooperative outcomes via tit-for-tat strategies found to be valuable for cultivating cooperation in repeated play scenarios (Axelrod 1984). Fisher and Ury's (1991) *Getting to Yes* represents another prominent illustration of the problem-solving approach to negotiation, in which the possibility of mutually beneficial outcomes or "dual concerns" is inherent to negotiation (Rubin, Pruitt & Kim 1994). Within the integrative approach, the focus is on enhanced communication and trust-building, in service of recasting the dispute in a way that generates mutually acceptable solutions from which all parties can benefit (Wagner 2008; Hopmann 1995, 2001; Fisher et al. 1996; Spector 1995).[2]

---

[2] Extensions of this model include Kemp and Smith's (1994) experimental research in the production of joint gains, Chigas' (1997) assessment of the prospects for parallel negotiation to (re)frame the negotiation process and improve negotiated outcomes, Odell's (2000) incorporation of "value-creating" behavior and integrative strategies into his theoretical and empirical analysis of economic bargaining, Yong's (2003) consideration of the impact of domestic and international factors on shifting bargaining strategies (positional and integrative) employed by the Republic of Korea in a protracted negotiation with the United States on agricultural policy, and the examination of the

The contention here is that those employing positional bargaining are more likely to favor a CM strategy when seeking to close out a negotiation. Conversely, the adoption of an integrative orientation naturally lends itself to an increased probability that negotiators will identify and pursue a CR strategy. Beyond the obvious variance in conceptions of utility maximization, the differential norms associated with each of the two styles further underscore the degree to which variable bargaining styles may help explain differences in strategy (CM vs. CR) on the part of negotiators at closure. As positional bargaining styles privilege entrenched positions, the more limited ZOPA associated with CM outcomes is likely to come to the fore at closure. Conversely, the problem-based orientation at the heart of an integrative bargaining approach enhances the prospects for creative, positive-sum solutions to disputes as well as to the generation of transformative relationship dynamics between parties.

The pivot point is the fundamental difference concerning conceptions of marginal utility and utility maximization. This point of departure informs two distinct sets of perceptions of costs and benefits, each strongly informed by the attitudinal dispositions of negotiators employing one or the other bargaining style. Thus, positional bargaining generates attitudes among negotiators that the costs of an outcome of more limited scope (i.e. one avoiding/accepting underlying disputes or adversarial relations) are outweighed by the associated benefits of the greater attainability of a (limited) agreement. Negotiators employing a positional bargaining style are also more likely to accept the enhanced potential for a breakdown in negotiations and/or a resumption of hostilities that is par for the course within the more limited purview of CM rather than striving for a transformational (and thus more risky or costly) outcome as associated with a CR strategy.

Conversely, integrative bargaining styles engender different attitudes toward the negotiation process and outcome, subverting (and not just inverting) the previous calculus. For negotiators operating along an integrative bargaining tack, it is not merely a matter of the costs of avoidance/acceptance of disputes and relationships outweighing the benefits of a more limited, if more immediately attainable, agreement. Rather, the calculus turns on a different denominator, namely an appreciation of the benefits of a comprehensive approach aimed at a transformational breakthrough both of the problems underlying the conflict and of the relational attitudes sustaining it.

interactive effects between time pressure and interest and value-based bargaining in an experimental setting by Harinck and De Dreu (2004).

Illustrations of this synergy between negotiation style and closing behavior are legion. One recent example was negotiations spearheaded by Russia and the United States in the fall of 2013 concerning the use of chemical weapons in the Syrian civil war, culminating in a framework agreement for international control and dismantling of the Assad regime's chemical weapons stockpile. Given the deteriorating relationship between the United States and Russia and their starkly divergent objectives relative to the desired outcome for the conflict, it is hardly surprising that each side employed a positional approach to the negotiations. Neither party wished to pursue a more ambitious tack, instead adopting a severely circumscribed CM strategy in which the primary objective was removing one form of materiel from the conflict. Pursuing a strategy oriented around such a narrow objective had the additional appeal of a favorable risk/reward calculus for both parties as well, since the continuation of the hostilities without abatement had little bearing on the actual or perceived success or failure of the negotiation process.

An illustration of a similar synergy between integrative bargaining and closing behavior is the oft-cited example of the transformation of the issue of the status of the Sinai over the course of the Camp David process (Joffe 2002). As the parties (prompted by the mediation of President Carter) moved away from a strict positional framework toward an integrative approach, the Sinai problem was cast in a different light, as the needs of the Israelis (for assurance that the region would not serve as a staging ground for an attack by Egypt) and Egyptians (for assurance of Israel military withdrawal from the region) were discovered to be compatible. This focus on resolving particular disputes, as well as the effort to fundamentally redefine the relationship (as reflected in, among other things, the Accord's codification of Egypt's recognition of Israel's right to exist) was very much emblematic of a CR approach itself underpinned by a shift toward an integrative bargaining style by involved parties.

Recurrent interactions between parties to the negotiation constitute a second process-oriented variable shaping closing strategies. Drawing on the game-theoretic concept of repeated games, the track record of dyadic behavior between negotiation parties preceding the endpoint in the negotiations is a crucial variable conditioning strategic calculations concerning expected payoffs, coalition formation, reservation or security points, ZOPAs, and the shadow of the future (Axelrod & Hamilton 1981, Bearce, Floros & McKibben 2009; Carpenter 2003; Brams 2003). Indeed, recurrent interactions both impinge upon the possibility of reaching a negotiated settlement in the present and influence expectations of future interactions, including expectations about the enforceability of any such settlement.[3]

Axelrod's (1984) seminal work on cooperation proved a crucial point of departure for consideration of the prospects for cooperation through the mechanism of reciprocity, a phenomenon often evident in iterated games. A plethora of experimental studies examining cooperation in repeated-interaction environments followed, seeking to account for factors including noise and complexity, limited information, social structure, familiarity between partners, fairness, and the like (Wu & Axelrod 1995; Majeski 1995; Majeski & Fricks 1995; Cohen, Riolo & Axelrod 2001; Diekmann 2004). Similarly, strategic interactions which may not be captured in formal models but are nonetheless crucial to understanding the negotiation process, such as back-channel communications, have attracted increased attention in process-oriented studies (Pruitt 2006, 2008; Wanis-St. John 2006). So too have considerations of actor linkages relative to the strategic calculations of negotiation parties (Bueno de Mesquita 1990; Carraro and Marchiori 2004; Tollison and Willett 1979).

In light of these findings, the duration of any recurrent dyadic interaction and the quality of the relationship between the parties in that dyad are key determinants of whether negotiators will pursue a CM or CR strategy. Antagonistic relationships point negotiators toward the easier exit point of CM. In incorporating the importance of iteration and learning to negotiation, Leng (1983, 1993, 2000) is especially instructive on this point; he finds that the lessons of prior interactions tend to be used by crisis actors in ways that increase hostility, reduce the prospects for successful bargaining outcomes, and work against effective crisis resolution. Given that such situations will be compounded by ubiquitous considerations of commitment and enforcement problems (Fearon 1998; Axelrod & Keohane 1985), it seems safe to suppose that in the event such prior interactions were in and of themselves hostile or antagonistic, there would be a multiplier effect which would further propel negotiators along a path of lesser resistance (CM) in the closing stages.[4]

---

[3] For our purposes, whether a particular repeated game is better understood as finite (set number of iterations; time period and termination point fixed and known) or infinite (potentially unlimited number of iterations; time period and termination point unknown) is less relevant than is the general applicability of recurrent interactions to the majority of negotiations.

[4] Fearon's introduction of distinct negotiation domains (bargaining and enforcement) muddies the waters. In disaggregating the two domains, he appropriates the projection of optimists that repeated interactions and recognition of the "long shadow of the future" by negotiation principals renders cooperation more likely and agreements more enforceable. The present inquiry rejects a stark disaggregation of bargaining and

Relative to the closing strategies of negotiators, the quantity of repeated interactions is also important. Here it would seem that, *ceteris paribus*, the longer the duration of the negotiation process, the greater the likelihood of parties resorting to a CM rather than CR strategy. A somewhat counter-intuitive application of the logic of social learning relative to its customary translation in negotiation settings underpins this supposition. Namely, in crisis or conflict negotiation settings, animosity and mistrust between parties persists *even as those parties engage in sustained interaction*. In such circumstances, the chief result of increased opportunities for interaction and understanding of the other party is an enhanced desire to settle for and thus pursue a CM strategy. This would seem to have much to do with the stakes involved, particularly the desire to ameliorate the consequences associated with continued violence or threats of violence born of enhanced familiarity and engagement between the negotiation principals.

Examples of this relationship abound, particularly in civil conflicts. For instance, the highly fraught nature of relations between Sudan and South Sudan since the latter's independence in July 2011 is clearly a holdover from persistent internecine struggles as well as two protracted civil wars within Sudan (1955–1972 and 1983–2005). The negotiation process producing the Comprehensive Peace Agreement (brokered in part with the assistance of regional-governmental-organization mediation from the Intergovernmental Authority on Development, IGAD), while certainly fruitful and widely heralded, was a highly pragmatic one focused on a specific set of issues and objectives as delimited by the principals themselves (Butler 2009). These self-imposed constraints were the product of mutual recognition of the parties that decades of recurrent violence greatly inhibited the prospects of reaching a comprehensive peace agreement (CPA). Hence the parties gravitated toward a more limited CM strategy with the hopes of terminating the active conflict itself. The result was an agreement that intentionally avoided adopting a CR methodology, failing to address a number of crucial matters that would be brought to a head by the referendum on independence that the CPA itself provided for. The preference of negotiators for a CM strategy served as a midwife to the conditions of state failure in South Sudan (Kimenyi and Mbaku 2011).

Most *second-image* analyses in the negotiation domain are indebted to Putnam's (1988) concept of two-level games, itself extending the notion of boundary role conflict introduced by Druckman (1977). Thorough

enforcement in favor of an understanding of reciprocal linkages between the two domains.

application of equilibrium analysis by Fearon (1994) demonstrates that audience costs are critical to signaling the intentions of negotiators, conveying relative preferences for CM or CR (versus war). Smith (1998) and Johns (2006) build on Fearon's work, reversing the second image in analyzing the signals sent to the domestic political audience by a leader's performance. Prins (2003) offers a further extension, examining the ways in which signaling and credibility relative to audience costs impact the credible communication of negotiator intentions. Similar factors are at work in the related dynamics of "outbidding" and "frontstage" behavior used by actors in attempting to frame issues and alter or command the course of complex negotiations such as those typifying the Oslo I process in the early 1990s (Donohue & Druckman 2009).[5]

The primary impact of the second image on closing behavior is evident in the relationship between audience costs and the choice of CM or CR strategies by negotiators. This draws heavily from the reciprocal dynamics among audience costs, dispute escalation, and the fortunes of political leaders (Fearon 1994; Bennett & Stam 1996). In extrapolating from this dynamic, real and perceived pressures emanating from domestic constituencies have real impact on attempts at crafting a negotiated settlement to a dispute. In a climate defined by close scrutiny and evidently expressed preferences on the part of the domestic audience(s), it stands to reason that politically astute negotiators are likely to alter their negotiation strategy in response to the nature of those preferences, in either a CM or a CR direction, depending on the salience of the issue(s) and associated audience costs.

The greater the domestic political pressure for delivering a minimally acceptable negotiated outcome and/or for disengagement from the process, the greater the likelihood that negotiators will be pushed toward a CM strategy as a way of managing or mitigating attendant audience costs. At a minimum, the greater attainability of a CM approach is likely to facilitate termination of the negotiation more expediently – providing an appealing "exit" to negotiators buffeted by domestic audiences. Conversely, if the background noise is lower, the more time-consuming and complicated efforts associated with a CR approach may be seen as more appealing (or perhaps less risky).

---

[5] Other examples of second-image studies introduce similar social and contextual variables via different methodological avenues; these include retrospective assessments of historical cases (Bick 2006), applications to recent and contemporary negotiations (Knopf 1993), and efforts to incorporate factors including governmental secrecy, institutional constraints, decision-making processes, and public opinion into the two-level framework (Lieberfeld 2008; Mo 1995; Iida 1993; Trumbore & Boyer 2000; Shamir & Shikaki 2005).

The appeal of CM strategies to negotiators due to their capacity to hasten closure should not be overlooked. This effect is particularly acute in protracted or complex negotiations where the outcome is likely to portend high costs on the domestic level. In such circumstances the issue(s) at the heart of the negotiation, and beyond that the negotiation process itself, are more salient to domestic audiences and hence audience costs are actually or potentially higher. Partly because of this heightened domestic salience, the stakes for the negotiators themselves are higher, creating a self-perpetuating dynamic of high political risk for the negotiation team (and the political officials they represent). This is typically the case in conflict negotiations, in which both the intensity of the issue and the involvement of the domestic audience raise the political costs and consequences for all concerned parties (Butler & Boyer 2003). In such circumstances it is not hard to envision how CM strategies may be perceived as an appealing means of containing domestic audience costs and placating domestic critics while retaining greater agency for the principals themselves. Unlike CR strategies, CM approaches allow negotiators a fuller hand in navigating the negotiation minefield in self-serving (if not problem-solving) ways.

This is not to say that higher salience and correspondingly higher audience costs automatically propel negotiators toward CM strategies and away from CR. Attitudes within domestic audience(s) are ultimately critical, such that an inverted scenario in which highly engaged domestic audiences seek transformative changes in a conflict dynamic may prevail, producing significant pressure for negotiators to resolve rather than manage. The negotiations between the Colombian government and FARC reflect this dynamic. Yet the larger point regarding endgame stands – that audience costs play an important role not only in nudging negotiators toward a CM (more likely) or CR (less likely) strategy, but, beyond that, in accelerating the process toward closure.

The process leading up to and producing the Oslo agreement establishing a Declaration of Principles (DoP) on Palestinian self-rule in September 1993 illustrates this point well. Direct negotiations between the Israelis and Palestinians demonstrated the extent to which domestic audiences propelled the principals toward a CM approach, while also helping craft (or reshape) the context of the negotiation in ways that proved favorable for a successful (if limited) outcome. Significant audience costs brought about by domestic political upheaval on both sides (in Israel, the defeat of Likud and the formation of a new Labour government; for the Palestinians, challenges to Arafat's position from within Fatah and especially from Hamas) helped trigger a prevailing sense of pragmatism. This was clearly reflected in the desire of both parties to leave the table with a concrete, though highly circumscribed, agreement on the question of Palestinian autonomy going forward (Lieberfeld 2008).

Context Variables

While the significance of process variables for the choice of closing strategy is self-evident, it is also important to account for contextual factors which may influence negotiators to pursue a CM or CR strategy. The intractability of a conflict, the nature of the act triggering a conflict, and the overall scope and intensity of the violence associated with it are also worthy considerations.

Intractable conflicts have three conceptual components: They are marred by the long-term persistence of armed violence; they are prosecuted in a fashion that comes to be seen as counter-productive by observers and protagonists alike; and they are marked by one or more failed attempts to contain or resolve them (Kriesberg, Northrup & Thorson 1989; Putnam & Wondolleck 2003). The main supposition concerning the effects of intractability on closing behavior is that intractable conflicts prompt negotiators toward CM rather than CR strategies. This hypothesis is not obvious; one of the defining features of any intractable conflict is that it has necessarily been subjected to some prior (failed) attempt(s) at peacemaking. Satisfaction of this definitional criterion could tilt negotiators toward a more ambitious attempt at breaking the cycle of intractability through a CR approach. The reason it doesn't is two-fold; first, that negotiation in protracted conflicts tends to be shaped by risk aversion, and secondly, that negotiators are likely to view the continued (violent) prosecution of the conflict as suboptimal. In light of the weight of these considerations, parties seeking a negotiated settlement to intractable conflicts are more likely to pursue a CM approach *by virtue of the very criteria defining intractability*.

While intractability is treated here largely as a contextual variable, there is a process-oriented element to the concept that also necessitates consideration. The dynamic quality of intractability is perhaps best reflected in Kriesberg's (2005) concept of a life-cycle of intractable conflicts (see Figure 8.1). The model is particularly important, allowing us to take into account the particular phase in which an intractable conflict resides at the time the negotiation in question approaches closure. Negotiations occurring in any of the ascending phases of the life-cycle are, as previously discussed, likely to feature CM strategies as the process approaches termination. However, if negotiations occur in the small minority of cases where an intractable conflict has undergone

Life cycle of an intractable conflict (adapted from Kriesberg, 2005)

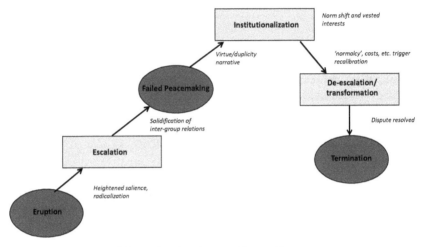

Figure 8.1. Life-cycle of an intractable conflict.

the normative and structural changes necessary to reach the tipping point of the model, distrust, risk aversion, and other factors mitigating against CR will have dissipated, thereby increasing the appeal of a CR strategy.

Conflict trigger, a proxy measure from the crisis literature used to overcome the difficulties inherent in identifying a single overriding dispute that can definitively be said to cause an armed conflict, provides a surrogate allowing rough characterization of the dispute on the basis of the nature of the act which sparked the conflict, with more provocative or violent triggers reflecting more intense and fundamental disputes (Table 8.1) (Brecher & Wilkenfeld 2000). The nature and type of the dispute(s) at the heart of any conflict have significant influence on whether CM or CR is employed in closing behavior (Burton & Dukes 1990; Atran & Axelrod 2008; Coleman & Lowe 2007).

The greater the severity of the trigger in a conflict, the more likely it is that negotiators at the closing phase will pursue CM rather than CR strategies. In the event that negotiation is employed at some later juncture, heightened perceptions of threat on the part of one or more parties are likely to increase the appeal of CM strategies and the more limited but attainable outcomes they portend. Given the stakes and risks involved, the perceived exigency of the quicker, more feasible outcomes associated with CM strategies would possess greater appeal to negotiators – even if, in fact, such an approach (unlike CR) leaves the dispute(s) at the heart of the conflict fundamentally unchanged.

Table 8.1 *Types of conflict triggers*

Category	Illustrations
Political/diplomatic act	Verbal threat, accusation, demand; act of subversion; adversarial alliance formation; treaty abrogation; diplomatic sanctions or severance of diplomatic relations
Economic act	Embargo or sanctions; nationalization or seizure of property; withholding or termination of economic aid
Internal challenge to regime or status quo of one or more conflict parties	Internal turmoil associated with governmental collapse, coup d'état, terrorism, assassination, riot, demonstrations, strikes, mass arrests, attempted or successful revolt
Structural change	Change in economic, technological, political, or military status quo in global system or regional subsystem
Indirect violent act	Show of force (e.g. war games or maneuvers); mobilization or change of force posture; violent revolution or insurrection in another state/society
Direct violent act	Border clash/crossing by outside military forces; violations of airspace or territorial waters; military incident (land, sea, or air); military attack on significant target

Adapted from Brecher and Wilkenfeld (2000).

One of many possible illustrations of this assertion is the tenor and scope of the negotiations during the conflict in Bosnia-Hercegovina in the early 1990s. The outbreak of militarized violence, which escalated dramatically as the theater shifted from Serbian Krajina to Bosnia, was in many ways adjacent to the dramatic changes to the political and social status quo occurring with the dissolution of Yugoslavia. This seismic shift underpinning the conflict itself offers one possible explanation for the limited horizons and self-serving negotiation strategies employed by the various delegations (led by the triumvirate of Milošević, Tuđman, and Izetbegović) throughout the duration of the conflict (Bose 2002). Indeed, one charitable interpretation of how the parties arrived at the *de facto* partition of Bosnia-Hercegovina codified in the Dayton Agreement is an unremitting pragmatism borne of the conditions inspiring the conflict in the first place (Chollet 2005).

However, a trigger effect may be an ambiguous indicator. A conflict precipitated by actual or threatened violence at the outset may not necessarily be defined by heavy violence throughout the duration of the conflict. For example, persistent tensions between the Democratic Republic of Congo (DRC) and Rwanda originated in the disastrous violence punctuating not only the DRC's civil war but also the 1994 genocide in neighboring Rwanda, and the presence of extremist Hutu militias based in refugee camps in the DRC. Despite these violent origins, much of the subsequent tension between the two states played out through diplomatic exchanges and periodic mobilizations rather than direct clashes, with both sides proving repeatedly amenable to UN, AU, and EU mediation and deployments (IRIN 2015; Reyntjens 2004). The reverse effect might also be present, as in the Falklands/Malvinas dispute where a heavily militarized interstate conflict was initiated by (literal) displays of flag waving and verbal salvos from each state's foreign ministry (GlobalSecurity.org 2015; Freedman 2007), calling for additional variables.

The greater the *centrality and severity of the violence* within a conflict, the more likely it is that parties engaged in negotiations at the closing phase will employ a CM rather than CR strategy (Butler 2007). The relevant logic underpinning this hypothesis is parallel to that advanced with respect to conflict trigger, namely conflicts in which violence is both more persistent and more egregious are conflicts in which negotiators are more likely to "settle" for a relatively easier path toward cessation of hostilities, given the stakes associated with the continuation of said hostilities. Centrality and severity are both continuous variables best assessed over the lifespan of a conflict. Whereas the centrality of violence pertains to the relative importance that parties attach to violence as a useful means of obtaining their goals and objectives, the severity of violence captures the intensity of violence employed by the parties to the conflict (both in terms of acute incidences of violence and in terms of sustained levels throughout the conflict). Taken together, these two related and mutually reinforcing measures provide valuable insights (both individually and jointly) into both the perceptions and the behavior of conflict parties with respect to violence – and also, by extension, into the closing strategy of negotiators seeking to delimit that violence.

Logically speaking, in the majority of cases one would expect the centrality and severity of violence to move conjointly. It would stand to reason that the greater the importance afforded to violence by the conflict parties, the greater the likelihood violence will persist at sustained high levels or that the conflict will be defined by occasional spasms of extreme violence, or both. This dynamic interaction is more likely over time to elicit negotiation behavior directed by the pursuit of CM outcomes as the scope and intensity of the violence on display in the conflict becomes untenable. Where these two dimensions of violence are disaligned, the perceptual dimension of centrality plays the more compelling part in shaping the decision of negotiators to pursue a CM strategy in the closing phase. The rationale for this claim borrows liberally from the logic of a mutually hurting stalemate; it is ultimately the perception of the (future) payoffs associated with continuation of violence that plays the greater role in getting conflict parties to the peace table. In this instance, the same can be said for the impact of this perceptual factor on the behavior of negotiators *already occupying a place at said table* to "settle" for the more limited outcomes associated with a CM strategy.

Relative to violence, the decision to adopt a CM footing as the closing strategy is most likely when the conflict dynamic reaches a "tipping point" – i.e. when the material dimension of severity remains high, but the perceptual dimension of centrality begins to wane. It is precisely at this point that a discrepancy between perceptions of the utility of violence and the persistence of that violence itself emerges, rendering a CM strategy more appealing. One apt contemporary example is the ongoing Colombian peace talks between the government and FARC, initiated in November 2012. The decision of the Colombian government to countenance and engage in direct negotiations with FARC representatives after decades of violence and official estimates of nearly a quarter-million casualties (National Centre for Historical Memory 2015) is clearly suggestive of a perceptual shift on the part of the government. While the severity of the violence in Colombia persisted, the shift toward direct negotiations was clearly indicative of a sharp decline in the perceived utility of a militarized approach. This is a stark reversal, particularly when considering the government's role in creating and supporting right-wing paramilitaries in the 1990s (Butler 2009).

Behavioral Manifestations in the Endgame

Once the negotiation principals have decided to pursue either CM or CR, how might their behavior unfold in the pursuit of that endgame? Are one or more of the behavioral typologies (Table 8.2) of mismatching, dueling, driving, and dragging more or less likely to correspond to and follow from a CM or CR strategy?[6]

Mismatching: If different strategic trajectories are evident in pursuit of CM or CR within the same negotiation setting, the most likely behavioral outcome will be mismatching. It is not hard to envision how divergences

---

[6] A fifth typology (mixed) is not included here, given the presumption that CM and CR strategies cannot be employed by the same actor simultaneously.

Table 8.2 *Typologies of closing behavior and associated strategies*

Typology of closing behavior	Defining characteristic(s)	Dominant strategy (*, more likely)	Contemporary example
Mismatch	Failure of bilateral logic to materialize	CM and CR	Russia/Ukraine
Dueling	Brinkmanship	CM	Greek debt
Driving	Synchronicity toward convergence	CM or CR*	Iranian nuclear disarmament
Dragging	Mutual pursuit of acceptable exit	CM* or CR	Colombian government/FARC

in negotiation behaviors might arise if one party is intent on the objective of containing, reversing, or ameliorating violent conflict, while the other has elected to focus on the fundamental disputes underlying that conflict. Such behavior is defined by suspicion and distrust between the parties, who not only are operating along a different strategic plane, but also may wrongly perceive the other party (or parties) to be following the same tack, producing sharp behavioral discrepancies. Negotiations between parties variously employing CM and CR strategies are therefore highly unlikely to produce a productive outcome of either type, and may break down entirely. Indeed, the mismatch of strategies (and associated objectives) is so basic and fundamental that even the time pressure and urgency associated with closure are unlikely to have much of a mitigating effect.

One telling example in this regard was the failure of bilateral negotiations (called for in UNSCR 502) between the United Kingdom and Argentina over the Falklands/Malvinas conflict in April 1982. The United Kingdom placed singular emphasis on the illegality of the Argentine use of force in seizing the islands; the result was a limited endgame defined by reaffirmation of the self-determination of the inhabitants of the islands through reversion of territorial control to the United Kingdom (Nielsson 1988). This proto-CM strategy was starkly at odds with the Argentine strategy, which – steeped in the conviction that British control over the islands constituted a case of "anachronistic colonialism" – contended that any bilateral negotiation should take up and redress fundamental legal and political disputes and questions concerning the origins of the status of British claims to the islands (Nielsson 1988). Not surprisingly, the mismatching between this more expansive CR-oriented strategy and the minimalist UK stance proved fatal to UN efforts to promote bilateral talks.

Dueling: Such closing behavior, akin to the game of chicken, in which the parties are locked in a positional game of competitive brinkmanship and are willing to hold out through the eleventh hour in the hope the other party concedes (Kitzantonis and Alderman 2015), is typically associated with (and encouraged by) the adoption of CM strategies. Parties engaged in dueling behavior at closure publicly accept the prospect of deadlock as preferable to significant concessions. It is not hard to see the similarities between this zero-sum behavior and the positional bargaining logic, risk-averse "satisficing" impulses, and domestic-audience pressures that often promulgate CM strategies. One relevant illustration of this is the Rambouillet talks concerning Kosovo between January and March 1999. The positions of the protagonists going into the talks concerning the future status of Kosovo were entrenched and irreconcilable. Fully aware of this dynamic, the Contact Group in concert with the parties employed a CM strategy in the hope of crafting a negotiated agreement aimed at containing the violence. However, adopting this strategy effectively reified the irreconcilability of the positions of the parties. Further, the inclusion of a provision within the Rambouillet Accords mandating that any agreement be implemented via imposition of a NATO force with free movement inside Kosovo and Serbia effectively scotched the possibility of a negotiated solution. The implications of such an arrangement for each side's security points made it a concession too significant for Milošević to bear, or for the Kosovar Albanians to drop (BBC 2000).

Dragging: Coming to the realization that the likely outcome toward which they are working is in fact undesirable, dragging parties mutually adjust their negotiating behavior toward a "soft landing" or safe exit that terminates the negotiations without significant damage. Whatever specific choices ensue are less important than the larger behavioral recalibration in which the parties work to extract themselves (and the other side) from a negotiated agreement which they have determined will be unworkable. The behavioral dynamic of dragging could emerge from parties employing either a CM or a CR strategy, though the premium placed on resistance points suggests a stronger correlation with the former strategy. Because CM is so closely associated with positional bargaining, intractable conflicts, sustained dyadic interactions, and mounting domestic-audience costs, the desire to identify a "safe landing" at the heart of dragging behavior is likely to have greater appeal to negotiators operating according to a CM logic in the first place.[7]

---

[7] One exception might be when parties engaged in bilateral negotiations are operating in accordance with a CR strategy, but in their efforts to address disputes defining the conflict come to realize that ripeness is not at hand and thus tabling certain issues or suspending talks in the interest of revisiting CR at a later date is necessary.

182   Causes

Recent developments (or lack thereof) in the Middle East peace process since the onset of the second *intifada* in 2000, and especially since the election of Hamas in 2006, bear all the hallmarks of dragging generated by a CM orientation on the part of the principals. Perhaps the clearest exhibits on both accounts are the recurrent short-lived ceasefires between Israel and Hamas (2008, 2012, and 2014). The narrow scope and short shelf-life of these agreements are evidence both of the dominance of CM strategies for both sides and of the shortcomings of CM approaches in the absence of any complementary attention to CR. Both Israeli and Palestinian leaders have effectively rejected all but the most skeletal notion of CM, which in turn explains the modality of dragging behavior that has defined the last decade or more of their infrequent and unproductive negotiated interactions.

Driving: Among the three coordinated behavioral types introduced in this volume, driving behavior constitutes a compelling departure. Here, a bilateral dynamic marked by the willingness to extend mutual concessions and compensations emerges, generating an interactive and reciprocal negotiating behavior in which the parties move toward a joint endgame. It is important to note motive here; driving behavior is precipitated not by altruistic or other-regarding motives, but rather by a perception by the parties that the cost of a breakdown in negotiations is perceived as higher than the expected benefit of an agreement (Pillar 1983). Hence driving is akin to an enlightened version of the Chicken Dilemma Game (CDG) where the parties are primarily motivated by avoiding a deadlock and thus strive to carve out a mutually enticing outcome (Goldstein 2005).

The underlying motive of driving behavior suggests that it is more likely to occur in conjunction with the use of a CR strategy. This association is explained by two compelling similarities between driving behavior and the internal logic of CR: first, driving behavior seeks to avoid the termination of the negotiation process, considering the absence of discursive exchange between the parties as tantamount to failure; secondly, the bargaining style on display tends toward facilitative–integrative rather than positional (as reflected in the extension and exchange of concessions and compensations). In light of these similarities, in cases where the negotiation process and/or context are more favorably disposed toward CR (say, when domestic-audience costs are low, and the friction between the parties as well as the severity and centrality of violence are on the decline), we are likely to witness not only a CR approach but also a behavioral manifestation in the form of driving behavior by the parties.

The negotiations between the Colombian government and FARC (ongoing at the time of writing) provide an apt illustration of this.

The opening of direct negotiations in November 2012 quickly proved the most significant effort in the decades-long civil war to address the underlying disputes at the heart of the conflict. Receiving the first ever signal of a genuine CR orientation on the part of the government, FARC quickly moved to take advantage of the opportunity to negotiate over long-held grievances such as the maldistribution of land in rural areas and the transition of FARC into a "legitimate" political actor (Miroff 2015). Parallel to this, driving behavior by both parties was also evinced in the jagged introduction of a series of unilateral and bilateral ceasefires. The Colombian case reflects both how the endgame as well as the concessions that define driving behavior overlap with CR strategies and how both CR outcomes and the driving behavior aimed at achieving them may still require an underlying platform of CM in order to maintain the momentum associated with each (Norwegian Peacebuilding Resource Centre 2013).

In the coordinated behavioral moves of dueling, dragging, and driving we can see manifest indications of endgame behavior which itself is determined by strategic orientation (CM or CR). In this, it appears more likely if not typical for the dynamic of closure to mitigate against CR efforts in favor of seemingly more feasible and attainable CM outcomes (i.e. a ceasefire rather than a peace accord). In cases where negotiators have already embraced a CM strategy, the closing phase propels them further in the direction of satisficing. The chief exception to this is the driving dynamic – as in the Colombian case – in which matching concessions can not only sustain but even encourage the persistence and flourishing of CR strategies as closure approaches.

Conclusion

This chapter provides a "first-cut" identification of several factors with bearing on the decision of negotiators to pursue conflict-management (CM) or conflict-resolution (CR) strategies as well as the behavioral manifestations of that choice in the endgames that result. In terms of process variables, bargaining style (positional vs. integrative) is an important determinant of negotiation strategy at closure, with the former more likely to produce a CM strategy and dueling behavior, and the latter a CR approach and greater associated potential for driving behavior. Similarly, the greater the domestic pressure for quick resolution or disengagement, the more likely the logic of expediency at the heart of CM will take over, and dragging behavior toward a quick exit will materialize. Conversely, less noise of this type increases the chance parties will employ a CR strategy reflected, again, in driving behavior.

Additionally, contextual considerations related to the conflict itself (including the severity of the trigger, the scope and intensity of the violence, and whether or not the conflict exhibits the criteria of intractability) have clear implications for the strategy adopted by the parties in the closing stage. Ultimately, the decision to pursue a CM or CR strategy should be understood neither as discrete nor as something linked to or bound by a given point in time early in the negotiation process. Rather, the strategy is likely (if not certain) to loom over the proceedings, shaping and reinforcing negotiation behavior and conceptions of the endgame.

9 Mediating Closure: Driving toward a MEO

Siniša Vuković

In the last moment of the mediated negotiations in Dayton, the Bosnian delegation was unenthusiastic with anything that had been proposed during the 20-day conference. In the last hour of the talks, Serbian President Milosevic and Croatian President Tudjman started discussing an option of bilaterally signing an agreement, thus excluding Bosnia's President Izetbegovic. For American mediators this partial signing was unacceptable. They had two options: try one last time to convince Izetbegovic, or concede failure of the talks.

"Chris [Warren Christopher]," I [Richard Holbrooke] said, "the next meeting may be the most important of your entire tenure as a Secretary. We can get this agreement – or we can lose it. Forget Washington. It is entirely in our hands. We must go into the meeting with an absolute determination to succeed."

Christopher listened silently, then nodded. Without stopping to talk to anyone else, we walked directly to Izetbegovic's rooms, where the three Bosnians waited for us. We outlined the offer from Milosevic. Silence. I repeated it, slowly and carefully. There were seven hundred journalists waiting outside the base, I said. They had been told by Sacirbey that the talks were over, and, in fact we would make such an announcement at 10:00am unless the offer to put Brcko under arbitration was accepted. Time had run out, and we needed an answer immediately.

There was a long, amazing pause. We watched Izetbegovic carefully. No one spoke. Finally, speaking slowly, Izetbegovic said, "It is not a just peace." He paused for what seemed like a minute, but was probably only three seconds. My heart almost stopped. Then: "But my people need peace" ... Leaning over to Christopher, I whispered, "Let's get out of here fast," and rose. Christopher shook Izetbegovic's hand and turned rapidly away. (Holbrooke 1998, 308–309)

The peace process in Dayton addressed a common problem in many contemporary international conflicts. Many of them are characterized by prolonged tensions, employment of destructive means, suspicion and mistrust, inflammatory rhetoric and polarized solutions that are usually presented as ultimatums. In such circumstances reaching a deal is nothing short of miraculous, as the parties are commonly resisting even the prospect of talking to each other. Owing to a complete breakdown of communication and high levels of uncertainty about the other side's capabilities and intentions, conflicting parties are generally either unable or unwilling to find a mutually acceptable solution on their own. As a consequence, in order to break this logjam, parties may seek or accept assistance from an outside party that can act as a mediator. Mediation represents a voluntary, non-coercive and legally non-binding form of assisted negotiation, where one or more external actors help the parties in dispute reach a mutually acceptable solution that they are either unable or unwilling to find on their own (Touval & Zartman 1985; Bercovitch 2002; Beardsley 2011; Greig & Diehl 2012; Vuković 2015a).

Beyond inability, the parties often do not feel the need to talk to the opponent to find a way to reduce their costs of conflict. They may need a mediator to ripen the perceptions of the conflict, fostering a sense of a mutually hurting stalemate (MHS) and promoting the utility of negotiations as a way out of the predicament (Zartman 2001; Zartman & De Soto 2010). Mediators acting as *ripeners* may set the stage for successful negotiations by encouraging the parties to recognize that they are in an unbearably painful deadlock, that their unilateral activities will not yield expected results, and that any attempt to escalate into victory is destined to produce even higher costs with no guarantee of success. Moreover, mediators may warn the parties of an impending catastrophe induced by their confrontational behavior. Ripe moments are a matter of perception. As noted by Zartman (2001, 9), "it is the perception of the objective condition, not the condition itself, that makes for a MHS." For this reason, depending on their capabilities and interests, either the mediators may facilitate communication and provide creative interpretations of the situation in order to induce the parties to recognize that they are in a mutually hurting stalemate, or they may actually ripen the conflict and create a stalemate by affecting the actual objective conditions on the ground.

Mediators may use information to manipulate the perceptions of the parties about the mutually hurting stalemate. This was the case in Bosnia, when US diplomats deceived the Bosnian authorities that after a massive Bosnian and Croatian offensive in the summer of 1995 the Bosnian Serbs were preparing a counter-offensive. Despite the fact that there was no evidence of this, the Americans used this information to depict a grim future and persuade the Bosnian authorities to accept the US initiative for mediated talks in Dayton; otherwise, the alternative was both uncertain and potentially very damaging (Silber & Little 1996).

But the push factor of a hurting stalemate is not enough for the parties to stay committed throughout the process and settle on a mutually acceptable solution. For this reason, mediators are tasked with a challenging role of providing mutually enticing opportunities (MEOs) that would pull the parties out of the conflict (Pruitt 1997; Pruitt & Olczak

1995; Ohlson 2008). As an essential aspect of the mediation process, MEOs represent a combination of creatively formulated solutions and attractive incentives offered by mediators with the aim of promoting inter- and intra-party trust and confidence in the peace process. More importantly, MEOs are designed and delivered during the negotiation process in order to encourage enthusiasm in the post-negotiated reality that will be characterized by interdependence. Therefore, MEOs exemplify the key tool at mediators' disposal which is used to keep the parties focused and committed until the very end of the peacemaking process. They help the mediators take up the work as *drivers* that can eliminate inter-party dueling and reduce potential dragging. When acting as drivers, mediators are entrusted with a delicate role of transforming the conflicting parties' negotiating behavior from competitive bargaining (characteristic for dueling) to problem solving, and guide (or leverage) them toward a mutually acceptable agreement.

A mediator's role is to bring out the MEOs in order to open and then consummate the endgame. As a result, MEOs represent an essential feature of the endgame. In the last moments of mediated processes, for the conflicting parties they denote the perceived utility of agreeing to end the talks with a mutually acceptable solution. They embody the ultimate degree of interest convergence from which the parties do not want to defect. Thus, the MEOs are mostly a matter of last moments. While they gain shape throughout the entire peacemaking process – starting with the preliminary diagnosis mediators make, continuing with the exploration of parties' interests and needs and acquisition of information, followed by the search for a formula for handling the conflict or problem – they are effectively projected in the last instants of the process. Mediators do this by resorting to incentives, which reflect their relevant material and non-material resources that can be used to induce the parties to settle. The present chapter aims to illustrate the driving role of mediators in the negotiation process, and to show the variety of tactical instruments used to leverage the parties into an agreement in the last segments of negotiation.

Mediators as Drivers: Breaking the Dueling

Strategies

In performing as a driver, a mediator has three strategies at their disposal: facilitation, formulation, and manipulation. *Facilitation* is occasioned by the fact that the conflicting sides generally develop high degrees of suspicion and distrust, and their behavior and decisions are inevitably conditioned by incomplete information about each other's capabilities and interests. This limits the likelihood that they will recognize mutually acceptable alternatives to a continued conflict. Consequently, the onset of negotiations in such conflicts is also characterized by competitive bargaining (Hopmann 1995). The parties primarily focus on their differences and frame potential gains as zero-sum. With limited information they are often unable to find any common ground. In such circumstances, the role of the mediator is to facilitate communication and provide the disputants with information that can reduce uncertainty and help them identify the range of mutually acceptable outcomes. In other words, mediators acting as facilitators helping the disputing sides recognize that they actually share a ZOPA and that an endgame is in view, as discussed by Chester Crocker in Chapter 17 (Zartman & Touval 1996; Beardsley *et al.* 2006; Vuković 2015b).

Facilitation is at the core of any mediation activity. Although in its most fundamental form it may be regarded as the least assertive form of mediator behavior, it is essential as it sets the stage for the process through which the parties may transform their confrontational relations. As the mediators provide the relevant information, they drive the parties into the process where they gradually start reframing their intransigent positions. With adequate information the conflicting parties may start realizing that their interests are not mutually exclusive. As noted by Hopmann (2001, 456), in such circumstances "the issue under negotiation is best defined not as a conflict between parties that must be resolved but rather as a common problem confronting all parties that must be solved."

When facilitation is not enough to complete the work of the endgame, a *formulator* may be needed. In order to drive the parties out of the deadlock developed by dueling and competitive bargaining and into closure, mediators need to encourage a more open information exchange. Even with the best intentions, information exchange does not automatically reduce high degrees of mistrust and suspicion between the parties. In fact, even when the conflicting parties start realizing that they might share a ZOPA, they may still be apprehensive to settle on a specific solution. Their decision may be conditioned by the prevailing skepticism about the other side's true intentions. As a consequence, the parties may interpret a variety of possible solutions – even those that are actually within a newly discovered ZOPA – as either unacceptable or mutually exclusive. In such situations, mediators are not only tasked to repair damaged communication; they are also called upon to enter into the substance of the process in order to redefine issues at stake, propose viable alternative formulas, and drive the parties toward a particular solution. According to Zartman & Touval (1996, 454), "formulas are the key to a negotiated solution to a conflict; they provide a common understanding of the problem and its solution or a shared notion of justice to govern an outcome." Acting more assertively, mediators may formulate creative and attractive solutions that can eliminate commitment problems among the parties; show how futile any future unilateral activity may be; promote the utility of cooperation and interdependence in the long run; and, most importantly, highlight that the present situation is unsustainable and requires immediate solution (Beardsley et al. 2006; Vuković 2015a). As a consequence, proposed formulas pull the parties to start realizing an opening of the endgame, and potentially capitalizing on it.

While driving the parties toward a specific outcome in the endgame, mediators are faced with the task of reducing the likelihood that conflicting parties will use mediation for devious reasons, such as regrouping, rearming, stalling, buying time, seeking international support and legitimacy, etc. and the utility for conflicting parties of doing so (Richmond 1998). In fact, accepting mediation does not automatically imply that the parties will be fully committed to finding a mutually acceptable solution. Owing to the voluntary nature of any mediation activity, participants maintain full autonomy over the decision regarding whether or not to accept proposed formulas. Walking away from the process is an option that each participating party may resort to if they are not satisfied with what was offered at the table. As every participant essentially has a veto power, manifested through the possibility of walking away, mediators are also faced with the challenge of formulating solutions that can overcome the "joint decision traps": situations that are prone to produce solutions that are reduced to the lowest common denominator, because the negotiators may otherwise veto each other's proposals (Scharpf 1988).

Building creative solutions often requires considerable resources from mediators, and hence a mediator as a *manipulator*. In order to make proposed agreements mutually enticing, mediators provide the disputants with various incentives that can take the form of immediate material gains, political cover that enhances domestic and international legitimacy, and guarantees of implementation assistance (Ohlson 2008; Beardsley 2011). In essence, these enticements are intended to help the parties reframe their relationships and promote cooperative behavior. However, such incentives are most needed in situations when facilitation and formulation fail to identify a ZOPA. When the parties lack enthusiasm to settle and are reluctant to compromise, more assertive third-party intervention is needed (Rubin 1980; Carnevale & Pruitt 1992; Sisk 2009; Bercovitch 2009). This type of mediation strategy is commonly referred to as "mediation with muscle" (Fisher & Keashley 1991;

Svensson 2007; Beardsley 2009) or manipulation (Touval & Zartman 2001; Beardsley *et al.* 2006). In such cases mediators use available material and non-material resources in order to affect the payoff structures of the bargaining process. Using various forms of leverage, the mediators increase the costs of the ongoing conflict, thereby reducing the appeal of non-compliance, while simultaneously enhancing the utility of a negotiated solution. These incentives induce the parties to recalibrate their preferences and develop a ZOPA, and encourage them to close the peacemaking process with a mutually acceptable solution.

Depending on mediators' abilities and interests, the three strategies are used intermittently throughout the process, and in the endgame specifically. While in the initial stages of mediation third parties may use the three strategies in order to ripen the conflict for resolution and sell the prospects of a way out through mediated negotiations – such as by using shuttle diplomacy to facilitate the initial softening up to diplomacy, conducting fact-finding missions to acquire relevant information, carrying out agenda-setting in order to narrow down the scope and give clarity to the process, including or excluding certain parties depending on their ability to participate in or spoil the process, applying diplomatic, economic, and military measures in order to decrease the utility of the ongoing conflict and increase the appeal of negotiations – in the endgame these three strategies are used to foster a sense of urgency to accept a presented formula. Using the relevant information acquired throughout the process, in the endgame mediators assume the responsibility to formulate and communicate the enticing nature of a proposed settlement, and if possible project a tailor-made set of incentives that can be realized only if the agreement is accepted. In order to effectively drive the parties through the endgame, mediators may inform them of an impending catastrophe if they don't immediately settle, use procedural tools – such as strict deadlines – to expedite the process, resort to ultimatums and threats of walking away in order to foster a sense of urgency to accept the settlement, and communicate the extent of political cover, implementation assistance, and international legitimacy they may grant to the parties if they promptly and constructively end the conflict. Evidently, the effectiveness in the endgame is contingent on mediators' ability to leverage the parties into accepting the negotiated terms forthwith.

Leverage

In order to stimulate concession-making behavior, mediators are not only required to provide the parties with creative formulas germane to the substance of the dispute. They are also expected to apply some form of influence that would drive the parties toward a specific formula within a newly developed ZOPA. The driving is contingent upon available resources at mediators' disposal. These resources are generally associated with mediators' leverage or power (Touval 1992; Touval & Zartman 2001). According to Bercovitch and his colleagues, leverage "enhances the mediator's ability to influence an outcome" (Bercovitch, Anagnoson & Wille 1991, 15). Therefore, mediation is commonly understood as a "process involving the exercise of power" (Smith 1994, 446). In international mediation, power represents "the ability to move a party in an intended direction" (Touval & Zartman 2001, 436). Moreover, for Zartman and Touval (1985, 40), "leverage is the ticket to mediation – third parties are only accepted as mediators if they are likely to produce an agreement or help the parties out of a predicament, and for this they usually need leverage." Following this line of thought, some scholars have argued that successful mediation is contingent upon mediators' ability to bring to bear sufficient leverage on the parties (Touval 1992; Svensson 2007).

Using French and Raven's (1959) study of social power, Carnevale classified seven types used in the peacemaking process: reward power; coercive power; legitimate power; expert power; referent power; information power; and relational power (Carnevale 2002). The common feature of all of them is that they are resource-based, both material and non-material in nature. The most material forms of all social power are the so-called carrots and sticks, reward and coercive power, or gratification (the ability to add resources to an outcome) and deprivation (the ability to withhold resources from one side or to direct them toward the other) (Touval & Zartman 2001, 437). On the one side, reward power entails mediators' capacity to compensate the parties for their cooperative behavior and reduce the appeal of dueling. This can be done through promises of economic aid, security guarantees, and implementation assistance. On the other, coercive power refers to various forms of threats and punishments – such as the use of diplomatic measures, the establishment of sanctions regimes, or the employment of military power – intended to limit defection and increase the costs of an ongoing conflict. The main purpose of carrots and sticks is to provide side payments intended to make the proposed MEO more enticing than a continued conflict. At the same time, they are used to expedite the peacemaking process in order to reduce or avoid potential dragging by the parties.

Given the tangible nature of carrots and sticks, these two types of power can be grouped into what Nye (2008) calls "hard power." Both are used to bring the parties to move toward a mutually acceptable solution, by means of the promise of rewards for compliance and the threat of penalty for defiance. However, since mediation is primarily a voluntary process, mediators need be apprehensive that hard power may produce adverse results: Putting more pressure on the parties may create more resistance, and as a result contribute to conflict intractability. In order to avoid such undesirable scenarios, mediators might be inclined to co-opt the parties into cooperation and acceptance of a proposed solution. Borrowing from Nye's concept of "soft power," through co-option a mediator may "get the parties to want the outcomes [it] wants" (Nye 2008, 96). Touval and Zartman (2001, 438) call this the power of persuasion, as it is aimed at reorienting parties' perceptions away from conflict and toward a compromise solution. In order to do so, mediators have to appeal to the parties through culture, political values, and foreign policies. In French and Raven's (1959, 154) terms, soft or persuasive power may be traced in the remaining forms of social power. On the one side, mediators may attract the parties into compliance with a proposed solution because of their expertise in the matter, or their ability to provide relevant information "which makes compliance with mediator's requests seem rational" (Carnevale 2002, 29). On the other, mediators may lead by example, by virtue of their institutional status, international reputation, or personal charisma, which can be used as tools of attraction. Finally, mediators may drive the parties toward a solution on the basis of the "belief that mediators have the right to prescribe behavior"; this legitimate power "derives from a norm that has been accepted by the disputants ... and influence rests on a judgment of how one *should* act, and the authority determines the standard" (Carnevale 2008, 28).

It is important to note that the field of international mediation is becoming increasingly crowded. Rarely does a single mediator have the capacity or the willingness to muster the resources needed for effective management of highly intractable conflicts. For this reason, mediators often engage collectively, conducting what is generally referred to as multiparty mediation activities (Crocker, Hampson & Aall 1999; Vuković 2015a). While these endeavors may lead to disastrous results if various mediators lack the ability to cooperate and coordinate their activities, the advantage of multiparty mediation processes rests on the fact that it allows mediators to pool their leverages, share responsibilities, and reduce relative costs of managing conflicts. However, this type of shared leverage is possible only once mediators have achieved coherence of action. More specifically, they need to show willingness to develop a shared diagnosis of the problem, work from a common script, accept their particular roles in order to avoid undermining each other's work, and most importantly apply the required leverages in a coordinated manner (Crocker *et al.* 2015, 2016; Vuković 2015a). This coherence of action is particularly important in the final stages of mediation processes. On the one hand, it will allow mediators to act as a united front that can incentivize and drive the disputing parties toward a solution in a way that would be impracticable for a single mediator. On the other, it will limit the disputing sides' maneuvering space for forum shopping and stalling.

Formulating MEOs

While various resources may be used to induce a sense of a mutually hurting stalemate – ranging from various forms of threats to promises – the same can be said about the formulation of MEOs, which are an essential feature of the endgame. As noted by Ohlson, "positive incentives and constructive elements, some form of MEO, conceived and born during the dialogue phase, has to be added in order to sustain the perception of ripeness, maintain the faith of the parties in the resolution process, hold out promises of future rewards and, thus, continue to reduce mutual distrust and fear" (Ohlson 2008, 148). The development of MEOs relies on the mediators' ability to persuade the parties that a proposed solution is in their best interest: While the parties may have to reformulate their intransigent positions, their essential interests and needs will be met in a way that outdoes the prolongation of the conflict and dueling. Solutions associated with MEOs are characterized by distinct features: *mutuality*, *interdependence*, *cooperation*, and *exclusivity*. As such, they acquire their final shape only in the endgame stages of the process, once all of the relevant information has been acquired and the mediators have accepted the challenge of formulating viable solutions backed by the necessary incentives.

As indicated by the name, MEOs represent outcomes that are formulated so that they do not favor one side over the other. The notion of acceptability or mutuality implies that the parties are driven to accept a solution that serves not only their interests, but also the interests of their counterparts. The reframing that is done under the mediators' guidance projects the interests no longer as a zero-sum, but as mutually compatible and complementary. Moreover, the reframing is done in such a way as to promote equity over equality, and fairness over parity. Both of these features are purely perceptual. While equality would imply equal distribution of value, regardless of the parties' actual interests, needs, and prevailing conditions (i.e. 50–50 solution), equitable solution favors an outcome where issue saliency for each party is taken into account in order to develop trade-offs that accommodate diverging interests and needs. These trade-offs are designed in such a way as to promote relative gains, instead of absolute ones. As a consequence, parties are encouraged to assess the outcome through the lens of fairness, which entails "an evenhanded process and equitable outcome" (Bercovitch 2005).

MEOs also represent solutions that promote interdependence. The newly established (micro)regime between the parties will be used to regulate future disputes over the matter in a predictable and controlled manner. The reason why they accept such constraints can be traced back to the "enticing" nature of these solutions. On the one side, MEOs represent opportunities that are unattainable to the parties through unilateral action, and are contingent upon their cooperative behavior. The benefits related to these solutions are available only as long as the parties are willing to cooperate. Defection terminates the benefits. On the other side, MEOs may also contain incentives provided by the mediators, intended to increase the attractiveness of cooperation and reduce the appeal of defection. These incentives are not only unattainable for parties through unilateral action, but also unachievable through bilateral engagement. In other words, they are *exclusive* to the mediated peace process. It is therefore the presence of mediators and their incentives that entices the parties to cooperate on two different levels – between the parties themselves, and between mediators and individual parties. Potential defection by the disputants will not only damage the (already fragile) relations between them, but would also ruin their existing or newly established relations with the mediators. Overall, MEOs are not just any type of solution. They represent a carefully designed set of incentives formulated and projected in such a way as to encourage parties to develop trust and confidence in each other, promote interdependence, and regulate their future relations. The ability of mediators to drive the parties away from dueling in the last stages of the peacemaking process is directly dependent on their capacity to formulate such solutions and persuade the parties that they are truly in their best interests.

Mediators as Drivers: Reducing the Dragging through Tactical Moves

The very exhaustive list of social forms of power does not address the core question: *How* do mediators use these leverages in order to make the parties accept a specific solution in the endgame? Therefore, it is very important to distinguish between what mediators *bring to* the table and what they *do* at the table, especially in the last phase of the talks. In other words, it is useful to discern a nuanced nature of power, which entails both the will and the skill of mediators (Komorita 1977; Lawler 1992). Treating power as a mere set of resources and possessions does not provide us with a clear idea of the actual effects and actions taken by mediators to produce those effects. As noted by Schelling (1960), the ability to muster extensive financial and military resources, and the capacity to withstand extensive costs, do not automatically translate into an advantageous negotiating position. On the contrary, these resources may be countered with specific tactical moves by a "weaker" party (in the sense of resources) such as bluffing, deceiving, making relational claims, projecting tailored information, or invoking specific rules, norms, and values. These tactical moves may favor a weaker party, as they put pressure on the stronger one to perceive those tactics as credible, and choose to accept such commitments instead of getting no agreement (Carnevale 2002, 28).

As noted by Touval and Zartman (2001, 439), "the mediator's leverage is based in the parties' need for the solution it is able to produce and on its ability to produce attractive solutions from each party." Accordingly, mediators exercise their tactical influence in a variety of ways, made possible by the very fact that they are present in the process (Pruitt & Carnevale 1993). There are several tactical tools that mediators may apply in order to drive the parties toward a specific outcome, minimize their dueling, undermine the temptation to use dragging to produce additional benefits, and ensure that proposed solutions are truly enticing, and that they represent a once-in-a-lifetime opportunity. These include various forms of control and manipulation of communication, reputation, procedure, and relations (Carnevale 2002, 33). As the following sections will echo, each one of these tools is applied in the endgame in order to create a sense of enticing opportunities, predictability in decision-making, and, most importantly, urgency to find a solution.

Mediators may use acquired information in order to *restructure concessions* made by the parties. While dueling may be characterized by maximalist demands and minimal concessions, mediators may provide (or impose) their own interpretations of these offers and indicate their relative utility, a possibility delineated in the discussion in Chapter 12 by Janice Gross Stein. Moreover, given the prevailing suspicion and mistrust between the parties in the last stage, they may also use mediators to propose specific solutions as trial balloons in order to avoid being perceived as weak and yielding by the other side. While mediators may accept such delegated responsibility, they may also use these inputs to formulate a final solution intended to end the process in a balanced and mutually enticing way. During the last days of mediated negotiations in Dayton, when the issue of Sarajevo was discussed, Milošević proposed a line along the river that would split the city in half, keeping large parts of the city (namely the neighborhood of Grbavica) in the hands of Bosnian

Serbs. Holbrooke knew that this proposal was inevitably going to be rejected by Bosnian Muslims. Instead of rejecting the proposal outright, Holbrooke informed Milošević that his novel suggestion for Sarajevo was a huge concession, and a move in the right direction, but not enough for Izetbegović to agree. He asked him to empathize with Izetbegović. After hearing this from mediators, Milošević stopped insisting on his proposal. Soon after that, when Warren Christopher drew a line that included Grbavica for Bosnian Muslims, and exclaimed "This is our line, the American line," Milošević did not object (Holbrooke 1998, 291).

Similarly, mediators might need to *redefine previously made agreements* that did not address the interests and concerns of specific parties. During the last days leading to the Good Friday Agreement, Mitchell had to cope with a negotiated formula between Blair and Ahern on Strand Two (i.e. North–South cross-border bodies) which he knew was unacceptable to the unionists in Northern Ireland. However, while this was certainly an impediment for the achievement of the final agreement, he used it as an opportunity: If Strand Two were amended sufficiently to accommodate unionist claims, he required simultaneous concessions from them on other issues in order to create mutually enticing solutions. The redefinition of Strand Two propelled the parties into an agreement (Mitchell 2000, 177).

In order to undermine dragging in the last segments of the talks, mediators may also use a specific type of information in order to *create a sense of urgency*. The anecdote from the introduction of this chapter is indicative of this tactical move. It was preceded by a demonstration of extreme frustration by Secretary Christopher, who voiced his discontent with Izebegović's intransigence and inability to perceive the enticing nature of the solution proposed to him. As a consequence, Christopher and Holbrooke used the *"threat of walking away"* as a way of putting an unyielding party under severe pressure: If the Americans were to walk away, all of the benefits proposed until that moment in Dayton would be eliminated, and it would inevitably have a damaging effect on Bosnia's future relations with the United States. It was the threat of losing these incentives that prompted Izetbegović to yield and agree to terms.

Closing the Endgame

If parties resort to threats of walking away, mediators may promote information that would invoke a similar *threat of damaged relations*. During the last days of the Camp David talks, dissatisfied with what had been proposed thus far, Sadat informed everyone that he and his delegation were leaving. As a demonstration of credible commitment to this threat he even made everyone in his delegation pack their bags. In reaction to this, Jimmy Carter (quoted in Quandt 1986, 239) wrote a letter to Sadat, where he emphasized the following points:

It will mean first of all an end to the relationship between the United States and Egypt. There is no way we can ever explain this to our people. It would mean an end to this peacekeeping effort, into which I have put so much investment. It would probably mean the end of my Presidency because this whole effort will be discredited. And last but not least, it will mean the end of something that is very precious to me: my friendship with you. Why are you doing it?

One of the main reasons why many mediated negotiations fail rests in the fact that parties may perceive proposed solutions as politically very costly and detrimental to their reputation. Mediators have to be sensitive to the fact that a potential solution can be found only within an overlap of domestic expectations and international possibilities. Hence conflicting parties may resist any agreement that they deem difficult to sell back home. In Bosnia, one of the main impediments to the final agreement was the inability to reach the infamous 51–49 formula for land distribution. This proved to be the most salient point for Milošević, who could not back away from a publicly stated commitment prior to his arrival to Dayton. At one point he even said "give me anything ... rocks, swamps, hills, anything, as long as it gets us to 49–51" (Holbrooke 1998, 302). By accommodating this request, mediators were able to elicit a substantial concession from Milošević, to place Brčko under international arbitration – a concession he could make as he had never publically addressed the issue, and thus regarding which he had more room to maneuver. Evidently, in order to drive the parties into acceptance, mediators may resort to specific *face-saving tactics* through which they clarify and provide constructive interpretations of the unfolding events, and provide political cover with the aim of encouraging concession exchange.

However, Milošević's last minute concession on Brčko was mainly induced by another tactical move effectively employed by the mediators. Faced with unyielding positions by all parties, despite the fact that "the conference was stalled within sight of its goal," Holbrooke and Christopher started contemplating the idea of accepting failure as a very likely outcome (Holbrooke 1998, 301). Instead of accepting defeat, they decided to test how the parties would react if proposed MEOs were given a rapidly approaching expiration date. For this reason they decided to *draft and distribute a statement of failure* intended to be made public at a specific time. The window between distribution and public announcement was intentionally reduced, and created an artificial sense of urgency, assuming the quality of an *ultimatum*: unless the parties complied with the mediators' request and accepted the terms, the public announcement would shift the blame for failure onto them, the "dead-cat effect" used by James Baker (Holbrooke 1998, 188, 204), coupled with the loss of MEOs and damaged relations with mediators.

Statements of failure can be also used to put more pressure on a specific party through *shaming and blaming* for the lack of cooperative behavior. This was a tactic used by Carter during the Camp David talks. In order to induce compliance and cooperation from Begin, Carter drafted a public statement (which was never used) where he would

> explain the gap had existed on the eve of Camp David. He would then announce that Sadat was prepared to make major concessions, which he would enumerate, such as full recognition of Israel, detailed security provisions, and an interim period of autonomy for the West Bank ... only two issues now prevented agreement. One was Begin's unwillingness to give up the settlements in Sinai. The other was his refusal to acknowledge that the withdrawal provision of the U.N. Resolution 242 would govern the final negotiations on the status of the West Bank and Gaza. On both points Carter was prepared to say that he sided with Sadat. (Quandt 1986, 240)

Mediators may also use specific procedural tactics in order to foster a sense of urgency. One of these is setting a very *strict agenda with strong deadlines*. Working with strict agendas and strong deadlines is a common approach among mediators. Holbrooke planned a seventeen-day conference, that would end around Thanksgiving week (Holbrooke 1998). Carter proposed a twelve-day conference (Quandt 1986). The Northern Ireland peace process was designed to last exactly fourteen days. According to Mitchell, the first four days were expected to be used in order to solicit comments from the parties about the situation at hand, and hear their suggestions of possible solutions. Then on the fifth day the mediators planned to produce a first draft of a comprehensive compromise agreement, which the parties would have over night to review. Days six and seven were intended to solicit reactions, which would be integrated into a second draft resolution on day eight. Finally, from day nine until day thirteen the parties would conduct final negotiations, which should be concluded on day fourteen. Despite such a strict agenda Mitchell knew that the endgame was not going to be easily controlled. For this reason, he made two very important procedural choices. First, he decided to use the highly symbolic nature of the Easter holidays, in order to elicit a sense of responsibility among the parties. Secondly, he set the official final deadline on Thursday prior to the holidays, knowing that in the likely case of it being breached, the parties would have to cope with mounting pressure to work and deliver something on the subsequent holiday (Mitchell 2000, 145). Two days before the scheduled end of the conference, faced with dragging behavior from Blair and Ahern on Strand Two, Mitchell (2000, 173) told them

> When we start on Thursday morning, it has to be clear to everyone that we'll continue until we finish, one way or the other. There can be no discussion of a pause or a break. I intend to tell the parties that I won't even consider such a request. If someone says to me, "We're nearly there but we're all tired, let's break until next week," I'm going to say "That's completely out of the question. There's not going to be a break, not for a week, not for a day, not for an hour. We're here until we finish. We'll either get an agreement or we'll fail to get an agreement. Then we'll all go out together and explain to the press and the waiting world how we succeeded or why we failed.

Deadlines, also discussed in Chapter 15 by P. Terrence Hopmann, are useful insomuch as they create psychological pressure on parties that MEOs may be lost unless they make an effort to make costly concessions. They give procedural clarity, and project potential responsibility for missing out on reaching an agreement. Most importantly, they are used to create a sense of desperation and exhaustion that induces the parties to make very politically sensitive deals. During the Dayton peace talks, most of the deals were made late at night after hours of excruciating negotiations. Even the "thirty-seven minute peace," where Milošević and Silajdžić agreed on a 51–49 formula, was reached at 4 in the morning. While the concessions that they made were certainly induced by timing pressures imposed by American mediators, the exhausting nature of such talks actually backfired, as it clouded everyone's judgment: In their euphoria over the agreement, they forgot to include the Croatian delegation, which, once presented with the deal, rejected it outright (Holbrooke 1998).

Finally, mediators may apply *pressure by using power from other third parties*, notably by going to a high authority, as Larry Crump also finds in Chapter 6. The final deadlocks in the Northern Irish and Bosnian peace talks were surpassed when mediators decided to have President Clinton use his reputation and relational power with the disputing sides in order to elicit final concessions from them and encourage them to sign an agreement (Mitchell 2000, 178; Holbrooke 1998, 302). Along with external pressures, mediators may use *intra-group pressures* as well. In Camp David, "the Americans tried to put pressure on Begin from within his own delegation, whereas they sought to give Sadat arguments to use to convince his advisors" (Quandt 1986, 237).

Conclusion

The final stages of any mediated negotiation process are characterized by rapid developments as each side has to decide which trade-offs are worth committing to. These are the crucial moments when parties accept to abandon previously defined non-negotiable positions, and opt for movement toward a solution previously perceived as unattainable and/or unacceptable. The rapid pace of these developments increases the likelihood of potential mistakes, which in turn threaten to push the entire process over the edge. In such delicate times mediators play a crucial role in driving the parties toward a carefully formulated and structured outcome. Although the mediators do not have the same level of responsibility for finding the solution as conflicting parties, their involvement makes them an essential piece of the peace puzzle.

Acting as drivers, the mediators facilitate communication between the parties, assist them in formulating viable alternatives to settle their dispute, and finally, if needed, provide attractive incentives in order to entice them to find a mutually acceptable solution. While taking the parties out of the conflict implies activities that will induce a perception among the disputing sides that their conflict has become unbearable and detrimental to their interests, moving the parties toward a peaceful solution is directly linked to mediators' ability to persuade the parties to accept a solution that offers enticing opportunities unavailable to them both through fighting and through bilateral negotiations. These enticing opportunities are projected toward each one of the conflicting parties in such a way as to emphasize mutuality, interdependence, cooperation, and the exclusivity of the solutions proposed by mediators. These mutually enticing opportunities represent inducements formulated and proposed as a way to encourage trust and confidence among the parties, promote their interdependence, and regulate their future relations.

In the most resistant cases, mediators embody the essential driving factor that moves the parties away from a potentially devious behavior in the peacemaking process and into an effective endgame. As the mediators become aware that the solution is within reach, in the final stages of the process they may opt to keep the parties mindful of an imminent catastrophe if they decide to defect from the process, they may use procedural tools to expedite the process and foster a sense of urgency to accept the deal, and they may project various incentives that they are ready to grant to the parties if they promptly and constructively end the conflict. Therefore, when parties are either unable or unwilling to end their conflict through peaceful means, the mediators assume the responsibility to construct the endgame for them and lead them through it in an effective manner.

10   Mediating Closure: Timing for a MHS

Isak Svensson

When is enough enough? This chapter will focus on the issue of *timing* in international mediation. The debate on timing (including the discussion about ripeness) has been one of the most important debates within the research on international mediation. The attention has been on identifying the conducive conditions for when constructive mediation and attempts at negotiation toward a solution of an armed conflict can be meaningfully initiated. Yet, relatively little attention has been paid to the other end of the spectrum: when it is most appropriate to *end* mediation efforts. This chapter, along with others in this volume, tries to address this lacuna. How do mediators draw mediation to a closure, and which tactical approaches are the most effective to reach the endpoint of third-party mediation? The focus here is on third-party mediation in internal armed conflicts, and the mediator's role in deciding between dragging and driving in the endgame, by outlining the broader conditions deciding the end point in mediation efforts. The following analysis is anchored in a rational cost–benefit analysis seen from the perspective of the mediators, an analysis that with all its limitations still gives us a good basis for thinking theoretically and conceptually about the termination of the mediation process.

The discussion here will focus on the conditions under which mediation efforts end, either through bringing the process to its end in an agreement (Type I), or alternatively when it is decided to end an unfruitful mediation attempt (Type II) and, in some cases, hand the process over to another mediator. Seen from the perspective of the mediators, the basic rationale for engagement depends on two major factors: the costs and benefits of the mediation engagement for the mediator versus the costs and benefits of the potential agreement. The benefits of the potential agreement are, in turn, determined by four factors: (1) the likelihood of gaining results through mediation; (2) the costs of the conflict at hand and potentially in the future; (3) the time it would take to reach a result; and (4) the value of a potential agreement (from the mediators' point of view). The value of the mediation efforts is a function of the perceived costs of the mediation efforts relative to the alternatives, as well as the perceived benefits that can arise from the fact that a mediator is engaged in a peace process, also relative to its alternatives. Consequently, the higher the chance of a settlement, the less important are the costs of the mediation engagement.

Getting to a Closure

One form of closure of a mediation engagement – in fact, the ideal form of closure – is through the reaching and signing of an agreement between the parties, which regulates their conflicting aspirations through a mutually acceptable deal. When the process is at a stage of closure, the conditions for bringing it to a successful end depend largely on the mediator's ability to utilize the incentives for settling the conflict. The role of the mediator is to continuously build confidence between the parties, as well as to maintain basic incentives for settling the conflict. At the end it is crucial to utilize the positive momentum of the process, and create space for settlement by identifying a focal point for the ending. The dynamics in the end of a negotiated peace process create a sort of dilemma for the mediator. Both sides would like to continue to negotiate in order to get a better deal, yet, neither the parties nor the mediator would like to risk the deal altogether. Zartman points to the underlying question of timing in the Introduction of this volume: "Should one continue to negotiate to try to get more, would pushing further push agreement out of reach, is there just or not quite enough to make for a positive outcome?" Thus, there is a trade-off to be made between continuing negotiations and reaching a deal. Parties engaged in the negotiation process will have incentives to try to get a better outcome in an agreement and it is therefore the mediators' job to try to get the parties to a closure.

The chance of getting a result depends on whether the underlying conditions are ripe – whether the parties perceive themselves as being stuck in a mutually hurting stalemate which is costly, whether the parties perceive openings for a solution (enticing opportunities), and also, to some extent, whether the parties have sorted out the question of valid spokespersons. Yet, these conditions can change throughout the process: Power relationships may shift, leading parties to re-evaluate the chances for making progress on the battlefield, and splinter dynamics or spoiler behavior may imply that the negotiation spokespersons are losing control over their own side's action and thereby cease to be valid spokespersons. Different external events may therefore end the moment of opportunity. An empirical example of when the issue of valid spokespersons meant an end (or rather a pause) to the mediation efforts is in Sri Lanka, when

President Kumaratunga carried out the mini-coup in November 2003, taking over control from the Prime-Minister Wickremasinghe. The Norwegian mediators decided to call off the mediation efforts until the authority question had been resolved on the government side (Höglund & Svensson 2011).

When the conditions are ripe – the existence of a mutually hurting stalemate, enticing opportunities, and present valid spokespersons – the momentum still has to be capitalized upon by the mediator. Hence, the mediator should bring a negotiation to an end before the conditions change, and at the same time try to sort out as many of the major disputed questions as possible. This creates a balancing act: The quality of the agreement would generally be enhanced the longer the negotiations continue, and by factors such as the inclusion of the civil society. However, including actors and sorting out problems take time, and processes that are drawn out risk losing momentum, creating space for spoilers to mobilize and the underlying conditions to change due to external events, or shifts in persons at the negotiation table. Thus, the mediator needs to weigh the time pressure to reach an agreement when the moment is ripe to settle against the quality of the agreement that would be enhanced by broader deliberations, the design of more robust post-conflict institutional arrangements, and by bringing up and sorting out more questions on the negotiation table. Therefore, timing the end of a mediation process depends on finding the optimal trade-off between the incentives for settling the conflict and resolving as many of the problems as possible. The situation when no more problems can be brought to the table without jeopardizing the incentive for terminating the conflict would be a situation in which mediators can bring the process to a meaningful closure.

This can help us to understand the sequencing of big or small issues toward the end phase. On the one hand, mediators have incentives to get the parties to reach a solution, capitalizing on the momentum gained in the process. Thereby, they may judge it to be worthwhile to wait with some of the larger issues in order to actually pin down an agreement, before the conducive conditions evaporate. The clock is ticking and, if an agreement is not reached, the moment may pass by. On the other hand, mediators have incentives to enhance the quality of the agreement by bringing up and resolving deeper and larger issues in the process. There is a tension between time and quality, and it is up to the mediator to assess the appropriate balance between these contradictory forces.

In the Israeli–Palestinian negotiations in 1993 the parties and mediators decided to start with smaller issues. The Oslo I Accord was concluded in 1993, with the help of a secret mediation channel, the so-called Oslo channel, that had been established in Norway. The accord was a partial peace agreement to establish Palestinian self-rule in Gaza and Jericho. The negotiations on permanent Palestinian self-rule were to begin within three years, and within five years a final peace agreement was to be concluded (Waage 2004, 135–136). More difficult questions, such as the status of Jerusalem and Israeli settlements on occupied land, were not addressed in the accord. Instead, these delicate matters were to be discussed and solved in the final peace agreement (Egeland 1999, 531). Another significant partial peace agreement, known as the Oslo II Accord, was signed in 1995. The agreement stipulated further withdrawal of Israeli forces from the West Bank (Egeland 1999, 540). After this agreement the process that had been initiated in 1993 in Oslo halted and the parties did not reach a stage at which they could conclude a final peace agreement.

A similar case is the mediation process in the Kosovo conflict. In 1999 a partial peace agreement, the Kosovo Peace Plan, was concluded between the government in Belgrade and the Kosovo Liberation Army. The main incompatibility, the political status of Kosovo, was not solved – it was left to be handled in the future. Instead, the plan stipulated the withdrawal of Serbian military and police from Kosovo and the establishment of an international force, led by NATO, in the area. The question of the political status was addressed in 2005 when the former President of Finland, Martti Ahtisaari, who had been one of three mediators in 1999, was assigned by the United Nations to negotiate between the parties and present a proposal to the Security Council on how to solve the political incompatibility.

One way for the mediator to handle this trade-off between quality (value) and chance (probability) of agreements is through *deadlines*, as discussed also by P. Terrence Hopmann in Chapter 15. The mediator in a negotiation process can try to deal with as many questions as possible, and to do this in as broad a manner as possible, within a given timeframe. That timeframe can be either one imposed by external events, or a self-imposed one. Former US President Bill Clinton's intensive mediation efforts in the Camp II process of year 2000 between Israel and Palestine is an example of a deadline imposed by external events, where the changing of presidents in the United States implied a watershed and a cut-off point in the process. There was an opening for a solution, with an American President committed to finding a comprehensive negotiated settlement to the conflict. There can also be self-imposed deadlines. The former Finnish President Ahtisaari imposed such a deadline when he was assigned to be the mediator in the Indonesia–Aceh peace process. Ahtisaari mediated on the request of the parties, and from the outset he told them that he would be available as a mediator only for six months. This meant that they should reach an agreement by the fall of 2006.

The timeframe generated an overall time pressure on the negotiations and made sure that the parties did not dwell too much on each issue (Merikallio 2006).

Ideally, agreements also entail regulations about the implementation of the stipulations, so that issues of disputes surrounding the implementation could be regulated. Yet, an agreement seldom means an entire end to the conflict; more usually it is merely the beginning of the end: Mediators may be needed throughout the implementation period to hinder the relapse of the conflict back into violence. Ahtisaari was invited back to the Aceh process after the peace deal had been reached in order to help negotiate issues also in the implementation phase (Merikallio 2006).

As these examples illustrates, the end dynamics of mediation is an essential element that needs to be taken into account in order to understand how mediation unfolds. How mediators time the closure, or relate to externally driven endpoints, is pivotal for understanding how mediation can contribute meaningfully in the process from war to peace.

When to End Unfruitful Mediation Attempts

There is also the question of whether mediation efforts should end, short of an agreement. Here again a basic cost–benefit analysis can help one to understand the logic of mediation termination. Mediators can have incentives to continue a mediation process even if the mediation effort has a low probability of reaching a result, just because the costs of the conflict are so high. This we have evidence of in the case when the UN mediation in the Syrian conflict was being led by the envoy Staffan de Mistura: The mediator still carried on, driven by consideration of the vast costs of a continuous conflict, even though many times the prospects for a positive outcome looked bleak. By contrast, when the mediation intervention is costly, when there are few possibilities to reach results (or it will take a very long time to obtain such results), or when the conflict is of little negative consequence for the third parties themselves, then we would expect mediators to end the mediation efforts. Thus, mediators will bring unfruitful processes to an end when the costs and risks of the mediation effort (including the risk that mediation merely serves as a rhetorical fig-leaf hiding the intentions of the belligerents) outweigh the benefits of mediation.

Mediation efforts are generally not particularly expensive compared with other types of third-party engagement, such as peacekeeping, international sanctions, and aid. Yet, if the third parties are at risk, then the parties may indeed decide to end the mediation efforts. The Norwegian mediation team in Sri Lanka came to such a situation in June 2006, when they decided to examine whether they should end their engagement, given that the security issue for mediators, or rather the unarmed monitors on the ground, rapidly deteriorated (Höglund & Svensson 2011).

The ending of mediation efforts can also be seen as a signal. It can be used by the mediators to send a strong message, for example, that the actors involved are not taking the mediation process sufficiently seriously. For example, the former UN Secretary General Kofi Annan ended his mediation effort in Syria partly in disappointment at the lack of commitment from the UN Security Council and its members. Also his successor, the Algerian diplomat Lakhdar Brahimi, stated that he also ended his mediation effort due to a lack of commitment from the warring parties and the international community (Lundgren 2016; Hinnebusch & Zartman 2015). When Swedish diplomat Jan Eliasson decided not to renew his mandate for mediating the conflict in Darfur in June 2008, he also wanted to send a clear signal to the warring parties and the Security Council that they were the main obstacles to reaching a peace agreement (Svensson & Wallensteen 2010, 98).

Even the threat of termination of mediation can, if it is credible, be an effective way to sharpen the minds of the participants in a negotiation process. According to Princen (1992), the termination tactic is the only source of leverage that all mediators have in common. When the Swedish diplomat Gunnar Jarring was mediating in the Middle East after the Arab–Israeli War 1967, he threatened to terminate his mission unless the parties agreed to make concessions in the process (Touval 1982). This was an effective tactic, but Touval (1982, 146) argues that the parties adhered to the demand probably because they feared being accused of being the party that terminated the mediation effort, rather than believing that the mediation process would succeed; this is the "dead-cat effect" identified by James Baker (Holbrooke 1998, 188, 200).

When an individual mediator or a mediation team steps down, the mediation process as a whole might continue with another third party. This has been the case in Syria: Kofi Annan was replaced by Lakhdar Brahimi, and Staffan de Mistura later replaced Brahimi. Annan chose not to renew his mandate as the UN–Arab League envoy after his six-point peace plan had failed. His successor, he said, might choose another path in order to solve the conflict (Lundgren 2016). Brahimi chose the same path, namely that of dealing with the great-power patrons of the two sides, and also failed (Hunnebusch & Zartman 2015). It should be mentioned that there could also be situations where new mediation efforts can be seen as new injections for the conflict mediation, while the old mediator might feel he/she has used all available tools. In 1971 Jarring presented a proposal to the conflicting parties in the

Arab–Israeli war. The proposal was met with negative reactions from all parties, who could not agree on even the basics of the proposal. Faced with this deadlock, Jarring felt that he had exhausted all the available options to mediate in the conflict. He remained as the official mediator until 1991, although his active phase as a mediator ended in 1971 (Mezagopian 2008, 188).

Lastly, there is the question of handing over the files: How do mediators lay the ground for subsequent third parties? There are many related questions here: How to identify a replacement? How to create institutional learning? The Swedish diplomat Jan Eliasson and his co-mediator Salim Salim decided to end their mediation efforts in Darfur, Sudan, in 2008 due to a lack of political will among the warring parties to reach a political settlement (Svensson & Wallensteen 2010, 98). In an attempt to reinvigorate the peace process in 2007, the mediation process had been set up as a cooperation between the United Nations (UN), represented by Eliasson, and the African Union (AU), represented by Salim. Throughout the process it became clear that having two lead negotiators at the negotiation table was not as fruitful as had been anticipated; on the contrary, the warring parties could play the mediators off against each other. In order to avoid this, Eliasson and Salim suggested that they should be followed by a single mediator who could represent both the UN and the AU. They had also realized that it would be better to find a mediator who was permanently stationed in the region and had a local context. They put a lot of effort into finding a suitable mediator from Africa who could step in as the lead negotiator in the peace process (Svensson & Wallensteen 2010, 100).

Mediation research, in particularly quantitatively oriented, has done a lot of work on the conditions explaining Entry of mediators. Yet, very little (if anything) has been done on explaining the conditions of various forms of Exit of mediators, and what kind of impact such exits have on the larger dynamics of conflicts. The framework here suggests some plausible ways in which we can theorize about the conditions under which mediators end their mediation efforts, and end them well. One potential future avenue for mediation research is therefore to examine empirically the point in time when mediation efforts are ended, and see whether we can bring light to bear on the termination dynamics of international mediation. It is to be hoped that this chapter, and this book as a whole, can contribute to that important endeavor.

11 Facing Impediments: Information and Communication

Andrew Kydd

What makes the end of a negotiation different from the beginning or the middle? While negotiations are ongoing, the alternative to an agreement now is more negotiations, and a possible agreement later. When the end is at hand, if an agreement is not reached now the parties will have to live without one for a while and the situation may deteriorate even further. This implies that the parties have greater incentives to make a concession when a negotiation is about to conclude than when the end is believed to be distant. In these moments of truth, the parties confront the possibility of failure head on and take a hard look at their own negotiating position, to see whether it can be adjusted to make an agreement more likely.

These last-minute concessions, however, need to be carefully managed to maximize the benefits and minimize the risks involved. The benefit of a concession is that it can be used to buy a counter-concession in exchange, and that, by moving toward the opponent's position, the concession should increase the chance that the opponent accepts the offer and a deal is struck. The downside of a concession is that it moves the potential agreement further from one's own ideal outcome, and may signal weakness to the other side, encouraging them to hope for further concessions. It may also signal weakness to domestic audiences on one's own side, leading them to undermine or reject the deal (Putnam 1988).

The communication strategies of the negotiators help to cope with these risks. There are two principal targets of communication within the negotiation, the other party and any third party or mediator who is present. Beyond these immediate audiences, one may also want to signal to the domestic audience at home and possibly the domestic audience of the other side.

When making a concession, negotiators strive to convey a number of things to their partner and mediator. First, they try to magnify the significance of the concession, so that the other side thinks they have achieved a big gain and so that third parties think the side making the concession has been reasonable and accommodating. This increases the perceived size of the concession and thereby should maximize the chance of acceptance. Secondly, they emphasize the difficulty in making the concession, how excruciating it was, how much of a sacrifice it was, how domestic audiences will find it difficult to accept, etc. Thirdly, they emphasize that there will be no further concessions, that this is the final offer. These strategies are in aid of minimizing inferences of weakness as a result of making the concession. Thus, the goal is to persuade the other side that the concession is huge, difficult to make, and final, as discussed further under concession aversion and loss aversion in Chapter 12 by Janice Gross Stein.

In addition to communicating to the negotiating parties, sometimes the parties like to signal to broader audiences that "a deal is near," or that "a deal is far away." A party that has just made an offer may wish to signal that the end is in sight, in order to put additional pressure on the other side to accept their concession. Rejecting it after an expectation that a deal is near has been generated looks additionally intransigent. A party that hopes for additional concessions will naturally want to say that a deal is far away, in order to increase the pressure for additional concessions.

The following discussion first shows how communication works in the three categories of negotiation, dueling, driving, and dragging. I then spell out the arguments made above in greater detail, looking at why concessions are likely in the endgame, how states strive to maximize their benefits and minimize their risks, and how they communicate with outside audiences to pressure their negotiating partners. It concludes with some thoughts on the role of creating value, destroying value, and the credibility of communication in the endgame.

Dueling, Driving, and Dragging

Zartman (in the Introduction to this volume) describes three types of negotiation. Dueling characterizes situations of extreme conflict of interest, where the parties see little prospect for joint gains and are very mistrustful. As a result, bargaining is very conflictual and focused on extracting concessions on zero-sum issues by making threats. This kind of negotiation is often observed in the context of civil wars and protracted conflicts like the Israeli–Palestinian conflict. Driving characterizes more positive-sum bargaining where the parties are more optimistic that there are joint gains to be had and believe it is worthwhile exploring to develop such gains. Driving is observed when parties have more businesslike relations, not characterized by mutual hatred or fear, but not especially friendly either. Dragging is a type of behavior seen when negotiators have given up on a particular negotiation but want to preserve the relationship between the negotiating parties. They therefore settle for a cosmetic agreement, or at least refrain from acrimonious casting of blame in the aftermath of what are essentially failed negotiations. This kind of behavior is seen among allies or trading partners when they realize an agreement is out of reach, but want to preserve the overall relationship and the possibility of future agreements.

Communication in dueling negotiations will be focused on committing to bottom lines, threatening punishment for lack of concessions, and casting blame for the failure of negotiations on the other side. In harsh, zero-sum negotiations, each side will entrench themselves in their bottom lines, striving to convince the other side that if they want peace it is they who must make the concessions. In order to extract concessions, threats will be used to persuade the other side that one is willing to walk away from the negotiations and return to conflict for as long as it takes to win. Finally, if, as is likely, the negotiations then fail, attention will shift to blaming the other side for the failure before third parties. The other side will be painted as aggressive, committed to illegitimate demands, and prone to bargaining in bad faith, while one's own side is presented as reasonable but under severe threat from the other.

In driving negotiations, communication will be more directed at searching and thrashing out areas of joint gains. The two sides will be in an exploratory mode, exchanging concessions that make both sides better off, and looking for more ways in which mutual cooperation could play out. In this context, shared or complementary interests will help assure honest communication about needs, interests, and capabilities, and so the parties will be able to clarify the scope of beneficial joint action. Negotiations between allies on how to fight a common enemy or between trading partners looking to maximize economic efficiency may have this characteristic.

Finally, dragging negotiations arise when partners decide a deal is not forthcoming but want to limit the political fallout from negotiating failure. Communication here will be targeted toward outsiders and will be designed to reassure nervous audiences that the relationship is still intact, that no backsliding is in evidence, and that forward momentum will resume in due course. This kind of communication accompanies failed rounds of trade negotiations and failed rounds of EU negotiations over deeper integration (Faure 2012). The parties sometimes devolve into bickering and casting of blame, but usually agree to limit such behavior in the interests of the ongoing relationship. Sometimes joint statements or non-binding resolutions are agreed upon that paper over the differences in the interests of presenting a facade of unity.

While communication is important in each of these three varied contexts, I argue that it is most important in the context of final concessions that, if made and accepted, make for a successful conclusion to a negotiation, and if not made or not accepted, spell failure. These concessions may arise in the context of the hard bargaining involved in dueling or the more businesslike bargaining of driving. When they are made, they are always packaged with appropriate communication, especially in dueling contexts, but in driving as well. This logic of communicating about concessions in the endgame needs further examination.

The Endgame

Negotiations take time because of information and uncertainty. If the negotiating parties could anticipate how they would turn out, who would make what concessions and what the eventual deal would look like, they would have an incentive to just implement that deal right away, rather than rack up the hotel bills. Conversely, if it could be foretold that a deal would not be possible, there would usually be no incentive to pretend to try, unless the parties were attempting to signal something to third parties. The uncertainty about whether a deal is possible and if so what it would look like is what negotiators are paid to resolve.[1]

The key thing that is uncertain is each side's bottom line, or the worst deal they would be willing to accept, defined by the best alternative (BATNA). If the bottom lines of each side were clear, and there were deals that both sides preferred over conflict, it would be relatively easy for them to pick one and implement it, and again, everyone but the hoteliers would be better off (Fearon 1995). However, we are not gifted with the ability to read minds, and minds are not always made up, so the preferences of others can only be guessed at, and this applies to their bottom lines as well.

Since the eventual deal must be located between the two sides' bottom lines, each side has a strong incentive to (a) discover the other side's bottom line, and (b) persuade the other side that one's own bottom line is as high as possible. Each side benefits by pushing the deal towards their opponent's bottom line. The question is, how far can you push? Each side wants to discover the other side's bottom line, to see how far they can push, and each side is attempting to persuade the other side that their bottom line is higher than it really is, so they will not push too far. Everyone realizes that this is what is going on, which makes straightforward communication about bottom lines so difficult, and subject to misrepresentation (Farrell & Rabin 1996). The pressure to abandon

---

[1] A similar analysis applies to war, which can be thought of as a very costly form of bargaining (Powell 2002).

subterfuge and lay one's cards on the table rises, however, as negotiations reach their conclusion.

Important and complex negotiations are often broken down into multiple issues that are negotiated by subcommittees of the two sides, or at least taken in sequence (Holbrooke 1998). Usually the easier or more technical issues are taken first, or assigned to lower-level people, while the most important "political" issues are reserved for later and for the highest-level negotiators, as illustrated in Larry Crump's Chapter 6. Progress can then be measured by how many tentative agreements are reached on the sub-issues. If there is little or no progress, then the negotiations will often peter out and end in failure without too much drama. If there is progress on the lower-level issues, however, then eventually there comes a moment of truth when the highest-level people must either complete the deal or walk away.

At these times, the pressure mounts. Negotiators start staying up late at night, drinking alcohol and coffee, smoking, eating bad food, sometimes talking for twenty-four hours at a time. This in itself is a signal of seriousness and the desire to reach a deal. Gone are the days when the parties would feign indifference as to whether a deal is reached or not, and fritter away time. The outlines of a deal have become clearer, and the parties now must decide whether or not to close on it.

The consequences of failing to agree therefore become stark. In the beginning and middle of a negotiation, failing to agree just means more bargaining. At the end, failing to agree means no agreement, at least for a while. This may mean simply the continuation of an existing bad situation, such as an ongoing civil war. Even in this case, however, the termination of negotiations eliminates for a time the hope of resolving the conflict, and so it makes the parties worse off, at least in expectation. When the Camp David negotiations mediated by President Clinton between Ehud Barak and Yasser Arafat in 2000 ended in acrimony, the two countries slid into the second intifada, in which thousands of Israelis and Palestinians lost their lives and the political (and physical) landscape was altered forever.

As a result, at these times the pressure to make concessions is the greatest. Negotiators are never too eager to make concessions in the early going, for fear of signaling weakness that will encourage the other side to hold out for more. As the end approaches and the consequences of failure become worse, negotiators start to consider carefully what concessions they could make and how they could be packaged to maximize their benefits and minimize their costs. So they begin to reinterpret positions, fudge differences, unlink things that have been linked, consider temporary deals, etc. When costs of disagreement are higher, then negotiators become more conciliatory.

Interestingly, negotiators may even have incentives to make concessions if they have concluded that an agreement is unlikely or even undesirable. If progress has been negligible, and the negotiations are about to fail, a last-minute concession that is unlikely to be accepted can serve to make a negotiating side look like it is striving for peace, while the other side bears responsibility for the failure of the negotiations. This could be useful with third parties and international audiences in the post-negotiations phase, when the two sides attempt to shift blame for the failure of negotiations on to the other. For instance, the aftermath of the Camp David negotiations generated extensive narratives that blamed the other side for their failure, with the Israeli narrative emphasizing the generosity of Barak's final proposals and the intransigence of Arafat, and the Palestinian narrative emphasizing the shortcomings of the Israeli proposal and the US bias towards Israel (Pressman 2003; Swisher 2004; Ross 2005). Another example is the Kosovo Liberation Army's acceptance of the Rambouillet accords, in the expectation that Serbia would reject them, leading to their preferred outcome of a war with NATO on their side (Daalder & O'Hanlon 2000; Kuperman 2008).

If concessions are to be made, however, they need to be made carefully, lest they give away more than is necessary and telegraph weakness to the other side and to domestic audiences. This dynamic was explored by Thomas Schelling (1966) in his discussion of how to duck out of commitments that have become inconvenient without encouraging further demands. A negotiator first has to decide how big a concession to make. The bigger the concession, the more likely it is to result in agreement. However, the bigger the concession, the more is given away, and the greater the criticism at home will be for having sold out the side. In addition, concessions may encourage intransigence on the other side by telegraphing weakness.[2] Once one side has retreated from previous demands, the following questions arise: How much further will you retreat? Where is your bottom line, now that we have discovered that it is not where you said it was, and why should we believe you now, when you say this is it, no further? The literature on reputation also suggests that initial weakness will lead to subsequent demands (Walter 2009).

Negotiators therefore strive to package their concessions in such a way as to minimize their cost, maximize their likelihood of acceptance,

---

[2] Somewhat strangely, even in multi-round incomplete-information models of bargaining, states tend to make initial offers that are either accepted, or are rejected leading to war, so this problem doesn't arise. See Fey, Meirowitz and Ramsay (2013); for an exception see Leventoğlu and Tarar (2008).

and minimize the impression of weakness conveyed by making them. This is the heart of communication in the endgame.

Communicating to Negotiation Partners

What do negotiators strive to convey about their concessions? First, they try to magnify the size of the concession and the extent to which it moves toward the other side's position. One's own concessions are always extraordinarily generous, and satisfy all reasonable demands that the other side could possibly have. This is a constant theme of the Israeli narrative of the Camp David negotiations, for instance; Barak's last proposal was unprecedented, generous, and gave the Palestinian side almost all it asked for. Indeed, one minimizes the remaining distance between the new position and the adversary's position, both to maximize the apparent size of the concession and to minimize the apparent size of the concession needed by the adversary to accept the concession and conclude the deal.

Making such a large concession is therefore proof of the reasonableness and moderation of the side making the concession, and an indication that a deal can be struck. However, negotiating parties also compete for the approval of any third party or mediator in the process, and, beyond the immediate negotiation, for support from external audiences who may view moderation favorably and intransigence unfavorably. Concessions are played up in this context to make the side look reasonable, willing to accommodate the legitimate interests of the other side, not fanatical, bigoted, or wedded to violence, etc.

As a result, to not accept the concession and conclude the negotiations on the basis of those terms would be a sign of fanaticism, extreme intransigence, or sinister intent. Since the concession satisfies all legitimate demands, to reject the concession and demand more is to pursue illegitimate demands. This message is probably not very effective with the other party directly, but it is primarily aimed at mediators and third parties, who then may put additional pressure on the other side to accept the proposal and conclude the deal.

To one's own domestic audience this message may be tailored further depending on circumstances. In some cases, maximizing the size of the concession is still good politics, particularly if it is rejected. A generous concession that is nonetheless rejected by the other side puts the country in the right and the adversary in the wrong in the post-negotiation competition for third-party support. However, if the concession is accepted, a deal is concluded, and the negotiator turns to the task of selling the deal domestically; all of a sudden the concession becomes minuscule, hardly noticeable, and really consonant in all but a few details with the essence of previous positions. This message is sent to avoid looking weak and to maximize the chance of ratification, or more generally, political support for the deal. We saw a similar effort by US Secretary of State Kerry to paint the nuclear deal with Iran in terms consonant with previous positions, despite the concessions that were made as the negotiations progressed, as Chapter 1 by Ariane Tabatabai and Camille Pease discusses.

Sometimes a concession is so generous that even after its acceptance it really cannot be plausibly reinterpreted as minimal. At this point the negotiators become experts in the other side's bottom line, and the deal is portrayed conclusively as the best that could possibly be obtained. The negotiators switch from doubting statements of the other side's resolve in order to extract more concessions from them to highlighting and endorsing statements of the other side's resolve, to prove to domestic audiences that this deal was the best that could be had. This is another manifestation of how negotiating opponents become allies in the ratification phase.

As a corollary to the framing of the size of the concession, the message is conveyed that the concession was incredibly difficult to make. The atmospherics may help get this message across: The concession should be made late in the negotiations, preferably late at night, after long hours of negotiation and after several near breakdowns in the negotiations. The concession is so large that it causes divisions within the negotiating team, with some team members openly hostile to it. These divisions will of course only be magnified back home, where the concession will be criticized by people who were too opposed to the negotiations to begin with to even be invited. This conveys the impression that even in the most positively disposed, pro-negotiations sample of representatives, the concession is so large as to cause divisions and controversy. The concession may have exceeded the negotiator's mandate, so it will require additional communication with higher authorities, who may not authorize it, in which case it will have to be withdrawn.

Another tactic that is employed to avoid the impression of weakness is to portray the concession not as a concession that gives away what was previously demanded, but as an "intellectual" breakthrough that "solves a problem," an example of reframing. This solution was arrived at through acts of supreme intelligence and creativity that reflect well upon the side making the new offer, rather than the supine abandonment of cherished goals. The side receiving the concession has an incentive to play along with this framing, to bolster the side making the concession in the hope of being on the receiving end of more intellectual breakthroughs. The negotiations that ended the Cold War were replete with examples of this kind of theater, when Gorbachev packaged concessions to the US or western position as intellectual breakthroughs and was encouraged to do so. For instance, at the Reykjavík summit in 1986 Gorbachev offered to accept the NATO proposal to eliminate intermediate-range missiles in Europe in exchange for US abandonment of the strategic defense initiative. Reagan refused and the summit broke up in acrimony. The next year Gorbachev broke the logjam by simply abandoning the linkage and accepting the western demand, despite the fact that the Soviet side gave up far more missiles than the NATO side. This may have made him look weak in US eyes, but it also served to build trust and boosted his popularity enormously, both in Europe and in the United States, sparking the era of "Gorbymania" (Kydd 2005, Chapter 8).

A related tactic is to reframe a concession as a high-minded commitment to a moral principle that was somehow overlooked before. That the moral principle happens to favor the other side in this instance is perfectly normal and acceptable; in other cases moral principles would favor one's own side and doubtless lead to concessions by the negotiating partner. Gorbachev pursued this tactic in the negotiations over German unification in 1990. The crucial question was whether a united Germany would remain in NATO or not. The Soviet position was that it should not, for obvious reasons, while the leaders of West Germany and the United States preferred that it should. Gorbachev realized, however, that Soviet leverage was weak, and so when western negotiators argued that states in general should be free to choose their alliance partners, Gorbachev agreed, much to the dismay of his negotiating team, as discussed further in Chapter 13 by Mikhail Troitskiy (Zelikow and Rice 1995). This kind of maneuver can be useful even if the other side is not taken in, if it impresses third parties with the moderation and enlightenment of the side making the concession, and if it can be used to sell the concession at home to domestic audiences.

All this is in support of the main message that needs to be conveyed, which is that no further concessions are to be expected. The negotiator's bottom line has been reached, the reservation value is on the table, and no deal would be preferred to anything even a smidgen worse. This is the final offer. The negotiations are about to end. Accepting the offer will result in a deal, proving the negotiator can accomplish the herculean task of selling such a huge concession at home. Rejecting the offer will result in no deal without a second's hesitation. The onus will be on the side rejecting such a concession, the "dead-cat" problem (Baker cited in Holbrooke 1998). This impression can be reinforced by theatrical tactics that underline that the negotiations are almost over, such as a demonstrative packing of the bags and bringing them to the lobby. For instance, Kerry reportedly "packed the bags" several times during the negotiations with Iran, as Holbrooke did at Dayton.

Communicating to Broader Audiences

In most high-profile negotiations there is some kind of agreement or understanding that the parties will not talk to the press while the negotiations are ongoing. However, this is sometimes breached. Secretary of State Kerry even occasionally tweeted about the ongoing negotiations (Gordon 2015). In some cases the parties leak details of the negotiations to the press, but this usually signals the breakdown of negotiations, and the parties are attempting to position themselves for the post-negotiations phase by casting pre-emptive blame on the other side. In other cases, however, broad and vague statements are sought by the press and provided by the negotiating parties. The parties in effect are allowed to express optimism that a deal is near or pessimism that a deal is far away. Why do the parties make such statements and what do they mean?

Parties have an incentive to say a deal is near after they have made a concession in order to put additional pressure on the other side to accept it and close the deal on those terms. If a general expectation of success can be created, then for the other side to reject the concession and demand more and have the negotiations fail on that account would be to dash the hopes that had been raised, leading additional blame to be allocated to the intransigent party. So in making a concession that one wishes to be final, one should strive to generate expectations that it will be accepted and that the deal is all but concluded.

Conversely, if one has not made a concession and is hoping for additional, reciprocal concessions from the other side, one should always hint that the negotiations still have a long way to go, the parties remain far apart, etc. It is, of course, the other side that is responsible for the remaining distance, because it has failed to make any significant concessions. If their behavior continues, it will unfortunately be impossible to conclude a deal. There is a slight hope that they will see reason and become more willing to come to a just and fair resolution, but there are sadly few signs of this so far. Kerry hinted that a deal was far away when the Iranians raised new demands over the conventional weapons embargo.

Creating Common Value

So far, it is communication primarily directed at convincing the other side to accept one's final proposal that has been discussed, as is common in dueling negotiations. Such communication is sometimes truthful; sometimes resolve is genuine, sometimes parties do lay their bottom lines on the table. Sincere communication can be designed to locate deals that both sides prefer to their respective bargaining positions, but what about the possibility of creating common value, as is more common in driving negotiations? This is rarer, in the final stages of negotiation, than it is claimed to be, even in the case of driving. For one thing, the negotiators have had a long time to thresh out the issues and have probably created as much value as they can by the end. Creating common value is what lower-level technical people are for; top-level negotiators step in at the end to make decisions on politically delicate concessions. For another, the dynamic discussed above kicks in, in which states making concessions wrap them in the language of creating mutual value to make them look less like concessions to international and domestic audiences. However, there may be instances in driving negotiations in which crucial last-minute proposals do benefit both sides in unexpected ways, in which case honest communication about them would be possible, especially if the information were self-evident once communicated.

Satisfying Honor, Saving Face, Fairness, and the Value of Destroying Value

A final interesting set of considerations concerns the related concepts of honor, face, and fairness. States are often extremely concerned with preserving their honor or saving face in the context of negotiations. The Iranian side in the nuclear negotiations has been highly focused on avoiding the perception that it is giving in to US pressure. In part, this can be understood as a typical bargaining tactic, if one can persuade the other side that one is so obsessed with honor that one cannot make concessions, then they may accept your position (Dafoe and Caughey 2016). However, these sorts of concerns for honor and face can lead to bargaining failure as well, if the two sides get locked into their positions and interpret any deviation from them as an unacceptable loss of face.

The concept of fairness comes in here, in that deals that can be portrayed as fair are more satisfactory from an honor or face perspective than ones that are obviously unfair. This helps explain why so many deals are written in abstract terms that theoretically apply to anyone. Even if each clause is in reality targeted toward specific states, the use of abstract terminology makes it look more general and fair. To paraphrase Anatole France, agreements, in their majestic equality, should forbid the rich and poor alike from sleeping under bridges. This becomes difficult when the subject matter of negotiation is inherently asymmetrical, as in the Iranian nuclear negotiations. In such cases, the less powerful negotiating partners are extremely alive to slights to their honor or any unfairness. This helps explain the Iranian insistence that Iran be accorded all its NPT-related rights.

One strategy that may help in these circumstances is the destruction of common value, rather than creation of it. Deals that are less efficient but more fair may have a better chance of succeeding than deals that are efficient but less fair. One example is the Iranian insistence on keeping Fordow operating, even if it is not enriching uranium. From the American perspective this is a waste of money, but from the Iranian perspective it means that the United States was not able to force Iran to close the facility, and hence is a victory.[3] That is, one can imagine three possible outcomes: The plant is open and enriching uranium (OE), the plant is open and not enriching uranium (ON), and the plant is closed (C). The American preference ordering is C > ON > OE, and they think the Iranian preference order should be OE > C > ON, because the plant is costly to operate and it produces no benefit if it is not enriching uranium. If that were true, ON would be inefficient, because both sides would be better off moving to C. However, the real Iranian preference ordering is OE > ON > C, because C is the United States' top preference and therefore it would be humiliating to accept it, and so ON is preferred to it, despite the financial cost. This makes ON efficient and the obvious split-the-difference outcome. In this case, communication about honor costs could be credible, since the Iranian willingness to accept ON and the attendant costs credibly conveys the honor cost they attach to C.

A Final Thought on Credibility

The end of negotiations is where the big concessions are made, if they are made at all. These concessions need to be justified and properly framed, to the other side, to third parties, and to domestic audiences. To the other side and to third parties they need to be magnified to look generous and hard to turn down, difficult to make, so that more cannot be expected, and therefore they are final. To domestic audiences, they need

---

[3] See Sanger and Gordon (2015). I thank Ahmer Tarar for bringing this example to my attention.

to be minimized to be reconcilable with previous positions going into the negotiations, so the negotiators cannot be criticized for giving the store away. Given the obvious incentives to convey these messages, their credibility is of course open to question. However, the very fact that they are sent at the end of negotiations bolsters their credibility. Presumably, if the parties have got this far, they have already done a lot of costly signaling about how tough they are, and how difficult it is to make concessions. When the negotiations are poised on the brink of success or failure, last-minute offers really are final, and so carry their own credibility.

There are still incentives to misrepresent, however, provided by the possibility, in some cases the certainty, of future negotiations over the same or similar topics. The 1994 North Korean nuclear deal was meant to be temporary, as indeed it was; the same parties negotiated over the same issue until the end of the Bush administration in 2009. In some cases the intervening conflict transforms the situation drastically; the United States and Japan did not negotiate ever again over the issues they negotiated over in 1941, nor did Britain and Germany revisit the Sudetenland agreement. However, states will have an eye to the distant future, and this gives them an incentive to be perceived as tough and resolute in defense of their interests. Nonetheless, the end of negotiating rounds is perhaps the moment in time when states have the greatest incentive to be truthful in discussing their bottom lines and making concessions. The cliché that these are moments of truth has some truth to it.

12 Facing Impediments: Prospecting

Janice Gross Stein

Exploring the factors that explain the end of negotiations is somewhat like explaining recovery from a long illness. The patient often does not know it is happening until after she has begun to feel better. In international negotiations, the parties often do not know that they are in the last phase until the negotiations are very close to, or at, their end; the markers are apparent only in hindsight. At other times, when negotiations are tightly structured and the parties demarcate the phases more clearly, they do know when they are in the endgame. At Taba in December 1999, as President Clinton prepared to hand over the presidency to George Bush, Israeli and Palestinian negotiators knew that they were in the last phase of negotiations that could take place with the assistance of the Clinton administration. The end of that process was externally demarcated.

Even when an international negotiation ends or collapses, there is almost always a tomorrow, a metagame, where another round can start, structured somewhat differently, under different auspices, with a different agenda. The failure of climate negotiators to reach even a framework agreement in Copenhagen certainly was the end of one round of negotiations, but simultaneously the beginning of preparations for another, differently structured negotiation where the parties learned from failure. An end to an international negotiation is rarely final, until the parties decide to resolve the outstanding issues, use coercion to change the bargaining climate, or put the issues aside as they recede in importance and the parties move on to other challenges.

This chapter explores the relevance of a cluster of concepts drawn from psychology and behavioral economics as explanations of the success and failure of negotiations in the final phase, as they end. I look particularly at the impact of framing effects and loss aversion, or what has come to be known as "prospect theory," and then at the three related concepts of the "certainty" effect, the "endowment" effect, and "hyperbolic discounting" that can, under certain conditions, amplify the impact of loss aversion.

To do so, I make a stylized assumption about the last phase of an international negotiation process. I assume that the parties to the negotiation have been through several prior rounds and know that this is the final phase in this particular process of negotiation. This simplifying assumption removes the uncertainty about whether or not the parties know they are in the endgame. It removes the possibility that one or more of the parties misperceive where they are in the process and do not appreciate that they are in the final phase. It also, for analytic convenience, removes the metagame from consideration and firmly establishes this round as final. Negotiators who think strategically tend to hold back making costly concessions until almost the very last moment in order both to avoid being pushed any further and to extract concessions from the other parties. The most serious and difficult exchanges usually take place in the final phase. This assumption of convenience that I make is a large one, but it helps to establish the terrain on which we can assess the impact of a cluster of psychological concepts in the final phase of an international negotiation.

Framing Effects and Loss Aversion

"Prospect theory," developed by Kahneman and Tversky (1979; 1984) and Tversky and Kahneman (1992), is a theory of individual decision-making under different conditions of risk. In a series of experiments, Kahneman and Tversky demonstrated that people's choices among prospects are shaping by "framing effects," namely the method, form, or sequence of presentation of options.[1] Secondly, people frame their choices around a reference point, and consider relative gains and losses from that reference point, rather than estimate the net expected value of their assets, as rational models of subjective expected utility expect. People generally choose the status quo as a reference point,

---

[1] In rational models of expected utility, preferences are assumed to be dominant, invariant, and transitive. Experimental results in psychology and behavioral economics demonstrate that all these axioms are violated by framing effects. Tversky and Kahneman define framing as "the decision-maker's conception of the acts, outcomes, and contingencies associated with a particular choice" (Tversky & Kahneman 1981, 453). Manipulation of framing effects can influence choice among options in a negotiation sequence. McDermott argues that because most people possess a natural aversion to extreme options, an advisor can create an extreme option and thereby encourage a decision-maker to choose a middle option that would have appeared unacceptable without the contrast effect (McDermott 2009, 92; Simonson & Tversky 1992). Advisors and negotiators, either accidentally or deliberately, can affect the outcome of decision-making by altering the framing of options. As McDermott argues, "Merely presenting the same choice in alternate ways, using differing wording, can affect decision making in significant ways" (McDermott 2009, 93).

but they occasionally use their aspirations or expectations as their reference point. What reference point they use is of central importance, because it is from that reference point that they assess the expected gains and losses of the options they identify. Finally, Kahneman and Tversky demonstrate that change is felt more strongly closer to the reference point, a matter of approach–avoidance discussed below by Dean Pruitt.

The fundamental argument of loss aversion that drives the theoretical argument and delivers the analytic punch is the unequal valuation of equivalent gains and losses. Kahneman and Tversky argue first that the pain of a loss is equivalent to twice the pleasure of an equivalent gain. Secondly, because losses are far more painful than gains, people are risk-averse with respect to gains and risk-acceptant with respect to losses. Leaders are less inclined to put at risk a gain they have achieved, or jeopardize a process that is going well. Conversely, after a major defeat, they are more inclined to take risks to recoup what they have lost. President Anwar el-Sadat came to office in 1970, three years after the devastating loss of the Sinai peninsula to Israel. Although Israel had unquestionable military superiority in the air, at sea, and on the ground, Sadat ordered his generals to work around these military advantages to design a high-risk strategy for Egypt's armed forces to cross the Suez Canal (Stein 1985). That high-risk strategy, which President Sadat chose because he was in the domain of loss relative to his reference point of Egyptian control of the Sinai, was an explicitly political strategy designed to jump-start a process of negotiation to persuade Israel to return the "lost" Sinai peninsula to Egypt. That strategy succeeded. Generally, people are willing to take greater risks to recover losses than they are to make gains.

Risk propensity is a function of the initial reference point a decision-maker chooses, but, once that reference point is known, prospect theory treats risk as situational rather than dispositional, although individual differences still matter. This situational dimension makes prospect theory especially suitable to the analysis of the phases of international negotiation; it mitigates in part the challenge of aggregating from the individual to the group level of analysis that can complicate the application of concepts drawn from psychology and behavioral economics to international behavior, where decision-making is frequently collective.

Five issues arise when prospect theory moves outside the lab to the analysis of international negotiation in international politics. First, economists and psychologists provide the frame in their experiments and then study the impact; in international negotiation the frame is not given and the theory provides only a partial account of framing through theories of "mental accounting."[2] Secondly, to test the impact of framing effects and loss aversion outside the laboratory in cases of international negotiation, reference points must be defined *ex ante*, independently of outcomes. More specifically, scholars must have evidence that decision-makers adopted a reference point at time t; that decision-makers subsequently perceive themselves as facing gains or losses relative to that reference point at time $t + n$; and, then, that the group's risk-taking behavior is in the predicted direction[3]

Third, even though risk is largely situational and individual differences are therefore less significant, there is still too little systematic work either in psychology or in behavioral economics on the impact of group dynamics on framing and choice. In a group context, choice shifts are specific cases of the more general phenomenon of group polarization, where group discussion leads to adoption of a more extreme position than the group average in the initially preferred direction.[4] However, group effects may be less important in international negotiations, where delegations are usually structured around a leader who is the arbiter of negotiation strategy and choices. Other members of the team function as information gatherers and as aids to information processing as well as advisors, but it is a more reasonable assumption that a single individual makes the final choices. From this perspective, the methodological individualism that underlies the experimental research and results in psychology and behavioral economics is far less

---

[2] Mental accounting "is a set of rules people use to choose reference points and categories for comparing various gains and losses" (Camerer & Kunreuther 1989, 573; Thaler 1985). These rules of mental accounting often violate the rules of economic decision-making. Other things being equal, people prefer the status quo because of the endowment effect (Knetsch & Sinden 1984; Thaler 1985). Mental accounting is one explanation of the shifts in reference points. Research shows, however, that framing effects can be reduced and even eliminated by changes in experimental design (Boettcher 2004; Kuhberger 1995; Levin, Schneider & Gaith 1998; Mandel 2001). Framing effects can vary as a function of domain, of the information in the prospects that decision-makers receive, of the outcome probabilities, and of emotion (Boettcher 2004; Schweitzer & DeChurch 2001; Carnevale 2008).

[3] Taliaferro formulates the requirements of an appropriate test of prospect theory in a related but somewhat different way. He argues that a careful test of prospect theory requires three observations: "(a) decision makers evaluated outcomes in terms of the reference point adopted at t; (b) decision makers perceive themselves as facing gains or losses relative to that reference point at $t + n$; and (c) the group's risk-taking behavior is in the predicted direction" (Taliaferro 1998, 109; see also Davis 2000; McDermott 2004).

[4] See Boettcher (2004) and Lamm (1988, 807). Social psychologists explain these group shifts in terms of the social milieu the group creates, through theories of social comparison, or by invoking the information-processing functioning of the group, through theories of persuasive arguments.

a problem in an explanation of negotiation outcomes than it is in descriptions of other kinds of state action and interaction.

This advantage can become a disadvantage. What is omitted from the testing of prospect theory in international negotiation is the basket of principal–agent dilemmas when senior leaders appoint representatives to lead negotiations on their behalf. The interests of the agents who are charged with responsibility for the negotiation do not necessarily converge with those of the principal who appointed them. Over time, for example, agents may become far more invested in a successful outcome of a negotiation than their principal, who remains removed and at a distance. As negotiations continue, agents invest more of their time and prestige, treat these assets as sunk costs, and become more willing to take risks to move toward agreement. Prospect theory can be helpful in unpacking these dilemmas. It is consistent with its expectations that agents should become risk-acceptant with respect to the losses they would experience as the negotiation proceeds should the process end in failure. In the final phase, the gap between principal and agent should grow. Heightened loss aversion by agents helps to explain the drive to agreement in the final stage, even when the terms of the bargain would violate the instructions of the principal. Some of these dynamics were apparent as Secretary of State John Kerry pushed hard for an agreement between Israel and Palestine while President Obama was reserved and stood way back over the horizon. The principal–agent relationship was ultimately not put to the test because Israel and Palestine used a combination of dueling and dragging strategies that ensured the negotiations ended in failure.

Finally, risk has emotional as well as probability dimensions. These emotional dimensions can accentuate individual differences and play out in several different ways. First, emotion influences the choice of reference points (Carnevale 2008). It also influences probability estimation. Risks that are particularly vivid or salient and frightening are systematically overestimated. In the wake of the attacks in Paris in November 2015, public estimates of the risk of a terrorist attack soared in Europe and North America. Risks that are uncontrollable are also feared even when they are statistically unlikely (Hall & Ross 2015; Kahneman 2011, 326–237; Loewenstein *et al.* 2001, 267; Mercer, 2005, 2010; Slovic *et al.* 2004). People generally rate the risk of dying in an airplane crash far more highly than they do that of dying in an auto accident, even though the likelihood of death on the highways is far higher.

Emotion also influences loss aversion directly. People *feel* the pain of loss more intensely than they *feel* the pleasure of gain. Tversky and Kahneman (1992) identified "enhanced loss aversion," or loss aversion that is associated with moral outrage. When legitimate rights are violated or a nation's flag is burned and an embassy destroyed, leaders are likely to feel the loss even more keenly as the effect of loss aversion is enhanced by feelings of humiliation and moral outrage (McDermott 2009). They are more likely to take risks to recover the loss and less likely to see concessions as compensating for the injury when emotion inflates the loss and feeling of injury. In reaction to the execution by Saudi Arabia of a prominent Shi'a sheikh in 2016, angry crowds in Tehran torched the Saudi embassy. Almost immediately, Saudi Arabia and several of its allies in the Gulf expressed their moral outrage at the sacking of the embassy and severed diplomatic relations. Even if the Saudi decision to break diplomatic relations was calculated and strategic, as it may well have been, the evidence shows that emotion and reason are deeply intermingled and reinforce the aversion to loss.

Experimental research has demonstrated that the strength of framing effects is not uniform but varies across conditions.[5] Domain has an impact on the strength of loss aversion: the tendency toward risk-seeking is greater in human life problems than in money problems (Mandel 2001, 71). Prospect theory is more likely to be relevant, therefore, to negotiations to end a war or agree to a ceasefire than it is to negotiations about international trade or international finance (Carnevale 2008; Kanner 2004; McDermott 2009). When their survival or the survival of those they represent is not assured, decision-makers are especially likely to be risk-acceptant.[6] Missing information, a common attribute of complex international negotiations, also enhances framing effects, but is likely to be less important in the final phase of a negotiation where the parties have had some opportunity to gather information (Mandel 2001, 60; Kuhberger 1995). Outcome probabilities also affect the strength of framing effects: certain/risky bimodal choices produce greater effects than do choices between two risky outcomes (Kuhberger 1998, 36; Boettcher 2004, 338). The final phase of a negotiation may have reduced some uncertainties, but some critical decisions even in the endgame may still involve a bimodal choice where framing effects will be more powerful.

---

[5] Framing effects vary by domain – medical diagnoses, betting, escalation of commitment; by the information contained in the prospects presented to decision-makers; by the descriptors associated with particular outcomes; and by the outcome probabilities. Kuhberger (1998) identified a wide range of framing effects across nine different domains. See also Boettcher (2004), Levin, Schneider, and Garth (1998), and Mandel (2001).

[6] In modeling outcomes of crisis bargaining, when decision-makers are risk-averse or risk-neutral, the predictions of rational choice and prospect theory are likely to converge. They are likely to diverge, however, when leaders on both sides are risk-acceptant because they feel that their survival is at stake. Both domain and individual heterogeneity matter (McDermott, Fowler & Smirnov 2008, 345; Schaub 2004).

Experiments have demonstrated that domain, missing information, outcome descriptors, outcome probabilities, and individual differences in emotion, identities, experience, and risk preferences can shift the selection of reference points and the impact of framing effects in systematic ways. Identification of these scope conditions, encompassing both situational and individual differences, and of threshold effects helps to establish when negotiators are likely to behave as psychological theories predict and when they are more likely to approximate rational choosers.

Reinforcing Loss Aversion: Certainty and Endowment Effects and Hyperbolic Discounting

Psychologists and economists have identified a series of pervasive biases and heuristics, or cognitive shortcuts, which people use to simplify complex-decision problems. Among those most relevant to loss aversion are the certainty effect, the endowment effect, and hyperbolic discounting.

The impact of loss aversion is amplified by systematic distortions in the weighting of probabilities. Individuals tend to be non-linear in the way they weight probabilities; when the probability of a consequence is low, people will tend to systematically underweight that probability; at the extreme, they will treat low-probability consequences as impossible. When the probability of a consequence is moderate or high, they will overweight these probabilities and treat high probabilities as certain.[7] The weighting function in prospect theory behaves poorly at either extreme. This tendency to treat what is probable as certain has an amplifying effect on loss aversion. When losses are probable, for example, non-linear probability estimation combines with framing effects to exaggerate the likelihood of loss, and consequently to increase risk-acceptance (Elms 2008, 247; Kahneman & Tversky 1984, 345; Schaub 2004, 399). In an elaboration of prospect theory, Tversky and Kahneman refine their general argument to accommodate the extremes. In experimental research they find a distinctive four fold pattern of risk attitudes: risk aversion for gains and risk seeking for losses of high probability and risk seeking for gains and risk aversion for losses of low probability (Tversky & Kahneman 1992).

As McDermott (2009, 104) observes, "The key insight from the certainty effect ... lies in the way this tendency encourages people to place less

---

[7] Economists have also advanced their knowledge of the threshold at which non-linear probability weighting shifts (Barberis 2012). Individuals tend to be non-linear in the way they weight probabilities; they shift from systematically overweighting to systematically underweighting the probability of outcomes somewhere between 0.30 and 0.40 (Camerer & Ho 1994; Tversky & Kahneman 1992; Wu & Gonzalez 1996).

value on uncertain outcomes, including those that may be harder to measure, than on certain outcomes that, while easier to measure, may not prove as valuable for the long-term stability of the relationship." The uncertain outcomes of a successful negotiation, such as trust, tend to be valued less highly than the certain outcomes with tangible benefits.

While the certainty effect works on processes of probability estimation, the endowment effect works on processes of value estimation. The results of repeated experiments suggest that people place a higher value on what they have than they would be willing to pay for an identical object in the marketplace (Thaler 1985; Kahneman, Knetsch & Thaler 1990; Jervis 1992; Goldgeier & Tetlock 2001; Plott & Zeiler 2005). When people overvalue what they currently possess, they tend to exaggerate the cost and losses of concessions that they make. The endowment effect amplifies loss aversion and makes it more difficult to persuade leaders to give up something that they already possess than to prevent them from taking something they do not currently have.

The endowment effect can make concessions even more difficult when both parties feel its impact. People tend to normalize much more quickly for gain than they do for loss. To return to Egypt and Israel, President Nasser of Egypt lost control of the Sinai in 1967 and never normalized for the loss. Israel quickly normalized for the gain, and attached great importance to the strategic depth that the Sinai provided in the event of an attack by Egypt. Repeated rounds of negotiation, mediated through third parties, took place between Egypt and Israel, but all ended in failure in large part because of the asymmetrical impact of the endowment effect on loss aversion. The new president of Egypt, Anwar el-Sadat, never normalized for the loss, and used as his reference point an aspiration level, the return of the Sinai to Egyptian sovereignty. The Sinai was Egypt's by endowment. Israel's leaders, who had quickly normalized for the gain, treated the status quo as their reference point and, as expected, exaggerated the value and the cost to them of the return of the Sinai to Egypt. The asymmetrical valuations made concessions more costly to Israel's leaders and increased the risk acceptance of Egypt's leaders for a limited use of force. Under these conditions, there was little chance that the negotiations held from 1971 to 1973 could succeed. After the war, however, when Sadat fully appreciated the limits of military force, the same preference structure led him again to take risks to push negotiations forward.

Behavioral economists and psychologists have also challenged the expectation of rational choice about the discount rate people use as they think about units of time (Coller & Williams 1999; Fowler & Kam 2008). Standard models assume that actors apply the same discount factor when comparing costs and benefits that arise between any two time periods. Experimental research suggests pervasive time inconsistency or "hyperbolic discounting" problems. People discount the future more and more heavily as they think further and further away from the present.

The impact of hyperbolic discounting on negotiation has not received much attention. Its effects can be paradoxical on the outcome. In climate negotiations, leaders significantly discounted the future as the consequences stretched out in time. That the effects of climate change were not likely to be seriously damaging for decades made it more difficult for leaders using a heavy discount rate to reach meaningful agreements. Loss aversion lost its strength as the future stretched out, largely due to processes of hyperbolic discounting as well as mobilized political interests that were focused on immediate losses (Hafner-Burton *et al.* 2017).

Hyperbolic discounting can also facilitate agreement in the end phase (Fearon 1998). As leaders discount future losses from agreement, they are better able to focus on avoiding the immediate losses from the failure to agree and on capturing any gains they may realize from agreement. The difficult final phases of negotiation between Iran and the United States over Iran's nuclear program are a case in point. As the zone of agreement became clearer to both parties in the final phases, so did the concessions that both sides would have to make and the costs (inflated by the endowment effect) of these concessions to the party that had to make them. That would generally preclude an agreement. But in this case, the losses from the failure to agree were immediate and large to both parties, while the large losses of agreement to the United States and its allies were postponed at least a decade into the future. It was this specific structure of present and future losses and a pattern of hyperbolic discounting by a president late in his last term that enabled this agreement.

Framing Effects and Loss Aversion in the Final Phases of Negotiation

In this volume, we are interested not only in explaining the outcome of negotiation processes, but also in characterizing the behavior in the final phases that leads to the outcome. Of particular interest here is the impact of framing effects, loss aversion, and associated biases and heuristics on behavior in the final phase that culminates either in the ability to reach an agreement or the failure to agree. I suggest a series of propositions that link loss aversion to bargaining behavior – dueling, driving, or dragging – and outcomes. I begin first with propositions derived from findings on loss aversion, or biased evaluation processes, and then move on to propositions that flow from knowledge of biased processes of estimating probabilities. In conclusion, I ask how negotiators can compensate for framing effects and loss aversion that vary across conditions.

Valuing Losses

1. *Loss aversion becomes stronger in the final phase as likely losses become clearer, and makes agreement more difficult.*[8] Consistently with the argument made by Pruitt in Chapter 14, as the negotiation progresses, the parties' estimates of the likelihoods of losses and gains from their reference points become clearer and their perception of the zone of agreement narrows as they become better informed about the reference points and options of others. In the final phase, the parties are especially likely to weigh their own concessions as losses and the concessions of others as gains. Because loss aversion is stronger than the desire for gain, each party sees itself as making greater concessions and enduring greater losses. Other things being equal, this pattern of asymmetrical evaluation is a significant obstacle to agreement.

In their analysis of arms-control negotiations, Quattrone and Tversky (1998, 460) illustrated the impact of asymmetrical evaluation in arms-control negotiations between the United States and the Soviet Union: "In negotiating over missiles, for example, each superpower may sense a greater loss in security from the dismantling of its own missiles than it senses a gain in security from a comparable reduction made by the other side."[9] When both parties have this asymmetrical pattern of perception, a pattern driven by loss aversion, the zone of possible agreement is narrowed in the final phase of negotiation and it becomes very difficult to reach agreement.

Experimental research confirms the impact of loss aversion. When negotiators in experiments are told to minimize their losses, they make threats that run a higher risk of deadlock and they reach significantly fewer agreements than do negotiators who have identical interests and are given the same information but are told to maximize their gains (Bazerman & Neale 1994).

2. *The unequal valuation of gains and losses characteristic of loss aversion leads to the systematic discounting of concessions that the other parties make* (McDermott 2009, 95, 96). Paradoxically, the willingness of one side to

---

[8] Pruitt in Chapter 14 reaches a similar conclusion in his analysis of the impact of approach–avoidance dynamics.
[9] McDermott (2009, 95) puts it well: "because each negotiator will consider his own losses as being greater than those incurred by the opponent, it becomes easy for both sides to see themselves as having given up more, gained less, and been placed at a disadvantage relative to the other side."

offer a concession in the final phase leads the other side to discount its value (Stillinger & Ross 1991). In the final phases of negotiation, concession aversion has pernicious effects on the outcome of negotiation. In important negotiations, where uncertainty is significant, parties tend to hold back their concessions until the last round, hoping that these will be seen as final, reflective of their bottom line, and that they will be interpreted as signals that there is no more room to move, as discussed by Andrew Kydd in Chapter 11. Insofar as the value of these concessions is discounted, by one or all of the parties, it becomes more difficult to reach agreement even when agreement would otherwise be possible. Loss and concession aversion is one explanation of "missed opportunities," or the failure to reach an agreement when observers can see a zone of possible agreement, given the preferences of the parties, but the parties miss the opportunity to reach agreement.[10]

3. *When negotiators have made a series of concessions over time, and some of these concessions are known to the public, negotiators treat these concessions as losses that have already been incurred.* When these concessions are publicly known, they can be considered as future "audience costs" (Fearon 1994). In the final phase of negotiation, three consequences can flow from sunk costs that are treated as losses from a reference point.

(a) These sunk costs may tip decision-makers into the domain of loss relative to their reference point. They then become risk-acceptant with respect to further losses and are willing to take additional risks to lock in an agreement. This pattern is quite common in spirals of military escalation when decision-makers have committed military assets to a conflict, have lost these assets, and yet continue to commit additional assets in the expectation that these additional resources will bring victory and justify the costs they have incurred. Much of President Johnson's decision-making in Vietnam has been explained by this kind of dynamic. A similar dynamic in negotiation would lead the parties to take risks and make additional concessions to secure an agreement. Secretary of State John Kerry's pursuit of an agreement with Iran in the final phase can be explained as an attempt to avoid losses that would have accrued from the sunk political costs had the United States and Iran been unable to agree.

---

[10] Research across thirty-two different studies of negotiation across more than 5,000 people found that negotiators failed to realize compatible issues about 50% of the time and participated in a lose–lose outcome (Thompson & Hrebec 1996). A lose–lose agreement is a negotiation situation in which parties had compatible interests on a few of the negotiation issues but fail to capitalize on compatible interests.

(b) Alternatively, when the sunk costs tip both sets of decision-makers into the domain of loss relative to their reference points, both parties become risk-acceptant but overvalue the cost of additional concessions in the asymmetrical pattern that I have described above. Under these circumstances, despite their risk-acceptance, they narrow the zone of agreement and miss an agreement that would have been available had their valuations been less asymmetrical. Research has not systematically identified the conditions when one or the other pattern is likely to occur, but the first pattern may be more likely when the parties are driving and the second more likely when they are dueling.

(c) Finally, as the last phase of negotiation begins, both parties may be in the domain of gain with respect to their reference points. Even after absorbing the sunk costs, they remain in the domain of gain, although their gains are less. Negotiations motivated by gain may happen far more quickly and easily than those motivated by loss. Here, even though the parties are risk-averse with respect to gains, in the final phase of negotiation they are open to persuasion about the benefits of agreement when additional concessions are framed as the price to achieve gains. Concessions can look far less consequential when they are regarded as the cost of achieving an agreement that brings benefits (Milburn and Isaac 1995, 338). This pattern should be more likely when negotiators on all sides are driving.

The context distinguishes these three stylized final phases of negotiation, two of which culminate in failure to agree while the third ends in agreement. The context is established by the reference points decision-makers use and whether or not they are in the domain of gain or loss in the final phase, by how likely the consequences of their choices are, and by how asymmetrical their valuations of their own concessions and those other parties make are. When there is a zone of possible agreement, these patterns shape whether decision-makers fail or succeed in the final phase in reaching agreement. It is these patterns that attenuate or amplify logics of driving or dueling.

4. *The endowment effect generally amplifies the effects of loss aversion and makes agreement less likely.* Because people overvalue what they have and therefore what they concede, endowment effects heighten the tendency to asymmetrical valuation of concessions and amplify the effects that I have described. Experimental research finds that partisanship enhanced the impact of the endowment effect and narrowed the zone of agreement beyond what impartial analysts would have identified.[11]

---

[11] Partisan attachments can have an impact very much like that of the endowment effect. In negotiation experiments, subjects were given roles as partisans or neutrals. The

Estimating Probabilities

5. *People's estimation of probabilities becomes especially distorted at the extremes in what is known as the "certainty effect."* They treat low-probability events as impossible and high-probability events as certain. Generally, although not always, these processes can make agreement less likely or narrow the scope of agreements that are reached. In the final phase of negotiation, people tend to discount low-probability but highly damaging events as impossible and leave them out of their calculations. A study of the behavior of a group of developing countries finds, for example, that negotiators often ignored the risks of bilateral investment treaties until they themselves became subject to an investment treaty claim. These results are consistent with those from field studies and experiments that people tend to ignore low-probability, high-impact risks if they cannot bring specific "vivid" instances to mind (Poulsen & Aisbett 2013).

6. *Hyperbolic discounting can either facilitate or complicate agreement, depending on the pattern of gains and losses.* Standard models assume that actors apply the same discount factor when comparing costs and benefits that arise between any two time periods, but experimental research suggests pervasive time inconsistency. Applying a strong discount factor to the future can have positive and negative effects in the final phase of negotiation. Hafner-Burton finds that when the shadow of the future weighs less heavily on the present, it becomes easier to negotiate trade agreements (Hafner-Burton, Hughes & Victor 2013).

The same dynamic was at play in the final phases of the negotiation between the P5+1, led by the United States, and Iran. The big powers discounted the future, and therefore gave less weight to the challenge that Iran would pose a decade later when it would be free to enrich uranium. Leaders replied to questions from critics who raised the prospect that Iran would be free to break out quickly after fifteen years and develop a nuclear weapon with the assurance that the Iranian government would evolve over time and, once it gained international acceptance, would be much less interested in weaponizing its program.

Israel's leaders also tend to heavily discount the future, but with negative consequences for agreement. In the final phases of the many negotiations with their Palestinian counterparts, when they have had to confront

---

partisans, who were given the same information as those who were told they were neutrals, significantly overestimated the value of their best options, underestimated the degree to which their objectives were compatible with those of the other side, and used a self-serving definition of fairness while thinking that their views were impartial (Lax & Sebenius 1986; Thompson 1995; Babcock & Lowenstein 1997).

difficult trade-offs in an uncertain environment, they have systematically discounted the future of an Israel with a majority of Palestinian citizens. They consistently trade present security benefits against discounted future costs of threats to their democratic political system and choose the status quo again and again. This same pattern bedevils international climate negotiations, where leaders discount the large costs of future damage to the environment from greenhouse-gas emissions and choose to make only limited agreements with limited costs in the present.

Moving Reference Points: A Research Question

Breaking the negotiation into demarcated phases suggests an interesting way of modeling the impact of reference points over time. As each new phase of the negotiation begins, in theory participants should choose as their reference point the status quo at that time, rather than the reference point they chose when the negotiation began. The central argument Kahneman and Tversky make is that people do not calculate net asset value, but instead calculate relative asset value, heavily weighted by losses, from a reference point they choose at the time they begin active consideration of their choice.

This argument should apply to the phases of a negotiation process. The reference point negotiators choose at the beginning of a process of pre-negotiation should move as the process of negotiation proceeds through its phases and move one last time as negotiators enter the final phase. If the reference point does not move, then by the time negotiators are in the final phase, they are calculating net value from the beginning of the process as a whole, rather than relative value as prospect theory expects.

There is anecdotal empirical evidence of the movement of reference points during negotiation processes. During the negotiations between the P5+1 and Iran, for example, the United States, behaving as a driver, moved its reference point from "no enrichment" at the beginning to 6,000 centrifuges in the final phase of the negotiation. Similarly, President Sadat of Egypt arrived at Camp David with an aspirational reference point in each of the two critical tracks of the negotiation. On the return of the Sinai, he moved not at all, but on the creation of an independent Palestinian state, he moved to an open-ended negotiation process that would define the boundaries of such a state over time. This asymmetrical pattern suggests that, in the final phase, he was simultaneously a "dueler" on the Sinai but a "dragger" on a Palestinian state. This pattern is consistent with the evidence that framing effects will vary across domains.

Whether the reference points the parties choose move with the phases of the negotiation is important to the explanation of the choices that the parties make. Yet we have no experimental, field, or archival research that systematically addresses the question of whether reference points shift as negotiation processes move through their phases.[12] Given the rich explanations that loss aversion and its related concepts bring to the outcome of negotiation, a priority research question should be to understand better how reference points move across the phases of negotiation.

Strategic Implications

Given the robust impact of loss aversion and its associated biases and heuristics, how can negotiators in the final phase of negotiations seek to mitigate the effects that reduce the likelihood of agreement when observers would agree that the preferences of the parties do create a zone of possible agreement? Five strategies may be helpful.

1. Pruitt (1983) suggests that *one party focus its strategy on helping the other to avoid loss, rather than on making gains*, a strategy also developed in his Chapter 14 in this volume. Since losses are more painful than gains are pleasurable, a strategy that helps an adversary to avoid an important loss is likely to weigh more heavily in an adversary's calculations. That strategy works best when one party's loss is not another party's gain. When the parties' losses are mirror images of one another, the trade-offs sharpen, and it becomes difficult to implement that kind of strategy in the final phase of a negotiation.

2. A related strategy is to *frame unavoidable costs as payments for larger benefits that will accrue from the agreement*. This kind of strategy should help negotiators reframe (heavily weighted) costs in the context of significantly larger gains. In environmental negotiations, the drivers worked to persuade the draggers that the future benefits from reduced environmental damage – better public health, preservation of low-lying societies, reduced damage from extreme-weather events – far outweighed the immediate costs of reducing greenhouse-gas emissions. This kind of strategy can work only when the gains of agreement significantly outweigh the costs; that asymmetry is necessary to compensate for the overweighting of loss.

Alternatively, negotiators can frame the costs of agreement in the context of the larger and, if possible, certain costs of failing to agree.

---

[12] Carnevale suggests the intriguing proposition that emotion may shift not only the direction of a reference point but also the nature of the reference point. Under positive affect, the shift may be to a reference point that derives from a collective outcome and the desire to do well together. Loss aversion would stem principally from collective rather than individual loss (Carnevale & De Dreu 2005; Carnevale 2008, 61).

When Secretary of State Baker was trying to persuade a very reluctant Prime Minister Shamir of Israel to attend the Madrid conference, he emphasized the losses that Israel would certainly incur should it fail to participate. When the problem was reframed, the prime minister agreed to join the negotiations.

3. Endowment effects and concession aversion amplify the effects of loss aversion. These processes of asymmetrical evaluation make agreements more difficult. To minimize this impact, *negotiators can ask neutral third parties, such as commissions or panels of experts, to estimate likely losses of the principal options and their value*. In the final phases of the complex negotiations on adopting the law of the sea, for example, parties invited neutral institutions such as international agencies and research universities to provide better technical information on the consequences, both costs and benefits, of adopting the law of the sea (Antrim & Sebenius 1992). Neutral third parties are not vulnerable to either endowment effects or concession aversion in their valuation of costs, and their estimates are more likely to be accepted as shared data by negotiators.[13]

4. *In multi-partner complex negotiations, one of the parties can sequence the negotiation by bringing partners on board in such a way as to progressively increase the losses that would accrue to later participants from a failure to agree* (Odell 2009). In the 1980s, Federal Reserve chairman Paul Volker wanted to build an international coalition in support of new rules requiring OECD banks to hold greater capital to strengthen the system against a chain default. He approached the United Kingdom first to secure its agreement; together they were home to a major share of the world banking system. Once he had secured British agreement, he then turned to Japan, a growing financial center whose banks were expanding into the US market. The losses to Japan's leadership of staying outside the agreement, now that it included Britain as well as the United States, were significantly larger. After a lengthy negotiation and significant modifications to the agreement, Tokyo agreed. The three governments then invited the European governments to join. European banks would by then have been at a significant disadvantage, if they failed to agree and

---

[13] In related research, Neale and Bazerman highlight the importance of third parties in helping adversaries reframe their conflicts in more neutral or positive ways in order to increase the likelihood of reaching agreement. How the parties frame their negotiation problem in the final phase is critical. When both parties define themselves in the domain of losses, agreement is especially unlikely. Loss-framed negotiators made fewer concessions, were less cooperative, and were more likely to reach an impasse (Neale & Bazerman 1985, 1992; Bottom & Studt 1993). The challenge for the third party is to persuade at least one, if not both, of the other parties to reframe so that they avoid the amplifying effects of loss aversion. De Dreu et al. (1994) find that frame adoption can be manipulated by communication.

were excluded from the three markets. In the final phase of the negotiation, the previously opposed Bundesbank agreed. Volker succeeded by progressively increasing the losses of the no-deal alternatives of outsiders in a phased strategy (Odell & Tingley 2014, 25; Sebenius 1996). The strategy depended on careful sequencing of partners who controlled market share to increase the losses that would arise from a failure to agree and deepen the impact of loss aversion.

5. Finally, complex multiparty negotiations often take place in a context of significant uncertainty, where losses are likely to be large, but are unknown. *To increase the likelihood of agreement and mitigate the effects of the certainty effect, negotiators can propose short-term agreements that can be renegotiated without penalty within a few years or provide escape clauses.* During the 1970s and 1980s, a time of significant economic uncertainties, G7 members negotiated agreements for macroeconomic coordination for short periods of time (Koremenos 2001; Rosendorff & Milner 2001).

The impact of framing effects, loss aversion, and a cluster of associated concepts on decision-makers' choices appears to be robust but variable across a set of conditions.[14] The impact of scope conditions on the impact of loss aversion in the final phase of negotiation and on the outcomes is an important area for future research. Also intriguing is the impact of shifts in reference points as negotiators move through the phases of negotiation. Further research could improve both the theory and the practice of international negotiation.

---

[14] There is some experimental research on the conditions that mitigate and occasionally reverse loss aversion. Decision researchers are integrating models of decision with affect and emotion (Haselhuhn & Mellers 2005; Lerner, Small & Loewenstein 2004; Novemsky & Kahneman 2005). One strand of this research suggests that affective systems underlie frame effects. De Martino *et al.* found that increased activation in the amygdala was associated with frame effects and suggest that framing effects are driven by affect nested in an emotional system (De Martino *et al.* 2006, 686; Bottom 1998; cf. Isen, Nygren & Ashby 1988). Carnevale argues that positive affect can impact a shift in reference points that in turn induces a downsizing of loss differences and an upsizing of gain differences. Usually a loss frame produces fewer concessions than does a gain frame. In experiments, when subjects were exposed to positive affect manipulation, they made *more* concessions when their outcomes were framed as losses, and fewer concessions when in the gain frame, both compared with controls (Carnevale 2008, 52). He suggests that the emotional state of the negotiator may be important not only in the direction of the frame effect by the size of the frame effect (Carnevale 2008, 59; Carnevale & De Dreu 2005). Individual differences matter as well. Pro-social people are more cooperative in a loss frame than they are in a gain frame, whereas pro-self people are more cooperative in a gain frame than they are in a loss frame (De Dreu & McCusker 1997).

13 When is "Enough" Enough? Uncertainty

Mikhail Troitskiy

This chapter analyzes the positive role of ambiguity in the closing phase of negotiations. For our purposes here, ambiguity means the lack of clarity about the meaning of an important aspect of negotiated agreement – whether substantive or procedural. The argument is that sometimes ambiguity in the negotiated deal does not prevent a constructive closure of negotiations. On the contrary, it can be conducive to closure and form the basis for a viable solution to the negotiated problem. If the sides agree to leave certain aspects of their agreement to chance – where the way these aspects get resolved will depend on future developments that are difficult to predict at the moment of closure – they may be able to conclude negotiations and portray the final agreement as Enough to provide for their common victory.

Good-faith negotiations, in which the sides are genuinely trying to derive benefits from a voluntary agreement that they believe is possible, can well end in "constructive ambiguity" – consent by all negotiating parties not to try to clearly define all conditions related to the uncertain future (Bercovitch 2009, 1/2). This allows all stakeholders to leave the negotiation table with their own vision of the future, hoping for the desired outcome to materialize even if their negotiation counterparts were reluctant to guarantee that outcome in the agreement that ended the negotiation. Asian negotiators have provided an example of leaving the final resolution of disputes to "future generations" (Ministry of Foreign Affairs of the People's Republic of China 2014; Steinberg & O'Hanlon 2016, 142). However, a more short-term approach to ambiguity whereby the final contours of the negotiated solution are supposed to transpire within several months or just a few years appears equally viable. This chapter discusses at least one case in which the sides set the deadline by which ambiguity was expected to be resolved by the flow of events.

In many instances, the quest for certainty can derail the agreement because it would reveal differences in expectations among the parties about the end result of the negotiations, the distribution of benefits, and possibly even the very rationale of negotiating. On the contrary, allowing for ambiguity can tamp down fears among the parties involved of being forced into an unfavorable deal. If the sides can live with ambiguity in the final agreement, flexibility in their positions increases and the chances of resolving their dispute go up. Negotiated agreements containing ambiguity are those in which Not Enough (from the perspective of initial expectations) Is Enough (to end negotiations constructively).

As Andrew Kydd notes in Chapter 11, the whole process of negotiation becomes useful and therefore possible because of the uncertainty surrounding the bottom lines of the negotiating parties. If they could openly put their utility and preference structures on the table, and agree on the principle guiding them to an optimal outcome, negotiation as a process would become unnecessary. In such a context, negotiation can then be seen as the business of mutual signaling and testing by the parties. Their signals are intended to communicate to the other side the configuration of their respective views of a ZOPA and the extent of commitment to particular solutions within that zone. Parties enter negotiation assuming that the outcomes that they announce as preferred can evolve as the parties engage and that at some future point in this process the gap between their preferred outcomes will eventually close.

This being an accurate rationalist description of the purpose and essence of the negotiation process, the clarity of the final agreement can supposedly differ. Negotiation can end with enough ambiguity surrounding the deal. For example, the language used to spell out some of its terms may allow for more than one interpretation, or the number of ways to implement the agreement may not be limited to one. The key to closure in uncertainty is the readiness of the negotiating parties to rely on the flow of subsequent events as the force that will determine the final solution.

Two factors play a crucial role in enabling "constructive ambiguity." The first is the difference in projections of the future by the negotiating parties. Reaching an agreement becomes easier if each party believes that, while the exact outcome still remains unclear, the future flow of events will be favorable to its interests. This would imply that the parties' expectations of the future are contradictory, if not mutually exclusive, but each party is nevertheless confident in its respective projection and willing to test it. The second is discounting of the future – underestimation of the possible losses in the distant future, explored in Chapter 12 by Janice Gross Stein as "hyperbolic discounting." If finalizing an agreement immediately provides tangible benefits to the negotiating parties while the costs of doing so are expected to materialize only in the relatively distant future, those costs tend to be discounted by the negotiators. This reconciles them to the ambiguity contained in the agreement and uncertainty with respect to the ultimate results of its implementation.

240   Causes

Drawing on the five patterns of behavior identified in the closing phase of negotiations, three cases illustrate the consequences of ambiguity in the final agreement. One of these patterns, *mismatching*, generates plenty of uncertainty in all phases of negotiation. However, as one of the two least productive patterns, it is not conducive to "hopeful ambiguity" at the closing stage. Mismatching negotiators often act for side effects and do not look for mutually satisfying solutions. As a result, they may only accidentally leave something to chance when parting ways at the end of their engagement session. The *dragging* pattern of negotiation may lead the sides to an ambivalent agreement, albeit less inadvertently than under mismatching strategies. An externally imposed deadline is required in order to close an inconclusive round of negotiation in "constructive ambiguity," otherwise the sides would be reluctant to take any associated risks upon themselves. Negotiators *driving* each other to an agreement, in accordance with the third pattern, would be most prone to ambiguous solutions given their demonstrated mutual interest in reaching a deal. They would be most willing to accept the future as their judge and abide by the agreement once its concrete terms had fully transpired. The pattern of *dueling* is geared toward winning big or losing big at the climax of an intense feud. Pursuing their brinkmanship strategies, players seek to prevail over opponents. An indisputable victory is hardly compatible with ambiguity in the negotiation outcome.

Dragging occurred in the process of searching for a sustainable solution to the conflict surrounding the breakaway parts of Ukraine between 2013 and 2015. Domestic political turmoil in Ukraine started in November 2013 over the country's association with the European Union and had morphed into a full-blown international crisis by spring 2014. Citing defensive motives but acting opportunistically, Moscow moved to take over the Crimean peninsula and support armed resistance to Kiev in the east Ukrainian region of Donbas (Charap & Colton 2017). Three major rounds of multilateral top-level negotiations, in Normandy, France in June 2014 and then in the Belarussian capital Minsk in September 2014 and February 2015, were conducted. Each Minsk agreement was expected to put an end to the armed conflict in eastern Ukraine. The warring sides and several mediators, including Russia, Germany, France, and the Organization for Security and Co-operation in Europe (OSCE), agreed twice on a ceasefire and a line of control.

The first Minsk agreement collapsed late in 2014 with the resumption of heavy fighting in the conflict zone. Minsk I was then superseded by a second accord that altered the line of actual control in the rebels' favor, but contained a more clear-cut and detailed, yet ambiguous, roadmap (Rojansky 2017). While at the time of signing both Minsk I and Minsk II were hailed by all the parties as successful outcomes, virtually all of their terms allowed for multiple (usually two opposing) interpretations.

Despite persistent contradictions, both rounds of Minsk negotiations led to a conclusion largely because the blueprint for conflict resolution embedded in the signed agreements was ambiguous. Successful closure was in the highest interest of the two mediators – German Chancellor Angela Merkel and French President François Hollande – who felt dismay at the inability to put an end to heavy fighting in the middle of Europe. In their turn, the conflicting sides – the presidents of Russia and Ukraine and the rebel commanders – were not as keen on reaching an agreement. Supported by Moscow, the rebels were on a successful offensive, while public opinion in Ukraine demanded a vigorous pushback from the country's president and armed forces, and was not ready for a compromise that smacked of defeat. However, their intransigence was reduced to a level allowing for a deal by ambiguity in the final document, each party agreeing because it expected its interpretation of the agreement's uncertain terms ultimately to prevail.

Another illustrative case of ambiguity to facilitate closure can be found in the negotiations on the reunification of Germany that took place between January and September 1990. At initial stages in these negotiations, top West German and US diplomats floated the idea of imposing restrictions on the future enlargement of NATO. The possibility of such a promise was then officially withdrawn, with the United States instructing allies to stop any discussion of the prospects for NATO enlargement with the Soviet leadership. Moscow, however, preferred to believe that the pledge of NATO's non-enlargement beyond unified Germany had actually been made and tried to invoke it as NATO began its expansion later in the 1990s. Irrespective of whether the Kremlin was deceiving itself or had legitimate grounds to demand that NATO should not enlarge itself into Central and Eastern Europe, such ambiguity helped to seal the deal of German reunification by September 1990. The West and the Soviet Union were mainly driving each other toward a solution. The most interested party – West Germany and its leader Helmut Kohl – was ready to make major concessions, including the 12 billion DM (US $7.7 billion as of 1990) to pay for the return home of the Soviet servicemen. Although hard-pressed by manifold economic challenges and interested in reaching an agreement on relocation of the Soviet troops withdrawn from East Germany, the Soviet leadership could have bargained much harder, rejecting the deal that eliminated the last material obstacle to the reunification. Signing the final document between the four former occupying powers and Germany was made easier by Moscow's belief that its security interests would be honored in the post-Cold War Europe. However, recent research points to possible attempts by Western powers to mismatch Gorbachev's cooperative strategy by attempting to extract maximum possible concessions, dueling-style, from the USSR (Sarotte 2014).

A final twin case of an ambiguous closure is provided by the negotiations between six world powers and Iran on Iran's nuclear program. These talks dragged for more than a decade – from 2003 to 2015 – and passed through two stages aimed at closure: in 2004–2005 and 2012–2015. Comparison of these two sub-cases provides important insights about the role of ambiguity in successful termination of negotiation. The unwillingness of the six powers to allow for sufficient flexibility in the final deal prevented them from reaching an agreement with Iran early in the talks. The full ban on enrichment activities turned out to be unacceptable to Tehran and delayed a compromise for about a decade (Lewis 2015). Tabatabai and Pease in this volume explain in detail how and why Tehran's determination to preserve at least some uranium-enrichment capability scuttled the first round of negotiation and became less of a stumbling block in the second round ten years later. When closure was finally reached, it came under criticism for failing to achieve such a ban (Kroenig 2015). The agreement did leave the six powers and the world with uncertainty about Iran's ultimate intentions in the nuclear field. And yet such uncertainty was enough to break out of the impasse and reap significant benefits, including a strengthened nuclear nonproliferation regime and a host of regional security issues in the Middle East being resolved.

While some of the deals examined below could still unravel – or at least were not being fully implemented according to the initial design – they did come to fruition at the time of their making, with all negotiating parties taking away a sense of success. The collapse of any of the discussed agreements was in no way pre-determined. If it happens, that would occur largely for reasons unrelated to the "hopeful ambiguity" inherent in the deals.

Minsk Agreements on Eastern Ukraine

A more detailed analysis shows the use of uncertainty in the Ukrainian negotiations. The level of antagonism in the Minsk negotiations on the fate of the east Ukrainian region of Donbas was extremely high. First, the negotiation game was zero-sum because the sides were essentially disputing control over a piece of land that could not easily be divided or shared. Secondly, the most powerful party – Russia – was not willing to acknowledge its direct involvement in the conflict, and was posing as merely a mediator capable of exerting limited influence on east Ukrainian separatists (Judah 2014). Thirdly, Russia and its allies in eastern Ukraine conducted offensive operations against Ukrainian forces in late August–September 2014 and January–February 2015 – right before the start of negotiations on Minsk I and Minsk II, respectively. By doing that, Moscow was upping the ante for Kiev and expecting the Ukrainian government to collapse in the face of critical military pressure and mounting economic challenges. While Moscow and its allies were not averse to the idea of negotiations, they were hoping for a fast depletion of Kiev's resources and therefore considered as favorable a "no war, no peace" situation with a constant threat of resumption of an offensive by the separatist and Russian forces (Freedman 2015).

Although Minsk I unraveled several months after it was signed and the political provisions of Minsk II were not implemented, as initially planned, by early 2018, they both exemplify successful conclusion of negotiations. Bringing the sides to the table and negotiating to a conclusion was no easy task. The Western mediators were nevertheless determined to achieve those goals by calibrated threats of sanctions against Russia and east Ukrainian separatists. An additional incentive for Moscow to join the negotiations was the opportunity to directly engage with major Western powers, supposedly "breaking the diplomatic blockade" that had been imposed on Russia through sanctions since the middle of 2014. However, bringing the negotiations to successful closure was a challenge of bigger proportions for Kiev and the Western mediators because of their limited ability to compromise on a final solution that, as they insisted, had to restore Ukraine's *de facto* territorial integrity. For Russia and its allies, a takeover of Donbas by Kiev – whether militarily or peacefully – would have amounted to defeat. In order to reach an agreement at each of the two closure stages, in September 2014 and February 2015, willpower and creativity were indispensable.

The Kremlin treated Minsk I seriously enough at the moment of signing. The signing of the protocol by the Russian representative, Moscow's ambassador to Ukraine, Mikhail Zurabov, indicates that the Kremlin considered it as acceptable and possible to implement. It is notable that Zurabov's signature on Minsk I came in contrast to the Kremlin's backing off at the last minute from participating in the February 21, 2014 agreement between Ukrainian then-President Viktor Yanukovich and the Maidan protestors. That agreement allowed Yanukovich to stay in power, but provided for an extraordinary presidential election within several months. Moscow sought a mediation role in that process, but according to the Russian official representative who was supposed to co-sign the agreement (along with an EU mediator), the Kremlin instructed him at the last minute to hold back. Such a decision was likely taken because Moscow possessed reliable information about the determination of President Yanukovich to "pull out of the game" and flee Kiev despite the personal security guarantees that the agreement extended to him. The Kremlin's calculus may have been to use the failed implementation of the Yanukovich–Maidan agreement to accuse the EU mediators (and the West in general) of unwillingness to enforce the deal that they had mediated and endorsed.

Indeed, when signing Minsk I, Moscow and the separatists were ready to raise the cost of a stalemate in the conflict for the Ukrainian side by resuming their offensive and defeating Kiev's forces on the ground. That move, undertaken in early January 2015, was likely aimed at undermining the position of Ukrainian President Petro Poroshenko, who had characterized negotiations and the first Minsk agreement as difficult decisions that had nevertheless to be taken in the wake of a major defeat of the Ukrainian army in late August and early September 2014 (Poroshenko 2014).

However, when it became clear that Minsk I was falling victim to the second major rebel offensive in January 2015, Western mediators did not restart negotiations from scratch; instead, they framed new talks as a bid to amend Minsk I. Supported by their NATO and EU partners, Merkel and Hollande not only prevented a cardinal revision of Minsk I, but also imposed a strict timeframe on the second round of negotiation. Although no new sanctions against Russia followed the resumption of hostilities in January 2015, the Western mediators made it clear that such sanctions would be forthcoming short of an immediate ceasefire and a final agreement on a lasting settlement. In that regard, the whole Minsk process can be seen as essentially one round of negotiation with two closure phases.

Determined not to let Minsk II follow the fate of Minsk I, German Chancellor Merkel and French President Hollande visited Russian President Vladimir Putin in Moscow on February 7, 2015 amidst the continuing offensive by the Donbas separatists apparently assisted by Russian troops that provided an urgency if not a deadline. They insisted on a new round of talks to acknowledge some of the changed realities on the ground, but at the same time to provide for a definitive resolution of the conflict (BBC News 2015). As the rebels were getting massive reinforcements from Russia and their advance was continuing at a considerable pace, the summit in Minsk scheduled for February 11 was largely believed to be the last chance for Ukraine to seek a compromise with the rebels. In turn, Putin was aware of the potentially grave consequences of deliberately scuttling the Minsk negotiations. His red line may have been the unconditional surrender of control over Donbas to

Kiev, judging by his earlier statements in which he called Kiev's takeover of eastern Donbas unacceptable because, according to Putin, that could result in a crackdown on ethnic Russians who live there and who have fought against Ukraine's nationalist authorities (Official Website of the President of Russia 2014).

Negotiations in the Minsk endgame began on the night of February 11. Given the worsening plight of the Ukrainian army, Berlin was ready to offer Moscow concessions focused on Crimea; while NATO allies were determined not to recognize Crimea as part of Russia, Merkel and Hollande could float the promise of lifting the EU's most painful sanctions (against Russia's banking, defense, and oil sectors) in exchange for returning control over Donbas to Ukraine (Pond & Kundnani 2015). Several other issues on the agenda were fully negotiable, with solutions on them in no way pre-determined. These included the shape of the line of control and the issue of withdrawal of heavy artillery from the conflict zone. However, it was clear that any final settlement could only take one of the following two forms: either a complete disbanding of the east Ukrainian "people's republics" and the restoration of *de facto* Ukrainian control over Donbas, or *de jure* separation of the republics from Ukraine through recognition of their independence by Russia with subsequent open organization of their defense by the Russian military. The second option could have proven almost as costly to Russia as a new major offensive against Ukraine as it would have triggered harsher sanctions by the West.

Given the inflexibility of both Moscow and Kiev, it was not possible to resolve the core strategic question of actual control over Donbas. Overall, it meant that neither a complete failure nor a definitive agreement was an option during Minsk II. At the same time, it was clear that Minsk II was indeed the endgame because postponing negotiations or continuing them indefinitely amid the Russian-backed rebel offensive was too costly for everyone – Ukraine, Russia, and the mediators. The sides were dueling but clearly dragging one another to an agreement in Minsk – walking away was not an option.

As a result, Moscow, Kiev, Berlin, and Paris opted for promising ambiguity by pushing the political phase of the peace plan back to the end of 2015 (as was initially expected) and hoping for an easing of tensions between February and December that would make a final resolution of the Donbas status problem possible. Russia and the separatists accepted that local elections in Donbas would be held until the end of 2015 "in accordance with the Ukrainian legislation [...] and relevant OSCE standards and [would be] monitored by OSCE/ODIHR." In its turn, Kiev agreed to amend the Ukrainian legislation up to the level of the constitution to grant Donbas a higher degree of autonomy. In addition, the Ukrainian government agreed that "questions related to local elections [would] be discussed and agreed upon with representatives of particular districts of Donetsk and Luhansk oblasts in the framework of the Trilateral Contact Group" (from the full text of the Minsk II Agreement, *Financial Times* 2015).

The document's key provisions were formulated in a deliberately opaque language while the time limits of its implementation were significantly extended. All sides preferred closing the negotiations with an "unfinished" agreement rather than accepting failure of the talks because of the high cost associated with the continuation of armed hostilities. For Russia and its allies on the ground it could have spelled more casualties and/or new Western sanctions; Ukraine could have imploded politically or collapsed economically; the EU would have had to live with a major armed conflict on its eastern borders; and the United States would have looked weak in the face of what was commonly characterized in the United States as "Russian aggression."

The sides opted for a deal with a significant element of uncertainty, assuming that the way in which it would eventually be implemented would depend on the evolution of the balance of forces and resolve in the conflict. Russia expected Ukraine to shatter under the economic pressures of war and the West to reverse course toward Russia because of "sanctions fatigue." In their turn, Ukraine and the West assumed that under the sanctions Moscow would re-assess its goals in Ukraine, stop supporting the separatists and sending fighters to eastern Ukraine, and possibly even agree to discuss the status of Crimea (Nelson 2017).

The rebels' January 2015 offensive in breach of Minsk I did not bring significant gains to them and Moscow. While the rebel-controlled territory marginally increased, the uncertainty embedded in Minsk II did not favor the separatists. Backed by threats of more sanctions against Russia, Minsk II set strict time limits for reaching a political solution in the form of return of control over the rebel territories to Kiev before the end of 2015. By that time, the conflict was not resolved, but effectively frozen; controversy still surrounded the sequencing of steps to implement the agreement. While Kiev insisted that elections under the Ukrainian law and the return of control over the eastern borders of Donbas to Ukraine should precede any serious discussion of a special status for the rebellious regions within Ukraine, both the rebels and Moscow argued that the incumbent separatist authorities had the right to conduct (that is, control and win) the elections. Only after these authorities had obtained recognition as a legitimate political force in Ukraine would they be ready to discuss the modalities of the border regime with Kiev. For the next four years and more, both Moscow and Kiev kept claiming that no viable alternative existed to Minsk II while accusing each other of dragging their feet on its implementation.

Acknowledging their failure to reach the required comprehensive settlement within the timeframe stipulated in the February 2015 document – by the end of 2015 – the leaders of Ukraine, Russia, Germany, and France decided in late December 2015 to allow for an additional year to implement Minsk II. Their continued verbal commitment to the agreement despite continued violence throughout 2015 and beyond confirmed that all sides were expecting the situation to eventually resolve in their respective favor, with resumed fighting or even a mere declaration of the impossibility of implementing the political part of Minsk II being considered the worst available option.

Both divergent assessments of the future outlook for the conflict and "hyperbolic discounting" played a role in facilitating the Minsk agreements. Moscow expected Ukraine to unravel under the weight of massive economic problems in the absence of a unifying challenge of the separatist rebellion in Donbas. In its turn, Kiev was counting on support from the West that was keeping Russia under the pressure of sanctions that many in Ukraine expected to lead to a change in Russian policy in the foreseeable future. Both sides appeared reluctant to consider a scenario in which none of those expectations would come into being, while the civil war in Donbas and the sanctions against Russia would continue to inflict pain both on Kiev and on Moscow over an indefinite period of time.

Even if, as of 2019, there are reasons to consider Minsk II impossible to implement and therefore a failure, its fate, just like that of anything else in the world, was not pre-destined – considerable chances existed for the agreement to be clarified and implemented. As the sides were facing an increasingly painful stalemate on the ground after signing the Minsk documents, they could have opted for a compromise on the most controversial issues of local elections and control over the separatist enclaves' border with Russia. In the absence of major breaches of the ceasefire, the Minsk process could have drained the resources both of Kiev (facing the constant threat of a financial meltdown or a new political rebellion) and of Moscow (suffering under Western sanctions) and eventually dragged them to a lasting political solution.

German Reunification

Negotiations between the USSR and the leading Western nations on the reunification of Germany began after the fall of the Berlin Wall in

November 1989 and concluded with the signing in September 1990 of the "4+2" agreement allowing the accession of what used to constitute the German Democratic Republic (GDR) to the Federal Republic of Germany (FRG). The speed with which these negotiations proceeded was astonishing. The Soviet Union not only agreed to pull out several hundred thousand troops it had kept on the ground in East Germany and other Central European countries and acquiesced to the removal from power of the most conservative elements in the East German government, but also relinquished political control over the GDR, thus allowing its absorption into the FRG.

Starting in late 1989, the Kremlin was facing a rapidly expanding array of challenges – from a full-blown economic crisis to ethnic hostilities in the peripheral republics of the USSR. By summer 1990, the Soviet leader Mikhail Gorbachev had realized that he would soon need external financial support in order to keep his country going. West Germany was willing to provide such support in exchange for removal of the last impediments to reunification. Regardless of the Soviet Union's predicament, throughout 1990 Moscow possessed enough bargaining power to delay closure in the reunification negotiations and prevent any deal from materializing. According to the historian Mary Elise Sarotte (2014, 9), "The Soviet Union had the ability to cause enormous problems for Kohl. Even though the USSR was on the verge of ruin, it held legal rights emanating from World War II and maintained roughly four hundred thousand troops in East Germany; these facts gave Gorbachev leverage regardless of his situation at home."

One of the most contentious issues in negotiating German reunification was the status of the unified Germany within NATO and the future of the European security order. Gorbachev initially expected to preserve the Warsaw Treaty Organization – the Soviet-led military bloc opposing NATO. Yet by the early months of 1990 it had become clear to him that it would be difficult to maintain the Warsaw Pact in its existing form, so the best Moscow could aspire to was a security order where NATO would continue to exist, but its role would be reduced, while a pan-European security institution would take the lead in managing European security. That would have required placing limits on NATO's ambitions in the post-Cold War world. A key constraint would have been a non-enlargement pledge that Gorbachev expected to receive from the North Atlantic Alliance.

Historians are engaged in a heated debate on the existence of non-enlargement guarantees extended to Gorbachev by the leaders of the United States and West Germany at different points in the reunification negotiations. Sarotte (2014) has pointed to documentary evidence of oral promises given by the US Secretary of State James Baker and the German Chancellor Helmut Kohl to Gorbachev in early February 1990 to forgo inclusion of the East German territory into NATO after reunification. Major West European leaders, such as the French President François Mitterand and the British Prime Minister Margaret Thatcher, were even willing to contemplate neutralization of Germany if the Soviet Union accepted German reunification.

Other scholars have suggested that the discussion on the status of East Germany within NATO did not in any case bear on the potential accession to NATO of other members of the Soviet bloc because in early 1990 these countries were still unable to make alliance choices (Kramer 2009). However, Sarotte insists that at least in the depths of policy planning at the US State Department and among Central European politicians, the prospect of expanding NATO eastwards was being discussed as Baker and Kohl were negotiating reunification conditions with Gorbachev. Sarotte's claims are backed up by more recent research suggesting that a discussion of the possibilities of offering restrictions on the enlargement of NATO did take place in the George H. W. Bush administration in 1990 (Shifrinson 2016).

The bottom line in that debate is that no written agreement on NATO emerged out of the February 1990 talks in Moscow. Therefore, even if any commitments were made during the negotiation, they did not bind future NATO policymakers. What is important is that between February 1990, when the promises were made, and September 1990, when the reunification actually happened, only a number of officials in the Bush administration were strictly opposed to any self-restraint on the part of NATO. Gorbachev and his team, as well as influential West European leaders – at least until late spring or summer 1990 – negotiated on the assumption that NATO would retain full freedom as a result of the German settlement. The US leadership acknowledged, according to Sarotte, that the Soviet Union could have bargained harder, although the willingness of NATO allies, including the FRG itself, to agree to tougher terms of the reunification was not pre-ordained.

The February 1990 negotiations created ambiguity around the prospects for NATO enlargement, and such ambiguity proved sufficient to close the reunification deal several months later. Even if the final agreement only banned the deployment of foreign troops and nuclear weapons on the former GDR territory while allowing the unified Germany to remain in NATO, the Soviet leaders may have been acting out of the belief that their fast retreat from Central Europe would not result in NATO promptly moving in to fill the vacuum. They were clearly susceptible to the "hyperbolic discounting" syndrome. Eventually, this ambiguity was dispelled when it became clear that post-Communist Russia would not be able to resist NATO's enlargement to Central and Eastern Europe, and the Clinton administration decided to move forward with it (Goldgeier 2016). Yet at the time of negotiation closure, such uncertainty untied Gorbachev's hands and convinced him not to thwart the reunification wholesale.

Negotiations on Iran's Nuclear Program

The P5+1 talks with Iran stalled for a decade from their beginning in 2003 until 2013 because the six negotiating powers insisted on absolute clarity about Iran's nuclear designs. They were insisting that Iran verifiably forswear any dual-use capabilities, and their demands included the dismantlement of all of Iran's uranium-enrichment equipment. Tehran was unwilling to do so, citing its right to a peaceful nuclear program under the NPT, which does not prohibit enrichment by non-nuclear-weapon states.

After a number of revelations made in 2002 and 2003 gave the international community grounds to suspect that Iran had been covertly developing dual-use (both peaceful and military) nuclear capabilities, the EU and the United States were quick to demand that Iran should immediately halt any enrichment of uranium. In November 2003 Tehran complied, and agreed to work with Brussels and Washington toward a comprehensive and permanent agreement on limitations upon and international control over Iran's nuclear program. The Western powers and Russia made it clear that they would be ready to supply Iran with light-water nuclear reactors, airplane engines, and electronics, and to support Tehran's bid to enter the World Trade Organization (WTO) in exchange for Iran's agreement not to pursue the full nuclear cycle and to allow rigorous inspections by the International Atomic Energy Agency (IAEA).

However, Iran continued to insist on its right to a limited uranium-enrichment program. A newly elected hard-line Iranian President, Mahmoud Ahmadinejad, announced, in late July 2005, that Tehran was resuming enrichment activities. That resulted in the six negotiating powers (China, France, Germany, Russia, the United Kingdom, and the United States) immediately toughening their stance and reiterating the no-enrichment demand. The IAEA indicated that it was ready to refer the Iran case to the UN Security Council, that would then come under much pressure to introduce sanctions against Iran. Russia and some of Iran's neighbors floated a proposal whereby Tehran would agree to send its uranium for enrichment abroad and get it back in the form of nuclear-reactor fuel rods unsuitable for remaking into weapons-grade material.

Tehran remained defiant, and in April 2006 informed the IAEA of its refusal to stop enriching uranium. In October 2006 Iran announced the launch of a second cascade of enrichment centrifuges. As a result, Security Council members in December 2006 united to pass Resolution 1737, banning all supplies to Iran that could be related to its nuclear program and demanding that all enrichment should be stopped within two months. UN sanctions were tightened in March 2007 by UNSC Resolution 1747, which imposed bans on state loans and exports of heavy arms to Iran, to be lifted only upon compliance with the no-enrichment demand. Further UN sanctions, including freezes of foreign assets for a number of Iranian organizations allegedly involved in the country's nuclear program, were introduced by Resolutions 1803 in March 2008 and 1929 in June 2010. In addition, the United States and its allies in Europe and Asia in 2010–2011 imposed stringent sanctions on Iran's oil industry, making investment into it extremely difficult and seriously restricting sales of Iranian oil.

Between 2011 and 2013 Iran's oil exports fell more than three-fold from the initial 2.2 million barrels per day, which resulted in the loss by Iran of tens of billions of US dollars in revenue. Iran's economy started tanking, with inflation becoming rampant (BBC World Service 2015).

However, Tehran continued to insist on its right under the Non-Proliferation Treaty to enrich uranium for peaceful purposes. The regional security situation was becoming tenser, with both the Israeli government and the Obama administration suggesting that the use of force against Iran was not being ruled out. That dynamic was clearly bringing the sides into an impasse until two major developments opened the door to a more constructive engagement.

The first was the election of a liberally minded (by Iranian standards) politician, Hassan Rouhani, as the president of Iran in August 2013. Rouhani was calling for a stepped-up dialogue with the United States, and his agenda was seemingly being supported by Iran's supreme leader, Grand Ayatollah Ali Khamenei. But equally important was the apparent readiness of the US government to discuss a nuclear deal that would fall short of a complete ban on enrichment.

Secret bilateral negotiations between the United States and Iran started the endgame soon after the election of Rouhani. As a major concession to Iran, the United States expressed a readiness to allow Iran to retain a certain enrichment capability in exchange for downsizing the key dual-use aspects of Iran's nuclear program. According to reports in major international newspapers, the reframing of the formula allowing for continued enrichment was developed late in 2012 by the team of US Secretary of State Hillary Clinton. Clinton reluctantly "recognized the difficulty of reaching a solution with zero enrichment," after her top foreign-policy aide reported from a preliminary round of negotiation with Iran in July 2012 that "zero enrichment" would be a non-starter for Tehran. US President Barack Obama either inspired or eventually got onboard with that approach, and proved ready to invest political capital into negotiating away the immediate risk of weaponization of Iran's nuclear program (Solomon & Meckler 2015). The five other negotiating parties endorsed the shift by mid 2013, and the deal acquired clear contours. It then took two more years of endgame negotiation to nail it down.

The resulting agreement between the six powers and Iran – the Joint Comprehensive Plan of Action (JCPOA) signed on July 14, 2015 – is discussed at length in Chapter 1 by Ariane Tabatabai and Camille Pease. Here it is important to note that by July 2015, negotiators were well in the endgame, into which they pushed themselves by agreeing to strict deadlines to conclude their talks and then agonizingly granting themselves brief extensions. The deadlines were imposed on the delegations primarily by the domestic politics in the United States and Iran, where opposition to the fledgling deal by Congress and Ayatollah Khamenei, respectively, threatened to become unsurpassable.

In such a situation of forced closure, the price the P5+1 had to pay for the nuclear deal with Iran was the preservation of significant uncertainty about Tehran's intentions in the nuclear field. Neither party pretended that the prospect of Iran acquiring a nuclear bomb was being discarded for good. Instead, the six powers argued that the deal would only extend the breakout period – the time necessary for diverting Iran's nuclear program to the military path and manufacturing a bomb. The six powers effectively relinquished their demand for full certainty about Iran's ultimate designs and reconciled themselves to achieving only an extension of Iran's breakout period.

While Tehran may not have been planning to manufacture a nuclear explosive device, the uncertainty about its intentions embedded in the JCPOA was beneficial to Iran as it could serve as a means of deterring or pressurizing Iran's regional rivals that had to take into account the possibility of Tehran breaking out of the agreement at a critical juncture in a putative regional stand-off. In any case, Iran would be free from most of the constraints imposed by the JCPOA, including those on Iran's nuclear-enrichment capability, within ten years of signing the agreement. Tehran may have been looking simply to postpone a major offensive against its regional and global rivals – after a decade's wait it could expect to emerge strengthened by unfrozen assets, a massive capital inflow, and expanded international trade. If the country's leadership never intended to change its approach to regional and international politics, it may have viewed the agreement as a strategic pause on the way toward a decisive reinforcement of its military capabilities, potentially including the nuclear bomb.

In their turn, the six powers gambled on the transformation of Iran's foreign policy and security aspirations upon greater integration into transnational business and social networks. The Iranian society and its leadership were expected to put religious intransigence and regional rivalries on the backburner while engaging in trade and attracting investment in a stable regional environment. Seeking to reap immediate benefits from an agreement with Iran, the six powers – and especially the United States – were prepared to discount major future risks of Iran, strengthened by unhindered economic engagement with the outside world, speeding up its missile program and eventually acquiring a nuclear bomb. In any case, the ambiguity inherent in the nuclear agreement with Iran allowed all sides to emerge victoriously from the protracted negotiation and achieve substantial progress in curbing the Iranian nuclear capability. That was just enough to stave off a crisis of the non-proliferation regime.

Conclusion: Ambiguity as a Deal-Maker

The uncertainty surrounding the outcome of the Minsk process in eastern Ukraine can be characterized as "positive" – one that expanded the room for maneuver on both sides. More generally, if the win-set of a negotiating party is defined as the set of outcomes with a satisfactory product of the outcome's utility and its probability, then thinking of outcomes in terms of ambiguity can sometimes expand the negotiating parties' win-sets. This happens because more positive outcomes will appear on the negotiation table once it becomes possible to push the judgment about an outcome's utility further into the future by describing this utility in probabilistic terms. For example, risk-prone negotiators could factor into their position new high-utility, but low-probability, outcomes that would be ruled out by a classical, non-probabilistic calculus. Generally, outcomes understood as probabilities are more easily comparable than "full-certainty" outcomes.

The flip side of the probability approach to assessing outcomes in negotiations is that negative – if low-probability and distant – outcomes will also have to be considered. For example, while the Minsk closure concerned only the fate of Donbas, Crimea loomed on the horizon during the talks as the next potential subject of negotiation. Moscow had pledged not to discuss the status of Crimea as a part of the Russian

Federation and even promised to deploy nuclear weapons on the peninsula to ensure its protection (Interfax-Ukraine 2014). And yet uncertainty about the West's approach to the issue of Crimea was lurking behind the Minsk accords. Two possibilities were discernible: Either the United States and its allies could agree to turn the page and refrain from pressuring Russia on Crimea, leaving only several symbolic sanctions in place, or the West could sustain its pressure, demanding negotiations and a settlement of the Crimea issue between Kiev and Moscow. It was not clear to the Kremlin which of these scenarios would materialize should Moscow stop supporting east Ukrainian separatists. A number of voices claiming to have an insight into the Kremlin's thinking complained that a compromise on eastern Ukraine could portray Russia as a weak player, prompting Kiev and the Western powers to raise the stakes and demand the return of Crimea (Charap & Colton 2017).

Overall, uncertainty during closure can provide a number of benefits to the sides. First, it can help the negotiators to convince second-level (usually, domestic) constituencies that no significant concessions have been made. Secondly, it can send the desired signals to third parties. The sides may wish not to become or appear weak in the eyes of third parties as a result of the agreement, so the availability of a number of interpretations of the negotiated agreement can help to fend off critics of the negotiators – for example, their domestic political adversaries. In the meantime, the negotiators will be able to claim credit for removing a disturbing and potentially costly dispute from their respective countries' agendas through peaceful and costless negotiations. For example, Iran's preserved enrichment capability showed its regional rivals that Tehran would be able to acquire a nuclear weapon should its vital interests come under threat. In its turn, by signing the Minsk agreements, Russia sought to convince the West that it was not opposed to Ukraine's territorial integrity (minus Crimea) while shifting the (potentially unbearable) burden of restoring that integrity to Kiev.

The cases examined here demonstrate that ambiguity in some aspects of the final agreement can sometimes be sustained until external developments hammer out a final resolution of the unsettled issues. Such resolution can materialize in different ways. In the negotiations on German reunification, the undecided issue lapsed in importance within several months of the deal having been reached – the Soviet Union broke up, and it took the newly independent Russian Federation at least two years to define its attitude to NATO enlargement. Even after Moscow had chosen to resist the geographic expansion of its former rival, for more than a decade the Kremlin's opinion was not being taken into account by NATO and its key member countries because Russia was not considered a formidable opponent any longer, and because NATO allies felt that their uncompromising cold-war posture had been vindicated by their ultimate victory.

At the time of writing, the jury was still out on the status of parts of Donbas, while the Iran nuclear deal seemed to be unraveling. Because of the change in US policy under the administration of Donald Trump, it remained in doubt. It remained to be seen whether the post-agreement flow of events would resolve to mutual satisfaction the issues left to chance. Even if they are inconclusive, these two cases suggest that the sides would be ready to accept the outcome if it did not significantly deviate from the status quo at the time of signing the deal. If some situation strongly favors one party over others, the temptation of the losing side to back out of the agreement after the "fog of uncertainty" has dissipated will be too strong for the agreement to hold.

14 When is "Enough" Enough? Approach–Avoidance

Dean G. Pruitt

Approach–avoidance conflict theory helps one to understand some of the events at the end of negotiation.[1] Approach and avoidance are fundamental building blocks of behavior which are controlled by different parts of the brain (Elliot & Covington 2001). They come into conflict when they occur simultaneously – we are attracted to an object, place, or action, but also repelled by it.

Approach–avoidance conflict often grows as we move toward an attractive object, place, or action. Approach is dominant as we start out, but as we get closer, reasons for avoidance come into focus. Is this really a good idea? Are we getting into trouble? Are we hurting ourselves? We become ambivalent and may pause to examine what we are doing? Consider, for example, Nowak and Vallacher's (1998) story of a hungry man who begins walking toward a refrigerator which he knows contains a tasty slice of pizza but then hesitates because he remembers that he is on a strict diet. What he does depends on the relative strength of the two sides of his ambivalence, but sorting that out takes time and effort.

Implications for Negotiation

A similar phenomenon often occurs in negotiation. The parties enter with some enthusiasm because the negotiation may help them achieve their goals or escape unwanted circumstances. But as the best possible agreement comes into view, one or both of them begin to have doubts. Is this what we were hoping for? Are we making a big mistake? Should we continue the talks? This is approach–avoidance conflict, and the pros and cons must be sorted out. Consider the following two examples.

---

[1] I wish to thank I. William Zartman for suggesting most of the international negotiation examples mentioned in this chapter.

The United States started the climate-change control process with the launching of the Framework Convention on Climate Change (FCCC) in 1992. But when it came to filling in the framework with action and policy commitments, the United States had second thoughts on the way to Kyoto and beyond. Then a different administration picked up the approach again, in Paris in 2015. Torn between the need to do something to mitigate the effects of global warming and the skepticism of parts of the public and government, the United States found the goal less attractive as it came face-to-face with the issue of implementation. Often parties head toward an improvement in their situation, only to see that the necessary actions are more than they can accept, and pull back.

Perhaps the most striking long-range example is the course of negotiations in the Middle East peace process, in which approach–avoidance conflict occurred again and again. Following UNSC Resolution 242 in 1968, which set the formula of "territory for security," negotiations began in 1973 for Israeli withdrawal from Egyptian and Syrian territories. However, in 1974, approach–avoidance conflict developed as Israel began to consider the prospects of a withdrawal from the Golan Heights, and the Syrian talks finally ground to a halt. Camp David followed in 1978, and, after much hesitation, an agreement between Israel and Egypt was signed. The next step was a renewed attempt to forge an Israeli–Syrian settlement, but avoidance again developed as the contours of a possible agreement came into sight (Rabinovich 1998). Jordan's turn came next, in 1994, and the approach prevailed over avoidance. Then in 1993, Israel and the Palestinian Liberation Organization reached a framework agreement at Oslo (Pruitt 1997), but avoidance took over when it came to implementation. The closer the parties got to a two-state solution, the more they disliked where they were heading, and the talks began dragging. Not only did movement toward the goal eventually stop, but the halt created worsening relations of disillusionment and distrust.

The reader may have noticed that the nature of the approach–avoidance conflict changed as we moved from individual decision-making (the refrigerator example) to national decision-making. When individuals are involved, the conflict is entirely intracranial. But in the case of nations (or smaller organizations), the conflict is likely to be both within *and between* people. Individuals or groups will often vie with each other to command the nation's decision-making, and some (the doves) are likely to favor moving to agreement while others (the hawks) favor making further demands or breaking off. Which side wins that sort of contest will depend on the strength of their arguments and their relative power.

Theory and Research on Approach–Avoidance Conflict

The original thinking about approach–avoidance conflict was based on observations of human behavior (Lewin 1935), and the theory was first used in explaining negotiations in Jensen's (1968) analysis of disarmament talks. The most important experimental research was done by Neil E. Miller (1944; 1971), who performed experiments with white Norway rats. These animals are like humans in their basic psychological makeup, though their thinking and range of action are much more limited. Miller trained hungry rats to run down a wooden alley to find food at the end. After they had been trained, he shocked their little feet at the end of the run when they were about to eat the food. When he put them back at the start point, most of them ran only part way and then got stuck, running short distances back and forth until the experimenter lifted them out. Clearly, they were in conflict between a hunger-motivated tendency to approach the end of the alley and a fear-motivated tendency to avoid it, just as a state might be caught between a peace-motivated tendency to end a conflict with a neighboring territory and a fear-motivated tendency to avoid the consequences of having an untrusted sovereign neighbor next door.

Figure 14.1 shows Miller's diagram of what happens inside humans or animals during approach–avoidance conflict. It is based on an earlier study in which Brown (1940) directly measured the strength of the approach and avoidance tendencies. The horizontal axis represents the floor of an alley or kitchen (in the refrigerator example), or, by extension, the path toward a negotiated agreement, with the start point on the right and the endpoint (where the food or agreement is located) on the left. The vertical axis shows the strength of the approach and avoidance tendencies.

The flatter line in the middle shows the strength of the approach tendency at each point in the journey – moderately strong at the start on the right and somewhat stronger as the actor gets closer to the endpoint. The steeper line shows the strength of the avoidance tendency. This tendency is quite weak at a distance from the endpoint but gets much stronger as the actor moves closer. Note that at the start, the approach tendency is stronger than the avoidance tendency, which is why the actor starts moving. But the avoidance tendency strengthens rapidly as the actor continues. At the point where the lines cross, the two tendencies are equal in strength, so the actor slows down or stops and shows signs of being in approach–avoidance conflict.

Why is the avoidance line steeper than the approach line in Figure 14.1? There are two possible answers, and both may be correct

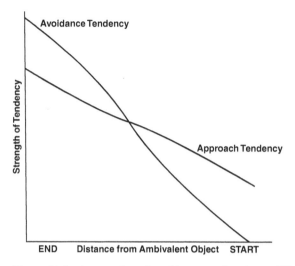

Figure 14.1. Approach and avoidance tendencies at different points in a journey. Approach–avoidance conflict is strongest where the lines cross. (Weiner 1972, 64)

since most behavior has multiple antecedents. One, advocated by Miller, is that the human or animal starts out with the motive (e.g. hunger) that is causing their approach and carries it with them as they move toward the end-point. That motive accounts for most of the approach tendency and stays constant as the actor moves along. The only thing that changes is the relative prominence of the endpoint in the actor's thinking, which "whets the appetite" for the object that is motivating the approach, somewhat increasing the approach tendency. However, the fear (or other repugnance) motive that engenders avoidance is produced by the prominence of the endpoint, rather than being dominant from the start. The avoidance tendency is not strong at first, because the endpoint is far away and not clearly envisioned. But the fear strengthens rapidly as action moves along, because the endpoint becomes clearer and more immediate.

The other possible answer derives from more recent research by Kahneman and Tversky (Kahneman 2011). Animals and humans are built in such a way that displeasure with negative events is much stronger than pleasure with comparable positive events, as discussed in Chapter 12 on prospect theory by Janice Gross Stein. Indeed, those authors find that human distress at losing a sum of money is about twice the happiness that is experienced on winning the same amount. Thus, loss looms larger than gain by a factor of two to one. It follows that as parties move toward an outcome and it becomes increasingly prominent in their thinking, the approach tendency will rise to some extent, but unpleasant implications and consequences of attaining the goal – the avoidance tendency – will rise twice as fast, as shown in Figure 14.1.

More Implications for Negotiation

So how does approach–avoidance theory apply to behavior at the end of negotiation? People commonly start negotiating because they envision an improvement in the status quo that can be achieved by a good agreement. Hence, they often begin with a strong approach motive and, as with the hunger drive in some of the examples cited above, they carry that motive with them as the talks progress. The avoidance motive is weak at first because it is hard for them to envision the end state. The other party's decisions and their own reactions to these decisions are not yet known. But as negotiation moves along, the best agreement they can possibly attain becomes increasingly clear and with it the expected cost (or risk) associated with that agreement. Approach–avoidance conflict sets in and the parties begin to examine whether that agreement is good enough. If the avoidance tendency becomes strong on either or both sides, it may cause the negotiation to drag and then end in failure. An outside observer might say that they are leaving money on the table, but remember that expected cost outweighs expected gain two-to-one in people's thinking.

Continuing with the Middle East narrative described earlier, renewed Israeli–Palestinian talks at Camp David in 2000 were making progress at first. But then PLO Chairman Yasser Arafat (who initially had protested that he was not ready for talks) dropped out psychologically, explaining that if he agreed to the terms under discussion, he would be murdered by some of his constituents. Thereafter he showed virtually no flexibility, dismissing all of the mediator's suggestions (Swisher 2004), and no agreement was reached. There are several possible explanations for his behavior. Perhaps he never intended to reach an agreement, or maybe Israel's best proposal did not meet an obvious bottom line, or possibly Israel made mistakes that reduced his freedom of choice.

But approach–avoidance conflict theory can also explain what happened. The avoidance line of thinking was present from the beginning but, as in Figure 14.1, it rose so fast that it overtook the approach line, despite the mediators' efforts to tamp it down. As the negotiation moved along, Arafat became increasingly clear about the range of possible agreements. At some point, he realized that the game of chicken was

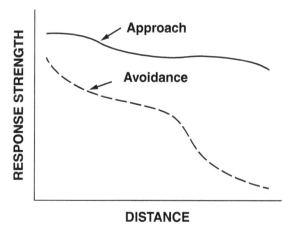

Figure 14.2. Approach–avoidance conflict when the approach tendency dominates over the avoidance tendency. (Miller 1971, 20)

near its end and Israel was unlikely to make substantial further concessions. Hence, the best agreement that he could obtain became prominent in his thinking, and with it the plusses and minuses associated with that agreement. On the positive (approach) side, the agreement would strengthen the Palestinian Authority, which was at least part of the reason why he got into the negotiation. But on the negative (avoidance) side, he would get into trouble with many of his constituents, who would insist that Israel make more concessions. Thoughts about constituent reactions – the "game of echoes" analyzed in Chapter 15 by P. Terrence Hopmann – may have produced rapidly growing fear which finally overwhelmed his desire for an agreement. That fear may have been strengthened by actual pressure from hawkish constituents who began to realize where the negotiation was headed. Constituent reaction was the reason he gave for dropping out.

One may wonder how agreements are ever reached, given these dynamics. The answer is that expected reward sometimes outweighs expected cost despite the latter's two-to-one advantage. This is shown in Figure 14.2. A negotiator's avoidance tendency rises as the likely agreement comes in view, and approach–avoidance conflict steadily increases. The result is soul searching and debate about whether to agree or to exit the negotiation. But the approach tendency wins out, which can happen in two ways: Either the developing agreement nicely improves on the status quo and is not so frightening, or the status quo is (or has become) so deficient that even a minimally favorable agreement seems better than none. Figure 14.2 models the situation in the 1963 Franco-German friendship negotiations that led to the Élysée Treaty, as described by Valerie Rosoux in Chapter 5; Figure 14.1 models her contrasting case, the failed 2004–2006 Franco-Algerian friendship negotiations.

The analysis also explains the situation where the option of continuing to negotiate is adopted. Negotiators will choose that option if, after reflection and consultation, the situation is so unclear that it cannot be assigned to either Figure 14.1 or Figure 14.2. Then they must kick the can further down the road and continue experiencing approach–avoidance conflict until a clearer picture develops. Something will change and they will eventually make a definitive decision, but for the moment they engage in dragging behavior. For example, under mediation by Norway and the Centre for Humanitarian Dialog (CHD), the Acehnese and Indonesians balked at the idea of "special autonomy," but then mediation by Martti Ahtisaari moved them on to accept "self-government" in 2005, ending a thirty-year rebellion.

Sometimes the approach and avoidance lines are so close at the end that a party wobbles publicly from one to the other. Richard Holbrooke (1998, 304–309) recalls that Bosnian President Alija Izetbegović refused an offer on November 20 but accepted it on November 21, reversing his refusal of the day before. The dueling negotiations over the 51%–49% land formula in the prior few days show how close approach was to avoidance for Izetbegović as the talks advanced to the end of the endgame (Holbrooke 1998, 293–299). Holbrooke recalls whispering to the US Secretary of State immediately after this reversal, "Let's get out of here fast" before he changes his mind again.

Suppose a negotiator reconciles his or her conflict by deciding to agree to the available terms. What then happens to the avoidance tendency and the fear on which it is often based? There is a study of novice parachute jumpers that may speak to that issue (Epstein & Fenz 1965). The researchers asked the men about their level of fear at several points before the jump. The results showed that fear steadily increased, as Miller would predict; but it sharply declined just before the jump. What may have happened at that point is that the parachutists made a definitive decision to go ahead with the jump and then steeled themselves for that event. Surprisingly, people have some control over their emotions and can even push away fear. That may be what happens in negotiation if a period of heavy approach–avoidance conflict produces a decision to reach agreement. In Zartman's words, they "[weigh their] values against the fearful hurdle and decide to go for it." The fear associated with that hurdle then fades away, along with the approach–avoidance conflict.

Conclusions

Two pieces of practical advice to negotiators and mediators are implied by the ideas just presented.

1. Toward the end of talks, negotiators will often be in severe conflict about whether to accept or reject the agreement that is shaping up. A researcher might be able to draw nice diagrams like those in Figures 14.1 and 14.2 to show how they will eventually decide. But the actual negotiators will be experiencing considerable uncertainty about what to do, because of approach–avoidance conflict. They must weigh their options and consult their validators. If the original motives that brought them into negotiation are strong enough, they and their validators may have to rethink their bottom lines and make additional concessions, accepting the available agreement. Or perhaps they can think of a new and better mutually acceptable option. Or, if their fears turn out to be stronger than their needs, they may decide to drop out. Clearly time is required to sort through these possibilities.

It follows that negotiators must be given time to work through their approach–avoidance conflict and not be required to make so quick a decision that they feel forced to withdraw. Imposing a deadline may be a good strategy when parties are close to agreement, but deadlines should not be totally rigid. Sometimes there needs to be wiggle room to allow negotiators and their validators time to think more deeply about what they want to do.

2. Knowing that cost looms larger than gain in people's thinking, it is particularly important to try to cut the other party's cost of reaching a viable agreement. There is a tendency to assume that the other party's hesitation about our offer is an effort to force us to make more concessions. While that may be true, the hesitation may instead reflect concern about the costs associated with what we are proposing, and we need to understand the nature of those costs and try to reduce them. Often cutting the other side's costs requires less sacrifice than one thinks.

Empathy with the other side – putting oneself in the other's shoes – will be helpful in discovering those costs. (Empathy is different from sympathy, though we need to be careful that the former not slide into the latter.) Understanding the other's costs may require us to believe what the other says, which is not always possible in a highly competitive situation. Hence, we may need to turn to trusted third parties who understand the other side.

The ideas presented in this chapter imply two other pieces of advice, this time for negotiation theorists and researchers.

3. The motives that impel a party into negotiation are likely to persist in that party's thinking and to affect the path of negotiation and the agreement reached at the end. These motives often derive from deficiencies in the status quo, including what Zartman (2000) calls a "hurting stalemate." The stronger a party's desire to escape the status quo, the more likely it is to make heavy concessions and accept an inferior settlement. Hence, one party's deficient status quo is a source of bargaining strength for the other. As Druckman (1994) has shown, there are many other variables that affect the likelihood of concession making; but the quality of a party's status quo is an important one and needs to be prominent in negotiation theory.

4. Approach–avoidance conflict usually is unpleasant, annoying, and distasteful – especially if it involves impassioned arguments between hawks and doves within our party. Unpleasantness usually motivates efforts to escape it, which in end-state negotiation may lead a party to lower its aspirations, to search for a novel mutually acceptable solution, or even to drop out of the negotiation and thus end the accompanying conflict. This line of reasoning has not yet produced any theory or research, but it deserves scholarly attention. To what extent does approach–avoidance conflict *per se* motivate action? If it does so to a significant extent, what sorts of actions may be so engendered and under what circumstances?

15   When is "Enough" Enough? Settling for Suboptimal Agreement

P. Terrence Hopmann

This chapter explores the issue of what may appear to be "premature closure," that is, a situation in which parties in a negotiation reach essentially satisfactory but suboptimal agreements that leave potential joint gains on the table. Many negotiated agreements are in fact suboptimal, in the sense that all parties could have achieved mutual gains through continued negotiation, but for various reasons to be elaborated below they conclude that an agreement is "good enough" and suspend negotiations before reaching the optimal outcome that might have further advanced the value for all parties if they had continued to negotiate. In the first systematic modern treatment of international negotiations, Fred Charles Iklé (1964, 59–60) asserted that at any point in a negotiation the parties face three choices: (1) to accept an agreement around which the parties have converged for whatever reason; (2) to terminate negotiations with no plans to resume them, or (3) "to try to improve the 'available' terms through further bargaining." This chapter analyzes the apparent dilemma of why so often negotiators opt for the first choice of accepting a "satisficing" agreement rather than the third possibility, that is, continuing to negotiate to seek mutually better terms of agreement.

The chapter begins with a theoretical introduction based upon game theory, which like all such analyses assumes that parties are rational utility maximizers, although each party's "rational" preferred outcome may be arrived at subjectively and thus be influenced by values and even by emotions. However, a puzzle arises when negotiators do achieve positive results for all parties and thus seize the moment and reach closure before exploring additional possibilities to enlarge their joint gains. The basic question is, "Why do the parties reach closure believing that they have achieved 'enough' benefit when they might have achieved more through continued efforts to negotiate?" Why are they often utility "satisficers" rather than utility maximizers?

The basic criteria for a "good agreement" include the values of efficiency (achieving maximum collective benefit), fairness (achieving agreements in which the parties' gains are approximately equal *relative to their security levels or their "best alternative to a negotiated agreement"* [BATNA]) (Fisher & Ury 1991), and stability and durability (achieving agreements that the parties have both the intent and the capability to implement over the long term) (Hopmann 1996, 28–30). Durability is closely related to the first two criteria, in the sense that the parties are most likely to want to implement agreements that provide them with maximum possible benefit and that they perceive to be fair; parties that believe that an agreement is unequal in favor of the other party(ies) and leaves them short of an optimal solution are less likely to have incentives to implement agreements fully over the long term. Conversely, the best guarantee of an agreement's survival is that all parties see it as fulfilling their interests, values, and needs to the greatest possible extent.

This chapter will explore the implications of these negotiation objectives in terms of the way they affect the timing of negotiation closure, especially why negotiations sometimes reach closure when they have only partly achieved these goals. It will focus here primarily on the efficiency criterion, while also considering fairness and stability as secondary factors, which should not be interpreted as suggesting that these latter factors are somehow less important than efficiency. The model that follows is just that, a model that is intended to elucidate the logic underlying the frequent failure to maximize mutual benefits in negotiations. It does not necessarily assume that optimality always represents a normatively superior outcome, especially in the formal sense, but I do argue that it is in the interest of all parties in a negotiation to achieve the maximum collective benefit possible in any given situation, especially when they can all reach superior outcomes simultaneously. Of course, the "value" of an agreement is subjectively defined by the parties, and benefits and costs to the parties cannot generally be identified objectively. They may include not only measurable, tangible values such as wealth, power, territory, and so forth, but also more subjective values such as normative principles like justice, status, saving face, defending identity, and self-respect. In this sense "optimality" lies in the collective beliefs of the parties to a negotiation. Cognitive, perceptual, and pragmatic considerations may all contribute to reaching agreements that are less than optimal for all parties, but a suboptimal agreement is not necessarily a "bad" agreement; in most cases it is preferable to Iklé's second choice of walking away without any agreement in the sense that it leaves all parties believing that they are better off than they would be if negotiations were suspended indefinitely. Nonetheless, it is also unfortunate that so many agreements leave value at the negotiating table that could have provided benefits for all parties simultaneously.

The Basic Model

The basic theoretical argument can best be represented by a classic game theory model, usually known as the "Battle of the Sexes," developed by Anatol Rapoport (1960) and Howard Raiffa (1995), depicted in an updated form in Figure 15.1. This model assumes a two-person, non-zero-sum negotiation, although it could be expanded into multi-dimensional space to account for multiparty negotiations.

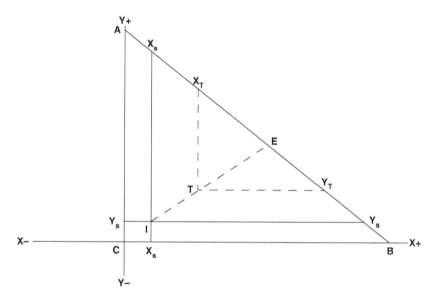

X: Value of agreement for party X (positive to negative)

Y: Value of agreement for party Y (positive to negative)

A–B: Frontier of optimal agreement

C: Point of neutral value (indifference) for both parties X and Y: value of agreement = value of non-agreement

X_s: Security Level (minimum acceptable agreement) for party X

Y_s: Security Level (minimum acceptable agreement) for party Y

I: Intersection of Security levels (minimum agreement for both parties)

Y_s–X_s–I: Zone of Possible Agreement (ZOPA)

E: Equilibrium outcome – maximum benefit and equal gains relative to non-agreement for both parties (optimal and "fair" outcome) – 45° angle to northeast from 1.

T: Hypothetical tentative agreement point

Y_T–X_T–T: Zone of Possible Improved Agreement (ZOPIA)

Figure 15.1. Leaving value on the table: suboptimal agreements.

The Y (vertical) axis represents the payoffs to party Y from positive to negative, and the X (horizontal) axis depicts the payoffs to party X relative to the status quo (point C). However, frequently it is possible for parties to receive positive payoffs from their own unilateral behavior without negotiating a cooperative relationship with the other, a point to which I will return below. The A–B line or northeast frontier, often referred to as the "Pareto-optimal" frontier, represents the maximum value that can be obtained within a given situation; in traditional economic theory this was often defined by "scarcity," namely the fact that limited resources would prohibit any gains beyond this frontier. In more general negotiation theory, this "upper limit" may be defined by whatever value is being negotiated: It may shift over time as conditions change, as values change, as new opportunities open up or as the issues under negotiation are reframed to allow for new ways of resolving the differences between the parties.

This line of "optimality" is, of course, largely theoretical, and given that negotiators seldom if ever have complete information about the parameters of their negotiating space, is usually unknown empirically by the parties in advance. Indeed, one of the purposes of any serious negotiation is for the parties to explore issues jointly, to learn about each other's preferences, and thus to increase their knowledge about what an optimal agreement might look like, even if it is never fully knowable. Nonetheless, positing such a "Pareto-optimal" frontier is necessary in order to understand the basic logic of the dilemma posed by reaching closure short of that frontier. Furthermore, this chapter assumes that the northeast frontier represents a fixed value that cannot be changed by the will of the negotiating parties. It thus represents the highest level of collective value to be divided within any given negotiation, but along this frontier any movement represents a gain in value for one party at the expense of the other party. Thus, any outcome within the A–B–C triangle is potentially positive for both parties, and point C serves as the status-quo point at which neither party can gain or lose value. Any agreement to the northeast of C represents a positive outcome for one or both parties until they reach the A–B frontier, beyond which no further increase in value is available to the parties collectively.

Therefore, two forces are always present in any given negotiation, called in the classic work of Walton and McKersie (1965) "integrative" and "distributive" bargaining. Integrative bargaining entails joint movement in a northeasterly direction, anywhere between 0° and 90°, where both parties increase their value. Distributive bargaining, on the other hand, seeks to move the outcome either in a northwesterly direction (between 280° and 360°) or in a southeasterly direction (between 90°

and 180°), so that one party gains value while the other loses value. In short, negotiations represent "mixed-motive" situations in which parties face simultaneous desires to produce mutual gains, while also facing competitive pressures to pursue unilateral gains at the expense of the other party. As long as the negotiation process moves in a generally northeasterly direction, even if deviating occasionally toward the northwest or southeast, the parties are pursuing mutual gains. However, when they reach the A–B frontier joint gains are no longer possible, and the negotiation essentially reverts to a zero-sum situation. Knowing this, however, may motivate negotiators to behave in a partly competitive fashion, even when they are far short of the A–B frontier, in order to assure a favorable outcome for themselves when they reach closure, whether at the A–B frontier or some place short of it but within the A–B–C triangle. However, tactics designed to "win" at the distributive game may undermine efforts by the parties to keep expanding mutually beneficial value by moving consistently toward the northeast, often causing them to end up well to the southwest of the A–B frontier. In this case both parties lose value relative to the possibilities inherent in the situation about which they were negotiating; in economic terms, such outcomes represent "opportunity costs" from the failure to seize the opportunity to discover and agree upon even more mutually beneficial outcomes. Any outcome that falls short of the A–B frontier is defined as "suboptimal," in the sense that there are outcomes from which both parties could have gained if they had kept on negotiating in order to move closer to the A–B frontier. Similarly, the "equity" of an outcome is defined by the degree to which an agreement falls along a 45° line from point I; agreements to the northwest of that line represent relative gains for party Y, whereas agreements to the southeast represent relative gains for party X. Agreements at point E thus constitute outcomes that are both optimal collectively and equitably distributed individually between the two parties.[1]

In order to determine the point of minimum benefit for both parties, that is point I, the available space for negotiation needs to be defined by another boundary, determined by what is often called the "security level." In game-theoretic terms, this is what the players could achieve by playing their "minimax" strategy as if it were a zero-sum game, thereby not requiring any cooperation from the other. In practical terms, this is often defined by the Best Alternative to a Negotiated Agreement (Fisher and Ury 1991); in theory this might be identical to the status-quo lines (X and Y), but in many situations actors have available alternatives

---

[1] This chapter is not focusing on alternative criteria for determining "equity," although there is a rich literature on that topic; see, for example, Bazerman and Neale (1995).

to a negotiated agreement that may also produce positive value above the status quo and that could be realized even if negotiations fail to come to closure. This "security" level is roughly equivalent to what economists traditionally identify as an "indifference curve" in the sense that it represents the value at which a party is indifferent between accepting a negotiated agreement or rejecting it and acting on its own. In the negotiation literature, this is also often referred to as the point of "minimum acceptable agreement" (Hopmann 1996), the "resistance point" (Walton & McKersie 1965), the "reservation value" (Raiffa 1995), or the "security point" (Zartman 1978, Brams 1990). These terms all more or less identify the same concept, namely the boundary below which a party will lose value from reaching a negotiated agreement. Therefore, an agreement at point I provides no increased value for either party over non-agreement and presumably any proposal falling outside the Y_s–X_s–I triangle would lead one or both parties to walk away rather than accept an agreement that produces no net benefit and even joint losses. No rational actor should accept an agreement that leaves it worse off than it would be without an agreement, so the two "security levels" define the limits of an acceptable agreement, and the space within the Y_s–X_s–I triangle represents what is often referred to as the Zone of Possible Agreement (ZOPA) (Raiffa 1995). In much of the negotiation literature this is depicted as a linear, one-dimensional space as in Putnam's (1988) concept of the "win space." However, this linear depiction fails to account fully for the dynamics of negotiation and doesn't distinguish between negotiations that produce optimal versus suboptimal outcomes, which is possible in the multi-dimensional depiction of the ZOPA as shown here.

In summary, the ZOPA falls within the triangle Y_s–X_s–I, that is above the security levels of both parties and yet within the frontier of possible optimal agreements. From any starting point within the ZOPA any move to the northeast (greater than 0° and less than 90°) is a positive-sum move in that both parties gain, although not necessarily equally. However, if we take the point of intersection of the two security levels, I, as an anchor point, then only moves at a 45° angle produce equal gains for both parties *relative to their security levels*. Therefore, agreement at point E represents the maximum gain for both parties, equally divided relative to their security levels, roughly corresponding to the classic Nash solution to the bargaining problem (Nash 1950, 1953). Any movement from point I between 0° and 45° represents absolute gains for both, but greater relative gains for X than for Y, whereas movements between 45° and 90° beyond I represent absolute gains for both but greater relative gains for Y than for X. Therefore, this model nicely depicts the dynamics of "mixed-motive" negotiations in which northeasterly moves within the ZOPA (Y_s–X_s–I) triangle represent joint gains, but moves toward the northwest or southeast away from the 45° line represent competitive moves. Obviously moves in a southwesterly direction represent joint losses for both parties, and therefore should not be undertaken by rational actors. It is this dynamics of "mixed motives," entailing both potential cooperation and conflict operating simultaneously, that makes the analysis of negotiation dynamics both interesting and complex.

This chapter, however, focuses primarily on one aspect of this complex dynamic, namely the issue of premature or suboptimal closure. In Figure 15.1, one may suppose hypothetically that two parties have reached a tentative agreement at point T. Agreement at this point has the nice property of producing equal positive gains for both parties relative to their security levels. That is, both parties are better off than they would have been had negotiations been abandoned, which would have left them at point I, since their joint movement has been toward the northeast. Furthermore, since in this example they also moved at a 45° angle from point I, their gains relative to their security levels are equal. So why not reach closure at this point? The answer is, of course, that they have left a lot of potential gains on the table. As Raiffa observes, "In looking for agreements, the parties might 'satisfice' on a Pareto inferior point X [T in Figure 15.1] without realizing that they are leaving potential gains on the table" (Raiffa 1995, 139). He notes that this point might be equitable but inefficient, in contrast to point E, which is both equitable and efficient. Therefore, any movement away from T between 0° and 90° would provide improved gains for both parties within the Y_T–X_T–T triangle, and if that movement were at a 45° angle the same equality could be preserved. In this regard, this may be considered to constitute the Zone of Possible Improved Agreements (ZOPIA). Nonetheless, if the parties are focused primarily on absolute rather than just relative gains, any move within the ZOPIA triangle through continued negotiations would be mutually beneficial rather than reaching closure at point T.

The remainder of this chapter will consider the question of why so many agreements end up reaching closure at suboptimal points like point T, or for that matter anywhere within the ZOPA (Y_s–X_s–I triangle) short of reaching the northeast (Y_s–X_s) frontier of optimal agreement. Why do negotiators so often leave potentially mutually beneficial joint gains on the table in the endgame by not exploring potential gains within the ZOPIA and settle instead on suboptimal outcomes anywhere within the larger ZOPA, when continued negotiations might have produced better results for both (Simon 1957, 198)? The remainder of this chapter thus focuses on some potential answers to this question.

Factors Contributing to Suboptimal Closure

Enough When? The Impact of Deadlines

Negotiation deadlines are a major factor contributing to premature closure of negotiations, often because time simply runs out on the negotiators and they have no choice but to accept the best agreement that they could reach as the deadline is approached, without the luxury of continuing to negotiate to get a better agreement. The general findings about the effect of deadlines in the literature on negotiations, both experimental and case-based, suggest that they are likely to facilitate reaching agreements, but that those agreements are likely to be suboptimal, unequal, or both. They facilitate reaching closure because they put pressure on the negotiators to move quickly toward an agreement – indeed, to accept any agreement that leaves them better off than the status quo or the intersection of their security levels. Time pressure tends to focus the mind on a rapid search for common ground, while reducing the time available to explore alternatives that might produce more efficient agreements. It also tends to reduce the impact of domestic pressures that may not have the time to influence the negotiators, a topic that I will explore further below. At the same time deadlines tend to discourage the use of problem-solving methods in the process of negotiating, since there is often insufficient time to explore fully all options to solve a particular conflict or to invent novel, but mutually advantageous, solutions to those problems that would have been more likely to produce outcomes closer to the optimal frontier.

It is important, however, to distinguish between two broad categories of deadline pressure – those that are imposed by external factors over which the negotiators have little or no control, and those established by the parties themselves on some more or less arbitrary criteria. These are not dichotomous, but they constitute ends of a continuum from externally imposed to internally created deadlines. The former tend to be characteristic of crisis negotiations, where some looming event creates a deadline for negotiations that must be completed before the escalating parties plunge together off the edge of a cliff. Such an event may be outside the control of the parties altogether, though more often it reflects the influence of different factions within the parties. For example, in a typical spiral of escalation the dynamics of military mobilizations creates a kind of pressure in which diplomats, trying to negotiate an end to a spiral of escalation or even measures to de-escalate a crisis, may find themselves confronted by their own internal political–military institutions that seem to be engaged in a virtually automatic spiral of escalation

When is "Enough" Enough?

that at some moment in the future will reach the point of no return. This prospect creates a decisive deadline after which a negotiated settlement may no longer be possible, or at least its options would be dramatically altered.

For example, during the 1962 Cuban missile crisis, the point at which Soviet intermediate-range missiles being deployed in Cuba would become operational constituted a clear deadline for the largely tacit negotiations between the United States and the Soviet Union to bring an end to that crisis before the strategic situation changed dramatically or war broke out. In fact, at the time the crisis was resolved the United States was within twenty-four hours of launching an attack against Cuba by some 40,000 US troops amassing in Florida. But unbeknownst to US decision-makers at the time, the Soviets had also deployed some 1,000 tactical nuclear warheads on the island which the Soviet commander, General Gribkov, had the authority and the intent to use against US forces invading Cuba, an event that could have easily set off a nuclear war between the United States and the Soviet Union. This clearly was serious deadline pressure, and so it should come as no surprise that the negotiations that ended the crisis failed to resolve the underlying dispute between the United States and Cuba, an issue that is only beginning to be resolved more than fifty years after the missile crisis.

A more uncertain deadline affected negotiations to prevent North Korea (the DPRK) from obtaining nuclear weapons. The "Agreed Framework" of 1994 between the United States and North Korea provided a plausible, if suboptimal, solution to this problem by requiring North Korea to cease efforts to develop a nuclear weapon and to accept international verification of its nuclear facilities. In exchange, the United States agreed to provide various forms of assistance to its non-weapons nuclear programs, especially the provision of light-water reactors to meet the DPRK's claimed need for peaceful nuclear energy. They further agreed to work in the future toward removing barriers to trade and to move toward a full normalization of political and economic relations. However, these negotiations postponed addressing the deeper issues of the political status of the two Koreas, a permanent peace agreement between the DPRK and the United States, or a mutual non-aggression pact; resolution of these issues would have constituted a superior agreement from the perspective of one or both parties, as well as the US ally in South Korea which was not a direct participant in the formal negotiations but had a vital interest in their outcome. Furthermore, issues such as the development of ballistic missiles and research on enrichment of nuclear fuels were largely disregarded as irrelevant so long as the DPRK could not develop and test nuclear weapons. Fearing possible rejection of a treaty by the US Senate, the Clinton administration opted to negotiate this as an agreed framework that was not fully binding on subsequent administrations (Oberdorfer and Carlin 2014, 274–280). However, these unresolved issues delayed implementation of some provisions of the Agreed Framework, and the opponents of the agreement in the administration of George W. Bush claimed that North Korea's behavior in some areas was not fully in compliance with the agreement, and the plans to negotiate a more comprehensive agreement led instead to the abrogation of the Agreed Framework by the Bush administration in 2002 (Oberdorfer and Carlin 2014, 362–364). Subsequently, efforts to prevent the DPRK from crossing the nuclear weapons threshold were then taken up in the Six Party talks (also engaging China, Russia, Japan, and South Korea) under a clear, if uncertain deadline, while North Korea continued its efforts to test a nuclear warhead. Once the first such test had occurred, the primary focus of the Six Party talks, namely to prevent this threshold from being breached, became largely irrelevant, and the negotiations ultimately broke up without reaching an agreement after the "deadline" had passed. The result was a missed opportunity to constrain the North Korean nuclear weapons program as well as to reduce tensions between the two Koreas and perhaps even to bring the DPRK into compliance with international norms and laws.

At an even subtler level, external deadline pressures may also apply, even if controversially, to negotiations on global climate change. To environmental scientists, at some point in the future, climate change will be so dramatic that its effects, such as the melting of arctic ice and the resulting rise in ocean levels, will become irreversible. The problem in this case is that the deadline remains uncertain, even among scientific specialists, who nonetheless agree that at some time in the relatively near-term future such a point of no return will be reached. This case, therefore, provides a good example of an externally imposed deadline until an unknown date. Thereby it creates some pressure on negotiators to reach agreement without creating a clear sense of urgency. As a result, it is also unclear whether this affords climate negotiators time to try to achieve a relatively optimal and fair agreement or whether it will allow them to "kick the can down the road" until such time as a disaster appears imminent, thereby perhaps facilitating agreement, but one more likely to be significantly suboptimal.

At the other end of the continuum, negotiating parties may impose deadlines on themselves to apply pressure to reach an agreement. Usually this implies that some external deadline exists at some indefinite point in the future, but, to avoid focusing on that external deadline, the parties will elect to impose a seemingly arbitrary deadline on themselves.

In some cases, the deadline may be purely arbitrary, due simply to the fact that busy diplomats need to conclude a particular set of negotiations so that they can turn their attention to other issues in a timely way. A good example of this situation applies to the negotiations in 2014–2015 between the P5+1 and Iran over the Iranian nuclear program, as analyzed in Chapter 1 by Ariane Tabatabai and Camille Pease. In this case, as in the North Korean case, an implicit deadline was imposed by the pace of Iranian nuclear development. In order to try to achieve an agreement prior to reaching either of these thresholds, the parties initially established a deadline for agreement of March 2015. At that point, they reached a "framework" for an agreement that appeared to be mutually beneficial and relatively "fair" to both sets of parties, but it also clearly achieved far less than the desired goal and also lacked important details necessary for its implementation. So the parties chose to ignore their self-imposed deadline and opted instead to create another deadline of June 30, 2015. However, having once moved a self-imposed deadline, the deadline itself became less credible, allowing an opportunity for yet another deadline to be allowed to elapse without a final agreement.

Closure was finally reached on July 13, 2015, shortly after the deadline had been passed, but whether the agreement produced a better outcome in terms of efficiency and fairness subsequently became a subject of debate. Some critics, mostly in the United States, charged that the agreement was less than optimal and that negotiations should have continued negotiating in order to find a "better" agreement; however, "better" was often defined only in terms of unilateral US interests. A "better agreement" might well have led to "no agreement" if it had been rejected by Iran. By contrast, those who defended the treaty acknowledged that it was perhaps not optimal, especially from a unilateral perspective, but nonetheless it was better than the "next best alternative" for the United States; that is, it fell within the ZOPA (Y_s–X_s–I triangle), the best that realistically could have been achieved within the internally and externally imposed deadlines. Although the internal debate within the Iranian government is less well known publicly, it appears likely that similar arguments occurred there as well. A suboptimal agreement was preferable to the alternative of a continued economic crisis imposed by the sanctions and the threat it placed on the stability of the Iranian regime. In short, the Iranian nuclear case illustrates very well the dilemma between agreeing to a suboptimal outcome in the short term or continuing to negotiate to get a better, more optimal outcome with the risk that events could overtake the negotiators and undermine their ability to reach any agreement.

In summary, deadlines exert a mixed impact on closure in many negotiations: They apply significant pressure to reach an agreement in a timely fashion, but they also risk producing suboptimal agreements or, where a tentative agreement is recognized but the parties seek to improve on those interim agreements, they may allow the deadline to pass without reaching any agreement. If negotiations do break down, the parties may realize no net benefits even though there may have been ample negotiating space within a broad "zone of possible agreement."

Failing to Get More Than "Enough": The Negotiation Process

The negotiation process itself can make a critical difference in the ability of negotiators to attain agreements that at least approach optimality. Standard bargaining processes of negotiation in which parties start out with proposals or demands that are highly favorable to themselves and then seek to narrow those differences through a series of reciprocal concessions leading to closure somewhere in the middle – often referred to as the "50% solution" – tend to frame negotiations in two-dimensional rather than three-dimensional space and thus often produce suboptimal "compromise" positions. The focus in this concession–convergence model of bargaining is on making reciprocal concessions toward some midpoint between the initial demands of the parties without any effort to increase value for all parties. By contrast, problem-solving approaches seek to reframe interests and values, and search for superordinate goals that incorporate the preferences of both (all) parties. The process of negotiating within three-dimensional space allows for mutually beneficial changes in positions rather than zero-sum changes, so negotiations are more likely to move effectively over the long term toward more optimal agreements rather than making simple compromises between the positions of all parties (Hopmann 1996, Chapter 6). Thus, the actual process that negotiators adopt to try to find agreement may make a significant difference in their ability to approach more mutually beneficial outcomes. Since the use of these problem-solving approaches still remains infrequent in many international negotiations, the reliance on concession–convergence bargaining often leads to agreement, but on outcomes that leave a good deal of value unrealized. These agreements may be equitable, but also bargaining tends to lead to outcomes that reflect power asymmetries between the parties, with agreements often weighted in favor of the parties able to exert greater pressure and influence within the negotiations. The bargaining process tends to enhance the relevance of power asymmetries and thus emphasizes the distributive aspect of negotiations, whereas problem-solving focuses more attention on the integrative process.

The Strategic Arms Limitation Talks (SALT) in the 1970s provide a good example of some of the consequences of concession–convergence bargaining. Throughout most of their history, the United States and the Soviet Union sought to reduce the size of the other's strategic forces in a competitive fashion, where each side wanted to keep as many intercontinental ballistic missiles (ICBMs), submarine-launched ballistic missiles (SLBMs), and nuclear bombers as possible, while the other side wanted to reduce the arsenal of its rival as far as possible. Throughout much of the history of this series of negotiations, the process resembled bargaining over the price of a used car along a single quantitative dimension, where one side wanted more and granted the other less. In their later stages, as the Cold War was winding down in the 1980s and the Strategic Arms Reduction Talks (START) began, the focus turned toward trying to change the quality of the forces to reduce potential first-strike weapons, while maintaining invulnerable second-strike forces on both sides. This was based on the belief, largely shared by both sides by that time, that "mutual assured destruction," in which each side knew that any attack it made against the other could not destroy the other's capability to retaliate, created a more stable nuclear world than one based on the threat of a "winning" first strike (Talbott 1979). Of course, the outcome still was not optimal, in the sense that a world without any nuclear weapons would likely have been even more mutually beneficial. Nonetheless, within the constraints of the Cold War international system, this effort to achieve mutually beneficial reductions in offensive, first-strike strategic weapons at least provided a superior outcome to mere quantitative reductions that had no relationship to weapons' quality or criteria of strategic stability in a nuclear world.

"Enough" for Whom? The Impact of Domestic Influences

Virtually all international negotiations are conducted by some collective entity, often a government or international institution, sometimes by a non-state actor pursuing an agenda that places it in conflict with the state's governing authorities. Hardly ever do these collective entities behave as unitary actors, however, as different internal factions almost always hold different preferences, values, and interests. This division manifests itself in various forms.

(1) The principal–agent relationship occurs whenever negotiators are serving as "agents" for governments or institutions back home,

namely the "principals" who ultimately determine when "enough" is enough.

(2) These principals, however, do not generally work in a vacuum, but may also be constrained by the political environment in which they operate, including opposition political parties or groups, domestic interest groups, and, in most democratic states and even some authoritarian states, by general public opinion.

(3) Outside of these more or less structured institutions, parties often appear that may be opposed to a particular negotiation altogether, often referred to as "spoilers" (Stedman 2000). These individuals or groups, which may exist either within the negotiating entity or outside it, may engage in disruptive behavior to prevent additional efforts to improve a negotiation that they reject and thereby try to create an outcome, if there is an agreement at all, that is as minimal as possible.

The principal–agent problem often operates through the "boundary role conflict," in which negotiators seek maximum gains with their counterparts, but then find that this effort to reach optimal agreements is opposed by their principals back home. In general, the negotiators' incentives push them to try to reach the best agreement possible under the circumstances to demonstrate their negotiating skill. However, such attempts to reach an optimal outcome may run into opposition from the principals back home for several reasons. First, the negotiators are in direct communication with their counterparts and are thus in a better position to understand how to reach an optimal and fair agreement that will be mutually beneficial; they may be persuaded by the other side to understand their needs and interests, and, as a result of this capacity to empathize with the other, they may be in a better position to understand how the interests of the other may be advanced without significant costs for their own side. However, the principals generally have little or no direct contact with their counterparts and thus generally encounter difficulty in empathizing with them in order to improve joint outcomes for absolute gains as opposed to advancing their own unilateral preferences for relative gains (Druckman 1978). This conflict seems to have played out as well in the negotiations between the P5+1 negotiations with Iran on the Iranian nuclear program that led to the Joint Comprehensive Plan of Action signed on July 14, 2015. The negotiators appeared to have a good understanding of the needs of each other, and even some capacity to empathize with the needs of the other party. However, opposition back home in the United States from a conservative Senate dominated by the Republican opposition and in Iran by the Ayatollahs and other hard-line leaders forced closure around a suboptimal outcome, with potential joint gains unrealized, albeit with an agreement that fell within the ZOPA and thus was perceived to be better than the next best alternative for all parties.

Secondly, domestic political considerations such as electoral cycles or the influence of various domestic interest groups may limit the extent to which negotiators can extend negotiations to find optimal and fair agreements. For example, in contemporary negotiations between the government of the Philippines and the Moro Islamic Liberation Front (MILF) as well as between the government of Colombia and FARC, both President Aquino of the Philippines and President Santos of Colombia pushed for a speedy conclusion to negotiations so that the process of ratification and implementation could get under way before their terms of office expired. In both cases, concerns that an electoral victory by the opposition might undo what they had accomplished in negotiations with these rebel groups increased their preference for achieving a "satisficing" agreement rapidly rather than risking negotiating beyond the deadline imposed by the end of their term in office, which might have led to an overall collapse of the negotiation process. In both cases, the search for a perfect agreement became the potential enemy of a "good" agreement, even if it was less than optimal. In the case of the Philippines, an incident created by a mistaken encroachment of the Philippines police into a MILF camp led to police casualties; this reverberated through the mass media and public opinion in Manila, which blamed the MILF for a crisis that had actually been created by the National Police. As a result, the Comprehensive Peace Agreement reached in early 2014 was put on hold until after the 2016 presidential election. The election in May 2016, in which Rodrigo Duterte, a hard-line "law and order" candidate, defeated President Aquino's personally endorsed successor, meant that ratification of the peace agreement that ended a long-standing and deadly civil war was delayed because of a process that was completed too late to be finalized during Aquino's administration. Similarly, the Colombian government of President Santos pushed hard in the Havana negotiations to achieve an agreement with the FARC rebels before its mandate ran out; even after the signing of the agreement in 2016, it was defeated by a very narrow margin by Colombian voters in a nation-wide referendum on the basis of opposition arguments that a military defeat of FARC was preferable to the negotiated agreement. However, re-opened negotiations enabled the parties to find improved terms that allowed the agreement to be passed by the Colombian Senate before President Santos' term expired only to be reopened by his successor.

Thirdly, specific interest groups back home may also lobby in various ways to prevent efforts to achieve an optimal agreement for the collectivity as a whole if it threatens their own specific interests. For example, in trade negotiations interest groups representing sectors of the economy that may be threatened by expanded trade agreements may seek to cut off negotiations before reaching an optimal agreement from the perspective of society as a whole. Labor unions, manufacturers, environmental groups, and consumer groups may all constrict the available ZOPA in order to protect their own specific interests. In virtually all negotiations of this nature, there are inevitably winners and losers within each party, and the latter may engage in active lobbying or other tactics to prevent an expanded agreement that would be better for each party collectively, but in which subgroups would still inevitably suffer losses. This factor has had a clear effect on the Trans-Pacific Partnership trade agreement that became a hot political issue in the 2016 election in the United States and was ultimately tabled by President Donald Trump as special interests from all sides of the debate pressured politicians and negotiators to act in accordance with their own interests, even if it meant reducing the collective benefits for the US economy as a whole, to say nothing of the potential impact on economic development for many key US partners in East Asia.

Fourthly, spoilers may also limit the potential search for mutually superior solutions in a negotiation. Of course, "total" spoilers seek to prevent any agreement from being achieved and thus try to disrupt the negotiation process altogether. On the other hand, "limited" and "greedy" spoilers seek to limit only those aspects of a potential agreement that affect their specific interests (Stedman, 2000). Like all spoilers, they usually pursue disruptive tactics that seek to complicate the negotiation process, but their goal is often to achieve a limited agreement that does not impinge directly on their private interests. Therefore, like all special interest groups, they may try to prevent negotiation of a comprehensive agreement that might contain provisions beneficial for society as a whole but that would impinge directly on their own specific interests. Again, the long history of negotiations on issues such as trade and global warming demonstrates the potential effects of spoilers, especially greedy spoilers, in preventing negotiators from pursuing their optimal goals. And once offsetting interests come to bear in a negotiation, they may restrain the outcome from all sides, producing "lowest common denominator" agreements that meet the minimal objectives of all parties, while maximizing the interests of none; the result is a form of the "tragedy of the commons" in which the pursuit of individual self-interests prevents realization of overall better agreements for the interests of the whole.

Focus on Relative Rather Than Absolute Gains and Avoiding Loss

In cases where relative gains matter more than absolute gains, negotiators may not seek to move beyond point T for fear that this may move the agreement away from the 45° line in a direction favored by the other party; even though one's own side may make some gains from further negotiation, if Y is concerned that this may lead toward an agreement near point X_T, they may believe that their own gains will be offset by greater gains for the other party. This calculus may be drawn directly by the official negotiators (the agents) or it may be the result of pressure from back home (the principals). For example, as a condition of ratifying the 1973 SALT I treaty on strategic nuclear forces of the United States and the Soviet Union, discussed above, the US Senate attached a provision requiring that any future agreement on strategic weapons would have to be based on equal ceilings for each component of the strategic force triad (bombers, ICBMs, and SLBMs). They insisted that this was necessary to assure that the Soviets could not obtain greater relative, quantitative gains in every strategic delivery system compared with the United States in future negotiations. However, this measure limited the negotiators for the SALT II Treaty (which was concluded in 1979 but never ratified) from exploring trade-offs across weapons systems, even though that approach could have produced greater gains for both parties (Talbott 1979). The result was an equal, but suboptimal, agreement in the SALT II Treaty, which was allowed to die quietly as the Cold War heated up after the Soviet military action in Afghanistan beginning in December 1979.

This tendency to focus on potential relative losses (even with modest absolute gains) may be reinforced by the predictions of prospect theory, as discussed in Chapter 12 by Janice Gross Stein, which suggests that parties will often overvalue the losses associated with continued negotiations in comparison with any benefits. Kahneman and Tversky (1979; 1995) argue that, in bargaining, aversion to loss is "likely to reduce the range of acceptable agreements because one's own concessions are evaluated as losses and the opponent's concessions are evaluated as gains" (Kahneman & Tversky 1995, 60). Thus, even if a rational analysis suggested that continued negotiation was likely to yield greater benefits than would closure at point T, it is possible that these benefits will not be perceived as outweighing the risk of relative losses from continued negotiations. Kahneman and Tversky (1995, 56) cite a hypothetical example of two countries negotiating about strategic missiles, in which each side evaluates missiles reduced by the other as gains, while reductions of one's own missiles are considered as losses: "If losses have twice the impact of gains, then each side will require its opponent to eliminate twice as many missiles as it eliminates – not a promising start for the achievement of an agreement." Yet this is more or less what happened in the SALT I and II negotiations in the 1970s, in which both sides feared that extended negotiations might enable the other side to press for greater concessions that might have led to an unbalanced agreement. Thus, settlement at quantitative parity in major strategic systems was widely viewed as suboptimal, but it at least averted the risk that negotiating more complex trade-offs of different and sometimes unequal limits on each side might leave one party relatively worse off. In the case of strategic weaponry, the fear of relative losses in comparison with a strategic rival seemed to carry existential consequences. Thus, fear by both sides of falling behind in the strategic arms race led to valuable, but suboptimal, agreements to try to limit that competition. In short, prospect theory suggests that negotiators may depart from the rational pursuit of optimal agreements, thereby forgoing mutual gains in order to avoid individual losses that are evaluated as extremely costly.

In addition, in cases of intensely hostile conflicts, parties may want to inflict losses on their enemies, even while negotiating a formal end to hostilities. In these situations, the search for mutually advantageous optimal solutions gives way to the search for "victory" through negotiations, for obtaining greater benefits than the opponent, or even inflicting pain on the other. Insofar as this feeling is mutual, as each side retaliates against the other's attempt to punish it, the result may push the parties away from the Pareto-optimal frontier, resulting in mutually inefficient agreements or, in extreme cases, causing negotiations to collapse even though a wide ZOPA was in fact open to them. The more each party feels painful losses due to gains by the other, the more they may be willing to accept modest losses compared with the most efficient outcome in order to inflict even greater losses on the other (Kydd 2015).

Bureaucratic Costs of the Search for Optimal Agreements

Similarly, the parties may feel under pressure in the endgame and believe that further improvements will simply be too time-consuming or difficult to be worth the effort. The literature on bureaucratic decision-making has long argued that policy decisions are normally based on a limited search through just a few options rather than a purely rational, "root and branch" search through all available options to locate the solution that maximizes benefits and minimizes costs for all parties (Lindblom 1959); there are likely many instances in which this finding applies to negotiations as well. Thus, in a classic satisficing mode, they may come to believe that a suboptimal outcome is simply "enough" in order to avoid the costly time and effort entailed in the continued search for a superior agreement. As noted at the beginning of this chapter, the Pareto-optimal frontier is seldom known in any precise way by the parties, and discovering optimal outcomes may require extensive joint exploration through a lengthy negotiation process in order to discover Pareto-superior outcomes. This process of search and mutual learning may be very time-consuming and costly for busy negotiators, and they may thus prefer agreement that is "good enough," even if not optimal. This phenomenon follows the logic of Herbert Simon's (1957) classic notion of "bounded rationality"; negotiators seek to find a satisfactory agreement that all parties can accept in the shortest possible time and with the least amount of costly search, rather than exploring superior outcomes that might enhance to the fullest possible extent the interests and needs of all parties to the negotiation.

For example, in the negotiations of the Partial Nuclear Test Ban, which reached closure in July 1963, the parties had initially sought an agreement on a comprehensive ban on testing nuclear weapons in all environments, but they ultimately settled on a lesser agreement that banned testing only in the atmosphere, under water, and in outer space, allowing underground tests to continue. A comprehensive ban required an extensive scientific analysis of the capability to reliably detect underground nuclear tests, especially to distinguish them from earthquakes, and to devise a mutually acceptable process to inspect possible test sites if such an event were detected on the territory of one of the nuclear weapons states (Hopmann 2014, 32–57). The verification and confirmation process was subject to technical debate among geophysicists, but more important was the heated domestic opposition from the nuclear weapons labs both in the United States and in the Soviet Union, opposition that spilled over into the domestic political arena, especially in the United States (Hopmann 1996, 293–296). The decision to abandon the effort to achieve a comprehensive ban was influenced by the belief on the part of US negotiators that a comprehensive agreement would likely not be ratified by the US Senate (Goodby 2005), even though most believed that such an agreement would have been more effective in the goal of limiting the nuclear arms race. The partial test ban produced some joint benefits by reducing pollution from atmospheric tests and by restricting testing by potential new nuclear weapons states that did not have a capability to conduct underground tests.[2] Therefore, the United States and the Soviet Union concluded that a partial ban was "enough,"

---

[2] Such countries, including France, China, India, and Pakistan, did not sign the Partial Nuclear Test Ban Treaty.

though inferior to a comprehensive test ban, in terms of serving their primary interest in limiting the development of more sophisticated and deadly nuclear weapons.

The Impact of Third-Party Facilitators and Mediators

Premature closure in negotiations may also be influenced by third parties serving as facilitators or mediators between the parties to a conflict. In principle, facilitators and mediators are supposed to assist the disputants to find the best possible agreement that maximizes their joint benefits, but frequently in practice third parties pursue other objectives that reflect their own values and interests, as Vuković argues in Chapter 9. This may affect premature closure in several ways. First, mediators are evaluated primarily in terms of their success or failure in promoting an agreement, with little regard for the content of that agreement. Their reputation is usually based on their success rate in producing agreements, but it makes little difference to their evaluation whether they produce an agreement at point T or at point E (the optimal and fair solution) in Figure 15.1. Since agreement at any point within the ZOPA may be considered to constitute a successful outcome, the mediator will likely achieve recognition for any agreement even if it falls far short of the optimum. Thus, mediators sometimes pressure the disputing parties to finalize an agreement at any point within the ZOPA, no matter how far short of the optimal outcome it may fall. In addition, some high-level mediators may find themselves under pressure to reach rapid, if suboptimal, agreements due to the many demands on their time. Time pressure may play an especially important role in conflicts mediated, for example, by the UN Secretary General and the Special Representatives of the Secretary General, who are frequently called upon to mediate major international disputes in addition to having to perform many other duties.

It is also often the case that third parties represent states, multinational institutions, or non-governmental organizations, all of which bring their own interests to the negotiation process and their own preferences for an outcome (Touval & Zartman 1985), which may not coincide with the optimal outcome from the perspective of all the disputing parties. For example, Russia mediated the war in 1992–1994 between Armenia and Azerbaijan over the breakaway region of Nagorno-Karabakh, and pushed for a hasty ceasefire along the existing line of contact between the opposing armed forces without any consideration for resolving the underlying issues that had led to the fighting. It appears likely that this served Russia's primary interest in ending a full-scale war in its "near abroad," while leaving a region of instability that served its long-term interests of gaining greater influence within the southern Caucasus. Similarly, as argued in Vukovič's Chapter 9 in this volume, US President Jimmy Carter at Camp David pushed for a rapprochement between Israel and Egypt that served US regional interests, while avoiding the more difficult and potentially sensitive task of seeking a solution to the Israeli–Palestinian conflict. The result was a "successful" agreement at Camp David that nonetheless fell far short of being an optimal solution to the most serious conflict in the region.

Conclusion

We generally tend to view negotiations as being successful when they reach closure and an agreement is consummated. However, agreement alone is only one criterion for evaluating the outcome of negotiations. Ideally agreements should be efficient, fair, and durable; however, reaching such successful agreements often requires a lengthy and laborious process of negotiations, and this chapter has argued that often this leads negotiators to "satisfice," to settle for less than optimal, fair, and durable agreements in the endgame. Often this premature closure still results in agreements that produce joint benefits for the parties and is therefore preferable to breaking off negotiations altogether; even a suboptimal agreement may be better than none if it at least provides superior payoffs than the next best alternative available to the parties (BATNA).

This chapter has proposed several possible explanations for why negotiators often reach closure before they are able to negotiate about all the potential benefits that might have been available to them if they had continued to negotiate. These include the impact of deadlines, of the negotiating process adopted, of internal pressures within each of the parties, of conflicts over relative gains and losses, of costs entailed in a lengthy search for optimal solutions, and finally of the self-interested behavior of third-party facilitators and mediators. Although this chapter has identified historical examples of the effects of each of these explanatory factors, systematic exploration of their impact requires further research; at this point, this chapter has essentially sought to identity potential hypotheses to explain why negotiators so often settle for suboptimal agreements and leave potential mutual benefits on the negotiating table. Those hypotheses need to be tested rigorously in future research.

Premature closure may produce sufficient satisfaction in managed conflicts that the parties fail, for long periods of time, to resume negotiations to extend the benefits that they left on the table, as discussed by Butler in Chapter 8. This often results in opportunities for enhanced cooperation through efficient, fair, and durable agreements being missed

(Jentleson 2000). For example, the agreement on a suboptimal outcome in the Partial Nuclear Test Ban Treaty of 1963 postponed the attainment of a Comprehensive Nuclear Test Ban (CTBT) until 1996. By that time, with the Cold War behind them, the pressures to ratify such an agreement had been reduced for the major nuclear weapons states, so that more than twenty years after the signing of the CTBT it had still not entered into force. Similarly, postponing extensive negotiations on the Israeli–Palestinian conflict at Camp David in 1978 also produced a historic agreement between Israel and Egypt that provided considerable benefit to both parties, but almost forty years later the underlying issue of Israeli–Palestinian relations remained unresolved and the situation on the ground was far less conducive to agreement than it had been forty years before. In short, suboptimal agreements are not necessarily bad agreements; indeed, the two examples just cited are often considered as major cases of success in the literature on international negotiations. Yet, if suboptimal agreements remove pressure to continue negotiating for better agreements, they often produce at best mixed successes, with significant missed opportunities.

16 Lessons for Theory

I. William Zartman

It goes without saying that there is no theory of closure; indeed, there is no authoritative theory of negotiation, despite several attempts. Were it not for the custom of books sponsored by the Processes of International Negotiation (PIN) Program at Clingendael – now at the German Institute of Global and Area Studies–Hamburg (GIGA) – to conclude – close – with a chapter on Lessons for Theory, this chapter should rather be entitled more restrainedly Lessons for Analysis.[1] This project is designed to open a debate and promote further research, so the usual lessons for theory are really challenges for theory. The book has drawn attention to clear behavioral patterns and effects in closure, and it has also brought to light further questions unearthed by analysis to date.

The first challenge is on the identification of the endgame itself. Much like the situation of ripeness before it was subjected to conceptual analysis (Zartman 1984, 2000), endgame is often referred to by practitioners (sometimes by different names) without any definition of its meaning. Like love, it has to be felt. The few works that have addressed the existence of a closure phase (Pillar 1983; Shell 1999; Gulliver 1979; Selten 1978) have suggested identifiably different behavior but have left the questions of turning points, conceptual boundaries, and alternative scenarios open for further investigation. This study reflects practitioners' testimony that an endgame can be identified in the course of a negotiating process, and that behavior in it is distinguishably different from the more tentative, testing activity up to the point when things get serious and an end is in sight. Obviously negotiation remains negotiation, at a high enough level of abstraction, but the focus, intensity, constriction, and behavior in the endgame set it apart from the preceding phases of the process, much as crisis characteristics and behavior have been accepted as distinguished from other phases of conflict (Brecher & Wilkenfeld

---

[1] I am deeply grateful to my two close colleagues, Terry Hopmann and Dean Pruitt, for excellent and timely help in composing this chapter.

2000). Studies of the whole negotiation process in the cases cited, and others, would be useful to bring out the difference even more clearly.

Much presentation and analysis has been offered here as to negotiators' behavior in the endgame, caught between deciding what is enough and striving to get more. That behavior has been typologized into a number of patterns or modes, although in fact negotiators often waffle among them. Those patterns have smoothed over the role of individual issues, sticking points, trade-offs, and breakthroughs in making the trip to agreement bumpy. Significant signposts such as turning points, ZOPAs, consensual formulas, reframes, implementing details, agenda agreements, mediation, and critical risk have been identified with greater precision than concepts hold over reality. Inherent impediments such as differential evaluation, manipulated information, approach–avoidance, unclaimed gains, deadlines, and principal–agent disjunctures have been analyzed, with more emphasis on their debilitating effects on progress than on the tricks negotiators use to circumvent them. In presenting and examining these elements, this work has opened them up to further dissection and has also created room for other behavioral characteristics that might play a significant role.

One should also investigate how neat the boundary is into the endgame. Evidence points to a recognized, shared sense of entrance into the final phrase. While that is an adequate working concept, in reality there are likely to be lingering uncertainties in the sensing, disjunctures in the sharing, and even retreats in the entrances. In dealing with a process where there is already debate over when it has really begun and really ended, this kind of fluffiness around the edges of a concept should not inhibit pursuit of an analysis into its essence and effects. Recognition signs as negotiators pass from the main course of their activity into closure would be helpful in sharpening the sense of the endgame, for they may be indicators of entry into a closure phase before it has been explicitly identified by the parties.

Then again, how reversible or extensible is its occurrence? All the patterns of behavior suggest that something may go wrong in the final process; are there warning signs, and, on the other hand, can the process be put back on track, presumably as driving? Pruitt in Chapter 14, after Jensen (1978), identifies behavior in which parties get cold feet as they take final steps toward closure, avoiding agreement as they approach it, a typical dragging behavior. When the movement to closure becomes bogged down, can it be revived within the same endgame or must a new endgame, with its turning points and reframing, be inaugurated, and how? The examples with which this study begins show closure phases of different lengths, sometimes long enough to raise the question as to whether the endgame began as early as claimed, was interrupted and revived, or actually began later in the period. It may be that length is merely a matter of culture, personality, weather, or *force majeure*, but it might also be a matter of other more scientifically determinable variables. Such pursuit, as given here, has opened the way for additional elaboration of behavior within the concept that can in turn be useful for the improvement of negotiating practice.

Several patterns or modes of negotiating in the endgame have been identified and used in the analysis presented here: dueling, driving, dragging, and mixed and mismatched, overcoming some earlier work that considered only driving (Gulliver 1979). There may be others, although these appear to be the prominent modes. Again, they may be found in different versions in earlier phases of negotiation, although they do not fit very well into either the diagnosis phase, with its search for basic positions, interests, and parameters (Stein 1989), or the formula phase, with its search for the elements (ZOPA, formula, definition of the problem) that constitute the material that endgame works with (Zartman *et al.* 1996). The difference, again, is that the modes identified then constitute the major paths along which the parties work toward a conclusion that they sense is possible within the endgame. It would be interesting to see whether other patterns can be identified and what they might be.

With these patterns clearly established, the next challenge is to address the most prominent questions in social science analysis: Which, When, Why? There are some indicators for when each of the patterns will be followed, opening the room for further, comprehensive analysis. In part this is because humans are capable of free choice, including some of the dumbest things and some of the most creative moments, and will not stay put in analytical boxes. In part, it is because parties can shift paths when the current one does not seem to be working. Since the first three patterns are reciprocal, the parties lock each other into the pattern, but can shift when the opponent does not seem to be playing the mode; that is, when the other gives signs of already shifting. In part, however, it is because answers have not yet been pursued beyond some general indications. It appears that patterns tend to be chosen as a continuation of preceding behavior, and also as a result of a turning point that may indicate a reframing of the issues or a confirmation of the current condition of the formula(s).

More specifically for each pattern, dueling is indicated when there is no agreed formula, a low critical risk (i.e. indifference between failure and success), and thus a security point that is close to the value of an agreement and is bearable for both parties or at least for one party.

Driving is indicated when there is a consensual formula, a high critical risk, a cost of breakdown much greater than the cost/gain of agreement, and a mutual dependence between the parties. A mismatch also follows when a formula is absent or is not reflected in emerging details of an agreement, although the latter may also predict dragging. Beyond these rough indications lies much room for a better understanding of the conditions leading to different patterns. These paths will not be determinate and inflexible, but an understanding of the behavior preceding each pattern will help negotiators plan where they are going and influence others to move in the same direction. Of course, the identified patterns themselves can be challenged and new or additional regularities of behavior discovered.

Dueling, either unilaterally as in mismatching or bi(multi)laterally as in reciprocal behavior, is the hallmark of "transactional bargaining" when stakes matter and relationships do not (Shell 1999, 160–175). Zero-sum hard bargaining has lost its favor among students of negotiation in the move to develop awareness of the advantages of positive-sum integrative problem-solving, and rightly so. But it remains a dominant mode of interaction among businessmen, lawyers, and diplomats, who probably make up the largest segment of negotiators. Putting the two together, if absolute gains are sought, it would be most advantageous mutually to break the dueling stand-off and seek a juncture of demands. At what point? When in the endgame demands have been made clear but before the parties have become irrevocably dug in before their publics. Which, when, how? "Negotiation analysis" has sought to determine the point statistically, by making everything quantifiable and squeezing politics out, but political reality has been squeezed out in most cases in the process (Raiffa 2005). Furthermore, when relative gains are the object, trade-offs become more difficult.

Yet some dueling suddenly reaches a balanced agreement: Which, when, why? At some point, one or more parties suddenly bring up a different critical risk calculation and – as in a real-life chicken game – see the impending crash as worse than they had originally calculated (a case of approach–non-avoidance, mooted in Dean Pruitt's presentation); they revise their calculations and can either swerve or start launching what-if openers as discussed by Siniša Vuković, or settle for a conflict-management outcome to at least stop the violence (CM) without full resolution (CR) as Michael Butler analyzes, among the most prominent alternatives explored in this volume. In these cases, one of the negotiators has gotten its message across: that breakdown really is more costly than concession for the other but not for the first party. It is a matter of psychology, or careful realistic calculation, or an external shock, among others, to impel the revised calculation. But all this needs further research, beginning from cases, to satisfy the "Which, When, Why" question.

Driving is a broad pattern, often mistaken as the only one again in the view of integrative negotiations. The cases and conceptual discussions amply show that there are many quirks of behavior as negotiators drive themselves and each other to a conclusion, and many slips during the game. Janice Gross Stein's chapter has identified some ways of overcoming the perils of prospect theory, Andrew Kydd has introduced some approaches to pursue in dealing with information theory, Terrence Hopmann has laid out principal–agent problems, and Dean Pruitt has shown how to favor approach over avoidance. Yet these obstacles and others are still present and identify the long ranges required for double-minded driving that characterized the cases that began this study as examples. In all of these cases and the concepts examined, the name of the endgame is persuasion, which invites much more work, in concept and in practice.

As the initial examples have suggested, dueling and mismatching do not always end in negotiation failure nor driving in success. So all of the patterns invite further investigation to help identify Which, When, and Why. As Daniel Druckman, Michael Butler, Larry Crump, Janice Stein, Terrence Hopmann, and Siniša Vuković have each suggested in their chapters, success may be achieved only by revising the goals and settling for something less than, or at least different from, the original aim. Such shifts are judgment calls, but greater insights into their opportunity would be helpful. The conclusion thus has wide support, which is not surprising; what is instructive is that Not Enough's being Enough is achieved and explained by a number of different approaches and paths.

In dealing with the concept of endgame and its modes or patterns, several contributing concepts appear prominently. They are *critical risk*, *security point* or *BATNA*, *reference points*, and *formula/(re)frame*. It is important to establish their meaning and role in the closure calculations and then to examine their dynamic quality. The concepts discussed here are often presented as linear, yet their course is no more linear than the negotiation process itself. The characteristics of non-linearity are an important further development once concepts have been identified. Coddington's (1966, 1968) criticism of Cross's (1966, 1969) work was that it left no place for brinkmanship, the strategic use of concessions distinct from the previous concession rates on which economists had based their theorizing (Young 1975). Similarly, on approach–avoidance, another subject that the discipline introduced and then dropped, what affects and effects a change in slope, a crossing of the lines, a change in the shape of the lines (which are certainly not straight): Which, When, Why? Here again the slope may be reversed: Approach–acceleration has often been noticed in a rush to closure; when does it overcome avoidance tendencies, and when does avoidance rein in the more common tendency to accelerate? Acceleration itself is an important phenomenon to investigate further, for it is often the cause for another endgame problem, that of gains left on the table, as Hopmann discusses in his chapter. Unrealized gains are easier to identify in concept than in reality, since the criteria for identifying what is actually realizable, like reframing, are a matter of creativity and learning outside the box before us. Haste may impede creativity, but it may be both necessary and natural in the final stretch to lock in gains in hand and neglect the two in the bush. "Let's get out of here," said the Dayton negotiators with a reluctant "yes" in hand.

Critical risk (the ratio between the difference between victory and losing and that between victory and deadlock [BATNA]) is the calculation that negotiators make in comparing potential losses and so depends on the negotiator's judgment as to whether she or he is in a Chicken Game or a Prisoners' Dilemma Game, or a Bluff vs. Called-Bluff Game (Snyder & Diesing 1977). Negotiating decisions are then made on whether losing to the opponent (agreeing to the opponent's demand) is worse than losing through a deadlock, in which the opponent loses as well. Critical risk calculations are made – more or less consciously and explicitly – by each party on each issue under negotiation, whether through concession, compensation, or construction (reframing, discussed below), but they also take into account the whole accord being negotiated: Is it worth jeopardizing the agreement in shape so far by holding out for/against a particular demand? These calculations of course are individual to each party, and are constantly under revision or at least subject to confirmation. Step-by-step analysis of negotiators' behavior in moving toward closure in the final phase would be highly enlightening.

Critical risk in turn hangs on evaluations of the *security point* or *BATNA*, the value of an outcome in the absence of closure on an agreement. BATNA calculations are the basis for the original decision to negotiate, as the parties decide to seek to overcome the costly stalemate in which they find themselves, and that awareness must be maintained until that status quo is replaced by a closed agreement. BATNA calculations take into account not only costs and benefits of the status quo but also costs of breaking off negotiations in the closure phase, and so are more costly in that phase than before the parties thought they were heading to an agreement. BATNAs too are constantly re-examined, and are open to negotiation as well; parties can make moves to influence the opponent's evaluation of its costs in case of breakdown. As seen in dueling, for example, parties are constantly telling the other, "I can stand a breakdown but you can't." So BATNA too is not fixed forever throughout the negotiations. It can change because of events and because of recalculations, but it is also negotiable. In driving, as in the Iran non-proliferation Joint Comprehensive Plan of Action, both parties felt that break-off was worse than acceptance of the terms of agreement, even though the terms were short of both sides' previous demands. In dragging, the parties agree that, after all, it is better to postpone or break off or maintain the uncertainty. Specific analyses of the dynamics of BATNA negotiations would yield a deeper understanding of the process and would be useful for negotiators seeking lessons for future practice.

Reference points are the basis of parties' evaluations of losses and gains in making their critical risk calculations at any time in the negotiation. Reference points are the values against which gains and losses are measured. Prospect theory indicates that initial evaluations tend to be made against the status quo and also that losses are given an inflated value compared with gains, rather than an intrinsic value. But while the latter comparison seems to hold throughout negotiations, the reference point evolves with the progress of the negotiations, involving not only BATNA but where things stand in the negotiation itself. How these reference points evolve and how that evolution affects the negotiation process as it proceeds toward closure is still not well understood; status quo within the negotiations vs. status quo without negotiations (BATNA) has also been compared with evaluation of the likely outcome vs. the desired outcome as a reference point (see the discussion of "levels of aspiration" in Pruitt 1981). "We are doing well compared with where we started, but what is the likely outcome toward which we are heading compared with where we wanted to be when we started?" is a continual four-sided box within which negotiating decision are made. Yes, the theory indicates that some of these reference points are often bypassed in the rush to conclusion, making conclusions possible but not necessarily optimal (depending on the reference for that judgment, of course) (Kahneman 2011). Empirical testing and application in the context of the most delicate part of the negotiation process, the endgame, is the next step.

Finally, the *formula* or *frame* for the negotiations is of defining importance in the final phase. A formula is an understanding of the nature of the problem under negotiation, the frame for its solution, the issues to be covered, the sense of justice to be applied, and the principles to be used to govern the final details of the agreement. As noted, these components tend to be agreed to as the parties begin driving toward an agreement; they may be agreed (as the nature of the problem) but not agreed *to* (solution to the problem) as the parties adopt a dueling mode of negotiation. However, it may turn out that the consensual formula is not adequate or appropriate for progress toward a conclusion, and needs to be revised. Put together or understood differently, the issues may be more amenable to negotiation. This happened in the middle of the Iran and Colombia endgames, but reframing may also mark a turning point that launches the endgame and makes it possible. Thus an agreed frame is essential in order to progress to a conclusion, but it may also need to be reformulated in the final phase. Dragging often happens when the agreed formula turns out to be inadequate but when the parties are also incapable of reframing a new formula that would allow them to proceed. From the beginning of its identification as a concept, formulation was declared to be a matter of trial and error (Zartman & Berman 1982); reframing is doubly so, and greater study is needed to understand the process.

In summary, these four major components – critical risk, security points, reference points, and formula/frame – are well enough established as concepts, and have been for a long time, but their dynamics remain to be explored, conceptually and in practice. Presented first as integral or, if dynamically, as linear, such concepts are constantly up for revision, negotiation, or evolution during negotiation and especially during the endgame. How these changes occur or are caused is still open to research, for it has a major impact on what is acceptable at closing time as opposed to at the opening of the closure phase. The deductive work has been laid out; inductive research on the ground or on the table is needed to complement it. In between, there is much room for experimental research, to generate hypotheses within the deductive layout and available for empirical testing. Negotiation was an important subject of inquiry in the 1970s among social psychologists, and Rubin and Brown (1975) is still a rich source of insights. But then it died, as research moved on to other tantalizing puzzles (Zartman & Rubin 2005). It needs to come back with experimental research as Daniel Druckman has done, specifically on behavior in the endgame.

Nothing exists if it does not have a name; the purpose of this collective work has been to identify and initiate a new topic of inquiry, and to establish it well enough for it to constitute a subject of analysis and practice. It is to be hoped the challenge will be picked up for continued study to further our understanding of an important phase of negotiation that has not previously been subject to focused analysis. The current volume is presented as the initiation and not the closure of the subject.

17 Lessons for Practice

Chester A. Crocker

This concluding chapter on lessons presents some reflections of a practitioner[1] about what works (or doesn't) when the endgame arrives. But when does the endgame start and what are the ingredients that make it emerge from the shadows of meetings featuring over-rehearsed restatements in plenary session? Sometimes such plenaries take place alongside separate working group meetings on individual problem areas (e.g. electoral systems, facilities for refugee repatriation, security provisions related to DDR). But since nothing is agreed – typically – until everything is agreed, issue-specific progress on such matters does not guarantee that the endgame actually gets launched; or, if it gets launched, that it will succeed to the point of agreement.

Experience suggests that the endgame begins only *after* a framework of principles has been agreed; *after* the guns have fallen silent or at least their use has been reduced; and *after* the right people have come to the table. Each negotiating team must be able to have some confidence that the other side is trying to think through the logic of the remaining gaps on the hard issues, rather than simply trying to wrong-foot or out-compete the adversary. As discussed in the concluding section of this chapter, the endgame arrives when the core matching commitments are clearly understood, at least in principle, so that they can be converted into details on all the major agenda items. But there are a number of conditions and factors influencing the likelihood of progress into closure on a deal.

Deadlines, Turning Points, Target Dates

Negotiators and mediators learn that there are situations where the comfortable default option is to keep on meeting and talking. This happens when the imagery of continued process becomes an important

---

[1] The writer has served as an official, state-based practitioner as well as a representative of an international organization and non-official organizations.

variable in its own right, rivaling the question of whether any real progress is actually being made. Meeting agendas are written with an almost inevitable item toward the end called "time and place of next meeting." When a process starts to look this way, a practitioner should be yearning for a means to shake things up.

There are several scenarios in which a stuck, stalemated process may be jolted into real movement. Each has its risks and potential rewards. The most common and often dramatic example occurs when one of the parties[2] experiences leadership term limits, or a leader is defeated or assassinated. Commentaries on the prospects for peace in Cyprus, the Philippines, or Colombia often appeared to turn on the question of leadership exit or defeat, creating a looming deadline. It is not obvious, however, how the deadline will be used by the parties – as a reason to accelerate decisions in order to grab the chance for a settlement before it slips away, or as an excuse for delay to see what a new leader might do (as discussed in Chapter 15 by P. Terrence Hopmann in this volume.) The interaction between democratic process and peace process has multiple variants that need little rehearsing here – e.g. the "complexity" of decision-making in relatively open, democratic systems; the question of whether followers will support the positions taken by their leaders; and the unknown durability of commitments made by leaders who could be thrown out at the next election.

Deadlines and target dates are often debated among practitioners. The risks are clear: Setting a deadline or a target date can expose the fragility of the negotiations and bring into question the influence of a mediator. There are two remedies for this dilemma. The first is to obtain buy-in from the conflict parties themselves or to encourage them to propose their own target dates. This was Mitchell's procedure as discussed here:

You have to be careful about that {deadlines}. Afterwards, at numerous press conferences, I was asked why didn't you set a deadline a year ago or six months ago. The answer was I think had I done so, I think the process would have failed. It was a risk. In retrospect it worked. But there is a risk involved and the time has to be right for it and I think the time was right for it. To me the critical act by the parties was their agreement to the establishment of a deadline. In mid-February [1998] ... I drafted a plan. I then went to each of the parties, the political parties and the governments, to get their assent. Each party agreed to a process which would involve a deadline. (Watt 2009)

A second remedy is to obtain agreement, as a certain-to-be-missed target date approaches, that it will be okay to set a new one since the

---

[2] The terms parties, conflict parties, and "sides" are used interchangeably in this chapter.

purpose of the negotiation is to resolve the outstanding issues, not to sweep them under the rug or devise verbal fudges. This occurred several times without serious ill effects during the final five months of the protracted Namibia–Angola negotiations in 1988 (Crocker 1992). Resetting a target date is actually a useful test of the parties' commitment. If the parties start fighting over who is to blame for a missed date, such behavior indicates trouble ahead and can be quite revealing.

Target dates set voluntarily by the parties themselves (not "imposed" by a mediator, as in the Mitchell example) illustrate a shared commitment to driving toward a conclusion. By contrast, deadlines may be "external" to the negotiating table and could flow from political, diplomatic, or legislative pressures that form part of the negotiating environment – e.g. in the case of the Philippines–Mindanao separatists during the final months of the Aquino administration or the Iran hostage case in the final months of the Carter administration. How such deadlines will influence the endgame can serve as a useful test of the parties' seriousness, or, in the terms of this study, of whether this is a driving or a dueling case. It could even shed light on whether this is a case of parties that are only interested in the ancillary benefits of being seen to negotiate – in order to buy time, to wrong-foot the other side, or to burnish their public image.

Creating Coherence in the Sides – Hawks, Doves, and Spoilers

There are several other aspects of the endgame dynamic that are of particular importance when mediation is involved. One is the potential impact of term limits for a mediator (whose home base may be about to experience a change of leadership) or of the replacement of a mediator by a third party of greater (or lesser) heft and skill. It made a difference when former UNSG Kofi Annan agreed to lead the diplomatic intervention in Kenya after serious electoral violence in early 2008, after other candidates had surfaced and then withdrawn. The impact of George Mitchell between 1995 and 1998 (alongside the British and Irish teams) is widely viewed as making a major difference leading up to Northern Ireland's Good Friday accord.[3] But even the most effective mediators are ill-advised to reference their own term limits as a reason for conflict parties to get down to serious business: Such action could backfire, letting doubters off the hook. On the other hand, the threat to suspend or even

---

[3] For a British insider account crediting Mitchell's contribution, see Powell (2008).

call off the mediation can be a form of leverage and pressure when the conflict parties are resisting the final movement needed in the endgame, as discussed by Svensson in Chapter 10 of this volume.

A standard principle of mediation practice (and theory) is that success depends on leverage (Touval & Zartman 2001). But leverage comes from diverse sources. Sometimes it is borrowed by a mediator from other parties that offer some measure of credibility and influence which the mediator may not possess. But leverage is diluted or lost altogether if the external political context of a conflict is incoherent or even polarized. The problem arises throughout a negotiation process, and it may even inhibit the start of serious talks, as the Syrian tragedy has richly demonstrated (Crocker, Hampson & Aall 2015b).

This problem becomes especially acute during the endgame when the negotiation can be thrown off course by outside actors who "export" their difference to the conflict parties. The risks here are multiple: Conflicting external signals may exacerbate divisions *between* the parties, but they also have the potential to create splits and fissures *within* the parties. At the very moment when negotiators are most in need of taking the final, toughest decisions to reach settlement, an outside intervention dissenting from the agreement terms that are gradually taking shape may re-open old wounds between the sides or undercut the position of a lead negotiator for one of the conflict parties.

The hawk/dove factional divisions that often characterize warring parties (Iklé 1971b) can be exacerbated by spoilers acting from within or outside the conflict. To a mediator, such activities send immediate signals of warning that require prompt action to counter the disturbance and, if possible, to neutralize the intervention. The art of managing spoilers depends on who they are and whether they can be bought off or quarantined, or must be deterred or coerced (Stedman 2000). The clear implication for mediation tradecraft is not to wait until spoilers show their hand, by which time it may be too late to shield the negotiation process from efforts to destabilize it. Instead, the challenge is to rally and reinforce an external coalition of interested parties with a stake in the enterprise – be they actual diplomatic partners in a "group of friends" (Whitfield 2007), or less supportive stakeholders who need to be persuaded to see that their interests are, in fact, compatible with a negotiated settlement of the conflict. There will be times when neutralizing a potential external spoiler will require a *quid pro quo*: some form of recognition, an acknowledgement of its stake and status in order to achieve buy-in or to minimize unhelpful interference. The goal is to corral the negotiating parties in order to encourage them to take the final big decisions and to make escape or "forum shopping" as difficult as possible.

Important as these measures are, the mediator also needs to focus on building internal coherence *within* the sides. The final choices about exit, settlement, or continuation of the negotiation are the most difficult and often the most divisive; making peace involves hard, legacy-defining choices that can lead to accusations of "sell-out" or even treason. Courageous deciders may face coups d'état or even assassination. As parties enter the endgame where the stakes are going up, the third party may need to be proactive, reaching out to affected constituencies through public diplomacy channels to underscore the upsides of the possible deal and to paint stark pictures of how much could be lost if the talks collapse, playing on the parties' risk calculations. These messages need to come from the party leaders themselves, but third-party support may be useful in relatively open political systems where such activity is not blocked by an authoritarian regime. When peacemaking leaders have failed to bring along their own constituents, the process may have dangerously shallow roots. The contrast between peacemaking in Northern Ireland and Nagorno-Karabakh serves to illustrate this point.

Two other things the mediator can do to strengthen party coherence in the endgame are, first, to reinforce the position and standing of a party's lead negotiators; and, secondly, to deploy fresh ammunition and arguments that might help key decision-makers to carry the day against doubters and opponents. The leaders of the parties' negotiation teams play even more critical roles at this stage. They need the strongest possible mandate from home as they are stretched between their domestic political and bureaucratic requirements, on the one hand, and the pressures flowing from the negotiating table, on the other. The mediator's best course at this stage is to respect their needs on the timing and rhythm of meetings and to encourage them to include whatever voices are needed at the table so that party unity remains intact. The mediator should also be searching on all sides for fresh information and evidence that could serve as ammunition to reinforce the strength of the process. Especially helpful is evidence of one side's seriousness of purpose that can be shared with the other party. Where there are signs of responsible media posture or of good-faith implementation of agreed initial steps, these can be useful ammunition. Where the evidence points the other way, steps by the third party to press that party for better behavior can also serve to enhance the other side's confidence in the process.

Chemistry and Empathy: Interpersonal Factors

Diplomacy is partly a people business in which a positive interaction between individuals can be a catalyst for closing the deal. In the practice of mediation, this interaction occurs between mediators and individual conflict parties as well as directly between the conflict parties. While the importance of interpersonal communication is important throughout a negotiation process, its impact is most significant at the delicate moments when personal chemistry can be explosive or reassuring. For this reason, mediators can look for opportunities to coach the sides about each other's doubts and fears and possible ways to address them. The sharing of confidences – informally or even when note-takers are present – can be a powerful tool. Especially powerful at such times is the sharing of confidence about the price (to one's own side) of continued fighting or about the attractions of potential peace dividends. A third party who succeeds in coaching the parties to do such things as a demonstration of their own strength and self-confidence, rather than as a sign of weakness, will reap dividends ("I don't need peace any more than you do, but it will be a happy and proud day when our troops come home having contributed to the settlement we are building").

Good chemistry can follow from empathetic gestures offered to a party (by the other party or by a third party), as elaborated by Daniel Druckman in Chapter 7 of this volume. Gestures can demonstrate one's awareness of particular cultural symbolism or shared universal values and attachments. Expressions of respect for another's painful moment of history when a particular loss or suffering occurred can be valuable currency in negotiation, and the more personal they are, the better.

From Endgame to Implementation: Making Commitments Credible

The "credible commitment" problem is well recognized in the field of peacemaking in civil wars (Walter 2001). As a negotiation process approaches the final stages, the parties are likely to raise ever more demanding questions about each other's capacity and intent to implement commitments in good faith. Part of the problem relates to trust and confidence in the other side's motives. Doubts may also exist about whether the other party is sufficiently coherent to maintain a steady course and to check the activity of its own potential spoilers. Questions inevitably arise about the security implications of ceasefires and the management of disarmament and demobilization plans. When a proposed settlement involves a changed political dispensation, there will be questions about how electoral procedures will operate in practice and who will assure their fair administration. The most significant overall uncertainty surrounds the question of what recourse an aggrieved party will have to pursue alleged violations of an agreement's terms. In a word, where is the court of appeal and who are the judges?

Wise negotiators do not wait for these almost inevitable questions to be raised. It is best to pre-empt them *during the endgame* by creating a mechanism to oversee performance during the implementation phase by a body representing the sides and any relevant third parties. There may be several things to oversee: monitoring of ceasefires, verification of troop movements and disarmament, creation of voters' rolls, protection of human rights, budget transparency and revenue flows, and party performance on political commitments such as media access or refugee returns. Monitoring requires the presence of observers whose role is to check on performance and issue periodic reports in order to instill confidence or to shine a spotlight on non-performance. Monitoring mechanisms can be organized on an *ad hoc* basis or by including a role for the UN or other international bodies (Gowan 2016). In the absence of monitoring and observing mechanisms, disputes are likely to flare up and potentially spin out of control.

In some cases, the risks of a security breakdown are sufficiently tangible that parties will opt to accept a role for external peacekeeping forces for a transitional period. The deployment of UN blue helmets can be viewed as a particular type of implementing mechanism, one that has prospects for success when there is a peace to keep (as distinguished from cases where outside troops are inserted in the midst of ongoing strife as peacemakers) (Dobbins and Miller 2013). UN peacekeepers should not, however, be the only element of the mechanism available during the transition.

By negotiating implementation arrangements during the endgame, parties are investing in the possibility of a settlement before it happens and, therefore, making an eventual agreement much more likely. If this is self-evident, how should the parties select an implementing mechanism and who should they look to – apart perhaps from the UN Security Council, the ultimate court of appeal – to help "guarantee" the eventual agreement? This is case-dependent, but since the problem is to overcome credible commitment issues, the mechanism needs to include non-conflict parties – e.g. representatives of an appropriate regional organization, of party allies or patrons, experts drawn from relevant fields such as law, economic development, security sector and ceasefire monitoring, constitutional/electoral systems, human rights, and refugee affairs. The mechanism needs to include professional military expertise dedicated to monitoring the end of the fighting and the implementation of other security provisions of the settlement. The establishment of military-to-military communications links with third-party participation should be considered by the parties; resistance to such proposals is not a good sign.

In third-party-assisted negotiation, the question arises as to what role should be played after the agreement by the mediator(s) and facilitators who have played a central role in the process. A strong case can be made that these third parties need to be included in the implementation phase. Although their role may change after the deal has been agreed, their continued engagement may be central to a successful implementation and should be discussed during the endgame. They know the conflict history and the parties better than newly arrived outsiders who descend on the scene "after" the negotiation. Their continued presence will give confidence to the sides that someone who knows and cares will still be around. The endgame is the time to send messages of continued interest and support for the morning after the deal is signed. The opposite message – of washing hands and moving on to the next problem – is precisely what is *not* needed at this moment in the process.

Above all, it will be important to include the third party in the mechanism because negotiation will continue for a period, perhaps a long one, after the settlement is signed. As argued by Elizabeth Cousens (2008), there are many reasons why this is the case: Some issues may have been set aside or postponed; elements of the agreement may need interpretation or renegotiation; new, unforeseen issues may arise that could polarize the parties; and electoral or constitutional challenges may call for the help of a mutually acceptable outsider.

Concluding Thoughts

In the Introduction to this volume, Zartman outlines five patterns of negotiating behavior that help determine whether the endgame results in closure or collapse. One focal point in this analysis is the question of how much (how many points) to include in an agreement while "omitting the bone that got stuck in all parties' throats." He further raises the question "When in the process is the decision made to push for the difficult issue or to drop it, and how does this issue figure in the endgame?" Theoretically, these are significant questions because experience points to examples (noted by Hopmann and Vuković in this volume) in which parties agree on settlement terms that leave out what appear to be major issues, thus producing agreements that can be described as incomplete, suboptimal, and likely to leave grounds for continued conflict in future. Experience points to a different way of looking at the problem. Diplomatic agreements seldom "end conflict"; rather they set the stage for the next phase of conflict, while, one hopes, reducing its violence. Progress comes in stages, and today's imperfect deals can become the incremental and even irreversible steps that set the stage and define the basis on which the next phase of negotiation is conducted. Most agreements are, not surprisingly, suboptimal because they are milestones rather than "final solutions."

It may be helpful to think of phases or stages. An early stage is when the parties and the mediator (if one is present) determine the shape of the agenda, and agree on a basis for negotiation – i.e. what issues are we going to talk about? The next phase could involve months or even years of "dueling" over a definition of the quids and quos, the matching commitments that the sides are hypothetically prepared to make. This process of dueling is not automatically a permanent stand-off (hang tough, the ball is in your court): It can – with or without the help of a mediator – sometimes generate the ripening necessary in order to move from dueling to driving. Dueling continues as long as there is no agreement on a Formula going into the endgame. The parties still hold different notions of the nature of the problem, the terms of trade, and the notion of justice underwriting the negotiation and hence the agreement. The critical step is the parties' ability (or not) to successfully establish the framework of principles (matching commitments) that will guide them to closure. A practitioner's view is that this should happen before the endgame; if there is no agreement on what issues to include without breaking the back of an agreeable agenda, there will probably be no endgame. This step represents the start of the endgame, after which the parties must turn their attention from the basic formula to the details of how those principles will be operationally defined, sequenced, and implemented.

References

Cases (see also pp. 320–340)

Chapter 1

Albright, David & Stricker, Andrea. 2014. A Note on Iran's IR-5 Centrifuge Feeding, Institute for Science and International Security, November 20, http://isis-online.org/uploads/isis-reports/documents/Note_IR-5_Feeding_Iran_Nuclear_JPA_20Nov2014-Final.pdf.

al-Faisal, Saud. 2015. Press Availability with Saudi Arabia Foreign Minister Saud al-Faisal, https://2009-2017.state.gov/secretary/remarks/2015/03/238177.htm.

Amano, Yukiya. 2012. Statement to Sixty-Seventh Regular Session of United Nations General Assembly, Vienna, November 5. www.iaea.org/newscenter/statements/statement-sixty-seventh-regular-session-united-nations-general-assembly.

Arms Control Association. 2015. The Lausanne Framework and a Final Nuclear Deal with Iran, April, www.armscontrol.org/Issue-Briefs/2015-04-14/The-Lausanne-Framework-and-a-Final-Nuclear-Deal-with-Iran.

Astill, James & Younge, Gary. 2004. Iranian Leaders Welcome Easing of US Sanctions, *The Guardian*, January 1, www.theguardian.com/world/2004/jan/02/usa.iran.

Balali, Mehrdad. 2015. Iran Sends High-Level Negotiators to Geneva Nuclear Talks, *Reuters*, February 21, www.reuters.com/article/2015/02/21/us-iran-nuclear-usa-idUSKBN0LP0SM20150221.

BBC. 2014. Direct US–Iran Talks on Nuclear Deal Begin in Geneva, *BBC News*, June 9, www.bbc.com/news/world-middle-east-27762147.

Borger, Julian. 2012. Iran Nuclear Talks: Settling for Confusion in Baghdad, Hoping for Clarity in Moscow, *The Guardian*, May 29, www.theguardian.com/world/julian-borger-global-security-blog/2012/may/29/iran-nuclear-talks-baghdad-moscow.

Borhani, Mihan & Fung, Ching N. 2014, Iran and the P5+1, British American Security Information Council, October, www.basicint.org/sites/default/files/iranfactsheet_21102014.pdf.

Buckley, Neil, Dombey, Daniel & Smyth, Gareth. 2005. Russia Hits at Tehran over Nuclear Stand-off, *Financial Times*, March 14 (accessed 2015; no longer available online).

Bush, George W. 2005. 2005 State of the Union Address, *The Washington Post*, February 2, www.washingtonpost.com/wp-srv/politics/transcripts/bushtext_020205.html.

Christopher, Warren & Kreisberg, Paul H. (eds.). 1985. *American Hostages in Iran: The Conduct of a Crisis*. Council on Foreign Relations.

Cotton, Tom. 2015. An Open Letter to the Leaders of the Islamic Republic of Iran, March 9, www.cotton.senate.gov/?p=press_release&id=120.

Corker, Bob. 2015. Sen. Bob Corker: Congress Should Reject the Bad Iran Deal, *The Washington Post*, August 17, www.washingtonpost.com/opinions/congress-should-reject-the-bad-iran-deal/2015/08/17/0c983c78-44f3-11e5-8ab4-c73967a143d3_story.html.

Crail, Peter. 2012. Iran Responds to Call for Talks, *Arms Control Today*, March 2, www.armscontrol.org/print/5232.

Crumley, Bruce. 2013. Why France Played Hardball at Iranian Nuclear Talks, *Al Jazeera*, November 11, http://america.aljazeera.com/articles/2013/11/11/why-france-playedhardballatirannucleartalks.html.

Dahl, Fredrik. 2013. Q&A – Iran's Arak Reactor Is Growing Nuclear Concern for West, *Reuters*, November 22, www.reuters.com/article/us-iran-nuclear-arak/qa-irans-arak-reactor-is-growing-nuclear-concern-for-west-idUSBRE9AL0HY20131122.

Dahl, Fredrik & Williams, Dan. 2013. Iran's Arak Reactor Looms into Israeli, Western View, *Reuters*, June 2, www.reuters.com/article/2013/06/02/us-iran-nuclear-israel-idUSBRE95103920130602.

Davenport, Kelsey. 2014. History of Official Proposals on the Iranian Nuclear Issue, Arms Control Association, January, www.armscontrol.org/factsheets/Iran_Nuclear_Proposals.

  2015. Official Proposals on the Iranian Nuclear Issue, 2003–2013, www.armscontrol.org/factsheets/Iran_Nuclear_Proposals.

Dixon, Darius & Everett, Burgess. 2015. Can This Man Sell the Iran Deal to Congress?, *Politico*, April 7, www.politico.com/story/2015/04/ernest-moniz-iran-deal-congress-116747.

Dunham, Will. 2014. U.S. Releases $450 Million of Frozen Iranian Funds after IAEA Report, *Reuters*, April 17, www.reuters.com/article/2014/04/17/us-iran-nuclear-usa-idUSBREA3G1W620140417.

Erdbrink, Thomas & Sanger, David E. 2015. Iran's Supreme Leader Says Sanctions Must Lift When Nuclear Deal is Signed, *The New York Times*, April 9, www.nytimes.com/2015/04/10/world/middleeast/iran-khamenei-rouhani-nuclear-agreement.html.

EU. 2012. EU Imposes Fresh Round of Sanctions on Iran, European Union External Action Service, January 23, http://eeas.europa.eu/top_stories/2012/230112_iran_en.htm.

  2014. Joint Statement by Catherine Ashton and Iranian Foreign Minister Javad Zarif following the talks in Vienna, 24 November 2014, European Union External Action Service November 24, http://eeas.europa.eu/statements-eeas/2014/141124_02_en.htm.

Fitch, Asa, Solomon, Jay & Lee, Carol E. 2015. Iran's Ayatollah Ali Khamenei Blasts Terms of Nuclear Framework Deal, The Wall Street

Journal, April 9, www.wsj.com/articles/ayatollah-blasts-terms-of-nuclear-framework-1428623508.

Ford, Christopher A. 2012. Iran, Nonproliferation, and the IAEA: A Legal History, Hudson Institute Security and Foreign Affairs Briefing Paper.

Gordon, Michael R. 2015. Outline of Iran Nuclear Deal Sounds Different from Each Side, *The New York Times*, April 4 www.nytimes.com/2015/04/05/world/middleeast/outline-of-iran-nuclear-deal-sounds-different-from-each-side.html.

Harf, Marie. 2014. State Department Daily Briefing, *C-SPAN* video, April 17, www.c-span.org/video/?318940-1/state-department-briefing.

Herszenhorn, David M. 2015. House Rejects Iran Nuclear Deal, *The New York Times*, September 11, www.nytimes.com/2015/09/12/world/middleeast/iran-nuclear-deal-house.html; Roundup: Where Do U.S. Lawmakers Stand on The Iran Nuclear Deal?, *NPR*, September 8, www.npr.org/2015/09/08/438473622/roundup-where-do-u-s-lawmakers-stand-on-iran-nuclear-deal.

IAEA. 2003. Implementation of the NPT Safeguards Agreement in the Islamic Republic of Iran, GOV/2003/69, September 12.

2004. Implementation of the NPT Safeguards Agreement in the Islamic Republic of Iran, GOV/2004/49, June 18.

2005. Implementation of the NPT Safeguards Agreement in the Islamic Republic of Iran, GOV/2005/77, September 24.

2011. Subsidiary Arrangement to the Agreement between the Government of [...] and the International Atomic Energy Agency for the Application of Safeguards in Connection with the Treaty on the Non-Proliferation of Nuclear Weapons, SG-FM-1170, February.

2012a. Implementation of the NPT Safeguards Agreement and Relevant Provisions of Security Council Resolutions in the Islamic Republic of Iran, GOV/2012/23, May 25.

2012b. Implementation of the NPT Safeguards Agreement and Relevant Provisions of Security Council Resolutions in the Islamic Republic of Iran, GOV/2012/37, August.

2013. IAEA, Iran Sign Joint Statement on Framework of Cooperation, November 11, www.iaea.org/newscenter/pressreleases/iaea-iran-sign-joint-statement-framework-cooperation.

2014a. Status of Iran's Nuclear Programme in Relation to the Joint Plan of Action, GOV/INF/2012/1, January.

2014b. Joint Statement by Iran and IAEA, May 21, www.iaea.org/newscenter/pressreleases/joint-statement-iran-and-iaea.

2014c. Implementation of the NPT Safeguards Agreement and Relevant Provisions of Security Council Resolutions in the Islamic Republic of Iran, GOV/2014/10, February.

2014d. Implementation of the NPT Safeguards Agreement and Relevant Provisions of Security Council Resolutions in the Islamic Republic of Iran, GOV/2014/43, September.

2014e. Implementation of the NPT Safeguards Agreement and Relevant Provisions of Security Council Resolutions in the Islamic Republic of Iran, GOV/2015/58, November 7.

Iran Watch. 2011. A History of Iran's Nuclear Program, March 1, www.iranwatch.org/our-publications/weapon-program-background-report/history-irans-nuclear-program.

Irish, John. 2014. France Tempers Iran Nuclear Stance in Nod to Wider Diplomatic Needs, *Reuters*, November 21, www.reuters.com/article/2014/11/21/us-iran-nuclear-france-insight-idUSKCN0J50M420141121.

Karami, Arash. 2015. Iranian Negotiator Discusses Talks with Moniz, Al-Monitor, August 5, www.al-monitor.com/pulse/originals/2015/08/iran-negotiator-salehi-moniz.html.

Kelley, Robert E. 2013. The International Atomic Energy Agency and Parchin: Questions and Concerns, Stockholm International Peace Research Institute, January 18, www.sipri.org/media/expert-comments/18jan2013_IAEA_Kelley.

Kerr, Paul. 2003. IAEA Presses Iran to Comply with Nuclear Safeguards, Arms Control Association, July 1, www.armscontrol.org/print/1327.

Labott, Elise. 2012. Iran Is Ready for Nuclear Talks, Negotiator Tells EU, *CNN*, February 16, www.cnn.com/2012/02/16/world/meast/iran-nuclear/.

Lewis, Jeffrey. 2014. The Iran Nuke Extension Is a Death Sentence, *Foreign Policy*, November 25, http://foreignpolicy.com/2014/11/25/the-iran-nuke-extension-is-a-death-sentence/.

Maddux, Catherine. 2014. Elusive Deal with Iran Could Yield Foreign Policy Legacy for Obama, *Voice of America*, August 31, www.voanews.com/content/iran-nuke-deal-may-offer-obama-foreign-policy-legacy/2431156.html.

Mostaghim, Ramin & Richter, Paul. 2015. Iran's Khamenei Adds a Twist to Tough Terms for Nuclear Talks, *Los Angeles Times*, April 9, www.latimes.com/world/middleeast/la-fg-iran-nuclear-khamenei-20150409-story.html.

Mufson, Steven. 2015. Energy Secretary Moniz Emerges as Obama's Secret Weapon in Iran Talks, *The Washington Post*, April 30, www.washingtonpost.com/business/economy/energy-secretary-moniz-emerges-as-obamas-secret-weapon-in-iran-talks/2015/04/27/ac9a5d58-e398-11e4-905f-cc896d379a32_story.html.

New York Times Editoral Board. 2016. A Safer World, Thanks to the Iran Deal, *The New York Times*, January 17, www.nytimes.com/2016/01/18/opinion/a-safer-world-thanks-to-the-iran-deal.html.

Netanyahu, Benyamin. 2015. PM Netanyahu on Holocaust Remembrance Day, April 15, http://mfa.gov.il/MFA/ForeignPolicy/Iran/Nuclear/Pages/Excerpt-PM-Netanyahu on Holocaust Remembrance Day 15 Apr 2015.aspx.

Nuclear Threat Initiative. 2018. Iran, www.nti.org/learn/countries/iran/.

Parker, John W. 2012. *Russia and the Iranian Nuclear Program: Replay or Breakthrough?* NDU Press.

Pfeffer, Anshel. 2015. Laurent Fabius, the "Bad Cop" of the Iran Negotiations, *Haaretz*, July 5, www.haaretz.com/news/middle-east/.premium-1.664555.

Phillips, Amber. 2015. Why the Iran Deal Is So Huge for Obama's Legacy, *The Washington Post*, July 31, www.washingtonpost.com/news/the-fix/wp/2015/07/31/why-the-iran-deal-is-huge-for-obamas-legacy/.

Psaki, Jen. 2014. Daily Press Briefing – November 10, 2014, https://2009-2017.state.gov/r/pa/prs/dpb/2014/11/233921.htm.

RFE. 2015. Iran's Hard-Liners Irked by Zarif's Geneva Stroll with Kerry, *Radio Free Europe – Radio Liberty*, January 21, www.rferl.org/content/persian-letters-zarif-kerry-walk-irks-hard-liners/26806490.html.

Richter, Paul. 2012. Hope Fades for Quick Progress in Iran Nuclear Talks, *The Los Angeles Times*, May 24, http://articles.latimes.com/2012/may/24/world/la-fg-iran-nuclear-talks-20120524.

Rouhani, Hassan. 2011. *National Security and Nuclear Diplomacy*. Center for Strategic Research.

Ryabkov, Sergey. 2015. Transcript of a Meeting with Russian Deputy Foreign Minister Sergey Ryabkov, in *The Nuclear Iran Deal: Russia's Interests and Prospects for Implementation*, conference held by the Center for Energy and Security Studies (CENESS), Moscow, August 14, http://ceness-russia.org/data/page/p1494_1.pdf.

Sanger, David E. 2004. The Khan Network, presented June 4–5, 2004, at the Conference on South Asia and the Nuclear Future, https://fsi-live.s3.us-west-1.amazonaws.com/s3fs-public/evnts/media/Khan_network-paper.pdf.

2015a. No. 2 Negotiators in Iran Talks Argue Physics behind Politics, *The New York Times*, March 28, www.nytimes.com/2015/03/29/world/middleeast/no-2-negotiators-in-iran-talks-argue-physics-behind-politics.html.

2015b. Saudi Arabia Promises to Match Iran in Nuclear Capability, *The New York Times*, May 13, www.nytimes.com/2015/05/14/world/middleeast/saudi-arabia-promises-to-match-iran-in-nuclear-capability.html.

Sanger, David E. & Gordon, Michael R. 2015. Clearing Hurdles to Iran Nuclear Deal with Standoffs, Shouts, and Compromise, *The New York Times*, July 15, www.nytimes.com/2015/07/16/world/middleeast/clearing-hurdles-to-iran-nuclear-deal-with-standoffs-shouts-and-compromise.html.

Singh, Michael. 2015. The Sino-Iranian Tango, *Foreign Affairs*, July 21, www.foreignaffairs.com/articles/china/2015-07-21/sino-iranian-tango.

Sinha, Satyabrat. 2005. The Paris Agreement and Iranian Nuclear Case, Institute of Peace and Conflict Studies, January 4, www.ipcs.org/article/nuclear/the-paris-agreement-and-iranian-nuclear-case-1606.html.

Sinha, Shreeya & Campbell Beachy, Susan. 2015. Timeline on Iran's Nuclear Program, *The New York Times*, April 2, www.nytimes.com/interactive/2014/11/20/world/middleeast/Iran-nuclear-timeline.html#/#time243_10489.

UNSC. 2006a. United Nations Security Council (SC), Resolution 1696, S/RES/1696 (2006), July 31.

2006b. United Nations Security Council (SC), Resolution 1737, S/RES/1737 (2006), December 23.

US State Department. 2014a. Implementation of the Joint Plan of Action from November 24, 2013 in Geneva Between the P5+1 and The Islamic Republic of Iran and Provision of Limited, Temporary, and Targeted Sanctions Relief, January 20, www.treasury.gov/resource-center/sanctions/Programs/Pages/jpoa_archive.aspx.

2014b. Extension of Iran Nuclear Talks, July 18 (accessed 2015; no longer available online).

2015. Joint Comprehensive Plan of Action, July 14, www.state.gov/documents/organization/245317.pdf.

US Treasury Department. 2012. United States Increases Sanctions against the Government of Iran and Its Proliferation Networks, July 12, www.treasury.gov/press-center/press-releases/Pages/tg1634.aspx.
    2013. Treasury Announces Sanctions against Iran, February 6, www.treasury.gov/press-center/press-releases/Pages/tg1847.aspx.
Zarif, Mohmmed Javad. 2015. Twitter post, April 2, https://twitter.com/JZarif and Iran Disputes US Nuclear Deal "Fact Sheet," *The Guardian*, April 4, www.theguardian.com/world/2015/apr/05/iran-disputes-us-nuclear-deal-fact-sheet.

Chapter 2

Agence France-Presse. 2015. Little Sympathy for Greek Woes in Eurozone's Poorer Nations, *NDTV*, www.ndtv.com/world-news/little-sympathy-for-greek-woes-in-eurozones-poorer-nations-741394.
Alderman, Liz & Herszenhorn, David. 2015. Putin Meets with Alexis Tsipras of Greece, Raising Eyebrows in Europe, *The New York Times*, April 8, www.nytimes.com/2015/04/09/world/europe/putin-russia-alexis-tsipras-greece-financial-crisis.html?_r=0.
BBC News. 2012. Eurozone Crisis Explained, November 27.
    2015a. Greece Debt Crisis: Athens Rejects Five-Month Bailout Extension, www.bbc.com/news/world-europe-33290361.
    2015b. Wolfgang Schaeuble: Germany's Man with a Grexit Plan, www.bbc.com/news/world-europe-33511387.
    2015c. Greece Crisis: MPs Back €85bn Bailout in Marathon Debate, www.bbc.com/news/world-europe-33925781.
Becker, Markus & Weiland, Severin. 2015. Grexit auf Zeit: Wie Wolfgang Schäuble die Genossen verwirrte, *Spiegel Online*, www.spiegel.de/politik/deutschland/griechenland-schaeubles-grexit-plan-bringt-die-spd-auf-a-1043296.html.
Bharati, Naik, Magnay, Diana, McLaughlin, Erin & Retiniotis, Mary. 2010. Greece Accepts Bailout Package, *CNN Money*, http://money.cnn.com/2010/05/02/news/international/greece_bailout/#TOP.
Blackstone, Brian. 2015. ECB Faces Dilemma in Greek Referendum, *The Wall Street Journal*, www.wsj.com/articles/ecb-faces-dilemma-in-greek-referendum 1435404254.
Bundesministerium der Finanzen. 2014. Lage des Euroraums: Länderanalyse Griechenland (accessed October 2015; no longer online).
Castle, Stephen. 2012. With Details Settled, a 2nd Greek Bailout Is Formally Approved, *The New York Times*, www.nytimes.com/2012/03/15/business/global/greece-gets-formal-approval-for-second-bailout.html?_r=0.
Chibber, Kabir. 2015. Sorry, Greece – You're Not Going to Get What You Want (Whatever That Is), *Quartz*, http://qz.com/337393/sorry-greece-youre-not-going-to-get-what-you-want-whatever-that-is/.
Christodoulakis, Nicos. 2015. *Greek Endgame, from Austerity to Growth or Grexit*. Rowman & Littlefield.

Chrysoloras, Nikos & Pals, Fred. 2015. Greece's Tsipras Is on a High Wire, *Bloomberg*, www.bloomberg.com/news/articles/2015-02-22/greece-seeks-to-reconcile-creditor-demands-with-election-pledges.

Clements, Lana. 2015. What Happens If Greece Defaults?, *Daily Express*, www.express.co.uk/finance/city/581754/What-happens-if-Greece-defaults.

Eddy, Melissa. 2015. Germany's Tone Grows Sharper in Greek Debt Crisis, *The New York Times*, www.nytimes.com/2015/07/17/world/europe/eurozone-greece-debt-germany.html.

EFSF. 2013. Frequently Asked Questions, www.esm.europa.eu/about/FAQ.htm.

ESM (European Stability Mechanism) 2012. ESM Annual Report 2012, in *Secondary ESM Annual Report 2012*.

    2013. ESM Annual Report 2013, in *Secondary ESM Annual Report 2013*.

    2014. ESM Annual Report 2014, in *Secondary ESM Annual Report 2014*.

    2015a. About Us, www.esm.europa.eu/about/index.htm.

    2015b. Financial Assistance – Cyprus, www.esm.europa.eu/assistance/cyprus/index.htm.

    2015c. Financial Assistance – Spain, www.esm.europa.eu/assistance/spain/.

European Commission. 2015a. Financial Assistance in EU Member States – Greece, http://ec.europa.eu/economy_finance/assistance_eu_ms/greek_loan_facility/index_en.htm.

    2015b. Information from the European Commission on the Latest Draft Proposals in the Context of Negotiations with Greece, http://europa.eu/rapid/press-release_IP-15-5270_en.htm.

    2015c. Statement on Greece by the European Commission in Liaison with the European Central Bank, http://europa.eu/rapid/press-release_STATEMENT-15-5493_en.htm.

Eurostat. 2015a. Unemployment Rate – Annual Data.

    2015b. Gross Domestic Product at Market Prices.

    2015c. Gross Domestic Product, Volumes.

    2015d. Real GDP Growth Rate – Volume.

Ewing, Jack. 2015. Jacob Lew Warns Time Is Running Out to Reach Greek Debt Deal, *The New York Times*, www.nytimes.com/2015/05/30/business/international/g7-g-7-greek-greece-debt-imf-lew-deal-default-eurozone.html?_r=0.

Financial Times. 2012. Eurozone Agrees Second Greek Bail-out, www.ft.com/cms/s/a3445f64-5c4c-11e1-911f-00144feabdc0,Authorised=false.html?siteedition=uk&_i_location=http%3A%2F%2Fwww.ft.com%2Fcms%2Fs%2F0%2Fa3445f64-5c4c-11e1-911f-00144feabdc0.html%3Fsiteedition%3Duk&_i_referer=&classification=conditional_standard&iab=barrier-app#axzz3kb5RuTaS.

    2015. German MPs Urged to Take Tough Line on Greece, www.ft.com/cms/s/0/fd51e310-bcd8-11e4-a917-00144feab7de.html#axzz3kb5RuTaS.

General Secretariat of the Council. 2015a. Remarks by President Donald Tusk ahead of the European Council Meeting, www.consilium.europa.eu/en/press/press-releases/2015/06/25-tusk-remarks-ahead-european-council/.

    2015b. Ministerial Statement on 27 June 2015, www.consilium.europa.eu/en/press/press-releases/2015/06/27-ministerial-statement/.

2015c. Remarks by Eurogroup President at the Final Eurogroup Press Conference on 27 June 2015, www.consilium.europa.eu/en/press/press-releases/2015/06/27-eurogroup-press-remarks-final/.

Generalsekretariat des Rates. 2015. Die Euro-Gruppe, www.consilium.europa.eu/de/council-eu/eurogroup/.

Ghosal, Sayantan & Thomas, Dania. 2015. Think the Eurozone Will Be Safe from Grexit Contagion? Think Again, *CNN*, http://edition.cnn.com/2015/07/06/opinions/eurozone-grexit-contagion-threat/.

Gourevitch, Peter A. 1989. Keynesian Politics: The Political Sources of Economic Policy Choices, in Peter A. Hall (ed.), *The Political Power of Economic Ideas: Keynesianism Across Nations*. Princeton University Press.

Guarascio, Francesco & Maltezou, Renee. 2015. Greek Creditors Seek Third Wave of Reforms before Loan, *Thomson Reuters*, www.reuters.com/article/2015/07/27/us-eurozone-greece-talks-idUSKCN0Q112G20150727.

Guo, Liang & Zhang, Juanjuan. 2012. Consumer Deliberation and Product Line Design, *Marketing Science* 31: 995–1007.

Hall, Peter A. (ed.). 1989. *The Political Power of Economic Ideas: Keynesianism Across Nations*. Princeton University Press.

Hellenic Republic Prime Minister. 2015. Prime Minister Alexis Tsipras' Address Concerning the Referendum to Be Held on the 5th of July (accessed October 2015; no longer online).

Hellenic Statistical Authority. 2014a. Labour Force Survey 2nd Quarter 2014, in *Secondary Labour Force Survey 2nd Quarter 2014*.

2014b. Labour Force Survey 4th Quarter 2014, in *Secondary Labour Force Survey 4th Quarter 2014*.

Hewitt, Gavin. 2015. Greece: The Dangerous Game, *BBC News*, www.bbc.com/news/world-europe-31082656.

Hjelmgaard, Kim. 2015. Greece to Receive Billions of New Loans after Bailout Approved, *USA Today*, www.usatoday.com/story/money/business/2015/08/14/greeces-parliament-approves-third-bailout/31694111/.

Hooper, John. 2015. Greek Referendum: Germany Says It Won't Leave Greece in the Lurch, *The Guardian*, www.theguardian.com/world/2015/jul/04/greek-referendum-germany-no-vote.

Horvat, Srećko. 2014. President Alexis Tsipras? Is That a joke?, *The Guardian*, www.theguardian.com/commentisfree/2014/jan/21/alexis-tsipras-european-commission-president-syriza.

Jacobsen, Henriette. 2015. Eurogroup Continues Talks on Greek "Plan B" without Varoufakis, *EurActiv*, www.euractiv.com/sections/euro-finance/eurogroup-continues-talks-greek-plan-b-without-varoufakis-315801.

Kathimerini in English. 2015. Greek Parliament Approves Third Bailout But SYRIZA Rebellion Grows, www.ekathimerini.com/200565/article/ekathimerini/news/greek-parliament-approves-third-bailout-but-syriza-rebellion-grows.

Kirby, Paul. 2015. Greece Debt Crisis: Has Grexit Been Avoided?, *BBC News*, www.bbc.com/news/world-europe-32332221.

Kitsantonis, Niki & Yardley, Jim. 2015. Greek Prime Minister Calls for Referendum on Bailout Terms, *The New York Times*, www.nytimes.com/2015/06/27/business/international/greek-debt-talks-enter-final-stages.html.

Kollewe, Julia & Wearden, Graeme. 2015. Greek Bailout Deal Gets Bundestag Green Light, *The Guardian*, www.theguardian.com/business/2015/feb/27/greek-reform-plan-given-unanimous-support-by-german-parliament.

Lienau, Odette. 2015. Greece: How to Default on Sovereign Debt, Greek Reporter, http://greece.greekreporter.com/2015/06/09/greece-how-to-default-on-sovereign-debt/.

Lynch, Suzanne. 2015. Greece, Eurogroup Agree to Four Month Bailout Extension, *The Irish Times*, www.irishtimes.com/business/economy/greece-eurogroup-agree-to-four-month-bailout-extension-1.2111060.

Maas, Stefan. 2015. Schäuble-Vorschlag sorgt für Kontroversen, Deutschlandfunk, www.deutschlandfunk.de/grexit-auf-zeit-schaeuble-vorschlag-sorgt-fuer-kontroversen.1766.de.html?dram:article_id=325216.

OECD. 2015. General Government Debt (Indicator).

Panke, Diana. 2015. Lock-in Strategies in International Negotiations. The Deconstruction of Bargaining Power, *Millennium* 43: 375–391.

Plickert, Philip. 2015. Wie viel Schulden Griechenland schon erlassen wurden, *Frankfurter Allgemeine Zeitung*, www.faz.net/aktuell/wirtschaft/eurokrise/griechenland/wie-viel-schulden-griechenland-schon-erlassen-wurden-ein-offener-und-ein-verdeckter-schuldenschnitt-13391476.html.

Protothema. 2015. Tsipras to Draghi: "I Must Honor Greek People's Mandate," http://en.protothema.gr/tsipras-to-draghi-i-must-honor-the-greek-peoples-mandate/.

Rankin, Jennifer & Traynor, Ian. 2015. Greece Bailout Talks Break Down Again, *The Guardian*, www.theguardian.com/business/2015/jun/25/greece-bailout-crisis-last-minute-search-deal.

Schelling, Thomas. 1980. *The Strategy of Conflict* (second edition). Cambridge University Press.

Siems, Mathias & Schnyder, Gerhard. 2014. Ordoliberal Lessons for Economic Stability: Different Kinds of Regulation, Not More Regulation, *Governance* 27: 377–396.

Simantke, Elisa & Schumann, Harald. 2015. Varoufakis: Greece's Creditors Have Turned Negotiations into a War, *EurActiv*, www.euractiv.com/sections/euro-finance/varoufakis-greeces-creditors-have-turned-negotiations-war-315247.

Sinn, Hans-Werner. 2015. Opinion: Why "Grexit" Could Be Good for Greece, *CNN Money*, http://money.cnn.com/2015/07/07/news/economy/greece-grexit-sinn-opinion/.

Smith, Helena. 2015. Alexis Tsipras Hints That Greece Is Nearing Compromise Deal on Debts, *The Guardian*, www.theguardian.com/business/2015/jun/14/greece-nearing-compromise-deal-on-eu-debts-says-alexis-tsipras.

Spiegel Online. 2015. Griechisches Parlament: Tsipras bringt drittes Hilfspaket durch – 43 Abweichler bei Syriza, *Spiegel Online*, http://www.spiegel.de/politik/ausland/griechenland-parlament-stimmt-fuer-drittes-hilfspakets-a-1048112.html.

Spiegel, Peter. 2015. Greek Bailout Talks Near "Drop Dead" Moment, *Financial Times*, www.ft.com/intl/cms/s/2/7f31597a-f4cd-11e4-abb5-00144feab7de.html#axzz3kepmTkSz.

References 313

Stamouli, Nektaria & Bouras, Stelios. 2015. Greek Prime Minister Alexis Tsipras Pushes to Keep Political Support, *The Wall Street Journal*, www.wsj.com/articles/greek-prime-minister-alexis-tsipras-pushes-for-political-survival-1436893758.

Steinhauser, Gabriele & Dendrinou, Viktoria 2015a. Any Deal on New Greek Bailout Funds Put Off Until Weekend, *The Wall Street Journal*, www.wsj.com/articles/greek-prime-minister-alexis-tsipras-resumes-talks-on-bailout-with-institutions-1435224154.

2015b. Eurozone Finance Ministers Reject Greek Request for One-Month Bailout Extension, *The Wall Street Journal*, www.wsj.com/articles/greece-bailout-eurozone-ministers-to-explore-plan-b-1435393252.

Stewart, Heather. 2015a. Varoufakis Refuses Any Bailout Plan That Would Send Greece into "Death Spiral," *The Guardian*, www.theguardian.com/business/2015/may/14/yanis-varoufakis-refuses-bailout-plan-send-greece-into-death-spiral.

Stewart, James B. 2015b. In Greek Debt Puzzle, the Game Theorists Have It, *The New York Times*, www.nytimes.com/2015/06/05/business/in-greek-debt-puzzle-the-game-theorists-have-it.html?_r=0.

The Economist. 2012. Greek Taxation. A National Sport No More, *The Economist*, www.economist.com/news/europe/21565657-greek-tax-dodgers-are-being-outed-national-sport-no-more.

2014. Greece's Shadow Economy. The Treasures of Darkness, *The Economist*, www.economist.com/news/finance-and-economics/21623742-getting-greeks-pay-more-tax-not-just-hard-risky-treasures.

2015a. Outgamed, *The Economist*, www.economist.com/news/europe/21644592-deal-struck-extend-bail-out-after-greece-caves-now-syriza-must-answer-its.

2015b. The Referendum and the Greek Banks. Nowhere to Get Money, *The Economist*, www.economist.com/blogs/freeexchange/2015/06/referendum-and-greek-banks.

2015c. Why Germany and Greece Are at Odds, *The Economist* (accessed October 2015; no longer online).

The Guardian. 2015. The Guardian View on Greece: Dangerous Brinkmanship, *The Guardian*, www.theguardian.com/commentisfree/2015/may/06/guardian-view-greece-dangerous-brinkmanship.

Thompson, Mark. 2015. Greek Bailout: Europe Strikes Deal after Marathon Talks, *CNN Money*, http://money.cnn.com/2015/07/12/news/economy/greece-bailout-europe-conditions/.

Traynor, Ian. 2015. Greece Warned to Expect No Favours as Bailout Negotiations Begin, *The Guardian*, www.theguardian.com/world/2015/feb/11/greece-warned-no-favours-bailout-negotiations-begin.

Tsipras, Alexis. 2015. Alexis Tsipras: « Non à une zone euro à deux vitesses », *Le Monde*, www.lemonde.fr/economie/article/2015/05/31/alexis-tsipras-l-europe-est-a-la-croisee-des-chemins_4644263_3234.html.

Wearden, Graeme. 2010. Greece Debt Crisis: Timeline, *The Guardian*, www.theguardian.com/business/2010/may/05/greece-debt-crisis-timeline.

2015. Greece Bailout Agreement: Key Points, *The Guardian*, www.theguardian.com/business/2015/jul/13/greece-bailout-agreement-key-points-grexit.

Chapter 3

Bagley, Bruce & Restrepo, Elvira María (eds.), 2011. *La desmovilización de los paramilitares en Colombia: Entre el escepticismo y la esperanza*. Ediciones Uniandes.

Bejarano, Jesús A. 1995. *Una agenda para la paz*. Tercer Mundo.

Botero, Felipe (ed.). 2010. *Elecciones, partidos y Congreso: 40 años de análisis de la democracia en Colombia*. Ediciones Uniandes.

Chernick, Marc. 1999. Negotiating Peace amid Multiple Forms of Violence: The Protracted Search for a Settlement to the Armed Conflicts in Colombia, in Cynthia J. Arnson (ed.). *Comparative Peace Processes in Latin America*. Woodrow Wilson Center Press and Stanford University Press.

2008. *Acuerdo posible: solución negociada al conflicto armado colombiano*. Ediciones Aurora.

Comisión de Superación de la Violencia. 1992. *Pacificar la paz*. IEPRI, CINEP, Comisión Andina de Juristas Seccional Colombia, and CECOIN.

Cosoy, Natalio. 2016. Las FARC "violan las reglas del juego" y empiezan a hacer política en Colombia, BBC Mundo, www.bbc.com/mundo/noticias/2016/02/160217_colombia_farc_politica_conejo_crisis_nc.

CNN, 2015. Santos: Acuerdo final con las FARC será firmado a más tardar en 6 meses, http://cnnespanol.cnn.com/2015/09/23/asi-es-el-acuerdo-de-justicia-entre-el-gobierno-de-colombia-y-las-farc/#0.

Dudley, Steven. 2008. *Armas y urnas. Historia de un genocidio político*. Planeta.

El País, 2016. Kerry se reúne con los negociadores de Colombia y las FARC para impulsar el proceso de paz, http://internacional.elpais.com/internacional/2016/03/21/colombia/1458577625_110283.html.

El Tiempo. 2015. "El que no diga la verdad, se va para la cárcel": Juan Carlos Henao, www.elespectador.com/noticias/paz/el-no-diga-verdad-se-va-carcel-juan-carlos-henao-articulo-639463.

Europapress. 2014. Las FARC asumen su responsabilidad por los actos de guerra en el conflicto en Colombia, www.europapress.es/internacional/noticia-farc-asumen-responsabilidad-actos-guerra-conflicto-colombia-20141030141253.html.

Folke Bernadotte Academy. 2016. FBA Supports Peace Initiatives in Colombia, https://fba.se/en/newspress/nyhetsarkiv/2014/FBA-supports-peace-initiatives-in-Colombia/.

García, Mauricio. 1992. *De la Uribe a Tlaxcala: Procesos de paz*. CINEP.

Gómez, Marisol. 2012. Proceso de paz: un arranque que dejó clara la magnitud del reto, eltiempo.com, October 21.

Gómez-Suárez, Andrei. 2007. Perpetrator Blocs, Genocidal Mentalities and Geographies: The Destruction of the Union Patriotica in Colombia and Its Lessons for Genocide Studies, *Journal of Genocide Research* 9(4): 637–660.

Gómez-Suárez, Andrei & Newman, Jonathan, 2013. Safeguarding Political Guarantees in the Colombian Peace Process: Have Santos and FARC Learnt the Lessons from the Past?, *Third World Quarterly* 34(5): 819–837.

Granada, Soledad, Restrepo, Jorge A. & Vargas, Andrés. 2009. El agotamiento de la política de seguridad: Evolución y transformaciones recientes en el conflicto armado colombiano, in Jorge A. Restrepo and David Aponte

(eds.), *Guerra y violencias en Colombia: Herramientas e interpretaciones*. Pontificia Universidad Javeriana.
Hartlyn, Jonathan. 2008. *The Politics of Coalition Rule in Colombia*. Cambridge University Press.
Haspeslagh, Sophie. 2016. Getting to Havana: The Transition of a Non-state Armed Group Labelled as a "Terrorist" Organization, paper presented at ISA 2016 (Atlanta).
Human Rights Watch. 2013. El riesgo de volver a casa. Violencia y amenazas contra desplazados que reclaman restitución de sus tierras en Colombia, www.hrw.org/sites/default/files/reports/colombia0913spwebwcover.pdf.
Isaacson, Adam. 2010. *Don't Call It a Model: On Plan Colombia's Tenth Anniversary, Claims of "Success" Don't Stand Up to Scrutiny*. Washington Office on Latin America (WOLA), www.wola.org/publications/colombia_dont_call_it_a_model.
Kline, Harvey. 2007. *Chronicle of a Failure Foretold: The Peace Process of Colombian President Andrés Pastrana*. The University of Alabama Press.
Leal, Francisco. 1993. La guerra y la paz en Colombia, in *Nueva Sociedad*, Nr. 125, http://nuso.org/media/articles/downloads/2250_1.pdf.
Licklider, Roy & Bloom, Mia. 2013. *Living Together after Ethnic Killing: Exploring the Chaim Kaufman Argument*. Routledge.
Machado, Absalón. 2009. *Ensayos para la historia de la política de tierras en Colombia. De la colonia a la creación del Frente Nacional*. Universidad Nacional de Colombia.
Mesa de conversaciones. 2015. 5. Acuerdo sobre las Víctimas del Conflicto: "Sistema Integral de Verdad, Justicia, Reparación y No Repetición", incluyendo la Jurisdicción Especial para la Paz; y Compromiso sobre Derechos Humanos; www.altocomisionadoparalapaz.gov.co/mesadecon versaciones/PDF/borrador-conjunto-acuerdo-sobre-las-victimas-del-con flicto-1450190262.pdf.
Molano, Alfredo. 2015. "Perdón Bojayá": Farc, www.elespectador.com/noticias/politica/perdon-bojaya-farc-articulo-603910.
Nasi, Carlo. 2007. *Cuando callan los fusiles. Impacto de la paz negociada en Colombia y en Centroamérica*. Grupo Editorial Norma-Universidad de los Andes.
  2009. Colombia's Peace Processes, 1982–2002: Conditions, Strategies and Outcomes, in Virginia Bouvier (ed.), *Colombia: Building Peace in a Time of War*. US Institute of Peace Press.
Nieto, Rafael. 2001. Economía y violencia, in *Colombia: conflicto armado, perspectivas de paz y democracia*. Latin American and Caribbean Center.
Nussio, Enzo. 2012. *La vida después de la desmovilización. Percepciones, emociones y estrategias de exparamilitares en Colombia*. Universidad de los Andes.
OAS. 2016. *Vigésimo Primer Informe Semestral del Secretario General al Consejo Permanente sobre la misión de apoyo al proceso de paz en Colombia de la Organización de los Estados Americanos (MAPP/OEA)*, www.mapp-oea.org/wp-content/uploads/2016/01/XXI-Informe-Semestral-MAPPOEA.pdf.
Pardo, Rafael. 2004. *Historia de las guerras*. Ediciones B.
Pecaut, Daniel. 1997. Presente, pasado y futuro de la violencia in Colombia, *Desarrollo Económico* 36(144): 891–929.

Pizarro Leongómez, Eduardo. 1990. La insurgencia armada: Raíces y perspectivas, in Francisco Leal Buitrago and León Zamosc (eds.), *Al filo del caos: Crisis política en la Colombia de los años 80*. IEPRI, Tercer Mundo.

Presidencia de la República de Colombia. 1988. *Iniciativa para la paz*.

Rettberg, Angelika. 2015. Victims of the Colombian Armed Conflict: The Birth of a Political Actor, in Bruce Bagley and Jonathan Rosen (eds.), *Colombia's Political Economy at the Outset of the 21st Century: From Uribe to Santos and Beyond*. Lexington Books.

  2016. Learning from the Past: The Colombian Private Sector in Colombia's Transition to Peace, working paper for the Josef Korbel School of International Studies, University of Denver's project on Non-Violent Action in Violent Settings.

Rettberg, Angelika & Daniel Quiroga. 2017. Más allá de la firma: Las elecciones legislativas (2014) y locales (2015) y el futuro de la implementación de la paz en Colombia, http://dx.doi.org/10.2139/ssrn.2718732.

Rosen, Jonathan. 2014. *The Losing War: Plan Colombia and Beyond*. SUNY Press.

Sánchez, Gonzalo & Meertens, Donny. 1983. *Bandoleros, gamonales y campesinos: El caso de la violencia en Colombia*. El Ancora Editores.

Semana. 2016. Autorizan bombardeos aéreos contra las bacrim, www.semana.com/nacion/articulo/autorizan-bombardeos-aereos-contra-bandas-criminales/472499.

Tickner, Arlene. 2003. Colombia and the United States: From Counternarcotics to Counterterrorism, *Current History* 102(661): 77–85.

United Nations. 2016. El Consejo de Seguridad establece misión política para Colombia, https://colombia.unmissions.org/sites/default/files/resolucion_2366_consejo_seguridad_naciones_unidas_segunda_mision_en_colombia.pdf.

Valencia, León. 2002. *Adiós a la política, bienvenida la guerra*. Intermedio.

Vargas, Alejandro. 2000. La insurgencia colombiana y el proceso de paz, in *El proceso de paz en Colombia y la política exterior de Estados Unidos*, Working Paper Series No. 247. Woodrow Wilson International Center for Scholars, www.wilsoncenter.org/sites/default/files/wp247_el_proceso_de_paz_en_colombia_y_la_politica_exterior_de_los_estados_unidos.pdf.

Villamizar, Darío. 1997. *Un adiós a la guerra*. Planeta.

World Bank. Overview Colombia, www.worldbank.org/en/country/colombia/overview.

Wilde, Alexander (ed.). 1978. Conversations among Gentlemen: Oligarchical Democracy in Colombia, in Juan J. Linz & Alfred Stepan, *The Breakdown of Democratic Regimes: Latin America*. Johns Hopkins University Press.

  1982. *La quiebra de la democracia*. Tercer Mundo.

Chapter 4

Baker, H. 1993. Symbolism in Cross-Cultural Trade: Making Chinese Symbols Work for You, in T. D. Weinshall (ed.), *Societal Culture and Management*. De Gruyter.

Blackman, C. 1997. *Negotiating China*. Allen and Unwin.

2000. *China Business: The Rules of the Game*. Allen and Unwin.
Brunner, James A. and Wang You. 1988. Chinese Negotiating and the Concept of Face. *Journal of International Consumer Marketing* 1(1): 27–44.
Buchan, N. 1998. *Culture, Fairness and Trust: Competing Influences on Negotiating Behavior and Outcomes in China, Korea, Japan and the United States*. University of Pennsylvania Press.
Chen, D. & Faure, G. O. 1995. When Chinese Companies Negotiate with Their Government. *Organization Studies* 16(1): 27–54.
Chu, Chin-Ning. 1991.*The Asian Mind Game*. Simon and Schuster.
Confucius. 1996. *The Analects*. Wordsworth.
Chung, M. 2008. *Shanghaied: Why Foster's Could Not Survive China*. Heidelberg Press.
2011. Doing Business Successfully in *China*. Woodhead Publishing.
Clissold, T. 2010. *Mr China*. Constable and Robinson.
Cremer, R. & Faure, G. O. 2017. Modernization with Chinese Characteristics, *Quarterly Journal of Chinese Studies* 5(2): 26–41.
De Mente, B. L. 1989. *Chinese Etiquette & Ethics in Business*. NTC Business Books.
DeBruijn, E. J. & Jia, X. 1993. Managing Sino-Western Joint Ventures. Transferring Technology to China by Means of Joint Ventures, *Research-Technology Management*, January–February, 17–22.
Eiteman, D. K. 1990. American Executives' Perceptions of Negotiating Joint Ventures with the P.R.C.: Lessons Learned, *Columbia Journal of World Business* 25: 4.
Fang, T. 1999.*Chinese Business Negotiating Style*. Sage.
Faure, Guy Olivier. 1998. Negotiation: The Chinese Concept, *Negotiation Journal* 14(2): 137–148.
2000a. Negotiation for Setting up Joint Ventures in China, *International Negotiation* 5(1): 157–189.
2000b. Joint Ventures in China and Their Negotiation, in Victor A. Kremenyuk and Gunnar Sjöstedt (eds.), *International Economic Negotiation*. Edward Elgar.
2008. Chinese Society and Its New Emerging Culture, *Journal of Contemporary China* 17(56): 469–491.
2009. Negotiated Risks across Cultures: Joint Ventures in China, in R. Avenhaus and Gunnar Sjöstedt (eds.), *Negotiated Risks: International Talks on Hazardous Issues*. Springer.
2011. Informal Mediation in China, *Conflict Resolution Quarterly* 29(1): 85–99.
Faure, Guy Olivier & Chen, D. 1999. Overcoming Negotiation Deadlocks in Business: Lessons from the Chinese, *The SIETAR International Journal* 1(2): 73–94.
Faure, Guy Olivier & Ding, Y. 2003. Chinese Culture and Negotiation: Strategies for Handling Stalemates, in I. Alon (ed.), *Chinese Culture, Organizational Behavior, and International Business Management*. Praeger.
Faure, Guy Olivier & Fang, T. 2008. Changing Chinese Values: Keeping up with Paradoxes, *International Business Review* 17(2): 194–207.
2011. Chinese Communication Characteristics: A Yin Yang Perspective, *International Journal of Intercultural Relations* 35(3): 320–333.

Faure, Guy Olivier & Rubin, Jeffrey Z. 1993. *Culture and Negotiation.* Sage.
Fernandez, J. A. & Underwood, L. 2012. *China Entrepreneur: Voices of Experience from 40 International Business Pioneers.* John Wiley & Sons.
Gao, Y. 1991. *Lure the Tiger out of the Mountains: The Thirty-Six Stratagems of Ancient China.* Simon & Schuster.
Graham, J. & Lam, M. 2003. The Chinese Negotiation, *Harvard Business Review* 81(10): 82–91.
Hall, E. T. 1976. *Beyond Culture.* Anchor.
Ho, D. 1976. On the Concept of Face, *American Journal of Sociology* 81: 867–884.
Hsieh, Cheng-Ho & Liu, Chiping. 1992. The Importance of Personal Contact in Trading with China, *Review of Business* 14(2): 41–42.
Hwang, K. K. 1987. Face and Favor: The Chinese Power Game, *American Journal of Sociology* 92: 944–974.
Kirkbride, P., Tang, S. & Westwood, R. 1991. Chinese Conflict Preferences and Negotiating Behavior: Cultural and Psychological Influences, *Organization Studies* 12(3): 365–386.
Lavin, Franklin L. 1994. Negotiating with the Chinese: Or How Not to Kowtow, *Foreign Affairs* 73(4): unpaginated, www.foreignaffairs.com/articles/asia/1994-07-01/negotiating-chinese-or-how-not-kowtow.
Lee, Kam-hon, Yang, Guang & Graham John L. 2006. Tension and Trust in International Business Negotiations, *Journal of International Business Studies* 37(5): 623–641.
Leung, T. K. P. & Yeung L. L. 1995. Negotiation in the People's Republic of China: Results of a Survey of Small Businesses in Hong Kong, *Journal of Small Business Management* 33(1): 70–77.
Lewis, D. 1995. *The Life and the Death of a Joint Venture in China.* Asia Law and Practice.
Lip, E. 1991. *Chinese Tactics for Success: 36 Stratagems.* Shing Lee.
  1995. *Feng Shui for Business.* Times Books International.
Lu, X. 1980. On "Face," in *Selected Works* (Vol. 4). Foreign Language Press.
Mann, J. 1989. *Beijing Jeep.* Simon and Schuster.
March, R. M. & Wu, S.-H. 2007. *The Chinese Negotiator: How to Succeed in the World's Largest Market.* Kodansha International.
McNeilly, M. 1996. *The Six Principles from Sun Tzu and the Art of Business: Six Principles for Managers.* Oxford University Press.
Purves, B. 1991. *Barefoot in the Boardroom: Venture and Misadventure in the People's Republic of China.* Allen & Unwin.
Pye, L. 1982. *Chinese Commercial Negotiating Style.* Oelgeschlager, Gunn, and Hain.
Seligman, S. D. 1990. *Chinese Business Etiquette.* Warner.
Shapiro, J., Behrman, J., Fisher, W. & Powell, S. 1991. *Direct Investment and Joint Ventures in China.* Quorum.
Solomon, R. H. 1987. China: Friendship and Obligation in Chinese Negotiation Style, in H. Binnendijk (ed.), *National Negotiating Styles.* Foreign Service Institute, US Department of State.
Yang, M. 1994. *Gifts, Favours, and Banquets: The Art of Social Relationships in China.* Cornell University Press.

Chapter 5

Ackermann, A. 1994. Reconciliation as a Peace-Building Process in Post-War Europe: The Franco-German case, *Peace and Change* 19(3): 229–250.
Baussant, M. 2002. *Pieds-noirs. Mémoires d'exils*. Stock.
Binoche, J. 1990. *De Gaulle et les Allemands*. Complexe.
Chirac, J. 2011. *Le temps présidentiel*. Éditions NiL.
de Gaulle, C. 1944. *Vers l'armée de métier*. Berger-Levrault.
1962. Speech in Hamburg, September 7.
Fackler, M. 1965. The Franco-German Treaty: The End of Hereditary Enemy, *The World Today* 21(1): 24–33.
Gerstenmaier, E. 1964. L'influence de la France sur le sentiment national en Allemagne, *Articles et Documents* 1606: 2.
Grosser, A. 1967. *French Foreign Policy under de Gaulle*. Little Brown.
Jauffret, J.-C. 2000. *Soldats en Algérie, 1954–1962. Expériences contrastées des hommes du contingent*. Autrement.
Ku, Y. 2008. International Reconciliation in the Postwar Era, 1945–2005: A Comparative Study of Japan–ROK and Franco-German relations, *Asian Perspective* 32(3): 5–37.
Kurbjuweit, D. 2010. Let Down by the US: Why Germany Needs Europe, *Der Spiegel*, December 14.
Pervillé, G. 2014. Une politique de l'oubli: La mémoire de la guerre en France et en Algérie, *Le sociographe* 46(2): 85–95.
Peyrefitte, A. 1994. *C'était de Gaulle, I*. Fayard.
Puchala, D. 1970. Integration and Disintegration in Franco-German Relations, 1954–1965, *International Organization* 24(2): 183–208.
Rosoux, V. 2014. Portée et limites du concept de réconciliation. Une histoire à terminer, *Revue d'études comparatives Est–Ouest* 45(3–4): 21–47.
Wallace, H. 1986. The Conduct of Bilateral Relationships by Governments, in Roger Morgan and Caroline Bray (eds.), *Partners and Rivals in Western Europe: Britain, France, Germany*. Gower.

Chapter 6

APEC. 2015. APEC History, www.apec.org/About-Us/About-APEC/History.
APEC Policy Support Unit. 2015. *Do FTAs Matter for Trade?* Asia Pacific Economic Cooperation.
Dupont, Christophe. 1996. Negotiation and Coalition Building. *International Negotiation* 1(1): 47–64.
McDonough, Patrick J. 1999. Subsidies and Countervailing Measures, in T. P. Stewart (ed.), *The GATT Uruguay Round: A Negotiating History – Volume IV: The End Game*. Kluwer International Law.
Reyna, Jimmie. 1999. Services, in T. P. Stewart (ed.), *The GATT Uruguay Round: A Negotiating History – Volume IV: The End Game*. Kluwer International Law.
Stewart, Terence P. (ed), 1999. *The GATT Uruguay Round: A Negotiating History – Volume IV: The End Game*. Kluwer International Law.

Winham, Gilbert R. 1987. Multilateral Economic Negotiation. *Negotiation Journal* 3(2): 175–189.
Yin, Robert K. 1989. *Case Study Research: Design and Methods* (revised edition). Sage.

Negotiations

Introduction and Chapters 7–17

Al-Jazeera (2014), Syria Mediator Brahimi Announces Resignation, May 14, www.aljazeera.com/news/middleeast/2014/05/syria-peace-envoy-brahimi-2014513151918573244.html.
Albin, Cecilia. 2001. *Justice and Fairness in International Negotiation*. Cambridge University Press.
Antrim, Lance N. & Sebenius, James K. 1992. Formal Individual Mediation and the Negotiators' Dilemma: Tommy Koh at the Law of the Sea Conference, in J. Bercovitch and J. Z. Rubin (eds.), *Mediation in International Relations: Multiple Approaches to Conflict Management*. Macmillan.
Appelt, K. C., Zou, X., Arora, P. & Higgins, E. T. 2009. Regulatory Fit in Negotiation: Effects of "Prevention-Buyer" and "Promotion-Seller" Fit. *Social Cognition* 27: 365–384.
Arnson, Cynthia & I. William Zartman (eds.). 2005. *Rethinking the Economics of War: The Intersection of Need, Creed, and Greed*. Johns Hopkins University Press.
Atran, Scott & Axelrod Robert, 2008. Reframing Sacred Values. *Negotiation Journal* 24(3): 221–247.
Axelrod, Robert. 1984. *The Evolution of Cooperation*. New York: Basic Books.
Axelrod, Robert & Hamilton, William D. 1981. The Evolution of Cooperation, *Science* 211(4489): 1390–1396.
Axelrod, Robert & Keohane, Robert. O. 1985. Achieving Cooperation under Anarchy: Strategies and Institutions, *World Politics* 38(1), 226–254.
Babcock, Linda & Loewenstein, George. 1997. Explaining Bargaining Impasse: The Role of Self-Serving Biases, *The Journal of Economic Perspectives* 11(1): 109–126.
Barberis, Nicholas C. 2012. Thirty Years of Prospect Theory in Economics: A Review and Assessment. *NBER Working Paper* 18621.
Bartos, Otomar. 1976. How Predictable Are Negotiations?, in I. William Zartman (ed.). *The 50% Solution*. Doubleday Anchor.
Bartos, Otomar J. 1995. Modeling Distributive and Integrative Negotiations, in Daniel Druckman and Christopher Mitchell (eds.), *Flexibility in International Negotiation and Mediation*. Sage.
Bazerman, Max & Neale, Margaret. 1994. *Negotiating Rationally*. The Free Press.
Bazerman, Max H. & Neale, Margaret A. 1995. The Role of Fairness Considerations and Relationships in a Judgmental Perspective of Negotiations, in Kenneth Arrow, Robert H. Mnookin, Lee Ross, Amos Tversky, and Robert Wilson (eds.), *Barriers to Conflict Resolution*. W. W. Norton.

BBC News. 2015. Ukraine Crisis: Leaders Upbeat after Moscow Talks, February 7, www.bbc.com/news/world-europe-31158925.
BBC World Service. 2015. Iran's Nuclear Crisis: What Are the Sanctions?, March 30, www.bbc.com/news/world-middle-east-15983302.
Bearce, David H., Floros, Katherine M. & McKibben, Heather Elko. 2009. The Shadow of the Future and International Bargaining: The Occurrence of Bargaining in a Three-Phase Cooperation Framework, *Journal of Politics* 71: 719–732.
Beardsley, K. 2009. Intervention without Leverage: Explaining the Prevalence of Weak Mediators, *International Interactions* 35(3): 272–297.
   2011. *The Mediation Dilemma*. Cornell University Press.
Beardsley, K., Quinn, D. M., Biswas, B. & Wilkenfeld, J. (2006). Mediation Style and Crisis Outcomes. *Journal of Conflict Resolution* 50(1): 58–86.
Beckett, Samuel. 1957. *Endgame* (play).
Bennett, D. Scott & Stam, Allan C. 1996. The Duration of Interstate Wars, 1816–1985, *American Political Science Review* 90(2): 239–257.
Bercovitch, J. 2002. *Studies in International Mediation*. Macmillan.
   2005. Mediation Success or Failure: A Search for the Elusive Criteria. *Cardozo Journal of Conflict Resolution* 7: 289–302.
Bercovitch, J. 2009. Mediation and Conflict Resolution, in Jacob Bercovitch, Victor Kremenyuk, and I. William Zartman (eds.), *The SAGE Handbook of Conflict Resolution*.
Bercovitch, J., Anagnoson, J. Theodore & Wille, Donnette L. 1991. Some Conceptual Issues and Empirical Trends in the Study of Successful Mediation in International Relations, *Journal of Peace Research* 28(1): 7–17.
Berton, Peter & Kimura, Hiroshi. 1999. *International Negotiation: Actors, Structure/Process, Values*. St. Martin Press.
Bick, Etta. 2006. Two-Level Negotiations and U.S. Foreign Policy: The Failure of the Johnson Plan for the Palestinian Refugees, 1961–1962, *Diplomacy & Statecraft* 17(3): 447–474.
Bishop, Robert. 1964. A Zeuthen–Hicks Theory of Bargaining, *Econometrica* XXXII(3): 410–417
Boettcher, William, A. 2004. The Prospects for Prospect Theory: An Empirical Evaluation of International Relations' Applications of Framing and Loss Aversion, *Political Psychology* 25(3): 331–362.
Bose, Sumantra. (2002). *Bosnia after Dayton: Nationalist Partition and International Intervention*. Oxford University Press.
Bottom, William P. 1998. Negotiator Risk: Sources of Uncertainty and the Impact of Reference Points on Negotiated Agreements, *Organizational Behavior and Human Decision Processes* 76(2): 89–112.
Bottom, William P. & Studt, Amy. 1993. Framing Effects and the Distributive Aspect of Integrative Bargaining. *Organizational Behavior and Human Decision Processes* 56(3): 459–474.
Boyer, Mark A., Urlacher, Brian, Hudson, Natalie F., Niv-Solomon, Anat, Janik, Laura L., Butler, Michael J., Brown, Scott W. & Ioannou, Andri. 2009. Gender and Negotiation: Some Experimental Findings from an International Negotiation Simulation, *International Studies Quarterly* 53(1): 23–47.

Brams, Steven J. 1990. *Negotiation Games*. Routledge.
  2003. *Negotiation Games: Applying Game Theory to Bargaining and Arbitration* (revised edition). Routledge.
Brecher, Michael & Wilkenfeld, Jonathan. 2000. *A Study of Crisis*. University of Michigan Press.
British Broadcasting Corporation (BBC). 2000. Rambouillet Talks Designed to Fail, 19 March, http://news.bbc.co.uk/2/hi/europe/682877.stm.
Brown, J. S. 1940. *Generalized Approach and Avoidance Responses in Relation to Conflict Behavior*. Unpublished dissertation, Yale University.
Bueno de Mesquita, Bruce. 1990. Multilateral Negotiations: A Spatial Analysis of the Arab–Israeli Dispute, *International Organization* 44(3): 317–340.
Bueno de Mesquita, Bruce, McDermott, Rose & Cope, Emily. 2001. The Expected Prospects for Peace in Northern Ireland, *International Interactions* 27(2): 129–167.
Burton, John W. 1990. *Conflict: Resolution and Prevention*. Macmillan.
Burton, John W. & Dukes, Frank. 1990. *Conflict: Practices in Management, Settlement & Resolution*. St. Martin's Press.
Burton, John W. & Sandole, Dennis J. D. 1986. Generic Theory: The Basis of Conflict Resolution, *Negotiation Journal* 2(4): 333–344.
Butler, Michael J. 2007. "Crisis Bargaining and Third-Party Mediation: Bridging the Gap," *International Negotiation* 12(2): 247–272.
  2009. *International Conflict Management*. Routledge.
Butler, Michael J. & Boyer, Mark A. 2003. Bosnian Peacekeeping and EU Tax Harmony: Evolving Policy Frames and Changing Policy Processes, *International Journal* 58(2): 389–416.
Camerer, Colin & Ho, Teck-Hua. 1994. Violations of the Betweenness Axiom and Nonlinearity in Probability, *Journal of Risk and Uncertainty* 8(2): 167–196.
Camerer, Colin & Kunreuther, Howard. 1989. Decision Processes for Low Probability Events: Policy Implications, *Journal of Policy Analysis and Management* 8(4): 565–592.
Carnevale, Peter J. 2002. Mediating from Strength, in J. Bercovitch (ed.), *Studies in International Mediation: Essays in Honor of Jeffrey Z. Rubin*. Palgrave Macmillan.
  2008. Positive Affect and Decision Frame in Negotiation, *Group Decision and Negotiation* 17(1): 51–63.
Carnevale, Peter J. & De Dreu, Carsten K. W. 2005. Laboratory Experiments on Negotiation and Social Conflict. *International Negotiation* 10(1): 51–66.
Carnevale, Peter J. & Pruitt, Dean G. 1992. Negotiation and Mediation, *Annual Review of Psychology* 43(1): 531–582.
Carnevale, Peter J. & Latané Drews, Julie. 1969. The Effect of Time Pressure, Time Elapsed, and the Opponent's Concession Rate on Behavior in Negotiation, *Journal of Experimental Social Psychology* 5(1): 43–60.
Carnevale, Peter J. & Olczak, Paul V. 1995. Beyond Hope: Approaches to Resolving Seemingly Intractable Conflict, in B. B. Bunker and Jeffrey Z. Rubin (eds.), *Conflict, Cooperation, and Justice: Essays Inspired by the Work of Morton Deutsch*. Jossey-Bass.
Carpenter, Jeffrey P. 2003. Bargaining Outcomes as the Result of Coordinated Expectations, *Journal of Conflict Resolution* 47(2): 119–139.

Carraro, Carlo & Marchiori, Carmen. 2004. Endogenous Strategic Issue Linkage in International Negotiations, in C. Carraro and V. Fragnelli (eds.), *Game Practice and the Environment*. Edward Elgar.

Caspi, Plia Vaisman, Olekalns, Mara & Druckman, Daniel. 2017. After the Fall: Regulatory Focus, Trust and Negotiators' Responses to a Crisis, *Journal of Trust Research* 7(1): 57–70.

Charap, Samuel & Colton, Timothy. 2017. *Everyone Loses: The Ukraine Crisis and the Ruinous Contest for Post-Soviet Eurasia*. Routledge.

Chasek, Pamela. 1997. A Comparative Analysis of Multilateral Environmental Negotiations, *Group Decision and Negotiation* 6: 437–461.

Chigas, Diana V. 1997. Unofficial Interventions with Official Actors: Parallel Negotiation Training in Violent Intrastate Conflicts, *International Negotiation* 2(3): 409–436.

Chollet, Derrick. 2005. *The Road to the Dayton Accords: A study of American Statecraft*. Palgrave Macmillan.

Christopher, Warren & Kreisberg, Paul H. (eds.). 1985. *American Hostages in Iran: The Conduct of a Crisis*. Yale University Press

Coddington, Alan. 1966. A Theory of the Bargaining Process: Comment, *American Economic Review* LVI: 522–530.

1968. *Theories of the Bargaining Process*. Aldine.

Cohen, Michael D., Riolo, Rick L. & Robert Axelrod. 2001. The Role of Social Structure in the Maintenance of Cooperative Regimes, *Rationality and Society* 13(1): 5–32.

Cohen, Raymond. 1997. *Negotiating across Cultures: International Communication in an Interdependent World* (revised edition). United States Institute of Peace.

Coleman, Peter T. & Krister Lowe, J. 2007. Conflict, Identity, and Resilience: Negotiating Collective Identities within the Israeli and Palestinian Diasporas, *Conflict Resolution Quarterly* 24(4): 377–412.

Coller, Marybeth & Williams, Melanie B. 1999. Eliciting Individual Discount Rates, *Experimental Economics* 2(2): 107–127.

Colosi, Thomas R. 1986. The Iceberg Principle: Secrecy in Negotiation, in Diane B. Bendahmane and John W. McDonald, Jr. (eds.), *Perspectives on Negotiation: Four Case Studies and Interpretations*. Center for the Study of Foreign Affairs.

Conlon, D. E., Carnevale, P. & Ross, W. H. 1994. The Influence of Third-Party Power and Suggestions on Negotiation: The Surface Value of a Compromise, *Journal of Applied Social Psychology* 24: 1084–1113.

Cousens, Elizabeth, 2008. It Ain't Over 'til It's Over: What Role for Mediation in Post-agreement Contexts? Background paper prepared for the Oslo Forum co-hosted by the Royal Norwegian Ministry of Foreign Affairs and the Centre for Humanitarian Dialogue, www.files.ethz.ch/isn/90795/Aint_Over_06_08.pdf.

Crocker, Chester A., Hampson, Fen Osler & Aall, Pamela. 1999. *Herding Cats: Multiparty Mediation in a Complex World*. US Institute of Peace Press.

2001. A Crowded Stage: Liabilities and Benefits of Multiparty Mediation, *International Studies Perspectives* 2(1): 51–67.

2015a. The Shifting Sands of Peacemaking: Challenges of Multiparty Mediation, *International Negotiation* 20(3): 363–388.

2015b. Why is Mediation so Hard? The Case of Syria, in Mauro Galluccio (ed.), *Handbook of International Negotiation*. Springer.

2016. Securing Leverage in Current Conflict Negotiations: The Quest for Coherence in Turbulent Times. *St Antony's International Review* 11(2): 15–37.

(eds.). 2007. *Leashing the Dogs of War: Conflict Management in a Divided World*. US Institute of Peace Press.

Crocker, Chester A. 1992. *High Noon in South Africa: Making Peace in a Rough Neighborhood*. W. W. Norton.

Cross, John. 1966. A Theory of the Bargaining Process: Reply, *American Economic Review* LVI: 531–533.

1969. *The Economics of Bargaining*. Basic.

Crump, Larry. 2006. Global Trade Policy Development in a Two-Track System, *Journal of International Economic Law* 9(2): 487–510.

2007. A Temporal Model of Negotiation Linkage Dynamics, *Negotiation Journal* 23(2): 117–153.

2010. Strategically Managing Negotiation Linkage Dynamics, *Negotiation and Conflict Management Research* 3(1): 3–27.

2013. International Trade Negotiations, in M. Olekalns and W. Adair (eds.), *Handbook of Research on Negotiation*. Edward Edgar.

2015. Analyzing Complex Negotiations, *Negotiation Journal* 31(2): 131–153.

Crump, Larry & Druckman, Daniel. 2012. Turning points in multilateral trade negotiations on intellectual property. *International Negotiation* 17: 9–35.

Crump, Larry & Zartman, I. William. 2003. Multilateral Negotiation and the Management of Complexity. *International Negotiation* 8(1): 1–5.

Daalder, Ivo H. & O'Hanlon, Michael E. 2000. *Winning Ugly, NATO's War to Save Kosovo*. Brookings.

Dafoe, Alan & Caughey, Devin. 2016. Honor and War: Southern U.S. Presidents and the Effects of Concern for Reputation, *World Politics* 68(2): 341–381.

Davis, James W. 2000. *Threats and Promises: The Pursuit of International Influence*. Johns Hopkins University Press.

De Dreu, Carsten K. W. & McCusker, Christopher. 1997. Gain–Loss Frames on Cooperation in Two-Person Social Dilemmas: A Transformational Analysis, *Journal of Personality and Social Psychology* 72(5): 1093–1106.

De Dreu, Carsten K. W., Carnevale, Peter J., Emans, Ben J. M. & van de Vliert, Evert. 1994. Effects of Gain–Loss Frames in Negotiation: Loss Aversion, Mismatching, and Frame Adoption, *Organizational Behavior and Human Decision Processes* 60(1): 90–107.

de Gaulle, Charles 1962. Speech to the German Military Academy, Hamburg, 7 September, cited in Jacques Binoche. 1990. *De Gaulle et les Allemands*. Complexe, 143.

De Martino, Benedetto, Kumaran, Dharshan, Seymour, Ben & Dolan, Raymond J. 2006. Frames, Biases and Rational Decision Making in the Human Brain, *Science* 313(5787): 684–687.

Diekmann, Andreas. 2004. The Power of Reciprocity: Fairness, Reciprocity, and Stakes in Variants of the Dictator Game, *Journal of Conflict Resolution* 48(4): 487–505.

Dixon, William J. & Senese, Paul D. 2002. Democracy, Disputes, and Negotiated Settlements, *Journal of Conflict Resolution* 46(4): 547–571.
Dobbins, James & Miller, Laurel. 2013. Overcoming Obstacles to Peace, *Survival: Global Politics and Strategy* 55(1): 103–120.
Donohue, William A. & Roberto, A. J. 1996. An Empirical Examination of Three Models of Integrative and Distributive Bargaining, *International Journal of Conflict Management* 7: 802–811.
Donohue, William A. & Druckman, Daniel. 2009. Message Framing Surrounding the Oslo I Accords, *Journal of Conflict Resolution* 53(1): 119–145.
Douglas, Ann. 1962. *Industrial Peacemaking*. Columbia University Press.
Druckman, Daniel. 1977. Boundary Role Conflict: Negotiation as Dual Responsiveness, *Journal of Conflict Resolution* 21(4): 639–662.
  1978. Boundary Role Conflict: Negotiation as Dual Responsiveness, in I. William Zartman (ed.), *The Negotiation Process: Theories and Applications*. Sage.
  1986. Stages, Turning Points and Crises: Negotiating Military Base Rights, Spain and the United States, *Journal of Conflict Resolution* XXX(2): 327–360.
  1993. The Situational Levers of Negotiating Flexibility, *Journal of Conflict Resolution* 37: 236–276.
  1994. Determinants of Compromising Behavior in Negotiation: A Meta-analysis, *Journal of Conflict Resolution* 38(3): 507–556.
  2001. Turning Points in International Negotiation: A Comparative Analysis, *Journal of Conflict Resolution* 45: 519–544.
  2002. Case-Based Research on International Negotiation: Approaches and Data Sets, *International Negotiation* 7(1): 17–37.
  2004. Departures in Negotiation: Extensions and New Directions, *Negotiation Journal* 20(2): 185–204.
  2005. Conflict Escalation and Negotiation: A Turning-Points Analysis, in I. William Zartman and Guy Olivier Faure (eds.), *Escalation and Negotiation in International Conflicts*. Cambridge University Press.
Druckman, Daniel & Harris, Richard. 1990. Alternative Models of Responsiveness in International Negotiation, *Journal of Conflict Resolution* 34: 234–251.
Druckman, Daniel & Olekalns, Mara. 2011. Turning points in negotiation. *Negotiation and Conflict Management Research* 4: 1–7.
  2013a. Motivating Primes, Trust, and Negotiators' Reaction to a Crisis, *Journal of Conflict Resolution* 57(6): 966–990.
  2013b. Punctuated Negotiation: Transitions, Interruptions, and Turning Points, in Mara Olekalns and Wendi L. Adair (eds.), *Handbook of Research on Negotiation*. Edward Elgar.
Druckman, Daniel, Olekalns, Mara & Smith, Philip. 2009. Interpretive Filters: Social Cognition and the Impact of Turning Points in Negotiation, *Negotiation Journal* 25: 13–40.
Earley P. C. 1997. *Face, Harmony and Social Structure*. Oxford University Press.
Egeland, Jan. 1999. The Oslo Accord: Multiparty Facilitation through the Norwegian Channel, in Chester A. Crocker, Fen Osler Hampson, and Pamela Aall (eds.), *Herding Cats: Multiparty Mediation in a Complex World*. US Institute of Peace Press.

Elms, Deborah Kay. 2008. New Directions for IPE: Drawing from Behavioral Economics, *International Studies Review* 10(2): 239–265.

Elliot, A. J. & Covington, M. V. 2001. Approach and Avoidance Motivation, *Educational Psychology Review* XIII: 73–92.

Epstein, S. & Fenz, W. D. 1965. Steepness of Approach and Avoidance Gradients in Humans as a Function of Experience, *Journal of Experimental Psychology* LDD: 1–12.

Evans, Peter B., Jacobson, Harold K. & Putnam, Robert D. 1993. *Double-Edged Diplomacy*. University of California Press.

Farrell, Joseph & Rabin, Matthew. 1996. Cheap Talk, *Journal of Economic Perspectives* 10(3): 103–118.

Faure, Guy Olivier. 2006. Stratégies chinoises de négociation, *Agir, Revue Générale de Stratégie* 53–64.

(ed.). 2012. *Unfinished Business: Why International Negotiations Fail*. Georgia University Press.

Faure, Guy Olivier & Rubin, Jeffrey Z. 1993. *Culture and Negotiation: The Resolution of Water Disputes*. Sage.

Fearon, James D. 1994. Domestic Political Audiences and the Escalation of International Disputes, *American Political Science Review* 88(3): 577–592.

1995. Rationalist Explanations for War, *International Organization* 49(3): 379–414.

1998. Bargaining, Enforcement, and International Cooperation, *International Organization* 52(2): 269–305.

Fey, Mark, Meirowitz, Adam & Ramsay, Kristopher. 2013. Credibility and Commitment in Crisis Bargaining, *Political Science Research and Methods* 1(1): 27–52.

Financial Times. 2015. Full Text of the Minsk Agreement, February 12, www.ft.com/cms/s/0/21b8f98e-b2a5-11e4-b234-00144feab7de.html#axzz3wUHFPozZ.

Fisher, Roger J. & Keashly, L. (1991). The Potential Complementarity of Mediation and Consultation within a Contingency Model of Third Party Intervention, *Journal of Peace Research* 28(1): 29–42.

Fisher, Roger & William Ury, with Bruce Patton. 1991. *Getting to Yes: Negotiating Agreement Without Giving In* (second edition). Penguin Books.

Fisher, Roger, Schneider, Andrea Kupfer, Borgwardt, Elizabeth & Ganson, Brian. 1996. *Coping with International Conflict: A Systematic Approach to Influence in International Negotiation*. Prentice Hall.

Fixdal, Monica. 2012. *Just Peace: How Wars Should End*. Palgrave.

Florea, Natalie, Boyer, Mark A., Brown, Scott W., Butler, Michael J., Hernandez, Magnolia, Weir, Kimberly, Johnson, Paula, Lin Meng, Mayall, Hayley & Lima, Clarisse. 2003. Negotiating from Mars to Venus: Some Findings on Gender's Impact in Simulated International Negotiations, *Simulation and Games* 34(2): 226–248.

Fowler, James H. & Kam, Cindy D. 2006. Patience as a Political Virtue: Delayed Gratification and Turnout, *Political Behavior* 28(2): 113–128.

Freedman, Lawrence. 2007. *The Official History of the Falklands Campaign, Vol. 1: The Origins of the Falklands War*. Routledge.

2015. Ukraine and the Art of Exhaustion, *Survival* LVII(5): 77–106.
French, J. R. P., Jr. & Raven, B. 1959. The Bases of Social Power, in D. Cartwright, (ed.), *Studies in Social Power*. University of Michigan Press.
Frey, James. 2016. *Endgame: The Rules of the Game*. Harper Collins.
Galtung, Johan. 1969. Violence, Peace, and Peace Research, *Journal of Peace Research* 6(3): 167–191.
GlobalSecurity.org. 2015. The Falkland Islands Conflict, 1982: Air Defense of the Fleet, www.globalsecurity.org/military/library/report/1984/HJA.htm.
Goldgeier, James, 2016. Promises Made, Promises Broken: What Yeltsin Was Told about NATO in 1993 and Why It Matters, *War on The Rocks*, July 12, http://warontherocks.com/2016/07/promises-made-promises-broken-what-yeltsin-was-told-about-nato-in-1993-and-why-it-matters/.
Goldgeier, James & Philip E. Tetlock, 2001. Psychology and International Relations Theory. *Annual Review of Political Science* 4(1): 67–92.
Goldstein, Joshua 2010. Chicken Dilemmas: Crossing the Road to Cooperation, in I. William Zartman and Saadia Touval (eds.), *International Cooperation: The Extents and Limits of Multilateralism*. Cambridge University Press.
Goodby, James E. 2012. Eight Negotiations – Seventeen Lessons, *International Negotiation* XVII(2): 213–236.
  2005. The Limited Test Ban Negotiations, 1954–63: How a Negotiator Viewed the Proceedings, *International Negotiation* 10(3): 381–404.
Gordon, Michael R. 2015. Iran Talks Still Face Difficult Issues, Kerry Says. *The New York Times*, July 11.
Gowan, Richard. 2016. It's Time for the U.N. to Refresh Its Neglected Cease-Fire Monitoring Skills, *World Politics Review*, April 16.
Greig, J. M. & Diehl, P. F. 2012. *International Mediation*. Polity.
Grieco, Joseph M. 1988. Anarchy and the Limits of Cooperation: A Realist Critique of the Newest Liberal Institutionalism, *International Organization* 42(3): 485–507.
Grieco, Joseph M., Powell, Robert & Snidal, Duncan. 1993. The Relative Gains Problem for International Cooperation, *American Political Science Review* 87: 729–743.
Gulliver, P. H. 1979. *Disputes and Negotiations: A Cross-Cultural Perspective*. Academic Press.
Hafner-Burton, Emilie M., Haggard, Stephan, Lake, David A. & Victor, David G. 2017. The Behavioral Revolution and the Study of International Relations, *International Organization* 71(suppl. S1): S1–S31.
Hafner-Burton, Emilie M., Hughes, D. Alex & Victor, David G. 2013. The Cognitive Revolution and the Political Psychology of Elite Decision Making, *Perspectives on Politics* 11(2): 368–386.
Hall, Todd H. & Ross, Andrew A. G. 2015. Affective Politics after 9/11, *International Organization* 69(4): 847–879.
Hall, W. E. 2014. *Turning Points in Environmental Negotiation: Exploring Conflict Resolution Dynamics in Domestic and International Cases*. Republic-of-Letters Publishing.

Harinck, Fieke & De Dreu, Carsten K. W. 2004. Negotiating Interests or Values and Reaching Integrative Agreements: The Importance of Time Pressure and Temporary Impasses, *European Journal of Social Psychology* 34(5): 595–611.

Harinck, Fieke & Druckman, Daniel. 2017. Do Negotiation Interventions Matter? Resolving Conflicting Interests and Values. *Journal of Conflict Resolution* 61(1): 29–55.

Haselhuhn, Michael P. & Mellers, Barbara A. 2005. Emotions and Cooperation in Economic Games, *Cognitive Brain Research* 23(1): 24–33.

Hedden, William. 2016. Cited in David Roberts, Grand Canyon on the Edge, *Smithsonian* XXXXVI(11): 69.

Higgins, E. T. 1987. Self-discrepancy: A Theory Relating Self and Affect, *Psychological Review* 94: 319–340.

Hinnebusch, Raymond & Zartman, I. William. 2015. *UN Mediation in the Syrian Crisis: From Kofi Annan to Lahdar Brahimi*. International Peace Institute.

Höglund, Kristine & Isak Svensson. 2011, Should I Stay or Should I Go? Termination as a Tactic and Norwegian Mediation in Sri Lanka, *Negotiation and Conflict Management Research* 4(1): 12–32.

Holbrooke, Richard C. 1998. *To End a War*. Random House.

Holmes, M. E. 1992. Phase Structures in Negotiation, in L. L. Putnam and M. E. Roloff (eds.), *Communication and Negotiation*. Sage.

Homans, C. G. 1961, *Social Behavior*. Harcourt Brace & Jovanovich.

Hopmann, P. Terrence. 1995. Two Paradigms of Negotiation: Bargaining and Problem Solving, *Annals of the American Academy of Political and Social Science* 542: 24–47.

   1996. *The Negotiation Process and the Resolution of International Conflicts*. University of South Carolina Press.

   2001. Bargaining and Problem Solving: Two Perspectives on International Negotiation, in Chester A. Crocker, Fen Osler Hampson, and Pamela Aall (eds.), *Turbulent Peace: The Challenges of Managing International Conflict*. US Institute of Peace Press.

   2014. The Verification Debate and Its Effects on the Negotiation Process, in Mordechai Melamud, Paul Meerts, and I. William Zartman (eds.), *Banning the Bang or the Bomb? Negotiating the Nuclear Test Ban Regime*. Cambridge University Press.

Hopmann, P. Terrence & Zartman, I. William (eds.). 2014. *Mindanao: Understanding Conflict 2014*. Conflict Management Program, Johns Hopkins University-SAIS.

Hume, Cameron 1994. *Ending Mozambique's War*. US Institute of Peace Press.

Iida, Keisuke. 1993. When and How Do Domestic Constraints Matter? Two-Level Games with Uncertainty, *Journal of Conflict Resolution* 37(3): 403–426.

Iklé, F. C. 1964. *How Nations Negotiate*. Harper.

   1971a. *How Wars End*. Columbia University Press.

   1971b. *Every War Must End*. Columbia University Press.

Interfax-Ukraine. 2014. Crimea Became Part of Russia, Which Has Nuclear Weapons According to NPT – Lavrov, December 15, http://en.interfax.com.ua/news/general/239978.html.

IRIN. 2015. 2004 Chronology of Events, www.irinnews.org/report/52561/rwanda-2004-chronology-of-events.
Isen, Alice M., Nygren, Thomas E. & Ashby, F. Gregory. 1988. The Influence of Positive Affect on the Perceived Utility of Gains and Losses, *Journal of Personality and Social Psychology* 55(5): 710–717.
Jensen, Lloyd. 1968. Approach–Avoidance Bargaining in the Test-Ban Negotiations, *International Studies Quarterly* XII(2): 152–160. (Republished as Soviet–American Behavior in Disarmament Negotiations, in I. William Zartman (ed.). 1978. *The 50% Solution*. Doubleday Anchor.)
Jentleson, Bruce W. 2000. Preventive Diplomacy: Analytical Conclusion and Policy Lessons, in Bruce W. Jentleson (ed.), *Opportunities Missed, Opportunities Seized: Preventive Diplomacy in the Post-Cold War World*. Roman and Littlefield.
Jervis, Robert. 1976. *Perception and Misperception in International Politics*. Princeton University Press.
  1992. Political Implications of Loss Aversion, *Political Psychology* 13(2):187–204.
Joffe, Josef. 2002. Mediation in the Middle East, *The Washington Quarterly* 25(4): 171–175.
Johns, Leslie. 2006. Knowing the Unknown: Executive Evaluation and International Crisis Outcomes, *Journal of Conflict Resolution* 50(2): 228–252.
Johnson, Hilde Frafjord. 2011. *Waging Peace in Sudan: The Inside Story of the Negotiations That Ended Africa's Longest Civil War*. Sussex Academic.
Judah, Tim. 2014. Ukraine: What Putin Has Won, *The New York Review of Books*, October 9, www.nybooks.com/articles/2014/10/09/ukraine-what-putin-has-won/.
Kahneman, Daniel. 2011. *Thinking, Fast and Slow*. Farrar, Straus and Giroux.
Kahneman, Daniel, Knetsch, Jack L. & Thaler, Richard H. 1990. Experimental Tests of the Endowment Effect and the Coase Theorem, *Journal of Political Economy* 98(6): 1325–1348.
Kahneman, Daniel & Tversky, Amos. 1979. Prospect Theory: An Analysis of Decision under Risk, *Econometrica* 47(2): 263–291.
  1984. Choices, Values, and Frames. *American Psychologist* 39(4): 341–350.
  1995. Conflict Resolution: A Cognitive Perspective, in Kenneth Arrow, Robert H. Mnookin, Lee Ross, Amos Tversky, and Robert Wilson (eds.), *Barriers to Conflict Resolution*. W. W. Norton.
Kanner, Michael. 2004. Framing and the Role of the Second Actor: An Application of Prospect Theory to Bargaining, *Political Psychology* 25(2): 213–239.
Keashly, L. & Fisher, R. J. 1996. A Contingency Perspective on Conflict Interventions: Theoretical and Practical Considerations, in Jacob Bercovitch (ed.), *Resolving International Conflicts: The Theory and Practice of Mediation*. Lynne Rienner.
Kelley, H. H. & Michela, J. L. 1980. Attribution Theory and Research, *Annual Review of Psychology* 31(1): 457–501.
Kelley, H. H., Beckman, L. L. & Fischer, C. S. 1967. Negotiating the Division of a Reward under Incomplete Information, *Journal of Experimental Social Psychology* 3: 361–398.

Kelman, Herbert. 1990. Interactive Problem-Solving: A Social-Psychological Approach to Conflict Resolution, in John Burton and Frank Duke (eds.), *Conflict: Readings in Management and Resolution*. St. Martin's Press.
  1992. Informal Mediation by the Scholar/Practitioner, in Jacob Bercovitch and Jeffrey Z. Rubin (eds.), *Mediation in International Relations: Multiple Approaches to Conflict Management*. St. Martin's Press.
Kemp, Katherine E. & Smith, William P. 1994. Information Exchange, Toughness, and Integrative Bargaining – The Roles of Explicit Cues and Perspective-Taking, *International Journal of Conflict Management* 5: 5–21.
Kimenyi, Mwangi S. & Mbaku, John Mukum. 2011. *South Sudan: Avoiding State Failure*. Brookings Institution Press.
Kitzantonis, Niki & Alderman, Liz. 2015. Greece Defers Payment, *New York Times*, June 5.
Knetsch, Jack L. & Sinden, J. A. 1984. Willingness to Pay and Compensation Demanded: Experimental Evidence of an Unexpected Disparity in Measures of Value, *The Quarterly Journal of Economics* 99(3): 507–521.
Knopf, Jeffrey W. 1993. Beyond Two-Level Games: Domestic–International Interaction in the Intermediate-Range Nuclear Force Negotiations, *International Organization* 47: 599–628.
Komorita, S. S. 1977. Negotiating from Strength and the Concept of Bargaining Strength, *Journal for the Theory of Social Behaviour* 7(1): 65–79.
Koremonos, Barbara. 2001. Loosening the Ties That Bind: A Learning Model of Agreement Flexiblity, *International Organization* 55(2): 289–325.
Kramer, Mark, 2009. The Myth of a No-NATO Enlargement Pledge to Russia, *Washington Quarterly* XXXII(2): 39–61.
Kremenyuk, Victor A. 2002. The Emerging System of International Negotiation, in Victor A. Kremenyuk (ed.), *International Negotiation: Analysis, Approaches, Issues* (second edition). Jossey-Bass.
Kreutz, Joakim. 2010. How and When Armed Conflicts End, *Journal of Peace Research* IIIL(2): 243–250.
Kriesberg, Louis. 1982. Social Conflict Theories and Conflict Resolution, *Peace & Change* 8(2–3): 3–17.
  2005. Nature, Dynamics, and Phases of Intractability, in Chester A. Crocker, Fen Osler Hampson, and Pamela Aall (eds.), *Grasping the Nettle: Analyzing Cases of Intractable Conflict*. US Institute of Peace Press.
  2007. The Development of the Conflict Resolution Field, in I. William Zartman (ed.), *Peacemaking in International Conflict: Methods and Techniques*. US Institute of Peace Press.
Kriesberg, Louis, Northrup, Terrell A. & Thorson, Stuart J. 1989. *Intractable Conflicts and Their Transformation*. Syracuse University Press.
Kroenig, Matthew. 2015. Why Is Obama Abandoning 70 Years of U.S. Nonproliferation Policy?, *Tablet*, June 15, www.tabletmag.com/jewish-news-and-politics/191479/obama-iran-nonproliferation.
Kuhberger, Anton. 1995. The Framing of Decisions: A New Look at Old Problems, *Organizational Behavior and Human Decision Processes* 62(6): 230–240.
  1998. The Influence of Framing on Risky Decisions: A Meta-Analysis, *Organizational Behavior and Human Decision Processes* 75(1): 23–55.

Kuperman, Alan. 2008. The Moral Hazard of Humanitarian Intervention: Lessons from the Balkans, *International Studies Quarterly* 52(1): 49–80.

Kydd, Andrew H. 2005. *Trust and Mistrust in International Relations*. Princeton University Press.

2015. Pie Uneaten: Hostility and Inefficiency in Bargaining. Unpublished University of Wisconsin manuscript.

Lamm, Helmut. 1988. A Review of Our Research on Group Polarization: Eleven Experiments on the Effects of Group Discussion on Risk Acceptance, Probability Estimation, and Negotiation Positions, *Psychological Reports* 62(3): 807–813.

Lawler, E. J. 1992. Power Processes in Bargaining, *The Sociological Quarterly* 33(1): 17–34.

Lax, David A. & Sebenius, James K. 1986. *The Manager as Negotiator: Bargaining for Cooperation and Competitive Gain*. Free Press.

Leary, K. 2004. Critical Moments as Relational Moments: The Centre for Humanitarian Dialogue and the Conflict in Aceh, *Negotiation Journal* 20: 311–338.

Leng, Russell J. 1983. When Will They Ever Learn? Coercive Bargaining in Recurrent Crises, *Journal of Conflict Resolution* 27(3): 379–419.

1993. Reciprocating Influence Strategies in Interstate Crisis Bargaining, *Journal of Conflict Resolution* 37(1): 3–41.

2000. *Bargaining and Learning in Recurring Crises: The Soviet–American, Egyptian–Israeli, and Indo-Pakistani Rivalries*. University of Michigan Press.

Lerner, Jennifer S., Small, Deborah A. & Loewenstein, George. 2004. Heart Strings and Purse Strings: Effects of Specific Emotions on Economic Transactions, *Psychological Science* 15(5): 337–341.

Leventoğlu, Bahar & Tarar, Ahmer. 2008. Does Private Information Lead to Delay or War in Crisis Bargaining, *International Studies Quarterly* 52(3): 533–553.

Levin, I. P., Schneider, S. L. & Gaeth, G. J. 1998. All Frames Are Not Created Equal: A Typology and Critical Analysis of Framing Effects, *Organizational Behavior and Human Decision Processes* 76(2): 149–188.

Lewin, K. 1935. *A Dynamic Theory of Personality*. McGraw-Hill.

Lewis, Jeffrey 2015. Why a "Bad" Deal with Iran Is Better Than No Deal at All, *Foreign Policy*, March 11, http://foreignpolicy.com/2015/03/11/why-a-bad-deal-with-iran-is-better-than-no-deal-at-all-tom-cotton-letter.

Licklider, Roy. 1993. *Stopping the Killing: How Civil Wars End*. New York University.

Lieberfeld, Daniel. 2008. Secrecy and "Two Level Games" in the Oslo Accord. What the Primary Sources Tell Us, *International Negotiation* 13(1): 133–146.

Lindblom, Charles E. 1959. The Science of "Muddling Through," *Public Administration Review* XIX(2): 79–88.

Loewenstein, George F., Weber, Elke U., Hsee, Christopher K. & Welch, Ned. 2001. Risk as Feelings, *Psychological Bulletin* 127(2): 267–286.

Lundgren, M. 2016. Mediation in Syria: Initiatives, Strategies, and Obstacles, 2011–2016, *Contemporary Security Policy* 37(2): 273–288.

Majeski, Stephen J. 1995. Generating and Maintaining Cooperation in International Relations: A Model of Repeated Interaction among Groups in Complex and Uncertain Situations, *International Interactions* 21(3): 265–289.

Majeski, Stephen J. & Fricks, Shane. 1995. Relations among Nation-States in a Changing Environment – A Model of Repeated Interaction between 2 Groups with Limited Information, *International Interactions* 19(4): 283–309.

Mandel, D. R. 2001. Gain–Loss Framing and Choice: Separating Outcome Formulations from Descriptor Formulations, *Organizational Behavior and Human Decision Processes* 85(1): 56–76.

McDermott, Rose. 2004. The Feeling of Rationality: The Meaning of Neuroscientific Advances for Political Science, *Perspectives on Politics* 2(4): 691–706.

  2009. Prospect Theory and Negotiation, in R. Avenhaus and G. Sjostedt (eds.), *Negotiated Risks*. Springer-Verlag.

McDermott, Rose, Fowler, James H. & Smirnov, Oleg. 2008. On the Evolutionary Origin of Prospect Theory Preferences, *The Journal of Politics* 70(2): 335–350.

McGinn, K. L., Lingo, E. & Ciano, K. 2004. Transitions through Out-of-Keeping Acts, *Negotiation Journal* 20: 171–184.

McManus, Doyle. 1981. *Free at Last!* Signet.

Melamud, Mordechai, Meeerts, Paul & Zartman, I. William (eds.). 2010. *Banning the Bomb or Banning the Blast? Negotiations for the Comprehensive Test Ban Treaty*. Cambridge University Press.

Mercer, Jonathan. 2005. Rationality and Psychology in International Politics, *International Organization* 59(1): 77–106.

  2010. Emotional Beliefs, *International Organization* 64(1): 1–31.

Merikallio, Katri. 2006. *Making Peace: Ahtisaari and Aceh*. Werner Söderström Bookwell Oy.

Mezagopian, Madeleine. 2008. UN–Swedish Impartial Mediation: The Gunnar Jarring Mission in the Middle East 1967–1973 (to be published in *Science of Mediation*. Sancta Simplicitas).

Milburn, T. W. 1972. The Management of Crisis, in C. F. Hermann (ed.), *International Crisis: Insights from Behavioral Research*. Free Press.

Milburn, T. W. & Isaac, Paul. 1995. Prospect Theory: Implications for International Mediation, *Peace and Conflict: Journal of Peace Psychology* 1(4): 333–342.

Miller, Aaron David. 2014. It's Iran, Stupid, *Foreign Policy*, February 12, http://foreignpolicy.com/2014/02/12/its-iran-stupid/.

Miller, N. E. 1944. Experimental Studies in Conflict, in J. M. Hunt (ed.), *Personality and the Behavior Disorders*. Roland Press.

  1971. *Selected Papers on Conflict, Displacement, Learned Drives, and Theory*. Aldine Atherton.

Ministry of Foreign Affairs of the People's Republic of China. 2014. Set aside dispute and pursue joint development, www.fmprc.gov.cn/mfa_eng/ziliao_665539/3602_665543/3604_665547/t18023.shtml.

Miroff, Nick. 2015. Colombian President, Rebels Announce Major Breakthrough in Peace Talks, *Washington Post*, September 23, www.washingtonpost.com/world/the_americas/colombia-and-rebels-expected-to-reveal-major-breakthrough-in-peace-talks/2015/09/23/98694be6-61f1-11e5-8475-781cc9851652_story.html.

Mitchell, G. J. 2000. *Making Peace*. University of California Press.

Mo, Jongryn. 1995. Domestic Institutions and International Bargaining: The Role of Agent Veto in Two-Level Games. *American Political Science Review* 89: 914–924.

Moore, Christopher W. 2003. *The Mediation Process: Practical Strategies for Resolving Conflict* (third edition). Jossey-Bass.

Nash, John F., Jr. 1950. The Bargaining Problem, *Econometrics* 18(2): 155–162.

1953. Two-Person Cooperative Games, *Econometrica* 21(1): 128–140.

National Centre for Historical Memory (Centro Nacional de Memoria Histórica). 2015. www.centrodememoriahistorica.gov.co/.

Neale, Margaret A. & Bazerman, Max H. 1985. The Effects of Framing and Negotiator Overconfidence on Bargaining Behaviors and Outcomes, *Academy of Management Journal* 28(1): 34–49.

1992. Negotiator Cognition and Rationality: A Behavioral Decision Theory Perspective. *Organizational Behavior and Human Decision Processes* 51(2): 157–175.

Nelson, Rebecca M. 2017. *U.S. Sanctions and the Russian Economy*, Congressional Research Service Report, November 17, https://fas.org/sgp/crs/row/R43895.pdf.

Nielsson, Gunnar P. 1988. *Mediation under Crisis Management Conditions: The U.N. Secretary General and the Falklands/Malvinas Islands Crisis, April 1–June 14, 1982*. Pew case study #110. Georgetown University Institute for the Study of Diplomacy.

Norwegian Peacebuilding Resource Centre. 2013. Challenges Facing the Colombian Peace Negotiations, www.peacebuilding.no/var/ezflow_site/storage/original/application/e0d5646f08cb959623b952bca6e27903.pdf.

Novemsky, Nathan & Kahneman, Daniel. 2005. How Do Intentions Affect Loss Aversion?, *Journal of Marketing Research* 42(2): 139–140.

Nowak, Andzej & Vallacher, Robin R. 1998. *Dynamical Social Psychology*. Guilford Press.

Nye, J. S. 2008. Public Diplomacy and Soft Power, *The Annals of the American Academy of Political and Social Science* 616(1): 94–109.

Oberdorfer, Don & Carlin, Robert. 2014. *The Two Koreas: A Contemporary History* (third edition). Basic Books.

Odell, John S. 2000. *Negotiating the World Economy*. Cornell University Press.

2001. Case Study Methods in International Political Economy, *International Studies Perspective* 2: 161–176.

2009. Breaking Deadlocks in International Institutional Negotiations: The WTO, Seattle, and Doha, *International Studies Quarterly* 53(2): 273–299.

Odell, John S., Tingley, Dustin with Hampson, Fen, Kydd, Andrew, Keohane, Robert, Leeds, Ashley, Sebenius, James, Stein, Janice, Walter, Barbara & Zartman, I. William. 2014. Negotiating Agreements in International Relations. (Prepared for the International Relations Working Group of the American Political Science 2013 Taskforce on Negotiating Agreements in Politics, co-directed by Jane Mansbridge and Cathie Jo Martin.)

Official Website of the President of Russia. 2014. Meeting of the Valdai International Discussion Club, October 24, http://en.kremlin.ru/events/president/news/46860.

Ohlson, Thomas. 2008. Understanding Causes of War and Peace, *European Journal of International Relations* 14(1): 133–160.

Olekalns, Mara & Druckman, Daniel. 2014. With Feeling: How Emotions Shape Negotiation. *Negotiation Journal* 30: 455–478.

Olekalns, Mara & Smith, P. 2005. Moments in Time: Metacognition, Trust, and Outcomes in Negotiation, *Personality and Social Psychology Bulletin* 31: 1696–1707.

Olekalns, Mara, Brett, J. M. & Weingart, L. 2003. Phases, Transitions and Interruptions: The Processes That Shape Agreement in Multi-party Negotiation, *International Journal of Conflict Management* 14: 191–211.

Owen, Robert B. 1985. The final negotiations, in Warren Christopher and Paul H. Kreisberg (eds.), *American Hostages in Iran: The Conduct of a Crisis*. Council on Foreign Relations.

Pillar, Paul 1983. *Negotiating Peace*. Princeton.

Plott, Charles R. & Zeiler, Kathryn. 2005. The Willingness to Pay–Willingness to Accept Gap, the "Endowment Effect," Subject Misconceptions, and Experimental Procedures for Eliciting Valuations, *American Economic Review* 95(3): 530–545.

Pond, Elizabeth & Kundnani, Hans. 2015. Germany's Real Role in the Ukraine Crisis, *Foreign Affairs*, March/April, www.foreignaffairs.com/articles/easterneurope-caucasus/germany-s-real-role-ukraine-crisis.

Poroshenko, Petro. 2014. President Commenting on Arrangements in Minsk: "I've Got No Illusions, But I've Got Hope," *President of Ukraine*, September 8, www.president.gov.ua/en/news/prezident-pro-domovlenosti-v-minsku-u-mene-nemaye-ilyuzij-al-33656.

Poulsen, Lauge N. Skovgaard & Aisbett, Emma. 2013. When the Claim Hits: Bilateral Investment Treaties and Bounded Rational Learning, *World Politics* 65(2): 273–313.

Powell, Jonathan, 2008. *Great Hatred, Little Room: Making Peace in Northern Ireland*. Random House – The Bodley Head.

Powell, Robert. 2002, Bargaining Theory and International Conflict, *Annual Review of Political Science* 5: 1–30.

Pressman, Jeremy. 2003. Visions in Collision: What Happened at Camp David and Taba, *International Security* 28(2): 5–43.

Princen, T. 1992. *Intermediaries in International Conflict*. Princeton University Press.

Prins, Brandon C. 2003. Institutional Instability and the Credibility of Audience Costs: Political Participation and Interstate Crisis Bargaining, 1816–1992, *Journal of Peace Research*, 40(1): 67–84.

Pruitt, Dean G. 1981. *Negotiation Behavior*. Academic Press.

1983. Achieving Integrative Agreements, in Max Bazerman and Roy Lewicki (eds.), *Negotiating in Organizations*. Sage.

1997. Ripeness Theory and the Oslo Talks. *International Negotiation* 2(2): 237–250.

2006. Negotiation with Terrorists, *International Negotiation* 11(2): 371–394.

2008. Back-Channel Communication in the Settlement of Conflict, *International Negotiation* 13(1): 37–54.

2015. Contributions to Readiness and Ripeness Theories: Three Peace Processes, in William Donohue and Daniel Druckman (eds.), *Searching for*

Better Agreements ... and Finding Them: Contributions of Dean G. Pruitt. Republic of Letters Publishing.
Pruitt, Dean G. & Carnevale, Peter J. 1993. *Negotiation in Social Conflict*. Thomson Brooks/Cole.
Putnam, Linda L. 2004. Transformation and Critical Moments in Negotiations, *Negotiation Journal* 20(2): 275–295.
Putnam, Linda L. & Fuller, R. 2010. Negotiation and Corporate Campaigns: The Case of the 2007–2008 Writers' Strike. (Paper presented at the Annual Meeting of the National Communication Association, San Francisco.)
Putnam, Linda L. & Shoemaker, M. 2007. Changes in Conflict Framing in the News Coverage of an Environmental Conflict, *Journal of Dispute Resolution* 1: 167–175.
Putnam, Linda L. & Wondolleck, J. M. 2003. Intractability: Definitions, Dimensions and Distinctions, in R. J. Lewicki, B. Gray, and M. Elliott (eds.), *Making Sense of Intractable Environmental Conflicts: Frames and Cases*. Island Press.
Putnam, Robert. D. 1988. Diplomacy and Domestic Politics: The Logic of Two-Level Games, *International Organization* 42(3): 427–460.
Quandt, William. B. 1986. *Camp David: Peacemaking and Politics*. Brookings Institution Press.
  1995. *Peace Process*. Brookings Institution Press.
Quattrone, George & Tversky, Amos. 1988. Contrasting Rational and Psychological Analyses of Political Choice, *American Political Science Review* 82(3): 719–736.
Rabinovich, Itamar. 1998. *The Brink of Peace: The Israeli–Syrian Negotiations*. Princeton University Press.
Raiffa, Howard. 1995. Analytical Barriers, in Kenneth Arrow, Robert H. Mnookin, Lee Ross, Amos Tversky, and Robert Wilson (eds.), *Barriers to Conflict Resolution*. W. W. Norton.
  2005. *Negotiation Analysis*. Belknap Press.
Ramsbothom, Oliver, Woodhouse, Tom & Miall, Hugh. 2005. *Contemporary Conflict Resolution: The Prevention, Management, and Transformation of Deadly Conflicts* (second edition). Polity.
Rapoport, Anatol. 1960. *Fights, Games, and Debates*. University of Michigan Press.
Regan, Patrick M. & Stam, Allan C., III. 2000. In the Nick of Time: Conflict Management, Mediation Timing, and the Duration of Interstate Disputes, *International Studies Quarterly* 44(2): 239–260.
Regehr, Ernie. 2015. *Disarming Conflict: Why Peace Cannot Be Won on the Battlefield*. Between the Lines.
Reyntjens, Filip. 2004. Rwanda, Ten Years On: From Genocide to Dictatorship, *African Affairs* 103(411): 177–210.
Richmond, O. (1998). Devious Objectives and the Disputants' View of International Mediation: A Theoretical Framework, *Journal of Peace Research* 35(6): 707–722.
Rohde, David. 1997. *Endgame: The Betrayal and Fall of Srebrenica*. Farrar, Straus & Giroux.

Rojansky, Matthew. 2017. The Ukraine–Russia Conflict: A Way Forward, *The National Interest*, February 1, http://nationalinterest.org/feature/the-ukraine-russia-conflict-way-forward-19282.

Rose, Gideon. 2012. *How Wars End: We Aways Fight the Last Battle*. Simon & Schuster.

Rosendorff, B. Peter & Milner, Helen V. 2001. The Optimal Design of International Trade Institutions: Uncertainty and Escape, *International Organization* 55(4): 829–857.

Ross, Dennis. 2005. *Missing Peace: The Inside Story of the Fight for Middle East Peace*. Farrar, Straus and Giroux.

Ruane, Abigail E. 2006. Real Men and Diplomats: Intercultural Diplomatic Negotiation and Masculinities in China and the United States, *International Studies Perspectives* 7(4): 342–359.

Rubin, Jeffrey Z. 1980. Experimental Research on Third-Party Intervention in Conflict: Toward Some Generalizations, *Psychological Bulletin* 87(2): 379–391.

Rubin, Jeffrey Z. & Brown, Bert. 1975. *The Social Psychology of Bargaining and Negotiation*. Academic.

Rubin, Jeffrey Z., Pruitt, Dean G. & Kim, S. H. 1994. *Social Conflict: Escalation, Stalemate, and Settlement*. McGraw-Hill.

Sanger, David E. & Gordon, Michael R. 2015. An Iran Nuclear Deal Built on Coffee, All-Nighters and Compromise, *The New York Times*, April 3.

Sarotte, Mary Elise. 2014. *1989: The Struggle to Create Post-Cold War Europe*. Princeton University Press.

Saunders, Harold A. 1985. Beginning of the End, in Warren Christopher and Paul H. Kreisberg (eds.), *American Hostages in Iran: The Conduct of a Crisis*. Council on Foreign Relations.

Scharpf, F. W. 1988. The Joint-Decision Trap: Lessons from German Federalism and European Integration, *Public Administration* 66(3): 239–278.

Schaub, Gary. 2004. Deterrence, Compellence, and Prospect Theory, *Political Psychology* 25(3): 389–411.

Schelling, Thomas C. 1960. *The Strategy of Conflict*. Harvard University Press. 1966. *Arms and Influence*. Yale University Press.

Schüßler, Rudolf (ed.). 2018. *Focal Points in Negotiation*. To be published.

Sharp, Gene. 1973. *The Politics of Nonviolent Action* (three volumes). Porter Sargent.

Schweitzer, Maurice E. & DeChurch, L. 2001. Linking Frames in Negotiation: Gains, Losses, and Conflict Frame Adoption, *International Journal of Conflict Management* 12(2): 100–113.

Sebenius, James K. 1996. Sequencing to Build Coalitions: With Whom Should I Talk First?, in Richard Zeckhauser, Ralph L. Keeney, and James K. Sebenius (eds.), *Wise Choices: Decisions, Games, and Negotiations*. Harvard Business School Press.

Selten, Reinhard. 1978. The Chain Store Paradox, *Theory and Decision* IX(2): 127–159.

Shamir, Jacob & Shikaki, Khalil. 2005. Public Opinion in the Israeli–Palestinian Two-Level Game, *Journal of Peace Research* 42(3): 311–328.

Shell, G. Richard. 1999. *Bargaining for Advantage*. Penguin.
Shifrinson, Joshua R. Itzkovitz. 2016. Deal or No Deal? The End of the Cold War and the U.S. Offer to Limit NATO Expansion, *International Security* XXXX (4): 7–44.
Shotwell, Peter. 2005. *GO Basics*. Tuttle.
Silber, L. & Little, A. 1996. *The Death of Yugoslavia*. Penguin.
Simon, Herbert. 1957. *Models of Man: Social and Rational*. Wiley.
Simonson, Itamar & Tversky, Amos. 1992. Choice in Context: Tradeoff Contrast and Extremeness Aversion, *Journal of Marketing Research* 29(3): 281–395.
Sisk, T. D. 2009. *International Mediation in Civil Wars: Bargaining with Bullets*. Routledge.
Slovic, Paul, Finucane, Melissa L., Peters, Ellen & MacGregor, Donald G. 2004. Risk as Analysis and Risk as Feelings: Some Thoughts about Affect, Reason, Risk, and Rationality, *Risk Analysis* 24(2): 311–322.
Smith, Alastair. 1998. International Crises and Domestic Politics, *American Political Science Review* 92(3): 623–638.
Smith, D. Leasel, Pruitt, Dean G. & Carnevale, Peter J. 1982. Matching and Mismatching: The Effect of Own Limit, Other's Toughness, and Time Pressure on Concession Rate in Negotiation, *Journal of Personality and Social Psychology* 42(5): 876–888.
Smith, James D. D. 1994. Mediator Impartiality: Banishing the Chimera, *Journal of Peace Research* 31(4): 445–450.
Snyder, Glenn H. & Diesing, Paul. 1977. *Conflict among Nations: Bargaining, Decision Making, and System Structure in International Crises*. Princeton University Press.
Solomon, Jay & Meckler, Laura. 2015. Hillary Clinton Opened Door to Key U.S. Shift toward Iran Nuclear Deal, *The Wall Street Journal*, September 8, www.wsj.com/articles/hillary-clinton-backed-key-u-s-shift-toward-iran-nuclear-deal-1441753099.
Spector, Bertram I. 1995. Creativity Heuristics for Impasse Resolution: Reframing Intractable Negotiations, *Annals of the American Academy of Political and Social Science* 542(1): 81–99.
Stanton, Frederik. 2010. *Great Negotiations*. Westholme.
Stedman, Stephan John. 2000. Spoiler Problems in Peace Processes, in Paul C. Stern and Daniel Druckman (eds.), *International Conflict Resolution after the Cold War*. National Academy Press.
Stein, Janice Gross. 1985. Calculation, Miscalculation, and Conventional Deterrence I: The View from Cairo, in Robert Jervis, Richard Ned Lebow, and Janice Gross Stein (eds.), *Psychology and Deterrence*. Johns Hopkins University Press.
  (ed.). 1989. *Getting to the Table: The Processes of International Negotiation*. Johns Hopkins University Press.
Stein, Janice Gross & Pauly, Louis (eds.). 1993. *Choosing to Cooperate*. Johns Hopkins University Press.
Steinberg, James & O'Hanlon, Michael E. 2016. *Strategic Reassurance and Resolve: U.S.–China Relations in the Twenty-First Century*. Princeton University Press.

Stillinger, Constance & Ross, Lee. 1991. Barriers to Conflict Resolution, *Negotiation Journal* 7(4): 389–404.
Svensson, I. 2007. Mediation with Muscles or Minds? Exploring Power Mediators and Pure Mediators in Civil Wars, *International Negotiation* 12(2): 229–248.
Svensson, I. & Wallensteen, Peter. 2010. *The Go-Between: Jan Eliasson and the Styles of Mediation*. US Institute of Peace Press.
Swisher, Clayton. 2004. *The Truth about Camp David: The Untold Story about the Collapse of the Middle East Peace Process*. Nation Books.
Talbott, Strobe. 1979. *Endgame: The Inside Story of SALT II*. Knopf.
Taliaferro, Jeffrey W. 1998. Quagmires in the Periphery: Foreign Wars and Escalating Commitment in International Conflict. *Security Studies* 7(3): 94–144.
Teger, A. 1980. *Too Much Invested to Quit*. Pergamon.
Thaler, Richard. 1985. Mental Accounting and Consumer Choice, *Marketing Science* 4(3): 199–214.
Thompson, Leigh. 1995. They Saw a Negotiation: Partisanship and Non-Partisan Perspectives, *Journal of Personality and Social Psychology* 68(5): 839–853.
  2009. *The Mind and Heart of the Negotiator*. Prentice Hall.
Thompson, Leigh & Hrebec, Dennis. 1996. Lose–Lose Agreements in Interdependent Decision Making, *Psychological Bulletin* 120(3): 396–409.
Tilly, Charles. 1985. Models and Realities of Popular Collective Action, *Social Research* 52(4): 717–747.
Tollison, Robert D. & Willett, Thomas D. 1979. An Economic Theory of Mutually Advantageous Issue Linkages in International Negotiations, *International Organization* 33(4): 425–449.
Touval, Saadia. 1982. *The Peace Brokers: Mediators in the Arab–Israeli Conflict, 1948–1979*. Princeton University Press.
  1992. The Superpowers as Mediators, in Jacob Bercovitch and Jeffrey Rubin (eds.), *Mediation in International Relations: Multiple Approaches to Conflict Management*. Palgrave Macmillan.
Touval, Saadia & Zartman, I. William. 1985. Introduction: Mediation in Theory, in Saadia Touval and I. William Zartman (eds.), *Mediation in Theory and Practice*. Westview Press.
  2001. International Mediation in the Post-Cold War Era, in Chester A. Crocker, Fen Osler Hampson, and Pamela Aall (eds.), *Turbulent Peace: The Challenges of Managing International Conflict*. US Institute of Peace Press.
Trumbore, Peter F. & Boyer, Mark A. 2000. International Crisis Decision Making as a Two Level Process, *Journal of Peace Research* 37(6): 679–697.
Tversky, Amos & Kahneman, Daniel. 1981. The Framing of Decisions and the Psychology of Choice. *Science* 211(4481): 453–458.
  1992. Advances in Prospect Theory: Cumulative Representation of Uncertainty, *Journal of Risk and Uncertainty* 5(4): 297–323.
Ury, William, Brett, Jeanne & Goldberg, Stephen. 1987. *Getting Disputes Resolved*. Harvard Program on Negotiation.
von Senger, H. 1991. *The Book of Stratagems*. Penguin.

Vuković, Siniša. 2015a. *International Multiparty Mediation and Conflict Management: Challenges of Cooperation and Coordination.* Routledge.
    2015b. Soft Power, Bias and Manipulation of International Organizations in International Mediation, *International Negotiation* 20(3): 414–443.
Waage, Hilde Henriksen. 2004. *Peacemaking Is a Risky Business": Norway's Role in the Peace Process in the Middle East, 1993–96.* International Peace Research Institute.
Wagner, Lynn M. 2008. *Problem-Solving and Bargaining in International Negotiations.* Martinus Nijhoff.
Wallensteen, Peter. 2011. *Understanding Conflict Resolution: War, Peace and the Global System.* Sage.
Walter, Barbara F. 1999. Designing Transitions from Civil War: Demobilization, Democratization, and Commitments to Peace, *International Security* 24(1): 127–155.
    2001. *Committing to Peace: The Successful Settlement of Civil Wars.* Princeton University Press.
    2009. *Reputation and Civil War: Why Separatist Conflicts Are So Violent.* Cambridge University Press.
Walton, Richard E. & McKersie, Robert B. 1965. *A Behavioral Theory of Labor Negotiations.* McGraw-Hill.
Wanis-St John, Anthony. 2006. Back-Channel Negotiation: International Bargaining in the Shadows. *Negotiation Journal* 22(2): 119–144.
Watkins, Michael & Rosegrant, Susan. 2001. *Breakthrough International Negotiation: How Great Negotiators Transformed the World's Toughest Post-Cold War Conflicts.* Jossey-Bass.
Watt, Nicholas. 2009. George Mitchell's Patient Diplomacy Shepherded Northern Ireland to Peace, *The Guardian*, January 23.
Weiner, B. 1972. *Theories of Motivation.* Markham.
Werner, Suzanne. 1997. In Search of Security: Relative Gains and Losses in Dyadic Relations, *Journal of Peace Research* 34(3): 289–302.
Whitfield, Teresa. 2007. *Friends Indeed? The United Nations, Groups of Friends, and the Resolution of Conflict.* US Institute of Peace Press.
Wu, George & Gonzalez, Richard. 1996. Curvature of the Probability Weighting Function, *Management Science* 42(12): 1676–1690.
Wu, Jianzhong & Axelrod, Robert. 1995. How to Cope with Noise in the Iterated Prisoner's Dilemma, *Journal of Conflict Resolution* 39(1): 183–189.
Yong Heun An. 2003. Politicians, Electoral Law and International Bargaining Approaches: A Case Study of Korea–U.S. Agricultural Trade Negotiation, *Pacific Focus* 18(1): 151–173.
Young, Oran (ed.). 1975. *Bargaining: Formal Theories of Negotiation.* University of Illinois Press.
Zartman, I. William. 1978. Negotiation as a Joint Decision-Making Process, in I. William Zartman (ed.), *The Negotiation Process: Theories and Applications.* Sage.
    1984. *Ripe for Resolution.* Oxford University Press.
    1997a. Justice in Negotiation, *International Political Science Review* XVIII(2): 121–138.

1997b. Explaining Oslo, in Dean G. Pruitt (ed.), *Lessons Learned from the Middle East Peace Process*, special issue of *International Negotiation* II(2): 195–215.

2000. Ripeness: The Hurting Stalemate Revisited, in Paul Stern and Daniel Druckman, eds, *International Conflict Resolution after the Cold War*. National Academy Press.

2001. The Timing of Peace Initiatives: Hurting Stalemates and Ripe Moments. *The Global Review of Ethnopolitics*, 1(1), 8–18.

2005. Comparative case studies. *International Negotiation* 10(1): 3–15.

2006. Ripeness Revisited: The Push and Pull of Conflict Management, in Corinna Houswedell, ed., *Deeskalation von Gewaltkonflikten seit 1945*. Essen: Klartext.

ed., 1976. *The 50% Solution*. Doubleday.

ed. 1978. *The Negotiation Process: Theories and Applications* (Beverly Hills, CA: Sage).

ed., 1994. *International multilateral negotiations: Approaches to the management of complexity*. San Francisco: Jossey-Bass.

et al 1996. "Negotiation as a Search for Justice," *International Negotiation* 1:79–98.

Zartman, I. William, and Rubin, J. (eds.). 2000. *Power and Negotiation*. The University of Michigan Press, Ann Arbor, MI, USA.

Zartman, I. William, and Faure, G. O. (eds.). 2005. *Escalation and Negotiation in International Conflicts*. Cambridge University Press.

1985. International mediation: Conflict resolution and power politics. *Journal of Social Issues*, 41(2), 27–45.

Zartman, I. William, and Berman, Maureen. 1982. *The Practical Negotiator*. Yale University Press.

Zartman, I. William, & De Soto, Á. 2010. *Timing Mediation Initiatives*. Washington, DC: United States Institute of Peace.

Zartman, I. William, and Rubin, Jeffrey Z. (eds.). 2005. *Power and Negotiation*. University of Michigan Press.

Zartman, I. William, and Kremenyuk, V. (eds.). 2005. *Peace versus Justice. Negotiating Forward- and Backward-Looking Outcomes*. Lanham: Rowman & Littlefield.

Zartman, I. William & Touval, S. 1985. International Mediation: Conflict Resolution and Power Politics. *Journal of Social Issues*, 41(2), 27–45.

1996. International mediation in the post-cold war era. *Managing Global Chaos: Sources of and Responses to International Conflict*, 445–461.

2009. *Negotiation and Conflict Management: Essays on Theory and Practice*. Routledge.

Zelikow, Philip, and Rice, Condoleeza. 1995. *Germany Unified and Europe Transformed: A Study in Statecraft*. Harvard University Press.

Zeuthen, Frederick 1930. *Problems of Monopoly and Economic Warfare*. Routledge.

Zubek, J. M., Pruitt, D. G., Peirce, R. S., & Iocolano, A. 1989. "Mediator and Disputant Characteristics and Behavior as they Affect the Outcome of Community Mediation," *2nd Annual Meeting of the International Association of Conflict Management* (Athens, GA).

Index

Aceh. *See* Indonesia
Additional Protocol, the, 30–32, 44
Adenauer, Konrad, 105–109, 113
Afghanistan, 35, 281
agenda setting, 15, 19, 68–70, 190, 198
Ahmadinejad, Mahmoud, 29, 31, 33, 44, 250
Ahtisaari, Martti, 204–205, 262
Algeria, 3, 13, 17, 104–105, 109–121
Angola, 13, 297
approach–avoidance, 12, 22, 291
approach–avoidance conflict theory, 256–264
Arafat, Yasser, 14, 174, 212–213, 260–261
Association of Southeast Asian Nations (ASEAN), 125
Australia, 124–125, 127–145

bargaining
  distributive. *See* hard bargaining
  hard, 5, 97, 167–170, 181, 211, 268–269, 276–277, 290
  integrative, 167–170
  positional. *See* hard bargaining
  problem-solving, 5, 167–170, 268–269, 272, 276–277, 290
best alternative to a negotiated agreement (BATNA), 8, 10–11, 15–16, 20–21, 35, 56, 60, 83, 115, 150, 164, 211, 266, 285, 292–293
Bosnia, 4, 15, 177, 185, 195–197, 199, 262
Bouteflika, Abdelaziz, 105, 110–115
brinkmanship, 7, 21, 90, 139, 180, 240, 291
Brunei, 125, 127–128, 130, 141
Bush, George H. W., 249
Bush, George W., 31–32, 36, 44, 131, 133, 138, 220–221, 274

Camp David, 170, 195–199, 212–214, 234, 257, 260, 285–286
Camp David I, 14
Camp David II, 14
Canada, 125, 127
Canberra. *See* Australia
Carter, Jimmy, 14, 170, 196–198, 285, 297
Chicken Dilemma Game (CDG). *See* Chicken Dilemma, the
Chicken Dilemma, the, 7, 9, 12, 16, 55, 61, 90, 101, 180, 182, 260, 290, 292
chicken game. *See* Chicken Dilemma, the
Chile, 68, 125–128, 134–135, 137–145
China, 27–28, 32, 83–103, 125–128, 238, 250, 274
Clinton, Bill, 134, 199, 204, 212, 221, 250, 274
Clinton, Hillary, 251
Cold War, 65, 216, 242, 248, 277, 281, 285
Colombia, 2, 14, 17, 62–82, 174, 179, 182–183, 279–280, 294, 296
compensation, 8–9, 12, 38, 92, 182, 292
concession, 3, 7–12, 20–22, 28, 37, 46–61, 68, 73, 78, 81, 83, 85, 88–89, 95–100, 102–103, 112, 114, 164, 181–183, 190, 195–199, 206, 208–220, 222, 226, 228–233, 236, 241–242, 245, 251, 254
  concession–convergence bargaining, 276–277
conflict management, 5, 15, 18–19, 164–184
conflict resolution, 5, 15, 19–20, 36, 164–184, 241
Congo, Democratic Republic, 178
convergence, 9, 36, 101, 112, 187, 276–277
cooperation, 8, 29, 31–32, 34, 36, 44, 98, 106–107, 110–111, 135, 162, 168, 171, 189, 192–194, 198, 210, 269, 271, 285
Crimea, 240, 245–246, 253–254

critical risk, 7, 9, 12, 14, 16, 19–20, 289–294
Cuba, 16, 64–66, 68, 78
 Cuban Missile Crisis, 9, 273
culture, 83–84, 92–94, 99–101, 103, 107, 109–110, 118, 132–133, 162, 167, 192, 289, 300
Cyprus, 48, 296

Darfur. *See* Sudan
Dayton Agreement, 2, 4, 15, 177, 185–186, 195–199, 217, 292
de Gaulle, Charles, 104–109, 113–114, 117–118
deadline, 1–4, 8, 12, 17–23, 36, 39, 45, 57, 61, 76–77, 85, 90, 99, 108–109, 111, 122–124, 133–134, 137–139, 142, 144, 149, 160–161, 164, 190, 198–199, 204–205, 238, 240, 244, 252, 263, 272–276, 279, 285, 288, 295–297
de Klerk, F. W., 12, 14, 22
disarmament, 2, 76–78, 258, 300–301
dragging, 5, 14–15, 17, 20–23, 28, 30–33, 44, 49, 84, 94, 112, 164, 179, 181–183, 187, 191, 194–196, 199, 201, 209–211, 225, 229, 240, 245, 257, 262, 288–290, 293–294
driving, 3, 5, 7, 9–15, 17–19, 22–23, 33–42, 45, 49, 63, 70–72, 80–81, 87, 90, 94, 97, 101–102, 112–113, 119, 127, 131, 133, 135, 137, 139, 161, 164, 179, 182–183, 201, 209–211, 218, 229, 232, 240–241, 289–291, 293–294, 297, 303

Ejército de Liberación Nacional (ELN), 65–66, 82
El Salvador, 14, 16
Élysée Treaty, 104–105, 107–110, 262
European Central Bank (ECB), 51, 55, 57, 61
European Union (EU), 9, 17, 33–34, 58–61, 119, 136, 240

Fabius, Laurent, 28
formula, 3–4, 8, 11, 14, 64, 70, 74, 79, 84, 87, 91, 99, 187, 191, 196–197, 251, 257, 262, 289–290, 293–294, 303
frame, 8, 17, 19, 68, 155–157, 173, 188, 222–223, 235–236, 276, 293–294

Framework Convention on Climate Change (FCCC), 22, 257
France, 13, 17, 29, 37, 43, 84–90, 92, 240–241, 244, 247, 249, 262
Fuerzas Armadas Revolucionarias de Colombia (FARC), 17, 62–82, 174, 179, 182–183, 279–280

gains
 absolute, 270, 278, 281–282, 290
 relative, 168, 194, 222, 269–271, 278, 281–282, 285, 290
game of echoes, 17, 19, 140–143, 261
General Agreement on Tariffs and Trade (GATT)
 Uruguay Round, 122–124, 139
Geneva, 9, 36–39, 128
 Geneva Conventions, 79
Germany, 3, 13, 15, 17, 27–30, 51–53, 56–57, 104–110, 113–121, 216, 220, 241–242, 244, 247–250, 254, 262
Gorbachev, Mikhail, 14–15, 151, 158, 216, 242, 248–250
Greece, 9, 17

hard bargaining, 12; *see* dueling
harkis, 116–117, 120
heavy-water reactor, 43–44
Hong Kong, 125, 127
Hussein, Saddam, 29

ideology, 164
IMF, 54–55, 58
Indonesia, 22, 127, 137, 204, 262
information distortion, 19, 21
International Atomic Energy Agency (IAEA), 27, 30–39, 44, 250–251
International Monetary Fund (IMF), 48–49, 51–52
intractability, 156, 164–165, 175–176, 181, 192
Iran, 1–2, 4, 12, 16–17, 158, 161, 215, 229, 231, 233, 242, 250–253, 255, 275, 278–279, 293–294, 297
Iraq, 29, 35, 135, 153–154
Ireland, 47–48
 Northern Ireland, 13, 196, 198, 297, 299
Israel, 9, 28, 43, 120, 156, 170, 174–175, 182, 198, 203–204, 206–207, 209, 212–214, 223, 225, 228, 233–236, 251, 257, 260–261, 285–286
Israeli, 221

Index

Jalili, Saeed, 28–35
Japan, 220, 236, 274
Jerusalem, 15, 204
Joint Comprehensive Plan of Action (JCPOA), 2, 12–13, 16, 42–44, 252

Kenya, 297
Kerry, John, 36, 39–41, 44, 78, 215–217, 225, 231
Khamenei, Ali, 40–41, 251–252
Khatami, Mohammad, 29–31, 44
Khrushchev, Nikita, 16
Korea
  North, 220, 273–275
  South, 125, 127, 135–140, 142–143, 273–274
Kosovo, 9, 15, 181, 204, 213

Libya, 32
light-water reactor, 43–44, 273
loss aversion. *See* Prospect theory
lowest common denominator (LCD), 15, 22, 113

Malaysia, 125, 127
mediation, 9, 13–14, 20, 22, 98–99, 102, 116, 151–152, 158, 161, 165–166, 170, 172, 178, 199–200, 208–209, 214, 240–245, 260, 262–263, 284–285, 288, 295–303
mediator, 94. *See* mediation
Mexico, 125, 127, 129, 131, 141, 143
Mindanao, 13, 297
mismatched, 5, 12–14, 33, 44, 112–113, 164, 179–180, 240, 242, 289–291
mixed, 5, 15–16, 101, 127, 135, 289
Moniz, Ernest, 40–41, 44
mutual dependence, 156–157, 159
mutually enticing opportunity (MEO), 12, 18, 20, 186–187, 191, 193–194, 197–199
mutually enticing outcome, 10, 182

Namibia, 2, 13, 16, 297
Netanyahu, Benjamin, 28, 41
New Zealand, 125, 127
Nixon, Richard, 16
non-governmental organizations, 115, 284
North Atlantic Treaty Organization (NATO), 108, 181, 204, 213, 216, 241, 244–245, 248–250, 254–255
Norway, 22, 68, 203–205
Nuclear Nonproliferation Treaty (NPT), 27, 30, 32, 219, 250

Obama, Barack, 27, 252
Oslo, 9, 15, 203–204, 257
Oslo Agreement, 174
Oslo I, 173, 203
Oslo II, 204

P5+1, 42–44, 250, 252
Pakistan, 29
Palestine, 9, 156, 174–175, 182, 203–204, 209, 212–214, 221, 225, 233–234, 257, 260–261, 285–286
Peru, 125, 127
Philippines, 125, 127, 279, 296–297
pieds-noirs, 116–117
Portugal, 47–48
positive-sum, 11, 169, 209, 270, 290
pre-negotiation, 3, 64, 68–70, 84, 158, 234
principal–agent relationship, 19, 22, 225, 277–278, 288, 291
Prisoners' Dilemma, 292
prospect theory, 8, 21, 168, 221–237, 259, 281–282, 291, 293
protracted
  conflict, 67, 172, 175, 209
  deadlock, 90–91, 98, 102
  negotiation, 164, 174, 253, 297
Putin, Vladimir, 54, 244–245

rapprochement, 28, 104–106, 113, 115–118, 120, 285
Reagan, Ronald, 14, 216
reciprocity, 5, 9, 13–14, 31, 35–36, 38, 171
reconciliation, 54, 119–121
reference point, 8, 21, 222–228, 230–232, 234–235, 237, 291, 293–294
reframe, 2–3, 9, 11–12, 19–20, 37, 113, 188–189, 193, 215–216, 235–236, 251, 276, 288–289, 292, 294
requitement, 10, 13
revolution, 27, 29, 36, 64, 65, 68
Reykjavik, 14–15, 216
ripe, 1, 13, 20, 116, 161, 166, 186, 190, 193, 201, 203, 287, 303
Ripeness Theory, 18
Rouhani, Hassan, 29–30, 35–36, 44–45, 158, 251
Russia, 27, 32, 44, 54, 85, 101, 127, 170, 240–247, 250–251, 253–255, 274, 284–285
Rwanda, 178

Sadat, Anwar, 14, 196, 198–199, 223, 228, 234
Safeguards Agreement, 30, 32, 38, 44
Salehi, Ali Akbar, 40, 44

satisficing, 5, 21, 181, 183, 265, 279, 282
Saudi Arabia, 28, 226
security point, 7–8, 10–13, 16–17, 21, 102, 112, 170, 181, 270, 289, 291–294
Singapore, 125, 127–131, 133–134, 140–141, 143
sovereign default, 47, 50, 52, 54–56, 58, 60–61
Soviet Union, 43, 106, 151, 158, 230, 241–242, 247–250, 254, 273, 277, 281, 283–284
Spain, 47–48, 149, 151
spoiler, 11, 17, 39, 45, 113, 116, 202–203, 278, 297–300
   greedy, 280–281
   limited, 280–281
   total, 280–281
Sri Lanka, 9, 14, 22, 202, 205
stalemate, 138, 244, 247, 292
   mutually hurting stalemate (MHS), 13, 17–18, 186, 193, 202
Sudan, 2, 12–13, 172, 206–207
Syria, 9, 20, 35, 170, 205–207, 257, 298

Tanzania, 158
terms of trade, 8, 34, 303
Thailand, 125, 127
The Strategic Arms Limitation Talks (SALT), 16, 277, 281–282
Troika, 47–60
trust
   affective, 97, 153, 156, 160
   cognitive, 97, 153, 156, 160
Tsipras, Alexis, 51

turning point, 12, 19, 28, 36, 62, 74, 95, 106, 115, 164, 287–289, 294–297
Turning Point of Closure, 3, 6, 22, 45
two-level game, 46, 53, 56, 167, 172

Ukraine, 15, 43, 240–247, 253–255
uncertainty, 19, 54, 95, 149, 163, 185, 188, 211, 222, 231, 237, 253–255, 263, 293, 300
United Kingdom, 28, 30, 180, 236, 250
United Nations General Assembly, 34, 36, 39
United Nations Security Council (UNSC), 27, 29, 32, 41, 135, 144, 204, 206, 250–251, 257
United States, 44–45, 47, 78, 125, 127–131, 137–145, 149, 151, 153–154, 158, 170, 197, 215–216, 218–220, 229–231, 233–234, 236, 241, 246, 248–254, 262, 273–275, 277–278, 280–281, 284–285

Venezuela, 67–68
Vietnam, 127, 231

World Bank, 69

Zarif, Javad, 29, 35–42, 44
zero-sum, 35, 87, 181, 188, 193, 209–210, 242, 269, 276, 290
Zone of Possible Agreement (ZOPA), 4, 11, 13, 28–37, 45, 84, 90, 112–114, 165, 169–170, 188–191, 239, 270–284, 288–289